# VAN DIEMEN'S
# WOMEN

# VAN DIEMEN'S WOMEN

## A HISTORY OF TRANSPORTATION TO TASMANIA

JOAN KAVANAGH & DIANNE SNOWDEN

The History Press Ireland

*Dedicated to the women and children
of the* Tasmania *(2) and especially
Eliza Davis and Margaret Butler*

First published 2015, reprinted 2016

The History Press Ireland
50 City Quay
Dublin 2
Ireland
www.thehistorypress.ie

British Library Cataloguing in Publication Data.
A catalogue record for this book is available from the British Library.

ISBN 978 1 84588 885 5

Typesetting and origination by The History Press
Printed and bound in Great Britain by TJ International Ltd

# Contents

Drawing, watercolour pencil, 'Barque Tasmania, 502 Tons, Capt A Jamieson, Becalmed
in Lat 17 S 30 W Long April 21st 1842', set under perspex, framed, unknown artist,
Mid Atlantic Ocean, 1842  OF. (Courtesy of the Powerhouse Museum, Sydney, NSW)

# Acknowledgements

The idea for this book germinated at the 1998 Irish-Australian Conference at La Trobe University in Melbourne. Seventeen years later, we are proud to present this book, the story of the women and children of the *Tasmania* (2).

Many people have been on this journey with us and we acknowledge their contribution with thanks.

For graciously agreeing to write the foreword for our book, we thank Mary McAleese, President of Ireland 1997–2011.

Dr Conor Fitzgerald GP and Dr John McManus GP for reading Surgeon Superintendent Lardner's journal and providing information about the shipboard complaints of the women and their children.

For shipping information, John Woods, Local Studies Library, Sunderland City Council and Captain John Barlow, Wicklow town harbour master.

In Ireland, the Director of the National Archives of Ireland, and the staff: Aideen Ireland, Gregory O'Connor, Brian Donnelly, Jennifer Dunne and the 'lads'. In the National Library of Ireland, Mary Broderick, David Phelan and Glenn Dunne. In the National Museum of Ireland, Lorna Elms, Finbarr Connolly and Noel Campbell. At Wicklow County Council, friends and former colleagues: Blaise Treacy, Tom Broderick, Eddie Sheehy, Lorraine Gallagher, Christine Flood, Seán O'Neill, Catherine Wright, Deirdre Burns, Aisling Lynch, Marion Fitzpatrick, the late Darragh Murphy, Pat Casey, the 'BTC' gang and Colin Fulham. Wicklow's Historic Gaol manager, Emeir O'Connell and the 'gaolers' Marie Comerford, Christine Murley, Patrick Mahood, James Murphy, Miriam Keegan and Tara Canavan. Lorraine McCann, archivist, Louth County Archives Service. The late Richard Bennett for bringing us around Grangegorman. Richard McCormick of the National Maritime

Museum, Dún Laoghaire; John Finlay and Joe Roberts for the photo of Wicklow Gaol; Martin Critchley for his maps. Stuart Rosenblatt of the Irish Jewish Museum and Catherine Cox of University College Dublin; Linda McKenna and Lesley Simpson, Down County Museum; Danny Cusack, an Aussie in Ireland; Fintan Vallely who searched the music archives for the 'The Irish Girl' and Emily Cox for her support; John Kearney and Amanda Pedlow, Offaly Historical and Archaeological Society; Sr Marie Bernadette, Sisters of Charity Archives.

A special thank you to Douglas and Linda Wilson in Wicklow for their generosity in opening up their home, Cronelea House, Shillelagh, where Eliza's life in Wicklow began.

Staff in the library and archives services throughout Ireland have been most helpful and courteous in responding to requests for assistance: Carmel Flahavan, Janette O'Brien, Clodagh Kinsella and Deirdre Condron, Carlow; Jonathan Smyth, Cavan; Peter Beirne, Clare; Kieran Wyse, Cork; Helen McNutt and Una Mathewson, Donegal; Nigel Curtin, Dún Laoghaire; Mike Lynch, Kerry; Mario Corrigan, Kildare; Jean Coughlan, Kilkenny; Bernie Foran and Bridget McCormack, Laois; Mary Conefrey and Thecla Carleton, Leitrim; Tony Storan, Limerick; Martin Morris, Longford; Alan Hand, Louth; Ivor Hamrock, Mayo; Tom French, Meath; Caitriona Lennon, Monaghan; Caitlin Browne and Richie Farrell, Roscommon; Mary Guinan-Darmody, Tipperary; Anne Lenihan, Waterford; Gretta Connell, Westmeath; Nicola McGrath, Wexford; and last but by no means least, Brendan Martin, Michael Kelleher, Robert Butler and all the staff in Wicklow County Library Service.

In England, the War Graves Photographic Project for images of the burial places of the descendants of the *Tasmania* (2) women and their prompt and efficient service.

In Australia, the staff of the Tasmanian Archive and Heritage Office; the Tasmanian Museum and Art Gallery (for the image of the solitary box); the National Archives of Australia; State Records of NSW (for the image of the *Anson*); State Library of Victoria (for the image of St Joseph's Orphanage); and the Powerhouse Museum (for the image of the *Tasmania*). To Brian Rieusset, Trudy Cowley and Mark Krause for sharing their images, and special thanks to Brian Andrews for the images of the reinterment of Judith Dooling, or Dowling, and for his interest in our project.

We also thank the Tasmanian Family History Society (formerly the Genealogical Society of Tasmania); the Friends of the Orphan Schools, especially Joyce Purtscher and Rosemary Davidson; the Female Convicts Research Centre; and Greta McDonald, site manager, Cascades Female Factory; Thelma McKay; the late Denise McNiece; Ray Thorburn; Coral Stubbs and Eddie O'Toole for kick-starting the research on Eliza Davis in Tasmania.

For information about Eliza Davis and photos of Eliza and her family, we thank descendants Bryan Lucas, Bronwyn Meikle, Gail Mulhern, Beverley Gellatly, the late George Hughes and Linda Hughes, and especially Bryan Lucas and Beverley Gellatly for generously sharing their photo collections and for providing additional information. Over many years, several of Eliza's descendants have provided information about this remarkable woman and we thank them for their interest and support. We also thank Georgia Wade at the Burnie Regional Museum for her interest in Eliza's story. For information about Margaret Butler and photos of her family, we thank descendants Les Butler; Betty, Cheryl and Sharon Whitney; Janet Hammon (for the photo of Margaret Lundie); and especially Beryl Snowden who, although not a descendant, has provided invaluable support and information over many years.

For information about the other women and their children, we are indebted to many fellow historians and researchers: for Esther and Mary Burgess, we thank Caroline and Emily Williams, Yvonne Jones, Peter Page; and for Ann Burgess, Barbara Simpson and Perry McIntyre. We especially thank Kevin Reed for kindly allowing us to use photos from his collection and for providing additional information; for Bridget Gallagher, we thank Harriet Taylor and Shirley Joyce in New Zealand; and for Mary McBride, Cheryl Griffin and Anne Kiely.

For taking time from his busy schedule, we thank the Hon. Michael Polley AM, former Speaker of the House of Assembly, Tasmanian Parliament, for showing the chair carved by W.P. Briggs to descendants Harriet Taylor and Shirley Joyce from New Zealand and for granting permission to take a photograph.

For encouragement and advice over many years, we thank Dr Perry McIntyre, Dr Liz Rushen, Dr William Nolan, and Professor Hamish Maxwell-Stewart. For their Irish hospitality, interest and friendship, we thank Siobhán Lynam and Barry Dowdall; and Joan's extended family, especially Marie Healy; Patricia Kavanagh; Frances Giles; Ena Havelin; Claire and Keith Malone; and Patricia and Richard Brady.

For persevering with our early drafts, we thank our readers Dr Bronwyn Meikle, Dr Bláthnaid Nolan, Marie Healy and Keith Malone as well as

Liz de Fegely for her specialist skills and Clodagh Jones for indexing. For her sound advice, Terri McDonnell. For proofreading, we thank Dr Jane Harrington and Dr Christine Leppard-Quinn, both always meticulous.

For their interest and support in our project, we thank our publishers The History Press Ireland, and especially Ronan Colgan and Beth Amphlett, always helpful.

And, finally, thank you to our families for their support and understanding through this long journey, and especially Bob, our 'chauffeur' and much more, in Ireland and Tasmania during our many research trips.

*Joan Kavanagh and Dianne Snowden, 2015*

# Foreword

For many Irish people the term 'bound for Botany Bay' is synonymous with the early history of colonial Australia and the political struggle for freedom in Ireland. Apart from the Irish political exiles transported in 1848, Van Diemen's Land, now known as Tasmania, is often overlooked as a place where Irish prisoners were sent. Yet it was just as important as Botany Bay. An estimated 40,000 Irish people were transported to Australian penal colonies between 1788 and 1867; nearly 11,000 of that number were sent to Van Diemen's Land. The majority of convicts were transported for non-political crimes, as in the case of the women of the *Tasmania* (2), who were exiled to Van Diemen's Land.

The story of the *Tasmania* (2) and its human cargo is one of remarkable resilience and survival. The ship was one of over twenty that sailed from Ireland to Van Diemen's Land carrying female convicts and their children. The *Tasmania* (2) left Ireland right on the cusp of the Great Famine on 2 September 1845. There were 138 women and 35 children on board. The voyage took just over three months to reach Hobart Town. On the journey Ellen Sullivan from County Kerry died, as did one child, while another child was born.

It has been said that the past is another country and this was certainly true for the convicts who made that long journey. The circumstances that led to their arrests, convictions and transportation tell of lives ground down by poverty. For the women of the *Tasmania* (2), a troubled past shaped their future destinies, thousands of miles from home, family, friends and everything familiar. We can sense their grief, desolation and apprehension and the loss felt by those they left behind. For many the fear of the unknown was overwhelming, for some there may have been a sense of starting afresh, but for all there was the virtual certainty of no return.

The story of these Irish women and their children has been told by
the authors, Joan Kavanagh and Dianne Snowden, with great sensitivity
and compassion. Their detailed and meticulous research not only skilfully
integrates the Irish and Australian narratives but takes us into the lives of
the convict women once they were free.

For the authors, this was a journey of a different sort and a much longer
one. A chance conversation at the 1998 Irish-Australian Conference at La
Trobe University in Melbourne, Australia, led to the discovery that both
authors had an interest in the *Tasmania* (2) but from different perspectives. At the time, Joan was working in Wicklow's Historic Gaol and had
developed a particular interest in the life of a young woman, Elizabeth
Davis, incarcerated in the gaol, waiting to be transported for infanticide.
Dianne's great-great-great-grandmother, Margaret Butler from Tullow,
was also on the ship, transported for stealing potatoes. Margaret, a widow
with six children, brought two young children with her, one of whom
was Dianne's great-great-grandfather.

The transportation of these women created bonds of affinity between
Ireland and Australia that resonate still down the generations. Those bonds
are revealed and strengthened in the telling of the story of the *Tasmania* (2)
and her cargo of bewildered women and children. One hundred and
seventy years after these women and children were 'banished beyond
the seas' to be punished, then forgotten and consigned to an obscure
corner of history, Joan and Dianne have brought them back to memory.
This is an extraordinary Irish-Australian story and the authors are to be
congratulated for giving it back to us.

*Mary McAleese (President of Ireland 1997–2011)*

# Abbreviations

| | |
|---|---|
| ADB | Australian Dictionary of Biography |
| Adm. | Admiralty |
| ANU | Australian National University |
| BPP | British Parliamentary Papers |
| CON | Convict |
| CON LB | Convict Letter Book (NAI) |
| CRF | Convict Reference File |
| CSORP | Chief Secretary's Office Registered Papers |
| HSD | Health Services Department (TAS) |
| LC | Lower Court (TAS) |
| ML | Mitchell Library (NSW) |
| NAA | National Archives of Australia |
| NAI | National Archives of Ireland |
| NLI | National Library of Ireland |
| POL | Police Records (TAS) |
| RGD | Registrar-General's Department (TAS) |
| SC | Supreme Court (TAS) |
| SRNSW | State Records NSW |
| SWD | Social Welfare Department (TAS) |
| TAHO | Tasmanian Archive and Heritage Office |
| THRA | Tasmanian Historical Research Association |
| TNA | The National Archives (UK) |
| VDL | Van Diemen's Land |

# Conversions

Original Imperial measures are used in this study.

| | |
|---|---|
| 1 inch (in or ") | 2.54 centimetres |
| 1 foot (1ft or ') | 30.5 centimetres |
| 1 yard (3ft) | 0.914 metre |
| 1 mile | 1.61 kilometres |
| 1 square mile | 2.59 square kilometres |
| 1 acre | 2.47 hectares |
| 1 pound (lb) | 454 grams |
| 1 ounce (oz) | 28.3 grams |
| 1 ton | 1.02 tonnes |
| 1 gallon | 4.55 litres |

## CURRENCY

All monetary amounts are in sterling, the currency of Great Britain.

One pound sterling (£) equalled 20 shillings (s). One shilling (s) equalled 12 pence (d). One guinea was 21 shillings, or a pound plus a shilling (£1.1.0).

In 1966, Australia introduced decimal currency, replacing pounds, shillings and pence (£, s, d) with dollars and cents. One pound equalled two dollars; one shilling, ten cents; one penny, one cent.

# Glossary

**Absolute pardon:** an absolute pardon is a full pardon or unconditional pardon that releases the wrongdoer from punishment

**Anson:** The HMS *Anson* arrived in Hobart as a male-convict transport in 1844 and was subsequently refitted as a probation station for female convicts. It was then towed to Prince of Wales Bay, Risdon, near Hobart, where it was moored. Between 1844 and 1850, this hulk housed female convicts during their six-month probation period upon their arrival in Van Diemen's Land.

**Assignment system:** Operated for female convicts from 1803 to 1843. Under this system, eligible convicts were assigned to employers (masters/mistresses) to work as domestic servants. The convicts were not paid a wage and could be returned for reassignment by their employer if they were no longer needed or were unsuitable.

**Assizes:** The courts of assize – commonly known as the assizes – were courts held in the main county towns and presided over by visiting judges from the higher courts. At the assize courts judges conducted trials dealing with serious offenders such as murderers, burglars, highwaymen, rapists, forgers and others who came within the scope of capital crime. Court verdicts were returned by locally picked juries of twelve.

**Branch factory:** Connected to a female factory but off-site; for example, Brickfields Hiring Depot.

**Brickfields Hiring Depot:** Located at the brickfields, New Town, where North Hobart Football Oval and Rydges Hotel now stand. Female convicts eligible for assignment or hiring as probation pass-holders were housed here between 1842 and 1852. It was a branch factory of the Cascades Female Factory.

**Campbell Street Gaol (also Hobart Gaol):** Established in 1821 as a convict barrack, from 1846 it served as a civilian prison. It became Hobart's main gaol in 1853 and the only gaol in the south from 1877, when Port Arthur closed. Campbell Street Gaol closed in 1960 when a new gaol opened at Risdon.

**Capital respite:** This was the process whereby a person sentenced to be hanged had their sentence commuted to transportation.

**Cascades Gaol:** Cascades Gaol was essentially the same establishment as Cascades Female Factory, but it operated under local-authority administration from 1856 until its closure in 1877, when the remaining female prisoners were removed to Campbell Street Gaol.

**Certificate of freedom:** Convicts were eligible to receive a certificate of freedom (also known as a free certificate) when they had completed their sentence of transportation (but not if they were sentenced to transportation for life). Not all convicts collected their certificate of freedom and some only did so several years after their sentence expired. The certificate allowed them to travel wherever they wished.

**Conditional pardon:** A convict became eligible to apply for a conditional pardon after a certain period of their sentence had expired. It was approved if they were of good behaviour. Convicts applied at their local police office and the application was sent to the king or queen for approval; this was usually given a year or so after the application. A conditional pardon gave the convict the status of a free person but limited travel to certain jurisdictions, usually the Australian colonies and New Zealand.

**Conduct record:** This is the main convict record used by the colonial authorities to record convict details. The conduct record contained slightly different information in the assignment period and the probation period. Original female records are held at the Tasmanian Archive and Heritage Office (TAHO) as the CON40 series for the assignment period and the CON41 series for the probation period.

**Crime class:** In the female factories this was the punishment class. Convicts sentenced to the crime class undertook hard labour. After a certain portion of their sentence was served and if they were of good behaviour, they could move to the second class. When their punishment sentence at the female factory was completed, they were moved to the assignable class for assignment or hiring.

**Description list:** This convict record provided local authorities with a description of convicts for identification purposes. The original records for female convicts are held at the Tasmanian Archive and Heritage Office (TAHO) in the CON19 series.

**Female factory:** A house of correction for female convicts used as a place of punishment, confinement and hiring or assignment. While in the factory, convicts were expected to work at a range of tasks. There were five female factories in Van Diemen's Land: Hobart Town, George Town, Cascades, Launceston and Ross.

**Free certificate:** See **Certificate of freedom**.

**Hard labour:** A punishment served in female factories, usually in the crime class. Two common forms of hard labour were washing clothes at the washtub and picking oakum. The washing was often conducted in wet, cold conditions and was heavy work; picking oakum involved unravelling the hemp fibres from old tarry rope and it often made the fingers bleed.

**Hiring depot:** A place where employers could hire convicts. The main hiring depot was Brickfields in Hobart, although there were also hiring depots in Launceston and Ross. At one time, a hiring depot also operated from a house on Liverpool Street, Hobart.

**Hobart Gaol, Campbell Street:** See Campbell Street Gaol.

**House of correction:** A place of punishment for convicts charged with offences (usually against convict discipline). Female factories were houses of correction.

**Indent:** This convict record was one of the three main documents used by colonial authorities to record details of convicts. Indents were not as detailed as conduct records and repeated a lot of the same information. In addition, however, indents provided information on living relatives of the convicts. Most of these records for female convicts are held at the Tasmanian Archive and Heritage Office (TAHO) in the record series CON15. Some indents are held in the Mitchell Library in Sydney.

**'Interior':** Any part of Van Diemen's Land outside the two main centres, Hobart and Launceston. Convicts were often sent to the interior to remove them from bad influences in the towns.

**Launceston Gaol:** Formerly the Launceston Female Factory. There was also a Launceston Gaol for male prisoners next door.

**New Norfolk Insane Asylum:** Built in 1829 at New Norfolk, it operated primarily as a mental-health institution from 1833 until 2000/2001.

**New Town Charitable Institution:** An invalid depot that operated on the site of the Queen's Orphan Schools at New Town from 1874 for women and from 1879 for men. It mainly housed ex-convicts and paupers.

**Nursery:** Many female convicts brought young children with them when they were transported or gave birth while under sentence. Those under three years of age were usually housed in a nursery. Nurseries were either part of female factories or in separate institutions, especially in Hobart, where nurseries existed at various times in a house in Liverpool Street, at Dynnyrne House and at Brickfields.

**'On the town':** This phrase usually meant that the female convict had worked as a prostitute.

**Permission to marry:** From 1829 to 1857, convicts in Van Diemen's Land were required to seek permission to marry from the Lieutenant-Governor, even if only one of them was a convict. It was usually the male who applied for permission to marry.

**Port Arthur:** The penitentiary at Port Arthur on the Tasman Peninsula operated from 1830 to 1877. It catered for reoffending male convicts.

**Probation**: From 1844 till the end of transportation in 1853, female convicts were required to serve six months' probation upon arrival in Van Diemen's Land. This probation period was designed to teach convicts desirable skills – including reading, writing, ciphering (numeracy), needlework, domestic service – and also to separate the newly arrived convicts from the more hardened criminals in the female factories. When the probation period was completed, a convict became a probation pass-holder.

**Probation pass-holder:** A probation pass-holder could be hired to work by an employer. They were paid a minimum wage of £7 per annum. The best-behaved convicts became third-class probation pass-holders, while the less well-behaved convicts were the first class, then second class, before progressing, through good behaviour, to third class.

**Probation station:** A probation station was where convicts completing their six-month probation period were housed and worked. For male convicts, probation stations were dotted all over Van Diemen's Land. For female convicts, the *Anson* hulk was the main probation station. New Town Farm operated temporarily as a probation station for female convicts in 1850.

**Queen's Orphan School(s):** Originally known as the King's Orphan Schools, this institution comprised three schools – the Male Orphan School, the Female Orphan School and the Infant Orphan School (from 1862). It was located at New Town in what is now known as St John's Park Precinct. Children of convicts were sent there when they arrived on convict transports or when their mothers were under punishment. It was later known as the Queen's Asylum for Destitute Children.

**Queen's Asylum for Destitute Children:** See **Queen's Orphan School(s)**.

**Ross Female Factory:** Opened in March 1848 and closed in November 1854. It was the healthiest of the factories.

**Ross Hiring Depot:** Operated from within the Ross Female Factory.

**Second class:** Prisoners in the second class at a female factory were those working their way up from first (or crime) class to third class and included those imprisoned for minor offences (i.e not undertaking hard labour) and those awaiting confinement.

**Separate apartments:** Punishment cells located in Yard 3 at Cascades Female Factory. They were completely dark when both the inner and outer doors were shut and locked. Silence prevailed.

**Separate working cells:** Solitary confinement cells that allowed light in above the door so that prisoners could work, probably picking oakum. Situated in Yard 3 at Cascades Female Factory.

**Solitary cells:** Cells in female factories and gaols where prisoners were kept apart from others. They were usually dark and cramped.

**Solitary confinement:** This punishment kept a prisoner separate from all other prisoners, locked in a small dark cell or separate apartment. They were often fed only bread and water while in solitary confinement. The maximum number of days a prisoner could spend in solitary confinement at one stretch was fourteen.

**Solitary working cells:** See **Separate working cells**.

**Surgeon Superintendent:** The medical attendant on board convict transports, responsible both for the medical care of the convicts and for their discipline.

**Surgeon's journal:** Recorded by the Surgeon Superintendent on board the convict ship during the voyage. It included a sick list, records of cases in the hospital and general remarks.

**Ticket of leave:** After serving a portion of their sentence and being on good behaviour, convicts could apply for a ticket of leave. This allowed them to work for whomever they chose, but it often restricted them to a particular police district. It was the first step towards freedom.

**Visiting magistrate:** Several visiting magistrates operated throughout the colony. They visited hiring depots, gaols and female factories to pass sentence on prisoners charged with major crimes within the establishments.

**Washtub:** A punishment usually given to female convicts sentenced to hard labour. Female convicts worked at the washtub in Yard 2 at Cascades Female Factory, washing clothes and linen. It was difficult, heavy, wet and cold work.

**Working yards:** The yards at the female factories where prisoners worked, mainly washing.

*(Adapted from www.femaleconvicts.org.au/index.php/resources/glossary.)*

# Authors' Note

The names of the convict women have been recorded according to the spelling on the convict conduct record [CON41/1/8], with three exceptions: Esther Burgess is referred to on her conduct record as 'Burges'; she appears as Burgess in the text. Mary Byrne's conduct record refers to her as 'Bryne' and on her indent she is Mary Byrne; she is referred to as Mary Byrne. Eliza Davis is referred to as Elizabeth Davis in the convict records but she was generally known as Eliza and is referred to as such in this book. All other spelling of names are according to the document being used. The difficulty caused by name variations is highlighted by Mary Byrne's son, 'James Burns', also known as 'James McCann'. Mary married as 'Bryan'. Similarly, Mary Griffen's children were consistently recorded as Griffin from the time they were in Grangegorman Female Convict Depot in Dublin. Alternative spellings are shown like this: 'Meagher' (for Mary Meaghar).

Because the one described in this book was the second voyage of the *Tasmania* as a convict ship, it was styled the *Tasmania* (2) and it is referred to in this way in the text.

Where two convicts of the same name arrived on a convict ship, they were differentiated by the addition of 1st, 2nd, or 3rd on their convict records. There were two women named Margaret Butler on the *Tasmania* (2). The colonial authorities labelled them Margaret Butler 1st and Margaret Butler 2nd to distinguish them.

Biographies of the 138 women and 35 children, with detailed references, will be available in 2016 on http://dsnowden.edublogs.org.

It is not always possible to determine if a particular record relates to a particular convict, especially for birth, death and marriage records. Where we consider a record is likely to be relevant, even though it is unsubstantiated, we have added it to the end of the individual biography.

# Introduction

# More Sinned Against Than Sinning?[1]

Over the course of eighty years of transportation to Australia between 1788 and 1868, 825 convict ships transported more than 167,000 convicts.[2] Of these, approximately 80,000 were sent to Van Diemen's Land. Nearly 11,000 convicts sent to the colony were Irish; not quite 4,000 were Irish women.[3]

This study, by looking at the individual lives of a group of Irish women and their children and the context in which they lived, examines not only the reasons behind their transportation – why they committed crime – but also the social impact of transportation on those transported and those they left behind.

Few historians have analysed the colonial experience of individual convict women, particularly in Van Diemen's Land.[4] These women often disappeared from the records once they emerged from the convict system and so can be difficult to trace. This study adds to the body of knowledge about the individual convict experience. It also briefly considers the 'convict stain' and the denial of a convict past and its impact on family history and popular memory.

On 2 September 1845, the convict transport *Tasmania* (2) sailed from Ireland with 138 women and 35 of their free children.[5] One of the convict women, Ellen Sullivan, died during the voyage.[6] One child died and another was born on board. The ship arrived in the River Derwent near Hobart Town on 3 December 1845 and on 9 December 1845 it unloaded its human cargo of 137 female convicts and their children.[7]

The individual stories of each of the women on board, and the children who accompanied them, are complex and diverse. The stories of two

women in particular, Eliza Davis from County Wicklow and Margaret
Butler 2nd from County Carlow, highlight this diversity.[8] They are key
individuals in this remarkable story of a group of Irish convict women
and their children.

## ELIZA DAVIS[9]

Eliza Davis, sometimes known as Elizabeth, was a foundling, an abandoned
child. She was admitted to the Dublin Foundling Hospital as an infant.
The Foundling Hospital grew out of the Dublin Workhouse, a Protestant
institution established in 1703 to remove deserted and destitute
children – many of whom were illegitimate – from the streets.[10] By 1819,
the Foundling Hospital had 8,740 children on its books. Administrative
changes, however, led to a decline in intake numbers: by the time Eliza
entered the institution numbers were less than 500.[11]

Life in the Foundling Hospital was harsh and regimented. Days were
long; Bible reading, prayer, spelling lessons and possibly some manual
work filled the day. Punishment included whipping and solitary confinement in a dark room. Mortality rates were high: between 1796 and 1826,
32,000 infants died of the 52,200 admitted.[12]

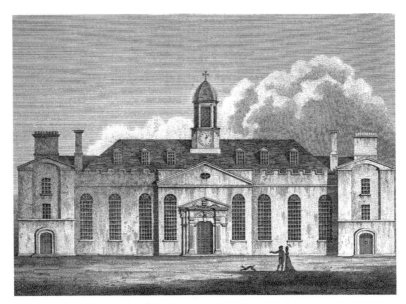

The dining hall of the Foundling Hospital, Dublin.
(NLI, ET B397, image courtesy of the National Library of Ireland)

When children were old enough, usually about 15 or 16, and if they were considered suitable, they were apprenticed for four years to masters and mistresses throughout Ireland. Formal indentures were signed and there were strict rules and regulations, which included attending church and Sunday school. Apprenticed children were clothed and their future expenses were covered by an annual payment of £1 made by the governors of the Foundling Hospital.[13]

Admissions to the Dublin Foundling Hospital closed in 1830 but it continued to bear responsibility for those children already admitted and those who had been apprenticed out.[14]

Nothing is known of Eliza's family circumstances or the parish she was from. In the hospital, she was raised as a Protestant. Much of the information about Eliza's early life, including information about her trial, comes from her detailed Convict Reference File.[15]

Eliza was apprenticed by the governor of the Foundling Hospital to a Protestant family, the Twamleys of Cronelea House, Shillelagh, County Wicklow. Cronelea is a townland covering an area of 470 acres of sloping hills in the south of the county.[16] The Twamleys were tenant farmers on the estate of Earl Fitzwilliam.[17]

Cronelea House, County Wicklow, built 1824, photographed October 2012. Eliza Davis was apprenticed here in 1841. (Authors' collection, reproduced with permission of Douglas and Linda Wilson)

There is confusion about the date on which Eliza's apprenticeship
commenced. At Eliza's trial, James Twamley stated that Eliza was apprenticed to him 'in or about the month of January 1841 for a period of four
years' and that she remained in his service up to the 'month of January 1845
when her term was up'.[18] According to the petition of the governor of
the Foundling Hospital at the time of Eliza's trial, she was apprenticed
'to a farmer in the County of Wicklow on the 6th November 1840' for
four years.

Eliza worked at the farm for the entire period of her four-year apprenticeship. She was often subject to epileptic fits and 'when so attacked she
would remain for several hours together in an incredible state and would
not come to her usual state of mind for many days afterwards'. In early
February 1845, when she was 19 and still living in Wicklow, Eliza gave
birth to a son. No information has come to light about the father of her
child; he was possibly a fellow servant who took advantage of her reduced
circumstances.

Eliza's infant son died tragically. On 3 March 1845, he was found
drowned in a pond at Coolkenny, near Cronelea. An inquest was held the
next day. The surgeon who attended the inquest and examined the body
told the court that 'the child had received injury on the head, but [he]
thinks the immediate cause of death was suffocation, it appeared previously to have been taken care of, it was a healthy male child'.

Eliza was charged with the murder of her son at the Wicklow Assizes on
8 July 1845: the indictment read that she 'did kill and murder it by throwing
it into a pond' on 24 February 1845. This was an extremely serious crime
and on 4 March 1845 Eliza was brought to the Wicklow County Gaol to
await her trial. More than four months later, Eliza appeared in court. Five
local women – Mary Deegan, Catherine Foley, Eliza Gahan, Bess Carr
and Margaret Hopkins – appeared to give evidence.

Eliza had lodged with Mary Deegan in the last days of her pregnancy,
confessing to Mary that 'she was not a married woman'. Eliza had left
Cronelea and had been living hand-to-mouth. It was Mary who gave
Eliza the baby clothes – a cotton gown and caps – which he was wearing
when he drowned. About a fortnight after the child's birth, Eliza and
her child left Mary's residence but it is not clear why. She seems to have
wandered with her baby through the countryside, meeting with occasional charity. Once a man invited her to come into his cottage for a
rest and a witness saw her sitting by the fire inside with her child. Other
witnesses saw her some days later without a child.

The most damning evidence was given by eyewitness Margaret Hopkins, a mother of eight, who testified that on the evening of 24 February:

> she was within six or seven perches of the girl when she saw her tie a black cloth or rag round the head of the child, and push it down into the pond by which she was sitting three times – that the prisoner passed her on the road immediately after without the child, yet she never asked her what she had done with it, never went to the water to ascertain whether it was there, dead or alive, nor did she ever relate what she had seen to any person until about a fortnight after the trial.[19]

Margaret saw this from the road on the far side of the pond. She watched as Eliza walked around the pond and up to the road, right past her. Asked by Eliza's counsel why she hadn't done anything to stop her, she replied that because she had a burden on her back she was not able to run down to the pond.[20]

No witnesses appeared to shed doubt on Margaret Hopkins' story. No one asked her why she did not go immediately to the police or why more than a week passed before the police constable from the Killybeg barracks was contacted. The case against Eliza appeared to be clear-cut.

The jury at the County Wicklow Assizes found Eliza guilty of murdering a male child, name unknown, and she was sentenced to death. The date of execution was scheduled for 16 August, just over five weeks from the time her sentence was handed down.

Evidence continued to be taken after the trial, and there were a number of petitions addressed to the Lord Lieutenant Governor and Governor General of Ireland in support of Eliza, aimed at staying her execution. Five days after the trial, a Justice of the Peace took a sworn statement from James Twamley, who said that he was:

> firmly convinced that the mind and reasoning faculties of the said Elizabeth Davis was greatly impaired and weakened … that at times [he] believes she was not legally responsible for her acts.

After her sentence, petitions were received from a range of individuals and groups, including the jury, the Quakers, the Foundling Home and the gentlemen of the borough of Wicklow town.

Two days after Twamley's evidence was received, another witness, Revd Solomon Donovan, came forward in support of Eliza. He knew Eliza when she was apprenticed to Twamley as he was a boarder there. He stated that Eliza was 'subject to fits of a very peculiar nature which frequently seized her while at work in the house and sometimes on the road'. She had 'remained as in a trance on those occasions sometimes the whole day, sometimes for twenty-four hours' and 'Very frequently [she] had a bewildered look and remained silent when spoken to as if in a state of amazement'.

Revd Donovan not only corroborated Twamley's account of Eliza's epilepsy but also frankly questioned the reliability of Margaret Hopkins' evidence, stating that it was 'wholly undeserving of the least credit'. If she had really witnessed Eliza drowning her child, 'she would not in my opinion have kept it secret so long'. He then attacked her motive for testifying: 'Margaret Hopkins and her husband are very poor and have a very large family', and once before when she gave evidence 'in a somewhat similar case', she received 'by order of the Court a sum of money to defray her expenses, which sum of money was in her estimation considerable'. Donovan suggested that 'a hope of obtaining a similar or greater sum was in my opinion the motive that induced her to volunteer her evidence against Eliza Davis'. He also attacked Margaret Hopkins' character, alleging that she had been imprisoned as a thief and since then had been 'known to make statements utterly false and without foundation'. Donovan's attack begs the question: why he did not give this evidence at Eliza's trial? Had he done so, the outcome for Eliza may well have been different.

The petition from the governors of the Foundling Hospital in Dublin noted that Eliza was visited each year by inspectors from the Foundling Hospital. They reported that her character and conduct were irreproachable until seduced by a fellow servant who was well aware of her destitute circumstances and who knew he would not be obliged to marry her, he being of the Roman Catholic persuasion and she being a Protestant.

The governors also criticised the legal representation at Eliza's trial, saying that:

> although the Crown most humanely assigned her both Counsel and
> Attorney at the time of the Assizes, yet the notice to these advocates
> was so very short (her attorney having only seen her the night previous
> to the trial) that it was impossible for them to prepare her case with

full deliberation or to procure such witnesses as she required for her
defence, the unhappy individual not having a friend in the world to
suggest a word in her favour.

As a result, there was no mention at her trial of her epilepsy and no case
mounted for accidental death 'whilst labouring under the effects of
one of those fits and not by premeditation'. Given these circumstances,
the governor 'humbly prayed' that the sentence of the 'unfortunate female
still under age' be commuted to any other 'sentence short of death as your
Excellency may seem fit'.

The *Nenagh Guardian* published a detailed account of the trial proceedings held in the Wicklow Assizes:

> These assizes commenced on Monday, when the grand jury having
> been sworn the business was immediately proceeded with, but no trial
> of any importance to the public took place.
>
> On Tuesday Eliza Davis was placed in the dock charged with the
> murder of her infant child on the 24th February last, at Coolkenny.
> It appeared by the evidence that the babe was "a child of shame," but as
> sworn to by Surgeon Morton, who examined the body, seemed to have
> been taken good care of up to the period (twelve days from its birth)
> when the foul deed was committed.

The jury, after a few minutes deliberation, returned a verdict of guilty,
and the judge (Chief Justice Doherty), after a suitable address, passed the
awful sentence of death on the unfortunate woman, who, with a loud
shriek, fell back into the dock, from which she was promptly removed:

> The Foreman, in a minute or two after, addressed his Lordship,
> stating that he had been requested by his brethren, unanimously,
> to recommend the convict to mercy – but received a reply that
> at that stage of the proceedings the recommendation, as far as he
> (the judge) was concerned, could not be entertained, but advised that
> a statement to that effect should be placed on paper and forwarded
> to the government.[21]

In July 1845, Eliza's sentence of death was commuted to transportation
for life through 'the interposition of the jury and several inhabitants of
the town'.[22]

Wicklow Courthouse, 2015. (Authors' collection)

She was given an opportunity to continue living but on another island at the other end of the world. Eliza left Wicklow Gaol on 12 August to go to Grangegorman, the Female Convict Depot in Dublin, where she joined other female convicts waiting for the arrival of a convict ship to take them to Van Diemen's Land. Eliza sailed from Dublin on 2 September 1845, a fortnight after she was due to be hanged.[23]

Wicklow Gaol before demolition of the tower block in the 1950s. (Courtesy of John Finlay)

There is no doubt that Eliza was more sinned against than sinning. The tragic circumstances surrounding the death of her infant son, the shambolic court case – the failure to take into consideration Eliza's epilepsy as a mitigating factor; the integrity of the main witness – the belated community support and all the unanswered questions surrounding the child's death combined to conspire against Eliza.

## MARGARET BUTLER 2ND

The story of Margaret Butler 2nd stands in stark contrast to that of Eliza Davis.[24] While Eliza's crime was serious and her sentence significant, Margaret was sentenced to transportation for seven years for stealing potatoes. The nature of Eliza's crime meant that she was very much alone whereas Margaret had the companionship of two of her children, who came with her, as well as that of the small group of Tullow women who were tried with her. The other women were Esther Burgess and her daughter Mary, and Mary Griffin. Another woman, Mary Byrne, was tried in Carlow for stealing potatoes on the same day in what appears to have been a separate crime. In all, eleven children came with this small group of women from Tullow.

Margaret Butler and her three fellow miscreants were tried at Tullow in April 1845. An account of the trial stated:

Tullow, Easter Quarter Sessions 1845, Thursday 3rd April.

Esther Burgess, Mary Burgess, Margaret Butler and Mary Griffin were indicted for stealing a barrel of potatoes of Richard Carr at Tullowland on 4 Feby last.

Tullow Courthouse, County Carlow, 2015. (Authors' collection)

Richard Carr sworn – lives at Tullow. On 4th Feby witness lost some potatoes from a pit at Tullowland on the land of Mr. Byrne – witness visited them 1/4 after six o'clock in the evening. The pit was then safe – he visited the pit again at about 1/2 past seven o'clock and found that about a barrel had been taken out. There were 4 kinds of potatoes in the pit – Russenden cups, Pink-eyes, Lumpers and Devonshires and an odd white cup thro' the others. On the same night about 9 o'clock witness found potatoes with the police corresponding with those which witness had lost.[25]

John Roddy, a constable, testified that he had hidden on the Dublin Road for two hours in the evening. He saw the four barefooted prisoners about eight o'clock, coming towards Tullow from the direction of Carr's potato pit.[26] Each had a bag of potatoes on her back so he arrested the women. Mary Griffen tried to spill the potatoes from her bag but he stopped her. He prevented Mary Burgess from running away. Carr afterwards identified the potatoes.

The women said they had gathered the potatoes 'thro' the country'. The constable, however, claimed to have a pair of shoes in the barracks belonging to Esther Burgess, contradicting his claim that the women were barefoot. The five nails in the shoe, he said, corresponded exactly with the tracks near Carr's pit. This is curious and contradictory information: did Esther remove her shoes and so was barefoot when arrested? He also found a mark of fresh clay on the hands and clothes of all four women.

Given the strength of this evidence and the apparent lack of any mitigating circumstances, it was not surprising that the jury found all the women guilty. The governor of the gaol reported that they had all been previously convicted of stealing potatoes: Esther Burgess three times and each of the others twice. The matron of the gaol stated that Margaret Butler and Mary Griffin were 'desperate characters and very ill conducted in Gaol'.[27] The women were sentenced to be transported for seven years and were sent to Carlow Gaol to await the next stage in the transportation process – admission to Grangegorman Female Convict Depot.

On 18 April 1845, Henry Hutton, assistant barrister for the county of Carlow, submitted the petition from Margaret Butler, written when she was in Carlow County Gaol. It was addressed to Lord Heytesbury, who was the Lord Lieutenant General and General Governor of Ireland. Like many of the petitions, it not only provided the context of the crime that was committed but also personal information about the person who committed it:

> To the Most Noble The Earl of Heytesbury – Lord Lieutenant General and General Governor of Ireland.
>
> The petition of Margaret Butler
>
> A Convict in Carlow Gaol –
>
> Most Humbly Sheweth
>
> That your petitioner was tried at the last quarter sessions of Tullow before Henry Hutton Esq – Assistant Barrister – for stealing a few potatoes and sentenced to seven years transportation.
>
> Petitioner begs most humbly to state that she was left a widow with six fatherless children who have been dependent on the bounty of a humane and charitable public for support. Hardship alone induced her and the tears of her wretched orphans compelled her to do what she was sentenced to leave her country for.
>
> Petitioner now throws herself on the mercy and clemency of your Excellency that you would be graciously pleased to commute her sentence to any length of imprisonment – but oh in pity to her orphans – do not send her from them as they would be thereon friendless outcasts

The front of former Carlow County Gaol, now a shopping centre, 2015. (Authors' collection)

on the world. Your Excellency will see by the undersigned signatures that poverty alone drove her to do what she has done.

Petitioner once more craves the clemency of your Excellency's prerogative on her favor and the Hands of her orphans shall be uplifted in prayer. And your petitioner as in duty bound will ever pray

From Margaret Butler a convict in Carlow Gaol Carlow April 16, 1845.[28]

Hutton's own view of the case took little account of Margaret Butler's pleadings, 'I am not aware of any mitigating circumstances which would render the Prisoner an object of mercy'.

According to her petition, Margaret had six children. Only two of her children, William and Mary Ann, were allowed to accompany her and there is no further mention of her other children.[29] From Carlow Gaol, Margaret and her children were admitted to Grangegorman Convict Depot to await the convict ship that would take them to the other side of the world.

As with Eliza Davis, there is a compelling case that Margaret Butler 2nd and the Tullow women were more sinned against than sinning. Margaret Butler 2nd and Esther Burgess were widows with several children; Mary Griffen, from Wicklow, was married with at least three children but her husband was in America. All resorted to scrounging for food in order to feed their young children and to survive the impoverished Irish conditions. It is difficult to see them as hardened criminals.

## A FLOATING DUNGEON

In December 1845, just after the *Tasmania* (2) arrived in Van Diemen's Land, a Hobart Town newspaper published an account of the scene aboard the *Tasmania* (2) before it sailed:

As it was expected that the above vessel would sail on Saturday from Kingstown Harbour, a number of persons proceeded to the pier to witness the impressive and melancholy sight. The day was beautiful, the sky serene, the sea unruffled, and everything indicated peacefulness and happiness; but when the eye turned to the gloomy form of a convict ship as it lay upon the calm blue waters, a floating dungeon, the prison, home of the felon exile, a sadness came o'er the mind from the reflection that no matter how bright and lovely, and joyous all things round it seemed to be, within its dark and tomblike bosom were enclosed many suffering spirits, whose crimes had expatriated them from their native land ... side by side knelt the miserable creature who poisoned her husband in Kilkenny and she who had drowned her infant in Wicklow when driven from the door of her seducer.[30]

Eliza Davis was the woman who drowned her infant in Wicklow.[31] The convict who poisoned her husband was Catherine Meany, aged 22, from Kilkenny. She was convicted of his murder after only three weeks of marriage.[32] Only the more sensational crimes were highlighted.

Each of the women on board the *Tasmania* (2) have individual and intricate stories. In the past, much of the writing about convict women ignored the complexity of individual convict lives and differences over time and place.[33] Looking at the lives of convict women in detail helps dispel the misconceptions and stereotypes which for too long were associated with them. Long-standing and persistent perceptions of female convicts as immoral prostitutes, for example, have been rejected.[34] Significantly, too, the long-held notion of a criminal class has since been discarded.[35] The stories of Eliza, Margaret and their shipmates show that their experiences were diverse and complex. As Reid concluded:

> The image makers have produced a series of one-dimensional characters; a range of cardboard cut-outs which all claim to be the convict woman. There are, however, no such fast and easy conclusions ... the sheer richness of the source material relating to female transportees should act as sufficient safeguard against the production of any one, thinly constructed image. It is more than possible, in other words, for historians to put 'some meat on the bones', and to produce a whole series of convict women.[36]

In some instances, putting 'meat on the bones' is made more difficult because records are not always available or accessible. Some women deliberately hid their convict past. Moreover, common names, variations in spelling and discrepancies in recorded ages complicate tracing the women, particularly once they had served their sentence and were free. Nevertheless, convict records provide a wealth of information, facilitating the re-creation of the lives of the women.

When Eliza Davis, Margaret Butler and their shipmates sailed from Kingstown in September 1845, they left an Ireland of poverty and hardship that was on the cusp of the Great Famine.

Widows such as Margaret Butler and single women like Eliza Davis were economically vulnerable in times of adversity. Those with children were particularly constrained in hard times. At the other end of the scale, the landed gentry lived in big houses in comfortable circumstances, with an abundance of domestic servants and farm labourers. It was a huge contrast.

Margaret Butler was born in around 1805, a time when most of the Irish population was extremely poor.[37] Her shipmates were born between the 1780s and 1820s, a period of social and political upheaval and rapidly changing economic conditions. These changes shaped the lives of the Irish people.

# 1

# Poverty Alone Drove Her to Do What She Has Done[1]

Centuries of colonialism had a huge impact on the native Irish, disen-franchising them and introducing a new culture and tradition. Tensions arising from religious, political, economic and land rights were endemic.

Poverty increased despite the continuation of the economic expansion of the latter half of the eighteenth century and the prosperity of agriculture, particularly during the Napoleonic Wars.[2] In 1815, the war ended and economic conditions worsened. The problem was exacerbated by rapid population growth. The Irish population increased significantly in the first half of the nineteenth century. An estimated 2.3 million people lived in Ireland in 1754. By 1841 this had increased to 8.1 million.[3] By 1845, it had reached about 8.5 million.[4] One in eight of those alive at the onset of the Great Famine, *An Gorta Mór*, perished.[5]

The population increase was particularly significant as the country relied upon agriculture; the labouring classes and small holders, especially in the west, could barely survive unless they supplemented the produce of their holdings with wages.[6] There was greater competition for land and increased unemployment. Agriculture was the main source of employment, although there was some industry in Ulster. Small farmers, usually renting over 15 acres, lived side by side with cottiers – those who rented about 5 acres of land but who also needed to work to supplement their income. At the bottom of this triangle were the labourers who rented 'conacre', usually plots of less than one acre on which to grow a single crop of potatoes. For those who could not find work as labourers in Ireland there was seasonal work in Scotland or work as navvies building the railways and canals in England. Others turned to begging.[7]

Begging for Alms. (NLI, 2033 (TX) 58(C), image courtesy of the National Library of Ireland)

Areas not usually ploughed were cultivated and land was divided into increasingly smaller plots.[8] According to Cecil Woodham-Smith, 'Unless an Irish labourer could get hold of a patch of land and grow potatoes on which to feed himself and his children, his family starved … the possession of a piece of land was literally a matter of life and death.'[9] For the agricultural labourers and cottier class in Ireland in the 1840s, the potato was a staple food; at least one third of the population was dependent upon it.[10]

Conditions were worse in the west and the south where population growth had been fastest and where holdings were the smallest; families living on the smallest holdings were entirely dependent on the potato.[11] By about 1840, the condition of the poor grew more desperate.[12]

The agricultural class of Limerick in 1837 was described in Samuel Lewis' topographical dictionary:

Women at field-work in Roscommon. (Reproduced with permission of Roscommon County Council: Library and Archive Services)

Cottages with a view of the obelisk at Killiney Hill, County Dublin, by Samuel Frederick Brocas. (NLI, 2064 (TX) 94, image courtesy of the National Library of Ireland)

The peasantry differ little in their manners, habits and dwellings from the same class in the other southern agricultural counties; their dwellings being thatched cabins, their food potatoes with milk and butter occasionally, their fuel turf, their clothing home-made frieze and cheap cotton and stuffs: their attachment to their neighbourhood of their nativity, and their love of large assemblages, whether for purposes of festivity or mourning, are further indications of the community of feelings and customs with their country men in their surrounding counties.[13]

About the same time, Alexis de Tocqueville, the French historian and philosopher, visited Ireland; he described the living conditions of the agricultural class in a village in Connaught:

All the houses in line to my right and my left were made of sun-dried mud and built with walls the height of a man. The roofs of these dwellings were made of thatch so old that the grass which covered it could be confused with the meadows on the neighbouring hills.

In more than one place I saw the flimsy timbers supporting these fragile roofs had yielded to the effects of time, giving the whole thing the effect of a mole-hill on which a passer-by has trod. The houses mostly had neither windows nor chimneys: the daylight came in and smoke came out by the door. If one could see into the houses, it was rare to notice more than bare walls, a rickety stool and a small peat fire burning slowly and dimly before four flat stones.[14]

## REGIONAL DIVERSITY

For administrative purposes, Ireland is divided into provinces, baronies, counties, parishes and townlands. The women of the *Tasmania* (2) came from thirty-one of the thirty-two counties of Ireland. Sligo was the only county not represented. Although geographically Ireland is a small island, historically it is characterised by regional diversity. The life experiences of the women living in the province of Ulster and those living in Munster, for example, were significantly different.

The circumstances of the Irish, and especially the poorer classes, can best be understood against a background of colonisation and suppression by the English Crown dating back at least to the sixteenth century. The surnames of the women on board the *Tasmania* (2) reflect the

Provinces, counties and main towns of Ireland. (Courtesy of Martin Critchley)

outside influences that dominated Irish history from the earliest times; the Norman invasion in 1169 and the plantations of the sixteenth and seventeenth centuries.[15] The surname Davis is of Welsh origin and the name Butler can be traced back to the Normans. While over eighty of the surnames of the women on board are of native Irish origin, the remainder stem from the Normans and English, Scottish and Welsh settlers, not forgetting those who came seeking trading opportunities and stayed. However, surnames that may appear to be non-Irish may in fact be anglicised versions of Irish names.[16]

Property was increasingly in the hands of English landowners, many of whom were absentee landlords who showed little compassion for those who worked the land. Land agents left in charge – sometimes a relative of the absentee landlord or a local person – could be particularly callous.

The suppression of the Irish was manifested in a number of political ways. As a result of the war between Protestant William III and Catholic James II, the Penal Laws, commencing in 1691, were enacted. These laws not only restricted the practice of Catholicism but prevented Irish Catholics purchasing or inheriting property, holding political, civil or military office, standing for political or public office, or voting in parliamentary elections. A Catholic landholder could also be dispossessed of his land by a Protestant relative. The laws were in place until 1829, when the Roman Catholic Relief Act was introduced.[17] In the eighteenth century, settlers of British extraction owned approximately 80 per cent of the land. This new Protestant ruling class, the Protestant Ascendancy, had exceptional influence on the way the country was governed. It ruled Ireland for the next two centuries. While the ruling elite inhabited grandiose buildings and townhouses in Dublin and on country estates, the majority of the population – constrained by religion and unable to own land – had restricted access to political and economic activities.[18]

Throughout the country the 'big houses' of the landlords were appearing on the Irish landscape, mirroring their counterparts in Britain: Castletown House in County Kildare; Westport House in County Mayo; Mount Wolseley, Tullow, County Carlow; Strokestown Park House in County Roscommon; Castle Ward in County Down; and Powerscourt House in County Wicklow are just a few of the imposing houses constructed in the eighteenth century. Landlords, some of whom were absentee, let their land to 'middlemen' tenants on very long leases with fixed rents. These 'middlemen', some descendants of the dispossessed Irish, in turn sublet to undertenants in order to generate an income. In the early years of the nineteenth century, once the leases expired, these middlemen were removed by many landlords in order to maximise the rents and also to extend grazing areas. This meant that less land was available for rent and in turn created tensions between Protestants and Catholics vying for what little land was available. This pressure was keenly felt in Ulster because of the depth of sectarian conflict there.[19]

The *Tasmania* (2) women from Ulster, ranging in age from 17 to 64, and their families most likely experienced a different life to those born in other parts of the country. Their families witnessed rapid agricultural and industrial growth in the eighteenth century, as well as considerable sectarian tension, especially in the north-east:

> No sooner did we enter Ulster than we observed the difference. The ground was cultivated just as in England, and the cottages were not only neat, but with doors, chimneys and windows. Newry, the first town we came to, (allowing for its size) is built much after the manner of Liverpool.[20]

Economic growth in Ulster was based on the linen industry, centred around Belfast. This industry transformed much of rural Ulster and brought an influx of rural people to the city in search of work.[21]

View of Powerscourt, County Wicklow, by A.F. Lydon. (NLI, ET B287, image courtesy of the National Library of Ireland)

## POVERTY AND SOCIAL AND POLITICAL UPHEAVAL

Living in parallel with the splendour of the elite were the wretched poorer classes.[22] As early as 1703, the Dublin Workhouse was established with the aim of removing beggar children from the streets of Dublin.[23] Education in the Protestant faith, and apprenticeships with Protestant masters only, became the cornerstone of public charities providing for impoverished children. The Dublin Workhouse became the Dublin Foundling Hospital in the 1730s. This was where Eliza Davis was admitted as an infant.

In the late eighteenth century, parliamentarians such as Henry Grattan advocated reform for the Irish Parliament in Dublin, to free it from restrictions imposed by the Penal Laws.[24] More radical organisations were also formed.[25] Political agitation was widespread. At the same time, other societies were also being formed with specific sectarian objectives. The mainly agrarian society known as the Defenders was a Catholic society in Leinster and south Ulster set up to protect its community from rival Protestant societies, especially the Orange Order, which had been founded in 1795 in County Armagh. Due to the demand for land and employment in Ulster, bitter rivalries arose between the groups.[26]

Rebellion was inevitable. From May 1798 it is estimated that over 30,000 people were killed and many of the leaders executed by the government. At least 400 men were sentenced to transportation to the penal colony of New South Wales between 1798 and 1805.[27]

The Irish Parliament merged with that of Great Britain following the movement for constitutional reform of the 1780s and the 1798 rebellion. British Prime Minister William Pitt argued that Ireland would be best served by a parliament in London. His proposal included freeing Irish Catholics from many of the restrictions imposed under the Penal Laws; this was known as 'Catholic Emancipation'. Opposition to Catholic Emancipation by King George III and Irish Protestants meant it was not included in the Act of Union 1800, which established the union of the two parliaments and two kingdoms.[28] On 1 January 1801, the United Kingdom of Great Britain and Ireland was formed; the Church of England and the Church of Ireland were merged into the 'United Church of England and Ireland' and the Union Flag was created.[29] Despite the promises, Catholic Emancipation did not occur for another thirty years.[30]

The Union with Britain meant that Ireland was ruled from London so it had little or no influence on how its affairs were managed. This Union was seen by the Protestant minority as offering protection, while the Catholic majority saw it as a symbol of oppression.

An Irish executive was kept in place to manage the country's adminis-tration, with the Lord Lieutenant as its head of administration in Dublin Castle. Usually a nobleman, he represented the sovereign. Under the Lord Lieutenant was the Chief Secretary, a politician and a member of the cabinet in London, who was required to attend Parliament in Westminster when in session. The Under Secretary, a permanent official, held an influ-ential post, liaising with the Chief Secretary in London and keeping the Lord Lieutenant informed on all aspects of the administration.[31]

Politically, the push for Catholic Emancipation continued, with radical lawyer Daniel O'Connell resurrecting the issue in the 1820s. He mobilised the Catholic population, holding large public meetings and encouraging those present to vote in the 1826 and 1828 elections for Catholic Association candidates rather than those endorsed by their landlords. The British government finally introduced the Roman Catholic Relief Act of 1829.[32]

Following this success, O'Connell turned to the other major political issue – the repeal of the union.[33]

## AGRICULTURE

Throughout Ireland, tillage farming also expanded in the late eighteenth century. The rising population in England's industrial towns and cities meant more grain was needed; Ireland's grain production expanded. The war in Europe (1792–1815) also stimulated the demand for cereals, meat and dairy products. The pressure for food produc-tion led to a demand for more land cultivation and a concomitant demand for labour. The potato was often planted on marginal land to prepare it for grain cultivation.[34] The signs of 'lazy bed' ridges dug into the hillsides can still be seen in many parts of Ireland today.

Lazy beds at Foher, Killary Harbour, County Mayo. (Courtesy of Perry McIntyre)

Economic expansion was

accompanied by population growth. By 1800, the Irish population was close to 5 million. It has been suggested that the consumption of potatoes in large quantities resulted in higher birth rates.[35] John Carr, a trained lawyer who pursued a career as a travel writer, visited Ireland in 1805, after the Act of Union was passed. He recorded the fact that on average the quantity of potatoes consumed in a day by a man, his wife and four children was 37lb (17kg).[36]

The Napoleonic Wars were followed by a severe economic downturn.[37] The price of grain fell and the textile industry collapsed throughout the country, except for north-east Ulster where the industry had become mechanised. In Munster the woollen industry also collapsed. Those dependent on this cottage-type industry (both linen and woollen) were forced to fall back on the potato patch to make a living. Poor harvests in 1816–17 and 1822 led to shortages of food and famine conditions and worsened an already difficult situation.

Unemployment increased and living conditions remained miserable. Social and economic divisions widened. The rural poor were dependent on the potato for their staple diet, supplemented with buttermilk and occasionally fish. The high yield and nutritional value of the potato, rich in vitamin C, made it an ideal food choice. It produced a more than generous crop on inferior soils; a half-acre could support a family. Contemporary travellers noted how poor and wretched the Irish looked, but, paradoxically, how taller and more athletic they appeared, nourished almost completely on potatoes.[38] The potato diet safeguarded the Irish poor from diseases such as scurvy. Ironically, it was the high yield of the potato that enabled large families to be supported on a small holding.

Seasonal food shortages intensified the problem. According to Ó Gráda, the 1835–1836 enquiry into the Irish poor referred to the 'hunger months' of June, July and August and the 'wretchedness' that they brought: 'the distress of the peasantry … is the most frightful evil in Ireland'. The poor resorted to eating nettles, wild mustard and other weeds in bad seasons.[39]

Numerous parliamentary enquiries were held into Irish poverty from 1819; there were also 114 Royal Commissions and 61 Special Committees of Enquiry held from 1800 to 1840, reporting on conditions in Ireland.[40]

In 1825, Daniel O'Connell described Irish living conditions to the House of Lords Select Committee on the State of Ireland:

The homes are not even called houses; they are called cabins; they are built of mud and covered with thatch partly and partly with a surface called scraws. Any continuance of rain naturally comes in.[41]

Asked about furniture and bedding, he responded:

It is a luxury to have a box to put anything into ... they generally have little beyond a cast iron pot, a milk tub they call a keeler, over which they put a wicker basket in order to throw the potatoes, water and all, into the basket so that the water should run into the keeler.

Nothing but straw and very few blankets. In general without bedsteads. The entire family sleeps in the same compartment; they call it a room; there is some division between it and the part where the fire is. And yet I do believe and indeed I am convinced that that species of promiscuous lying amongst each other does not induce the immorality which one would expect from it.[42]

O'Connell was also asked about diet:

Except on the sea coast, [diet] consists of potatoes during the greater part of the year; potatoes and sour milk during another portion; they use salt with their potatoes when they have nothing but water.[43]

The 1841 census provides a picture of the Ireland in which the *Tasmania* (2) women lived. Two thirds of the houses were single-roomed mud cabins without windows. Only seven out of every hundred farms in Ireland were of 30 acres or more and farmers formed only a quarter of the rural population. Extremely poor labourers and cottiers comprised the rest of the population, living on small tenant holdings which had been divided and subdivided again as the population increased.[44]

Many initiatives were introduced into Ireland; these were usually undertaken by English landlords on a voluntary basis. The Irish landlords either did not have the will or the means to finance local initiatives as their counterparts in England did. The prevalence of the notion of laissez-faire politics meant that interference by government was strongly opposed. The choices for the government were repression or action. The obvious choice was to take action to alleviate the chronic wretchedness of a growing poorer class. Parliamentary enquiries and reports in 1836 and 1837 resulted in the introduction of the Poor Law

system in 1838 and the construction of 130 workhouses to accommodate the marginalised and vulnerable.

For some of the women, minor famines, subsistence, poverty and
wretched conditions were a familiar occurrence. Many Irish people had
no choice but to beg, to wander the countryside or to migrate. How much
crime was a response to the social and economic conditions is impossible
to determine but certainly the rise in crime was frequently remarked upon
by social commentators and reported widely in newspapers. Agrarian
unrest in the form of secret regulatory societies began to emerge in the
1830s, as it had in the early decades of the eighteenth century and again
towards the last quarter of that century. The grievances were similar to
those of the previous century: the paying of tithes for the upkeep of the
clergy of the established Church, high rents, particularly for conacre, wages
and the price of goods and especially the change to pastoral agriculture.[45]
As Ó Tuathaigh stated, 'the social problems of Ireland, chiefly poverty,
ignorance and violence were becoming, if anything, more acute as time
went on'.[46] In 1844, in County Tipperary, for example, it was observed that:

> At the Thurles quarter session … Serjeant Howley, after a few prefatory
> observations, thus concluded his address to the jury:—I ought not to pass
> over, without remark, the crimes—the many heavy and dreadful crimes—
> which have been lately perpetrated within this riding of the county.[47]

In June 1845, the *Dublin Evening Packet and Correspondent* reported:

> The accounts from the disturbed parts of Leitrim, Roscommon, Cavan,
> and Fermanagh, continue to be of a very afflicting nature. One of the last
> reports from Leitrim gives the particulars of nine cases of robbery of fire-
> arms. Roscommon and Fermanagh furnish cases of threatening notices.[48]

The link between poverty and crime has been well documented.[49]
Although poverty arising from the famine was unparalleled, the Irish
people were subject to hard economic conditions for many years before
1845.[50] In the years preceding the famine in Ireland, there had been a
number of reports of crimes associated with poverty and distressed
circumstances − what Rudé refers to as 'survival crime', often food-
related.[51] Distress was often cited as a mitigating factor.[52]

The women of the *Tasmania* (2) were the descendants of those who had
lived through the traumatic events of the previous 250 years in Ireland.

They were products of a country that had lost control of its destiny at various times and to varying degrees until the ultimate loss of control in 1801. While officially Ireland was part of the United Kingdom of Great Britain and Ireland, it was in fact another colony. For the women of the *Tasmania* (2), transported to Van Diemen's Land, it was a case of replacing one colony with another.

In 1845, the previously unknown fungal disease *Phytophthora infestans* was introduced to Ireland, resulting in potato blight.[53] Famine was not a new experience for the Irish but the blight, which returned in following years, was cataclysmic;[54] One in eight of the population perished.[55]

As they sailed from Ireland on 2 September, the women could not have known of the tragic events about to unfold in their country: within a few short years, a million of their fellow countrymen and women would be dead from starvation and diseases such as typhus, cholera and tuberculosis. A further million would leave Ireland, never to return.

2

# The Law Must Take its Course[1]

Not only were the lives of the women of the *Tasmania* (2) influenced by
their impoverished conditions and the context of the Ireland in which
they lived; they were also shaped, to a large extent, by their experience
of the legal process in Ireland. Their crimes and subsequent trials, at
which they were all sentenced to varying terms of transportation, determined their fate. Information about the participation of the women in
the legal process is limited to newspaper accounts of the proceedings
and, in a small number of cases, to petitions or memorials written by
or on behalf of the women seeking clemency from the Lord Lieutenant
of Ireland, the Crown's representative in Ireland.[2] While many records
were destroyed in the Four Courts fire in 1922 at the beginning of the
Irish Civil War, a considerable amount of material survived, providing a
snapshot of the legal process in nineteenth-century Ireland.[3]

The Irish prison system was regulated by the Prison Act of 1826.[4]
Under this legislation, the management and maintenance of gaols was
overseen by a Board of Superintendence, appointed by grand juries,
which carried out local administration in Ireland.[5] From 1823, annual
reports by Inspectors-General of Prisons were presented before the
House of Commons in England, detailing the accounts of their inspec-
tions of each county gaol, bridewell and lunatic asylum in Ireland. It is
in these reports that much of the information about contemporary gaol
conditions is revealed.[6]

| PUBLIC RECORD OFFICE OF IRELAND. | | | | | | |
|---|---|---|---|---|---|---|
| Records of the CLERKS of the CROWN and PEACE  *County Clare* | | | | | | |
| DATE AND DESCRIPTION OF DOCUMENT *Peace Office.* | Final position in Record Treasury | | | Temporary position in Record Treasury | | |
| | Bay | Shelf | Sub-Number | Bay | Shelf | Sub-Number |
| *Crown Files at Quarter Sessions* (cont.) | | | | | | |
| 1840  Ennis | | | | 3 B | 11 | 14 |
| 1840  Ennistymon | | | | | | 15 |
| 1840  Kilrush | | | | | | 16 |
| 1840  Sixmilebridge (including Killaloe) Tulla & Miscellaneous. | | | | | | 17 |
| 1841  Ennis and Ennistymon | | | | | | 18 |
| 1841  Kilrush | | | | | | 19 |
| 1841  Sixmilebridge (including Killaloe) Tulla & Miscellaneous. | | | | | | 20 |
| 1842  Ennis & Ennistymon. | | | | | | 21 |
| 1842  Kilrush | | | | | | 22 |
| 1842  Killaloe, Sixmilebridge, Tulla. | | | | | | 23 |
| 1843  Ennis & Ennistymon | | | | | | 24 |
| 1843  Kilrush | AR IARRAIDH | | | | | 25 |
| 1843  Killaloe, Sixmilebridge, Tulla. | 1922 | | | | | 26 |
| 1844  Ennis & Ennistymon | NOT SALVED | | | | | 27 |
| 1844  Kilrush | | | | | | 28 |
| 1844  Killaloe, Sixmilebridge, Tulla. | | | | | | 29 |
| 1845  Ennis & Ennistymon | | | | | | 30 |
| 1845  Kilrush | | | | | | 31 |
| 1845  Killaloe, Sixmilebridge, Tulla. | | | | | | 32 |
| 1846  Ennis & Ennistymon | | | | | | 33 |
| 1846  Kilrush | | | | | | 34 |
| 1846  Killaloe, Sixmilebridge, Tulla. | | | | | | 35 |
| 1847  Ennis, Ennistymon | | | | | | |

A page from the Records of the Clerks of the Crown and Peace, County Clare, annotated 'not salved'. (NAI, CC/2006/35/5, reproduced with permission of the National Archives of Ireland)

## ARREST

For the women of the *Tasmania* (2), their first contact with the legal process was generally with a member of the police force, who became involved once a crime was discovered.

For centuries, policing in Ireland was based on the local appointment of constables and nightwatchmen.[7] This proved ineffective; corruption was common and the system was unable to deal with the agrarian and political agitation occurring from the 1770s. Policing was eventually centralised and in 1836 the Irish Constabulary was formed.[8]

Encounters with over-zealous or vigilant members of the Irish Constabulary led to the arrest of some of the *Tasmania* (2) women. Catherine Hughes, for example, had the misfortune of being watched at the fair at Banagher in King's County (now County Offaly) in September 1844 by a member of the Irish Constabulary as she picked a pocket. Information at her trial recorded that:

> Constable Hayes proved that he had been watching Prisoner for 2 hours and saw her several times make attempts to pick pockets and saw her close to Hannah Tobin whom he observed to put down her hand as if she had been robbed, went up and asked her, where she informed him she had been robbed, he followed Prisoner into a house and saw her seated in a back place on a chair, saw her throw back her hand, he went over and stooped and found a purse and a 5s piece. The purse was identified by Tobin as her property and prisoner had in her hand 3s and she also had something in her mouth which she swallowed.[9]

Catherine was accused of being part of a gang of 'marauders frequenting fairs'. She claimed that she was convicted on circumstantial evidence for taking silver from a woman she did not know.[10]

At Ellen Cahil's trial for stealing £10.10, two sub-constables gave evidence:

> Sub-Constable John Connell proved that he arrested Ellen Cahil the morning after the robbery in the Market-house; on being arrested she said "Oh! the deuce may care – I'll never go younger." He found 6s on her person.
>
> His Worship then recapitulated the evidence for the jury, and in doing so took occasion to pay a high compliment to Sub-Constable John Connell. He was very sorry that he was not rewarded; and if promotion was due to merit, the man (Connell) might be promoted.[11]

Similarly, the four Tullow women, Margaret Butler 2nd, Esther Burgess, Mary Burgess and Mary Griffen, were victims of a watchful constable. Constable John Roddy had 'concealed himself from about six o'clock to eight in the evening' when he saw the four prisoners each with 'a bag of potatoes on her back' coming from the direction of Richard Carr's potato pit. He arrested them. The constable also carried out some forensic detective work, concluding that the shoe nail prints at the site of Carr's pit matched those of shoes claimed by Esther Burgess in the police barracks.[12]

The arrest of Catherine Hughes, Margaret Butler 2nd and her compatriots, and no doubt other women of the *Tasmania* (2), can largely be attributed to the zeal of the Irish Constabulary.

Once the women were arrested, they were taken to the local police barracks. Sworn information relating to the offence was recorded. The offender was then brought before a magistrate who decided whether there was sufficient evidence to commit to trial. If so, the magistrate could either commit the suspect to gaol or release her on bail. In the case of the *Tasmania* (2) women, all were committed either to a county or city gaol to await the second stage in the process: appearing before a judge at either the assizes or quarter sessions.

## GAOLS

By 1844, some counties had erected new gaols or built extensions, largely as a result of penal reform advocated by Sir Jeremiah Fitzpatrick, MD, John Howard and Elizabeth Fry, who argued that old and new offenders should be separated.[13] The New House of Correction in Belfast, County Antrim, containing 300 cells, was completed in 1844. A new gaol had been built at Nenagh and extensive additions were added to county gaols at Wicklow, Wexford and in Ennis, County Clare. Additions or improvements were also underway in other counties; there were large additions to the Fermanagh county gaols at Enniskillen and Armagh; an extension at Kilkenny; a few cells on the separate system at Donegal County Gaol at Lifford; and a large addition for female prisoners at Kilmainham, Dublin's county gaol. In an effort to establish a separate system, some counties, including the county gaols at Tralee and Limerick, had erected large sheds in the yards, 'divided into separate workshops for all kinds of trades or industry, properly ventilated'.[14] Attention was drawn to the shortcomings in some county and city gaols; Louth, Kerry and Roscommon county

Cell block of Wicklow Gaol, 2009. (Authors' collection)

gaols and the city gaols of Dublin at Newgate, Kilkenny and Waterford were all in need of renovation.

As well as the separation and classification of offenders, work was also considered an important part of reform; the 1844 report noted that 'industrious habits' – including spinning, knitting, needlework and washing – had been established in all the prisons.[15] Schooling was carried out in almost every gaol and prison dress was the norm. A 'wholesome diet, at a very modest expense' was given to prisoners. Women were placed in the care of female officers, usually a matron.[16]

In 1844, Carlow County Gaol – where Margaret Butler 2nd was held – was run by 'zealous officers'.[17] A new wing allowed the separate system to be put into place but in the old section the cells were limited in size and were 'miserable abodes to subject any human being to be shut up in them for many hours'. The female accommodation was harshly criticised:

> The female division of the prison is much too limited in accommoda-
> tion. The cells and day-rooms are wretchedly small and dark; and as
> it is impossible to cause a proper classification of prisoners, according
> to the nature of the crimes, it is of the utmost importance that there
> should be a most strict system in every well-regulated prison, of
> having the most hardened and ill-behaved classes separated from
> those less practiced in vice.[18]

Wicklow Gaol, where Eliza Davis was imprisoned, had a new cell block with 40 cells for prisoners under the separate system.[19] The women were trained in spinning hemp, carding and spinning wool, knitting stockings, sewing and washing and were provided with basic schooling. A medical report commented on general health; it noted the preva-lence of catarrh, diarrhoea, dyspepsia and constipated bowels. Venereal diseases were also common. The cases of dyspepsia were numerous and could 'be accounted for by the confinement, want of usual active if not laborious employment, together with restrictions to one kind of food'.[20] This sounded an ominous note for those facing the long voyage to Van Diemen's Land; the diseases identified in the medical report mirrored those documented by Mr Lardner, Surgeon Superintendent of the *Tasmania* (2).[21]

## COURT PROCEEDINGS

As already noted, all the *Tasmania* (2) women were committed either to a county or city gaol to wait for the second stage in the legal process: appearing before a judge at either the assizes or quarter sessions. Serious cases, such as murder, were heard at the assizes, usually before one or two senior judges, travelling around the country and held in the spring or summer.[22] Quarter sessions, as the name implies, were conducted quarterly. They were presided over by an Assistant Barrister, later to be known as a county court judge.

The full pomp and ceremony of the state was demonstrated with the arrival of the judges in town, travelling on circuit in their carriages, escorted by police and military on horseback. The judicial attire – black robes trimmed with ermine – added to the spectacle: 'All was bustle and confusion, noise, dirt and distraction'.[23] The judges were assisted by the Criers at assizes and sessions. In many towns, fairs and balls were held attended by the gentry and members of the grand jury.[24] It was a huge event.

Just as impressive were the Irish courthouses constructed in the early nineteenth century. Wicklow Courthouse was built in 1824 and Tullow Courthouse about 1825. The two-storey stone Tullow Courthouse was smaller than most courthouses but was still imposing. Wicklow Courthouse was also a striking building. Adjoining the county gaol, it provided easy access for prisoners through the gaol yard into the cells in its basement to wait until it was time to be brought to the dock. The significance of such intimidating stone structures would not have been lost on the poor and destitute whose circumstances brought them there.

A sample of fifty-seven cases of the *Tasmania* (2) reveals 74 per cent were tried at the quarter sessions in the counties in which they had committed their crime. The remaining 26 per cent were tried at the spring or summer assizes in either 1844 or 1845.[25] Margaret Butler 2nd was tried at the quarter sessions in Tullow Courthouse before Assistant Barrister Henry Hutton.[26] Eliza Davis was tried at the summer assizes in Wicklow before Chief Justice John Doherty.[27]

For some of the *Tasmania* (2) women, there was no delay before they appeared in court: Margaret Randall and Anne Williams waited only a day. For others, it was a different story: Mary Barry, Honora Cullen, Ann Daly, Bridget Fanning and Ann Wall waited over fifty days to be tried. Eliza Davis was in custody for over eighteen weeks while she was waiting to come before the grand jury.

Before the women appeared in court, the Crown solicitors, acting on behalf of the Attorney General who oversaw all prosecutions, prepared the cases for the Crown counsel.

The Clerk of the Crown swore in the members of the grand jury, the most important local body in Ireland.[28] Once the local government business was completed, the hearing of witnesses and the presentation of evidence took place. The grand jury decided whether there was sufficient evidence to bring the offenders to trial before a petty jury. If twelve members of the grand jury considered there was sufficient

# NOTICE

## OF
## QUARTER
# SESSIONS.

### COUNTY OF CARLOW.

The next General Quarter Sessions of the Peace will be held at CARLOW, on Thursday, the 17th day of Oct., 1839; at BAGENALSTOWN, (for Civil Bills,) on Monday, the 21st day of Oct., 1839; at TULLOW, on Wednesday, the 23rd day of October, 1839.

The Clerks of the Petty Sessions, are required to forward Informations and Recognizances to the Office of the Clerk of the Peace, pursuant to the 6th and 7th Wm. IV, chap. 34.

The names of Persons who serve Notice to register their Votes will be called in CARLOW, for the Borough and for the Division of CARLOW, at 10 o'Clock; and in TULLOW, for the Division of TULLOW, at the same hour on the first morning of each Sessions; the Lists to be called in Alphabetical order.

Persons applying for Licences to sell Spirits, &c. must give 21 days Notice in writing, to the two next resident Magistrates, the Churchwardens of the parish, and to the Clerk of the Peace.

All persons who have obtained, or shall obtain, a License for the sale of Spirits, are to serve a notice on the Clerk of the Peace describing the situation of their house, with the name and residence of their sureties, within 6 days after, under a penalty of 10 Pounds.

At the conclusion of the Registry at Carlow and Tullow, the names of persons applying for License to sell Spirits will be called

All persons who intend to register Fire-Arms at said Sessions, will be required to produce a Certificate from the Magistrates at Petty Sessions, previously held nearest to their respective residences, setting forth that they are proper persons to be entrusted with Fire-Arms, also the number of Arms to be stated, and that they are qualified according to Law.

All Civil Bills, Ejectments, and appeals, to be lodged the day previous to each Sessions with the Clerk of the Peace, that they may be entered in alphabetical order, and the Attorney's name must be endorsed on each.

Dated 1st day of July, 1839.

**ALEX. J. HUMFREY,**
Clerk of the Peace.

Civil Bill Processes will be called at the sitting of the Court on the second day of each Sessions (if the Registry be then concluded), and the Criminal business will be proceeded on at twelve o'clock on the 2nd day of each Sessions, if the Registry be concluded.

The grand Jury will be sworn at the termination of the Registry in each Division.

Lahee, County Printer, Dublin-street, Carlow.

Notice of the holding of the quarter sessions for the County of Carlow, 1839.
(NAI, OP/1839/132, reproduced with permission of the National Archives of Ireland)

evidence to merit a trial they 'found a true bill against the prisoner', who was then indicted with the offence.[29] In the case of Eliza Davis, her indictment stated 'for that she being the mother of a male child, name unknown, did kill and murder it by throwing it into a pond etc on 24th of February'.[30]

The next step in the legal process was the arraignment. The prisoner was brought to the dock, and the indictment was read. The prisoner was asked to plead. If the prisoner pleaded not guilty, the case would proceed.

Swearing in a petty jury could take some time, with dozens of people called by the County Sheriff. Once the jury was selected and sworn in the trial began. The Crown counsel opened the proceedings, stating the Crown's case and calling witnesses. The defendant usually only had a junior counsel; in the case of destitute prisoners, he was often appointed by the judge. Defence counsel for Eliza Davis was only appointed the night before her case came to court.[31]

At the conclusion of the hearing of witnesses, the Crown counsel could again address the jury. He was followed by the judge, who summarised the evidence.

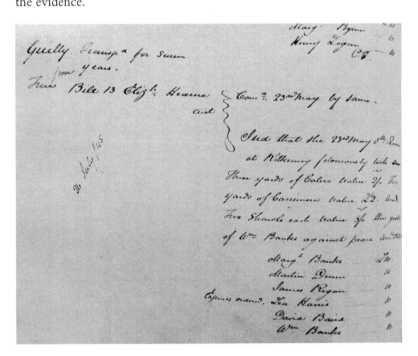

A True Bill was found against Elizabeth Hearns in the summer assize court. (NAI, CC/Kilkenny Assize Book 1833-46, reproduced with permission of the National Archives of Ireland)

As Niamh Howlin points out in a review of Irish murder trials, the discovery of a body usually triggered a trial.[32] The coroner was informed by the constabulary of any suspicious death. He then arranged for an inquest, empanelling a jury to examine the body, listen to the testimony of witnesses and to give a verdict. Eliza Davis and Catherine Meany went through this additional legal procedure.[33]

As already noted, an inquest into the death of Eliza's child was held the day after his body was found. Evidence was given that the cause of death was most likely suffocation.[34]

Similarly, the inquest for newly married Thomas Meany was held shortly after he died. The verdict was 'Wilful Murder against Catherine Meany, by administering Spanish Flies to her husband the deceased Thomas Meany from poisoning'. The magistrate stated he had been notified that a man was 'dangerously ill in a public house in Freshford'. He interviewed the man there, taking his dying declaration that he had been poisoned by his wife. Catherine Meany admitted she had given him the poison in a raspberry drink, procured by a man named Thomas Lennon. It appeared

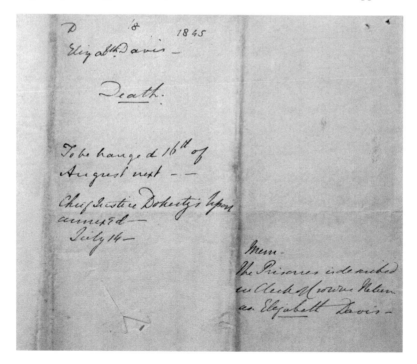

Eliza Davis' CRF. She was sentenced to death with planned date of execution 16 August 1845. (NAI, CRF 1845 D18, reproduced with permission of the National Archives of Ireland)

that Catherine had carried on an intrigue with Thomas Lennon for some
time before she married Thomas Meany and that he induced the woman to
poison her husband for the purpose of getting some money Thomas Meany
had collected to take Lennon to America.[35] Catherine was committed to the
Kilkenny County Gaol where she waited for over eight months to be tried.
Found guilty, she was sentenced to be 'transported beyond the seas for Life'.[36]

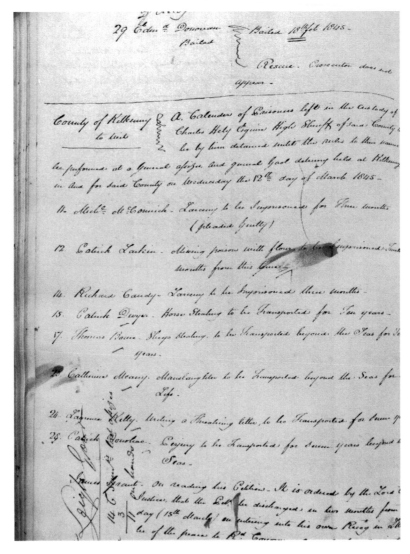

A calendar of prisoners left in the charge of Charles Hely Esquire High Sheriff
of County of Kilkenny, March 1845, listing Catherine Meany. (NAI, CC/Crown
Book Assizes Kilkenny 1833-46, reproduced with permission of the National
Archives of Ireland)

Before the judge passed sentence, information was sought about the behaviour of the women in gaol. In Carlow, the Tullow women were all found guilty. Their previous sentences were taken into consideration and Margaret Butler and Mary Griffin were described by the matron of the gaol as 'desperate characters & very ill conducted in Gaol'. They were then sentenced to transportation for seven years.[37]

Once the verdict had been reached and the judge had passed sentence, the Clerk of the Crown recorded in the quarter session or assize book the names of those found guilty. In Catherine Meany's case, her name was one of eleven listed on 'A Calendar of Prisoners left in the Charge of Charles Hely Esquire High Sheriff of County of Kilkenny, to be by him detained until their names be performed at a General Assize and general Gaol delivery held at Kilkenny in and for said County on Wednesday the 12th day of March 1845'.[38] As the records of the trials have not survived, there is no way of knowing how long the trials lasted. Vaughan, assuming that the judge sat for thirty hours over a period of five days at the Monaghan spring assizes in 1833, calculated that each trial of the ninety-five people before the court took on average twenty minutes.[39]

For many of the women of the *Tasmania* (2), the apprehension and anxiety experienced while they waited for trial must have been daunting. No doubt, the pageantry and formal language of the courts was an intimidating and overwhelming experience for most. The language used by the protagonists – Clerk of the Crown, solicitors and judges – was anything but simple or straightforward.

## PETITIONS

It is through the petitions or memorials that the voices of those convicted of a crime can be heard. Petitioning was the means by which those found guilty of a crime could appeal to the Lord Lieutenant, the Crown's representative in Ireland, for the 'prerogative of mercy to commute their sentence'.[40] The petitions, known as Convict Reference Files from 1836, provide two perspectives on the one event: the view of the officials involved in the case and that of the perpetrator. The petitions are remarkable documents for the wealth of information they provide about an individual and her circumstances.

Eighteen of the *Tasmania* (2) women sentenced to a term of transportation in 1844 and 1845 petitioned for clemency while they were in their respective county or city gaols. All except one were unsuccessful.

According to Rena Lohan, between 1791 and 1853, approximately 7,000 petitions were presented to the Lord Lieutenant by men and just under 1,000 by women. Taking into account the number of men sentenced to transportation in proportion to women, Lohan suggests that women petitioned on average only half as often as men.[41]

Margaret Gardiner, tried in January 1844 and sentenced to nine months' imprisonment for stealing, petitioned Earl De Grey in May that year. Committed to Queen's County Gaol in Maryborough in November 1843, she requested that her sentence be mitigated to the period she had already spent in gaol, 'afraid her poor aged Mother will die with want and hardship'. The opinion of Judge John Scholes was forwarded to Dublin Castle for the Lord Lieutenant's information. It did not paint a very positive picture of the petitioner:

> The case (picking pockets) was clearly proved, and the prisoner is a prostitute, of notorious bad character. The only doubts the Court had, was, whether she ought not to have been sentenced to transportation. In my humble opinion, a mitigation of her term of imprisonment would be of no benefit either to herself or to the community in which she was a nuisance. The prisoner has some solitary imprisonment yet to undergo, which may be salutary.[42]

In 1845, Margaret was sentenced to seven years' transportation for stealing but she did not petition again. She most likely knew that her next conviction would be a more severe sentence and that petitioning, under the circumstances, would be futile.

The petitions were usually written in the third person, on behalf of the prisoner, although Anne Kelly appears to have written her own petition.[43] Some petitions contain additional letters from family members: for example, Ann Flannery's father, Patrick, and Margaret Lee's sister, Catherine Fox.[44] The petitions were written in a stylised legal format. It is possible that prisoners or their families paid legal clerks to write the petitions. Hamish Maxwell-Stewart described colonial petitions as 'elaborate things, embellished with gothic capitals and elegant flourishes that curved across the paper directing the eye to their obsequious words'.[45] The Irish experience was no different.

Gaol chaplains may also have written petitions on behalf of their flock. This was certainly the case in Wicklow Gaol where the Church of Ireland chaplain, Revd Robert Porter, wrote letters seeking clemency for those in his charge.[46]

The petitions were written in a deferential and subordinate manner, addressing the Lord Lieutenant respectfully. The petitioner usually emphasised the compassion and humanity of the Lord Lieutenant, believing that he would consider the extenuating reasons. The closing line was generally 'and in duty bound will ever pray', showing the Lord Lieutenant that he would forever have the gratitude and prayers of the petitioner if he would but favour him or her with a successful outcome. Bláthnaid Nolan concluded that 'Irish convict women engaged in tendering petitions divulged an understanding of the power system they found themselves in'.[47] For some it worked. Lohan revealed that 49 of the 103 petitions submitted between 1845 and 1852 received a positive response.[48]

Promising to turn away from a path of wrongdoing, to which they had often been led by others, was one of the strategies used to achieve a commutation of sentence.[49] Others outlined the potential suffering for their family if they were transported. Of the petitions submitted only one – that of Ellen Sullivan from Camp, County Kerry – admitted guilt.[50] Catherine Hughes, aged 17, wrote three petitions from Tullamore Gaol. Described in her petition as a 'charwoman and merchant late of Aughrim in County Roscommon', she stated she had been convicted on her first offence for 'taking a few shillings'. She claimed, too, that the evidence against her was circumstantial and in her desperation petitioned not only the Lord Lieutenant but also 'Her Most Gracious Majesty Victoria the 1st', appealing to her as a mother:

> Your Majesty has given birth to Royal offspring who one day will sway the Sceptre of England and consider in your Royal Benevolent clemency the love you have towards your Royal children and although memorialist is the daughter of humble parents they are impregnated with the same paternal affection.

Catherine pleaded not to be sent from her native land, 'from the bosoms of all she holds dear, an aged mother, and five orphan'd Bros and sister, your Supplicant once their prop and stay for maintenance and support, but now their cause of shame their total ruin'.[51]

Sarah Ann O'Neill claimed she was the sole support for her mother who was 'dumb'. Both Sarah Ann and her mother were charged with the same offence, but her mother only received a sentence of imprisonment.[52] Elizabeth Wright, charged in Londonderry of having instruments for base coining in her possession, stated that her six children, ranging in age from

6 to 19, who had 'been entirely depending on her for support', would be 'left without the smallest means of subsistence'. While Chief Justice Pennefather 'could not make any change to the sentence' as she had been tried before with her husband for the same offence (he was transported but she escaped this fate then), he did suggest that the children could go with her.[53] Two children were granted permission to go with their mother; however, for whatever reason, Elizabeth did not bring any of her children with her.

When the petition arrived at Dublin Castle, the Lord Lieutenant read it and then officialdom sprang into action; reports, observations and notes were requested from those who had been involved in the case or who could give some insight and background to the character of the petitioner. This meant the judge at the trial, gaolers or individuals. The judges were asked if the petitioner was a proper object of mercy or if there were any circumstances which would enable the Lord Lieutenant to use his 'prerogative of mercy to commute their sentence'. Unfortunately for the petitioner, all too often the judges' responses contained the phrase 'no mitigating circumstances in this case'. Despite the women's pleadings, the response was invariably the same: the law must take its course.

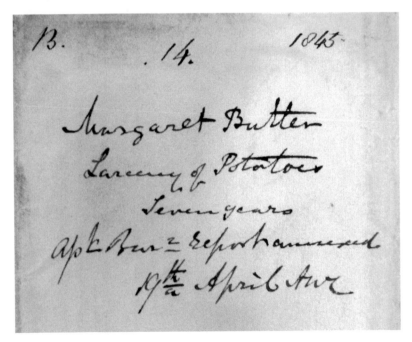

Margaret Butler 2nd's CRF cover page. (NAI, CRF 1845 B14, reproduced with permission of the National Archives of Ireland)

Few petitions were successful. As already noted, Eliza Davis' petition led to the commutation of her death sentence to transportation for life, while Margaret Butler, who begged to be allowed to remain with her children and not to be sent from Ireland, was ignored.[54]

Jane Bradshaw, a single mother aged 26, petitioned from Maryborough Gaol in Queen's County. She was described as 'an unprotected orphan', with a 'fatherless orphan scarcely ripe from her breast', and her petition stated:

> That your Petitioner, who is the Mother of an Infant Child, and left without a Father's protection or support is heartily sorry for having incurred the displeasure of the Law, to which she promises the strictest obedience in the future.

Jane had been charged with having a small frying pan, 'alleged to have been stolen', in her possession. She claimed to have borrowed it from a woman whose husband, from some 'private pique', was being obnoxious to her; when he found it in her possession, he prosecuted her. Her petition was in vain:

> The prisoner (who is the mother of an illegitimate child) stole the article in the Indictment, out of the house of a neighbour. She had been twice before convicted of Larceny, besides having been imprisoned for Vagrancy and Trespass.[55]

Perhaps not surprisingly, given this summary, there were no mitigating circumstances to consider. Jane's young daughter, Mary Jane Connor, accompanied her mother to Van Diemen's Land.

Honora Cullen was convicted of stealing a pound note on her first offence. A plain laundress from Tipperary, she was 'about 20 years of age'. Her petition, from Nenagh Gaol, stated that she was:

> a poor Orphan and earned her Bread by servitude, where she was seduced by a promise of marriage, and when she found herself pregnant, she was induced to take this money from her cousin to follow the person who brought her to misfortune as he was in a distant part, in hopes that he would fulfil his word.

She hoped to be 'left to rare her unfortunate offspring that she had the misfortune to bring into the world'. At her trial she was not able to afford a lawyer's fee.[56] About six weeks before her petition, and after eight months in gaol, she gave birth to a son, James Keegan, who came to Van Diemen's Land with her.[57]

An additional document was written from the victims of her crime, Bridget and Judy Ryan, seeking compensation in order to emigrate out of the country as they were in fear of 'sustaining violence from friends of the Traverser of whom there are a very powerful and a wicked faction in the country'. It was not successful.[58]

Judith Dooling, a widow aged 60, 'late of the Parish of Saint John Kilkenny', petitioned from Kilkenny Gaol. Judith and her son John were found guilty of 'receiving and having in their possession, one horse cover, the property of a Doctor Ryan of the 5th Regiment of Foot'. They were both sentenced to seven years' transportation. John pleaded guilty but 'positively declared' that his mother 'had nothing whatever to do with it'. Judith declared this was:

> the fact and truth, and consequently the Jury who tried her felt a great unwillingness to find her Guilty, but they could not avoid so doing, in as much as Petitioner and her said Son were tried under a Joint Indictment for such Offence, and the Barrister also expressed his regret at passing said sentence.

It seemed to be a great injustice resulting from a quirk of the law. Judith stated:

> that she's now upwards of twelve years a poor Widow and has endeavoured by her hard labour and industry to rear four fatherless children the youngest of who is only about twelve years of age. And Petitioner also begs leave most earnestly to state that should her said sentence be carried into execution, the youngest of her said children will be placed in a most forlorn and destitute state of indigence and misery, bereft of either Father or Mother, to rear or protect them, which is truly heart rending to your Excellency's aged, and alas heartbroken Petitioner.

Several merchants, shopkeepers and other inhabitants of the city of Kilkenny pleaded for clemency on Judith's behalf, including the mayor and former mayor, as well as the foreman of the jury. The Assistant Barrister Nicholas Purcell O'Gorman was requested to state whether the convicts were 'proper objects' for mercy or diminution of severity of sentence. He responded:

The Convicts were tried before me at the last October Sessions for Kilkenny in No. 11 for that they were receivers of certain stolen goods at Nelson Road to wit one suit of horse clothing the goods of Lewis Corcoran in No. 12 for that they did receive one trousers the goods of Martin McDonnell knowing same to have been feloniously stolen.

Henry Brook, a soldier proved that his master lost a suit of horse clothing, Sub S Bard proved his having searched in prisoner's house for those articles and found them concealed in the bed in which the female prisoner was lying, he was obliged to make her get up in order to find the stolen articles, when witness was taking the prisoner away in custody, the prisoner John then said the articles were his property, those articles were duly identified by both witnesses.

The prisoners produced no testimony … the Jury … without hesitation convicted the prisoners, neither of whom pleaded guilty.[59]

On 19 March 1845, in response to Judith's petition, Earl Heytesbury, Lord Lieutenant General and General Governor of Ireland, determined that the 'Law must take its Course'.

Ann Flannery, aged 24, was tried on her first offence, burning a house. Her father Patrick petitioned for clemency for his daughter, unsuccessfully, and she was transported for fifteen years:

That your Excellency's Petitioner has served many years in the Army – with credit to himself and the Corps (the 6th Dragoon Guards) in which he served until discharged at the General Reduction in the year 1814 – and in consequence of not having served his Second Period, got no Pension – that he subsequently served in the Roscommon Militia until disembodied and always supported a good character – that since the Militia was disembodied Petitioner has held a position of land at Roscommon – upon which by hard labour and industry he has hitherto supported his family – a wife and four children all of whom were born in the carabiniers –

That unfortunately in an evil hour the youngest daughter of Petitioner fell into error having become the victim of a designing villain who seduced her under pretence that he would marry her – that since that, she became acquainted with others who encouraged her to keep aloof from Petitioner – notwithstanding he tried every possible way to reclaim her to no purpose – until at length she in company with some other unfortunate girls who with another person, a man named Luke Fannon, were arrested about the 26th October last for

having attempted to burn a house. That Petitioner's daughter was
tried and convicted at the last General Assizes held in Roscommon
and sentenced to be transported for fifteen years – tho' Fannon was
acquitted on the same evidence. That Petitioner declines making any
remark on the conduct of and evidence given by the other parties –
who became the prosecutors of his daughter.

That Your Excellency's Petitioner, now an old gray headed man of
more than seventy-eight years – with a wife of about the same age –
a son who has been paralyzed since his infancy – and another son serving
with credit in the 9th Dragoons in India with a married and widowed
daughter who resides with Petitioner since the death of her husband,
a soldier, who died abroad – must eventually go with unparalleled sorrow
to the grave – If your Excellency does not take his wretched case into
your gracious consideration, and in your accustomed clemency, grant a
commutation of the sentence passed upon his daughter Ann Flannery –
which Petitioner humbly and earnestly implores your Excellency to do
and your Excellency's Petitioner will pray.

The petition was supported by the governor and surgeon to Roscommon
County Gaol and Infirmary. Despite the testimonies, Ann Flannery's
sentence was upheld.[60]

Anne Kelly was in Carlow Gaol when she successfully petitioned
in August 1845. Tried for stealing a pair of shoes, she was sentenced to
transportation for seven years. Anne argued that she committed the crime
because of her poverty:

> poverty alone induced her to commit the act which has been the cause
> of banishing her from her native home. She has two little boys who are
> now in the Poor House … the cries of her starving orphans was more
> than a mother could bear.[61]

She promised to never reoffend (she had already been to prison twice, for
three months and for twelve months). She argued that she was 'thrown on
the world very young without the protection of a mother or friend' and
that this was the cause of all her misfortune. Her petition was no different
to many others but her plea was heard and her sentence was commuted
to two years' imprisonment in the county gaol.[62] In September 1845,
the *Carlow Sentinel* published the following article, under the heading 'A
Fortunate Convict':

At the Quarter Sessions of Carlow, some time back a woman named Anne Kelly was sentenced to seven years transportation, being an old offender, and having been convicted of larceny on two previous occasions, being in fact a notoriously bad character. Shortly after her sentence she forwarded a memorial to the Lord Lieutenant without a single signature to it except her own. The memorial was referred to Henry Hutton Esq., the Assistant Barrister to report upon it and he stated the sentence of the court, and that the convict had been twice before convicted for larceny but declined recommending her petition to a favourable consideration. In a few days after we understand a communication was forwarded to Mr. Hutton by Sir Thomas Freemantle stating that the woman's sentence was commuted to two years imprisonment – a proceeding at which, we understand, the barrister was somewhat surprised.

It certainly is an unprecedented proceeding to have a convict's sentence commuted upon a bare statement of her own uncorroborated by a single signature, and what is still more singular, without any recommendation from the local authorities, and without even consulting them on the occasion.

What renders the case still more extraordinary is that about a year ago the prisoner was sentenced by the Judge to seven years transportation. On that occasion she petitioned the Judge before he left town, and made the same impression on his Lordship that she has now made on his Excellency.[63]

Esther Burgess, Margaret Butler's partner in crime, also had some success with her petition. Esther petitioned twice while she was in Carlow Gaol, the first time in April 1845:

Your Excellency's petitioner had no way to support herself and her large helpless family, but merely what petitioner could earn by her dayly labour, and being out of employment in February last petitioner had no means of any kind to purchase food for her miserable children, and the poor creatures were crying for something to eat, which caused the greatest affliction, and almost deranged Petitioner, at the impulse of the moment, and without reflection Petitioner unfortunately with her little daughter went out and brought in some Potatoes from a Neighbour's field, to keep Petitioner's wretched family from starvation.

The Lord Lieutenant was not moved by the cries of 'wretched orphans'. His abrupt and unambiguous response was 'The Law must take its Course'. Esther, however, was persistent: she sent a second petition in June 1845, pleading for her remaining child to be sent with her to 'New South Wales'. Her own plea for commutation of her sentence to imprisonment having been rejected, Esther Burgess wrote again, this time with the imprimatur of the Carlow Board of Superintendents, all of them Carlow landlords:

> To His Excellency Lord Heytesbury Lord Lieutenant General and General Governor of Ireland.
> The humble Petition of Esther Burgess a Prisoner under sentence of Transportation in Carlow Gaol—Humbly Sheweth
> That your Petitioner has a Daughter 13 years of age with no person to look after her and must ultimately come to utter ruin if your Excellency with your usual clemency and humanity will not allow her to go along with your Petitioner to New South [Wales]. That the Girl's Father being dead and having no friend or relative to look after her Petitioner humbly implores your Excellency will be graciously pleased to issue an order to have her sent to New South Wales along with your Petitioner and she shall ever pray.
>
> Esther Burgess
> Carlow Gaol, 2 June 1845.
> We believe the above statement to be true and we recommend the case to the favourable consideration of His Excellency the Lord Lieutenant …
> If I have the power of granting the prayer of this Petition, let the necessary steps be taken for that purpose. June 14th 1845 Heytesbury.[64]

Esther brought five of her seven children to Van Diemen's Land. Her eldest daughter, Mary, was tried with her and also transported on the *Tasmania* (2).[65]

The law did take its course for all who petitioned, except for Anne Kelly. For many the period between being committed to gaol to being tried and then awaiting word from Dublin Castle must have been a difficult time. As Oscar Wilde penned from his own experience in his *The Ballad of Reading Gaol* almost fifty years later:

I know not whether Laws be right,
Or whether Laws be wrong:
All that we know who lie in gaol
Is that the wall is strong;
And each day is like a year,
A year whose days are long.[66]

The waiting was not yet over. The transfer to Grangegorman Female Convict Depot to prepare for their long and arduous journey to Van Diemen's Land, for a number of the women, was still some time away.

For many, their anguish at being sentenced to transportation beyond the seas, forced to leave the country of their birth and undergo a sea voyage of over 12,000 miles to a strange land can only be imagined. For others like Mary Liston, Margaret Lee and Maria Lynch, who indicated that they wanted to be transported, receiving such a sentence appears to have been their objective.

# 'These Unfortunate Females': The Women of the *Tasmania* (2)[1]

Transportation to the penal colony of New South Wales ceased in 1840 and Van Diemen's Land became the main penal colony, receiving over 36,000 convicts between 1840 and 1853, when transportation there ended.[2] The Irish made up almost one third of that figure. The convicts' clothes and food were provided by the settlers in return for cheap labour. Those who behaved could look forward to earning a ticket of leave, which allowed them relative freedom and the right to work for wages. The granting of a conditional pardon or absolute pardon normally followed some time later.

Nearly 12,500 women were transported to Van Diemen's Land, mostly for petty theft. This was roughly the same number sent to New South Wales. Two thirds of the women arrived after 1840.[3]

Much of the historiography of convict women discounts the complexity of individual convict lives. Detailed studies of convict women demonstrate that their experience was individual, diverse and complex. As part of the exercise of putting 'some meat on the bones' of the *Tasmania* (2) convicts, this chapter considers demographic information about the women and the crimes they committed.[4]

Who, then, were the women on the *Tasmania* (2)?

## TRIAL PLACE

According to Williams, only 18 per cent of the women transported from Ireland came from the cities; most were rural women from the counties.[5]

The women of *Tasmania* (2) were tried in thirty of the thirty-two counties of Ireland. No *Tasmania* (2) women were tried in Sligo or Galway. The greatest number of *Tasmania* (2) women were tried in the province of Leinster (39.5 per cent), followed by Ulster (32 per cent), Munster (26.5 per cent), and Connaught (4 per cent).

## NATIVE PLACE

Most of the *Tasmania* (2) women were from Dublin, followed by Tipperary, Cavan and Fermanagh. The *Tasmania* (2) women came from thirty of the thirty-two counties of Ireland; no one came from Sligo. Dublin (county and city combined) had the highest number of convicts: 12.3 per cent, followed by Antrim with 8 per cent. Sligo and Galway were the only counties not represented.[6]

In rare instances, the recorded native place was quite specific: Elleanor McKiverigan, for example, was from Newry, County Down, and Catherine Foy was from Enniskillen, County Fermanagh. Catherine Hughes was from Athlone, Westmeath. Mostly, however, the recorded native place was simply the name of the county.

Nenagh Gaol, County Tipperary, 2014. (Authors' collection)

At least 26 per cent of the women were tried away from their native place. Being tried away from a native place could complicate matters at trial, even if it was in the same county. Honora Cullen, convicted on her first offence, stated in her petition from Nenagh Gaol that she was unable to pay for a lawyer 'to speak on her behalf as she was in a strange place where she was tried'.[7] According to her convict records, Honora was tried in Tipperary and her native place was Tipperary.

## LENGTH OF SENTENCE

The majority of women on the *Tasmania* (2) – 83 per cent – were sentenced to transportation for seven years, with twenty sentenced to ten years, two to fifteen years and two, Catherine Meany and Eliza Davis, sentenced to transportation for life.

|  | 7 | 10 | 14 | 15 | Life |
|---|---|---|---|---|---|
| **All Irish Female Convicts VDL (%)** | 83 | 10 | 1 | 3 | 3 |
| *Tasmania* (2) Convicts (%) 1845 | 83 | 14 | — | 1.5 | 1.5 |
| *Australasia* Convicts (%) 1849 | 84 | 8 | 1 | 3 | 5 |

Table 1: Percentage comparison of sentences of all Irish female convicts (n=3687) with *Tasmania* (2) convicts (n=138) and *Australasia* convicts (n=200).

## THE CRIMES

Classification of crime was an integral part of the convict system, although it was less significant in the colony where the crime committed was not as relevant as behaviour and skills. The length of sentence was only important for administrative purposes. Nevertheless, examining the types of crimes committed helps build a profile of the convict women.[8]

### Crimes against property: felony, burglary, larceny, stealing, receiving stolen goods

As with most convicts, the majority of *Tasmania* (2) women – 89 per cent – were transported for crimes against property.[9] Many of these property crimes were distinguished only by subtle differences.

Larceny, defined as the unlawful taking away of personal goods, accounted for 67 per cent of crimes committed by *Tasmania* (2) women and 74 per cent of property crimes.

The term felony related to an offence of a heinous or shocking character, while burglary was breaking into a house after sunset with intent to commit a felony. In some instances, the classification of crimes appears inconsistent: why were some cases of theft classed as felony when they appear no more serious than others? Stealing a watch, for example, could be classified as a felony, larceny or stealing.

Felony included various types of theft, including theft of money, clothing, ribbon, blankets and potatoes. Sixteen women were charged with felony of one sort. Anne Agnew, a Dublin dressmaker and milliner, was charged with felony for stealing a gold watch; Maria Johnson, for stealing a brass lock and lead pipe; and Mary Russell, for stealing potatoes.[10]

Two women were transported for burglary. Ellen Sullivan, who died during the voyage, was sentenced to transportation for ten years for burglary. It was her first offence.[11] Eleanor Shaughnessy, aged 19, was also convicted on her first offence and received a ten-year sentence. She admitted to burglary and stealing a veil.[12]

The offence of larceny was often broken down into specific types of larceny, such as stealing clothes (including boots and shoes) or cloth and stealing a watch. Thirteen stole money – amounts varied from 2/- to £43.[13]

Mary Hurley, from Kerry, had recently served three weeks for stealing when she was again charged with larceny and sentenced to transportation for seven years – she admitted to stealing a gown and a petticoat from her cousin.[14] The *Tralee Chronicle* reported:

> Mary Hurly pleaded guilty to stealing goods, the property of Michael Hurly of Tralee. Being one of those unfortunates creatures on the town and being found guilty of a larceny at the last sessions the Court said there was no use in expecting to have her reclaimed in this country and sentenced her to seven years transportation.[15]

Deborah Connor, aged 18, was tried at the Listowel Quarter Sessions in Kerry in April 1845 for stealing several items of clothing. She was sentenced to seven years' transportation.[16]

One of the most unusual accounts of stealing clothes was that of Catherine Riley, who admitted, 'I was living 10 years in men's clothes, I was an ostler at an Inn'.[17] Catherine, aged 30, was tried in Roscommon in October 1844 and was sentenced to transportation for seven years. She stated her offence to be stealing a suit of clothes. She had already been imprisoned for four months for the same offence.

According to the *Roscommon and Leitrim Gazette*, Catherine had stolen seventeen articles of clothing. The newspaper report revealed that Catherine, 'the traverser', had represented herself 'as having been ill-treated and deserted by her husband, who she alleged had gone off with another woman'. She sought shelter and after a few days 'decamped taking with her the sundry articles of clothing of the entire family':

> It appeared the … unfortunate woman was an old offender – and one in whose pursuit the … [arresting] policeman [James Mahon] was frequently engaged. She had been married twice – once in Mayo, under the name of Catherine Reilly to a man named Maley, by whom she had one child. After the death of the child she plundered this man's house of £25 – the money, in order to secure it she handed to her sister, but [her sister] turned the cash to her own account, and with it purchased some sheep; Catherine, after some time found her [sister] living at Belmullet, co. Mayo – took the sheep from her, and beat her so severely that her life was despaired of, for this latter offence she was tried at the Sessions of Ballina and sentenced to 7 years' transportation; when on her journey to Dublin (under the charge of … the Governor of the Mayo prison) the car broke down and [he] was dangerously injured; the country people having assembled wanted her to escape, but this she declined to do declaring her determination to attend him till his wounds were healed and his health restored … and on the recovery of [the Governor] he represented her conduct to the Lord Lieutenant which resulted in her sentence being commuted to two years' imprisonment. After the termination of the two years she procured a suit of men's clothes and returned under the name of James Reilly; there she engaged as a labouring man and for five days worked in the same field, with her brother! From thence she went to Killala, hired there as a servant boy, and after some months stole some clothes, she fled to Ballaghaderreen; in this town she hired with Mr. P. Gallagher, where she attended his stables and when time permitted worked in the fields with the men.

Catherine successfully masqueraded as a man for some time but was found out when she married:

At last she got married to a young woman, named Nelly Brett, with whom she lived for about 4 months, when, by mere accident, circumstances led to the report that the reputed husband was an imposter!

Nelly applied to Thomas Phillips, Esq., JP, of Clonmore, who issued a warrant for Catherine's arrest. After Catherine's apprehension, a note was sent to her native place and it was revealed that there was another warrant, issued because of the clothes she had stolen in Killala. She was sent to Ballina to await her trial and was sentenced to one month in prison. Catherine then returned to Ballaghaderreen. She met up with Nelly and they resolved to travel together, committing robberies as they went. Warrants were issued for their apprehension and 'the zealous and efficient' Constable Mahon 'at length succeeded in bringing to justice the … notorious and dangerous character':

> After our Assistant-Barrister had passed the sentence of 7 years' transportation the unfortunate woman left the Court singing in a good style "The Irish Girl".[18]

Like larceny, stealing was broken down into specific categories. Four women were charged with stealing rather than larceny. Two stole watches; one stole money and clothes; and one stole 6 yards of cashmere.[19]

Some of the women were transported for stealing animals. Mary Leonard, from Fermanagh, was 31 and had two children. She was sentenced to transportation for seven years for larceny – stealing a cow at her native place.[20] Ann Burns, from Tipperary, was transported for seven years for stealing five sheep.

Mary Meagher, transported for ten years, was part of a Tipperary sheep-stealing gang. Her son and father-in-law were transported for the same offence.[21]

As already noted, Margaret Butler 2nd stole twelve potatoes. Of the other women from Tullow, Esther Burgess stole 6 stone (38kg) of potatoes and Mary Byrne stole 2 stone (12.7kg). Esther's daughter Mary Burgess stole an unspecified quantity, as did Mary Griffen.

The Tullow women were not the only women transported for stealing potatoes, which seems to have been commonly done in small groups. Bridget Gallagher, her mother Rose Fitzpatrick and her brother James Gallagher were all transported for stealing potatoes. Rose admitted to stealing 10 stone (63.5kg); James to stealing about 7 or 8 stone (44.5 or 50.8kg); and Bridget simply to stealing potatoes.[22]

Margaret Maguire and her mother Mary Scallon were tried in Fermanagh for stealing potatoes.[23] Both had previous convictions for stealing poultry.

Tried together in Kildare, Ann Delany and Mary Russell were charged with felony (stealing potatoes). Ann, who was only 17, admitted to stealing 8lbs (3.7kg) of potatoes. She confessed to three previous offences of stealing potatoes. Mary stated that she stole eight barrels of potatoes. She also confessed to having been imprisoned for three similar offences as well as six weeks for assault.[24]

In all, nine women were transported for stealing potatoes.

At least twelve women were transported for receiving stolen goods.[25]

## Coining

Elizabeth Wright was tried in Londonderry on 17 March 1845 for having instruments for coining (a mould) in her possession. It was her first offence and she was sentenced to transportation for ten years. Elizabeth Wright's husband, John Wright, was convicted of passing base coin in Londonderry in 1842. He admitted to having lived for two years by selling base coin. He arrived in Van Diemen's Land on the *North Briton* in 1843.[26]

## Perjury

Two women were tried for perjury. Elizabeth Waring, a widow aged 40, was tried in Down in March 1845. It was her first offence. Sentenced to transportation for seven years, Elizabeth stated: 'Some people robbed me and then got witnesses to prove that they did not'.[27]

Bridget Stankard, aged 24, was also convicted on her first offence. Tried in Leitrim in December 1844, Bridget stated her offence: 'I swore that a man named Armstrong and another broke into a church. I was drunk at the time.'[28]

## 'A bunch of vagrants'[29]

Williams linked prostitution (or 'being on the town') and vagrancy.[30] Both were forms of survival in tough economic times. Eight women on the *Tasmania* (2) were transported for vagrancy.[31]

Bridget Cunningham, aged 20, was tried in Longford in July 1844 and was sentenced to transportation for seven years for vagrancy.[32] It was her first conviction. She stated that her offence was 'obtaining money by means of begging letters' and this was borne out by a report in the *Longford Journal*:

> William Harding, a smart or pert looking little man, apparently about 30 years of age, dressed in a scuffed green body coat, shabby brown surtout and Bridget Cunningham, a young woman of about 20, with an old worn out cloak, and a shabby black and white straw bonnet, were indicted as vagrants, having no settled place of residence, strolling about without any honest means of making out a living.
>
> Police Sergeant Peter Harvey, of Kenagh, deposed that on the 22nd June he received a message which caused him to arrest the prisoners, and on searching them found a great number of 'begging letters' in their bundle and on their person ... and which showed they made a regular trade of imposing on the charitable and humane.
>
> The reading of these documents attracted the attention of all in court, and excited some laughter from the ingenuity which with they were written, and several of them were addressed to gentlemen in every county from this down to Cork.
>
> The judge having explained the law, the jury returned a verdict for the prosecution.
>
> The prisoners were sentenced to be imprisoned for three months to afford them an opportunity of procuring two solvent sureties in £5 each, and themselves in £10 each, to keep the peace for seven years, in case they did not procure the required securities, to be then transported for seven years each.[33]

Bridget Egan and Mary Liston were tried with Mary Mansfield.[34] The *Nenagh Guardian*, reporting the North Tipperary Assizes, wrote:

> Biddy Egan, Mary Mansfield, and Mary Liston were indicted as vagrants. The two former pleaded Not Guilty, and the latter Guilty.
> Biddy Egan and Mary Mansfield, were then given in charge as vagrants.
> Mr. John Hart, of Borrisokane, deposed to their being vagrants.
> Mr. William Lavarette, also deposed to their being vagrants and being drunk about the town.
> Sub Constable Richard Revell, proved that he often took Egan up for being drunk; took the other prisoner to gaol for breaking Mr. Lavarette's windows.

Cork Gaol, 2014. (Authors' collection)

The Jury found them guilty, and his Lordship sentenced them to 7 years transportation, if they did not find two sureties in £5 each, within 3 months, for their good behaviour. He also remarked, that if they adopted the advice they were likely to receive, previous to their leaving this country, they would find they would end their days more happy than if they remained at home.[35]

## Arson

Two of the *Tasmania* (2) were convicted of arson.[36] Many more Irish women were transported for arson than English women, even before the famine.[37]

Ann Flannery, aged 24, was tried in Roscommon in July 1845 and was sentenced to transportation for fifteen years. Ann stated her offence to be burning a house. Although her gaol report stated that Ann had no previous offences, she admitted to being imprisoned for three days for stealing a watch and to being three years 'on the town'.[38]

Maria Lynch, like her arsonist shipmate Ann Flannery, was tried in Roscommon in July 1845. She stated that she set fire to a cart house; her prosecutor was in Galway.[39]

## Infanticide

As noted previously, there was one case of infanticide: that of Eliza Davis, tried in Wicklow for the murder of her infant child and sentenced to transportation for life.

## Manslaughter

Catherine Meany stated her offence to be poisoning her husband with cantharides: 'I was only married 3 weeks and 3 days, I was instigated to it by another man, Thomas Connor'.[40] Like Eliza Davis, she was sentenced to transportation for life.

| Offence | All Irish Female Convicts (%) | *Tasmania* (2) Convicts (%) 1845 | *Australasia* Convicts (%) 1849 |
|---|---|---|---|
| Larceny/Burglary | 60 | 80 | 57 |
| Animal stealing | 16 | 2 | 30 |
| Arson | 7 | 1.5 | 9 |
| Vagrancy | 3 | 6 | 1 |
| Receiving | 6 | 6.5 | 1 |
| Murder/Manslaughter/Assault | 2 | 1 | 2 |
| Other | 1 | 3 | 1 |

Table 2: Comparison of offences committed by all Irish female convicts (n=3,687), *Tasmania* (2) 1845 convicts (n=138) and *Australasia* 1849 (n=200).

## CONVICTIONS

In his study of Irish convicts, John Williams discovered that 64 per cent of Irish convicts, 70 per cent of English convicts and 93 per cent of Scottish convicts had previous offences.[41] Most of the *Tasmania* (2) women had been convicted before, usually only once or twice. Bridget Clifford, a vagrant, claimed to have been convicted twenty times.[42]

By their own account, 82 per cent of the women on board the *Tasmania* (2) were repeat offenders, some with numerous previous convictions.[43] When the women arrived in Van Diemen's Land, they were questioned about previous convictions; some, like Anne Dogherty, Ellen Cummane and Mary McVeagh, were economical with the truth.

In January 1845, the *Longford Journal* remarked that Anne Doherty was 'a strolling lady, who was acquainted with the vicinity of the gaol before from her previous visits to it'.[44] Anne was sentenced to seven years' transportation at Longford Quarter Sessions for stealing a goose and a gown.[45] When she arrived in Hobart Town, Anne admitted to having only one previous conviction.[46]

Like Anne, Deborah Connor, from Kerry, also admitted to only one previous conviction when she arrived in Hobart Town, a sentence of four months' imprisonment for stealing clothes.[47] The judge at her trial at the Listowel Quarter Sessions made note of this when he commented:

> it appeared the unfortunate woman was a hardened offender, and had been sentenced no later than the session before last to four months imprisonment. His Worship was sorry to perceive, that the sentence had no effect on her, as she still continued her former course of life and felt it his duty, his brother magistrate agreed with him, to sentence her to transportation for seven years.[48]

In Van Diemen's Land, Mary McVeagh admitted to only one previous conviction.[49] However, evidence in Ireland suggests that this was far from the truth. In the Lurgan Quarter Sessions (County Armagh), in November 1844, Mary appeared before Judge Edward Tickell, who stated:

> The Jury found the Prisoner guilty and in consequence of the exceedingly bad character given for the Prisoner by the Chief Constable and some of the other Police stationed near her residence this Bench decreed that further enquiry should be made about her … it appears that she had been previous to this gaol conviction, tried 3 times for larceny and had been twice convicted, her house was described by the Constable as a receptacle for thieves and when a robbery was committed was the one usually searched first.[50]

Mary's legal encounters, from the records supplied by the governor of Down County Gaol, dated back to 1839, when she received a sentence of two months with hard labour for stealing ducks. A year later, under the name of Mary Lavery, she was found not guilty of stealing a bed quilt and thirty hanks of yarn. In February 1841, she was charged with stealing fowl and spent a year of hard labour in Down Gaol.[51]

Mary was also creative with her age. In her petition, she claimed to be 'an old woman of nearly 80 years of age and a widow and mother of eight children, 3 sons and 5 daughters, 2 of her sons in the army but one of them drowned about 4 years ago'.[52] In fact, she was more likely to have been in her early fifties.[53] The Down County Gaol records stated that Mary was 49 in 1839, which would make her 54 in 1845. The governor of Armagh Gaol, Mr Turner, in his correspondence gave her age as 58.[54]

Anne Daley was tried and convicted in her native county of Tipperary in July 1845 for stealing a cloak, and was sentenced to seven years' transportation. In Van Diemen's Land, she confessed to a previous conviction for stealing a watch; she served a six-month sentence for this and was also convicted six or seven times for drunkenness. The Clonmel Gaol Register indicates that Anne was an inmate of the gaol on at least twenty occasions from December 1840 to the time she was sentenced to transportation in July 1845. Between 1840 and 1845, she was convicted of a range of offences: 'disorderly vagrant', 'drunk and disorderly and a common whore', 'prostitute', 'idle and disorderly', assault and larceny. She was also charged with 'attempting to drown herself and attempting to destroy

Clonmel Courthouse, County Tipperary, 2014. (Authors' collection)

Clonmel Gaol, County Tipperary, 2014. (Authors' collection)

herself in the workhouse'.[55] In a number of instances, Anne was released one day only to be re-committed to the gaol the following day. Anne was committed to Clonmel Gaol on 11 May 1845 for stealing a cloak. When she was sentenced to transportation, the resident magistrate noted that she was '23 times convicted'.[56]

Eliza Perry, a native of County Wicklow, was another repeat offender. In Van Diemen's Land, Eliza confessed to being imprisoned twice for three months for pledging. She was described as pock-pitted.[57] She was committed to Grangegorman Female Prison in January 1845 for a felony – stealing a watch and money in Dublin. She was sentenced in Dublin City to transportation for seven years. A woman named Eliza Perry from Wicklow appeared twenty-five times in the Dublin City Gaol Registers. Another entry for the same name, but with a native place of Hacketstown, a town in County Carlow bordering Wicklow, also appears in the register.[58] Eliza's first offence was in 1834, when she was charged with stealing money; she was imprisoned for three months. She committed a similar crime in 1837, serving six months in prison. The majority of her committals were for disturbing the peace and being disorderly; sentences imposed went from twenty-four hours to six months. Her trade, on two occasions was described as 'street walker', on others, as a 'servant'.[59]

Surviving gaol registers for the 1830s and 1840s list some women with similar names to those on the *Tasmania* (2); they may well have been the same women.[60] It is not always possible to prove that those of the same name were those transported on the *Tasmania* (2). From evidence in the registers, however, it is obvious that a number of the women had

Louth County Gaol, Dundalk, 2014. (Authors' collection)

considerably more contact with the law than they admitted to on arrival in Hobart.[61]

Anne Agnew from Dundalk, County Louth, stated she had been convicted once before for stealing, receiving a sentence of thirteen months.[62] An Ann Agnew, also from Dundalk, was committed to Grangegorman Female Prison in 1836 for three months for stealing a watch. In both records, her trade was listed as milliner.[63] It is likely that she was the woman who arrived on the *Tasmania* (2).

Mary Barry was sentenced to a term of transportation for seven years at the Limerick City Summer Assizes in July 1845 for stealing a sheet.[64] On arrival in Van Diemen's Land, Mary admitted to six months in prison for stealing 1s 8d. This is confirmed in the Limerick Gaol Register. She was discharged on 6 May 1845, having completed her sentence. If this is the same Mary Barry, she was back in Limerick Gaol in May, awaiting trial for the offence for which she was transported.[65]

Mary O'Brien 2nd admitted to three previous convictions but at her trial in July 1845:

His Lordship said this was the fourth time the prisoner had been convicted of robbery and the sixth time she had been in custody. Therefore, it was useless to allow her to remain in the country. The sentence of the Court was that she be transported for 7 years.[66]

It is not known how many previous convictions Ellen Cummane really had but she seems to have had a reputation for being troublesome. Ellen was convicted of larceny at the Tralee Quarter Sessions (County Kerry) in October 1844. She admitted to having been previously sentenced to twelve months for assault. The newspaper report remarked that 'having been convicted before she was sentenced to seven years transportation; the bench declaring their intention of weeding such characters out of this town'.[67]

Several of the women – 22.5 per cent – were convicted on a first offence. As already noted, Eliza Davis was transported for life on her first offence.

## MOTIVES BEHIND THE CRIMES

There was a strong link between poverty and crime. Women such as Margaret Butler 2nd asserted that poverty and distress drove them to crime:

Margaret, widowed with several children to feed, claimed that the crime she committed was the result of hardship and 'the tears of her wretched orphans'.[68]

Margaret Sloane, in her petition from Omagh Gaol, stated that 'in a time of extreme destitution and distress she was tempted to an old calico gown hardl[y] value[d] at one shilling'. She was tried in Tyrone for stealing a gown and a quilt, and sentenced to transportation for seven years.[69]

Some of the women confessed to deliberately committing crime in order to be transported.[70] Margaret Lee stated that she stole a shawl, adding, 'I committed this offence to follow my sister'.[71] Her sister, Anne Lee, was tried in 1843 in Monaghan for larceny.[72] While a petition seeking mercy was submitted on behalf of Margaret by another sister, Catherine Fox, Margaret gave 'no account of herself' at the trial at the Newry Sessions in October 1844. She was found guilty of stealing a shawl in a shop in the town of Newry, where she was unknown and no character witnesses were called. Was Margaret's silence her way of ensuring a sentence of transportation?

Mary Liston pleaded guilty to vagrancy in July 1844 at the North Tipperary Assizes.[73] The *Nenagh Guardian* reported:

> Court – Does she know she will be transported if she plead Guilty.
> Mary Liston – I do, my lord.
> Judge – Then you wish to be transported?
> Liston – I do, Sir.
> Judge – Then, if she doesn't get bail, two sureties in £5 each, within three months, let her be transported for 7 years.[74]

Arsonist Maria Lynch at her trial in Roscommon asked to be transported, as the *Roscommon and Leitrim Gazette* reported:

> Maria Lynch, Arson, by her own admission on the 23rd May, of a house between Knockeroghery and Athlone – The Prisoner, on being placed at the bar, pleaded guilty, and begged that his Lordship transport her.[75]

## PROSTITUTION: BEING 'ON THE TOWN'

Female convict records routinely recorded those involved in prostitution or being 'on the town', even though prostitution was not an offence. In all,

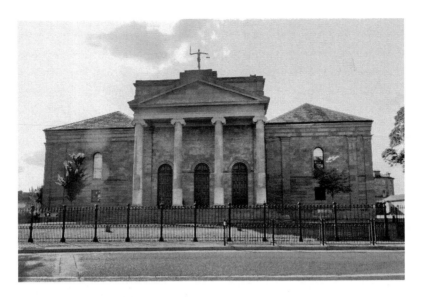

Nenagh Courthouse, Nenagh, County Tipperary, 2014. (Authors' collection)

the records of forty-four of the *Tasmania* (2) women were annotated in this way. This lifestyle was reflected in the medical complaints of some en route.[76]

Most of those who had been 'on the town' were transported for theft of some kind, although there were exceptions, including arsonist Ann Flannery who admitted to being three years 'on the town'.[77] Four women transported for vagrancy also confessed to being 'on the town'.[78]

Ellen Callaghan, a plain laundress or house servant in her 20s, stated her offence to be stealing money from a man. She admitted to previous offences – two or three times for stealing money – and added that she had been five or six years 'on the town'.[79]

Bell Amos, a farm servant from Fermanagh at the time of her trial, admitted to being three years 'on the town'. She was only 19 and so would have been 'on the town' from the time she was about 16.[80]

Bridget Dignan, a widow from Drogheda aged 22, confessed to a year.[81]

## TRIED TOGETHER

Some of the women were tried in pairs or small groups. Ann Collins and Margaret Daley, who both confessed to being 'on the town', were tried together in Cork for receiving stolen goods.[82] Jane Gallagher and Sarah Jane Marrow were tried together in Antrim for stealing money.[83]

Catherine Keeffe and Johannah Murray were tried in Cork on New Year's Day 1845 for receiving stolen goods (blankets).[84] Johannah stated that she was tried with Catherine 'Keath'.

Mary McBride and Elleanor McKiverigan, tried in Down, were both transported for ten years for larceny (stealing a handkerchief).[85] Mary stated that she was tried with 'Elleanor McKinowan'.[86]

Mary Sullivan 1st stated she was tried with Henrietta Beresford on board.[87] Mary, a widow with one child, was tried on 3 January 1845 in Limerick. She stated her offence to be stealing 16/-. Henrietta Beresford was tried in Limerick on 18 October 1844 for stealing muslin; her native place was Waterford.[88] The evidence of the two women does not match but it is difficult to say why.


## TRIED OR TRANSPORTED WITH FAMILY

As already mentioned, Tullow mother and daughter Esther and Mary Burgess were part of a small group transported for stealing potatoes. Transportation for the Burgess women was a family affair: not only was Esther Burgess tried with her daughter, but she brought five of her children with her.[89]

Potato stealing seems to have been a common group activity and was perhaps necessary for survival. Rose Fitzpatrick, aged 45, was tried in Cavan with her daughter Bridget Gallagher, aged 19, and her labourer son James Donovan, aged 23, who was transported as James Gallagher 1st.[90] Rose's older sister Ann, aged 54, was also transported on the Tasmania (2).[91] She was also tried in Cavan but for having stolen goods on her person.

Mary Meaghar, a widow aged 46 with ten children, was part of a family sheep-stealing gang, three generations tried together in Tipperary.[92] Mary Meagher's young son, Stephen Meagher, arrived on the Ratcliffe (1) in 1845. Because he was only 13, he was sent to Point Puer, near Port Arthur, when he arrived.[93] This was the place where juvenile male convicts were sent. Stephen was only 4ft 6in tall; he was Roman Catholic and could read a little. On board with Stephen were his grandfather, John Meagher 1st, aged 48; and uncle John, aged 25.[94] Grandfather John was sentenced to transportation for ten years for sheep stealing; Stephen, described as a labourer from Tipperary, and his mother Mary were transported for ten years for the same offence. Grandfather John's indent recorded that he was tried with his son and grandson on board; he was a quarryman from County Tipperary, a widower with eight children. He stated that his daughter-in-law 'Mary Rowan' (Mary Meaghar) was also transported.[95] Mary's brother-in-law John was tried for felony in a dwelling and putting in fear; he stated his offence to be stealing a gun.[96]

Judith Dooling, or Dowling, and her son John Dooling were tried together in Kilkenny but John was transported twelve months before his mother, arriving on the *Ratcliffe* (1) in 1845.[97] On his indent, John stated: 'Mother Judy transported coming out. Brothers Michael Patrick and Jerry, sisters Biddy and Honor'.[98] Both Judith and John died in tragic circumstances: Judith was accidentally killed in 1856 and John was murdered in 1859.[99]

Harriet Madine and Bell Rooney were cousins, both aged 28. Harriet was tried in County Down on 18 June 1845 for stealing £5. Bell was also tried in County Down on the same day for stealing 19/4d from the person. Both women had been 'on the town', Harriet for five years and Bell for eight months.[100]

Some of the women on the *Tasmania* (2) had family members who had been transported. This information was included on the convict indent.[101]

In some instances, it has not been possible to trace those family members who were transported. Variations in the spelling of names, common names and the use of maiden names for married women complicate the process. In addition, some family members may have been transported to other penal colonies.

Mary Salmon or Lyons, for example, had a brother, James, transported (according to her) 'about 6 years ago'.[102] He has not been located in the Van Diemen's Land records under Salmon or Lyons.

Sarah Jane Morrow's brother Patrick was transported but he has not been traced in the Tasmanian records.[103]

Mary Meehan, from Clare, also had a brother, Patrick, transported. He was her only living family member. According to her indent, he was transported 'about 14 years ago' but he also has not been located in the Van Diemen's Land records.[104] Similarly, Bridget Kelly's brother Patrick, transported about 1840, has not been traced.[105]

Margaret Lee had a sister Anne 'transported 2 year ago'. Anne arrived on the *East London* in 1843. Her indent stated that she was from Cavan and had three sisters: Rosa, Catherine and Margaret, all in Cavan.[106]

The husbands of at least four women were also transported. These are discussed in Chapter 9.

## BACKGROUND

### Religion

Overwhelmingly, the women of the *Tasmania* (2) were Roman Catholic: 78 per cent gave this as their religion. Another 21 per cent stated that they were Protestant (Church of England). One woman, Elizabeth Waring, a widowed servant tried in County Down, was recorded as a Jewess in the colony but a Protestant in the Grangegorman register.[107]

### Literacy

Most of the women were illiterate. The majority – seventy-two – could neither read nor write; fifty could read; while sixteen claimed that they could read and write (although some of these only a little).

### Age

The oldest of the convicts on board was Anne Gardiner or Harrison, who was 64.[108] There were eight others in their 60s. The youngest, Bridget Fanning, was 16.[109] Most of the women – 64 per cent – were in their 20s.

In comparison to other convict ships on which age studies have been carried out, the *Tasmania* (2) had fewer young convicts (aged between 10 and 19) and more older convicts (aged 50 and above), as shown in Table 3.

| Ship | 10–19 | 20–29 | 30–39 | 40–49 | 50+ |
|---|---|---|---|---|---|
| *Rajah* 1841 (England) | 20 | 56 | 15 | 5 | 4 |
| *Australasia* 1849 (Ireland) | 23 | 62 | 12 | 2.5 | 0.5 |
| *Tasmania* (2) 1845 (Ireland) | 6.5 | 64 | 14 | 9 | 6.5 |
| *Duchess of Northumberland* 1853 (England) | 25 | 47 | 20 | 7 | 1 |

Table 3: Comparison of ages.

### Trades

Most of the *Tasmania* (2) women who came into Grangegorman, including Margaret Butler 2nd, had no trade or occupation. There were some exceptions: in all, thirty-one – 22.5 per cent – had some form of trade and another nine were recorded as 'spinster' in the trade section. Eliza Davis was a servant. By the time the women arrived in

Van Diemen's Land, all had some form of occupation recorded, tailored to the economic requirements of the colony. This is discussed more fully in Chapter 6.

## PHYSICAL DESCRIPTIONS

All convicts who arrived in Van Diemen's Land between 1817 and 1853 were physically examined and their descriptions recorded. Physical descriptions were an aid to identification.

Eliza Davis was 5ft 1in (1.55m) with a fresh complexion, brown hair, grey eyes, oval head, high forehead, pointed nose, wide mouth and large chin.[110] Margaret Butler 2nd measured 5ft 3¼in (1.61m). She had a fresh complexion, round head, high forehead, brown hair, grey eyes, a small nose, a wide, large mouth and round chin. She had a 'hair mole' on the left side of her chin, two matching ones on the right side of her chin, and one on her right eye.[111]

The shortest convict, Margaret Connor, aged 25, was 4ft 6¾in (1.39m), one of thirty-eight women under 5ft (1.52m).[112] The tallest was 28-year-old Bell Rooney, who was 5ft 8¾in (1.75m), followed by Annie McCarmack, aged 22, who was 5ft 6½in (1.69m). Fanny Doherty, aged 27, and Ann Williams, aged 26, were 5ft 6in (1.68m).[113] Bridget Clifford's height was variously recorded: 5ft 8¼in (conduct record and description list) and 5ft 1¾in (indent).[114]

Ellen Sullivan's height was taken in Grangegorman – she was 4ft 11in (1.50m). Judith Dooling was also recorded in Grangegorman and was 4ft 9in (1.45m).[115]

Overall, the *Tasmania* (2) women were a motley group. Ellen Maguire and Margaret Sloane were freckled.[116] A small number had physical deformities; others were pock-pitted or scarred or blemished. Several had tattoos.[117]

Like Margaret Butler 2nd, some of the women had moles or other blemishes. Judith Dooling, for example, had a large mole at the side of her chin.[118] Eliza Hunter had a blue mark on her nose and a scar over her right eye.[119] Catherine Stewart had a large flesh mark under her right eye.[120]

Twelve women, ranging in age from 18 to 27, were pock-pitted, indicating that they had been scarred by smallpox or another eruptive disease. Some had scars or blemishes as well. Vagrant Bridget Egan, aged 20, was pock-pitted and had several brown marks on her left arm.[121]

About twenty women were scarred, mostly on the face. Anne Dogherty, 'a strolling lady' from Longford, had a scar over her left eye and a scar on her right arm.[122] Bridget Clifford, a vagrant who had been 'on the town' for six or seven years, had a scar over her left eye.[123]

Most of the physical deformities were minor. Anne Daley and Anne McAvine both had broken fingers.[124] Both were farm servants and there is no evidence that their deformities had an impact on their colonial work. Ellen Neill, who suffered terribly during the voyage, was lame in her right leg.[125]

Fanny Doherty, aged 27, was missing front teeth.[126] Ann Fitzpatrick, aged 54, had also lost some front teeth, as had Mary Lynam or Egan.[127] Ann Wade was missing a tooth in her upper jaw.[128] Bridget Stankard had a scar on her forehead and had lost one tooth in her upper jaw.[129]

Four women had problems with their eyes. Eleanor Shaughnessy had a squint and a scar over her right eye.[130] Mary Sullivan 1st was blind in her left eye and squinted.[131] Mary Meagher was blind in one eye.[132] Mary McCarthy had lost sight in her left eye. Mary McCarthy had been treated for a syphilitic condition in Grangegorman Hospital.[133]

Margaret McMackin or O'Neil, a widow from Tyrone in her 40s, was recorded as 'dumb'.[134] In a strange twist, the *Colonial Times* in February 1850 reported:

> Singular Circumstance.—There is now residing in Hobart Town a female named Margaret M'Mechan, who was married in Ireland and had three births, the last of twins. At this period she was suddenly deprived of speech, indeed became perfectly dumb, but what is rather unusual in such circumstance retained the faculty of hearing. The woman was subsequently transported to this colony whilst in that state, and remained so until the birth of her child in the Factory a short time since, when her speech which had left her upward of 14 years was suddenly restored to her, although not quite so perfectly.[135]

## Tattoos

The tattoos worn by the *Tasmania* (2) women were simple: mostly initials or dots. In all, fourteen women were tattooed. The initials on tattoos are not always easy to read.

In a study of 3,000 or so convicts transported to New South Wales in 1831, David Kent found about 30 per cent of the men and 10 per cent of the women were tattooed. The tattoos were etched into the skin with soot and black sediment from lamps. They recorded hopes, beliefs, disappointments and loves.[136] In many cases, the meaning of the tattoos is lost in the mists of time. Interestingly, many convict tattoos appear to have been created during the voyage.[137]

Two women wore tattoos that included hearts. Margaret Gibson, a housemaid or plain laundress aged 24, was born in Woolwich but her family were in County Down when she was tried. Margaret's tattoo, on her right arm, read 'N.C.M.C.J.G. Heart'.[138] Cavan widow Rose Fitzpatrick, who had a large scar on her forehead, was decorated with 'HS heart JM' on her right shoulder.[139]

Some of the tattoos were long and complex. Antrim woman Jane Gallagher had 'P.G.S.C.J.C.A.D.C.M.H.D.M.' tattooed on her right shoulder.[140] Jane's living relatives were her mother Ann, brothers Pat and James and sisters Catherine, Sally and Biddy. Perhaps their initials were incorporated into the tattoo. Margaret Sloane, a freckled widow from Tyrone, was tattooed with 'D X D MDHM' on her right arm.[141] Some of the longer tattoos are believed to represent messages or phrases.

Initials were a popular form of tattoo. Mary Carroll bore 'M A G' on her right shoulder and 'W' on the same shoulder.[142] Martha Merryfield had 'MM JJ' on her right arm.[143] Mary Francis had 'JM' on her left arm.[144] Mary McManus had 'HB' on her left arm.[145] Anne Mullan had 'A M I F P' on her right arm.[146]

Some of the women simply had dots tattooed. Arsonist Ann Flannery, from Roscommon, had seven dots on her left arm.[147] Mary Hurley had seven dots on her right hand.[148] Vagrant Bridget Cunningham had three blue dots on her right hand and Bridget Fanning had a blue dot on her left hand.[149] The meaning of the dots is not known.

In summary, then, the average age of the convicts on the *Tasmania* (2) was 29 years, the oldest was 64 and the youngest was 16. Most of the women received sentences of seven years, although there were two sentenced to transportation for life, two to fifteen years, and twenty to ten years. The overwhelming majority were convicted of stealing – mostly clothes, watches, and other property, but occasionally sheep or potatoes. Some were convicted of receiving stolen goods, others of vagrancy. Of the two transported for life, one was convicted of poisoning her husband; the other of infanticide. Most of the women had previous convictions and several had been 'on the town' for varying periods. A few had family members who had been transported, some were tried with their family members or had family members on board. A majority of the women were from

Front cover of the convict conduct records for the Tasmania (2). (TAHO, CON41/1/8, reproduced with permission of the Tasmanian Archive and Heritage Office)

Dublin and were servants when they were tried. Over two thirds were single but there were more widows than married women. The richness of convict records, in Ireland and Van Diemen's Land, allows an understanding of the complexity of the lives of individual convict women: who they were; where they were from; and why they were transported. These details, meticulously recorded in huge registers, not only demonstrate the importance of transportation to the British and colonial authorities but also provide a window into the lives of the convict women.

# 4

# Banished Beyond the Seas

That from and after the commencement of this act every person convicted before any court of competent jurisdiction in Great Britain, of any offence for which he or she shall be liable to be transported or banished, shall be adjudged and ordered to be transported or banished beyond the seas, for the term of life or years for which such offender shall be liable by law to be transported or banished.[1]

Grangegorman Female Depot, 2013. (Courtesy of Bob Gordon)

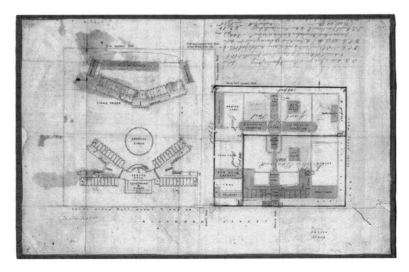

Richmond Gaol Plan, undated. (NAI, GPB, reproduced with permission of the National Archives of Ireland)

The women of the *Tasmania* (2) were all sentenced to be transported, banished beyond the seas. These legalistic words disguise the human cost of transportation for the convict women, their children and those they left behind. After they had been sentenced, the women waited in gaol for word that they would move to the next stage of their convict experience, relocation to Grangegorman Female Convict Depot in Dublin. Before this took place, a convict ship needed to be chartered and fitted out. The fate of the convict women who sailed on the *Tasmania* (2) was at the mercy of the authorities and an extremely bureaucratic system. The organisation of transportation was complex and based on a series of legislative requirements. Sentencing offenders to be transported 'beyond the seas' sounds relatively simple, but it was a complicated affair in which a number of government departments, private contractors and the Royal Navy were engaged from 1786 up to the cessation of transportation in 1868.[2]

Grangegorman, originally called the Richmond Penitentiary, was the first purpose-built prison for convict women in the British Isles. Its primary purpose was as a prison for women convicted in the City of Dublin and sentenced to imprisonment. It was also 'intended to receive the whole of the Females under sentence of Transportation in transit from their respective Counties to the Convict Ships' and contained an average of 200 to 400 prisoners.[3] Transportees were housed separately from the city prisoners in about fifty cells.

Part of the rationale for the convict depot was to provide the convict women with domestic skills – laundry, cooking and cleaning – which they could then use in Van Diemen's Land. The standard period of domestic training was three months. It was part of a strict daily routine of industry and education, which not only provided women with skills but also promoted discipline within the institution.[4] The women received 'moral instruction and advice' as well as religious instruction: 'The moral teaching given to convicts was to help reform their character and make them regret their crimes, while the advice given to them was supposed to help settle into a new life, free of crime, abroad.'[5] Revd Kirby was 'frequently engaged in the prison for hours' and 'on Sundays the duties are most laborious'. The Protestant chaplain, Revd Adams, claimed that he attended on average forty to fifty inmates daily.[6] The Sisters of Charity also attended the women in Grangegorman every Sunday, giving religious and moral instruction to the Roman Catholic women. 'Much good' was reported to have resulted from their visits.[7]

Diet in Irish prisons was regulated under an Act of Parliament:

> The diet was designed to be plain but sufficient and economical, so as not to act as an inducement to the poor classes to commit crime. Officially, the general diet in Grangegorman penitentiary consisted of eight ounces of oatmeal in stir-about, a pint of new milk for breakfast, four pounds of potatoes with a pint of buttermilk for dinner. The bread diet consisted of two pounds of bread and two pints of new milk per day which was supplied to the sick, to mentally ill inmates on medical authority, and to infant children.[8]

Lawlor suggests that it is doubtful that the inmates received their full entitlement of rations.

In order for a convict ship to be chartered, there first needed to be a sufficient number of convicts – a critical mass. This was based on the numbers housed in Grangegorman. In June 1845, a letter was sent from Grangegorman to the Convict Office in Dublin, stating that there were 109 female convicts in custody and, as the summer sessions and assizes were approaching, it was considered advisable to organise shipping for 150 women and children to Van Diemen's Land to arrive in Kingstown Harbour before the end of August. A letter was sent to Whitehall, the centre of government and administration in London, for approval. This letter also stated that 136 suits of clothing and 36 suits for children

The yard of Grangegorman Female Depot, 2013. (Courtesy of Bob Gordon)

were required. A further 40 sets of clothing and shoes for the convicts were to be 'of a larger size than those usually sent'.[9] It is not known why larger sizes were needed.

In July 1845, Dublin Castle ordered the removal of women from a number of county gaols to travel under escort to the depot in Dublin to join those already there and wait while their convict ship was prepared.[10]

## CHARTERING THE CONVICT SHIP

Organising the ship was quite a process. The British Admiralty advertised for tenders from private contractors to enter into a contract, known as a charter party, to provide a suitable vessel. The vessels for voyages from Ireland were fitted out in London.

In 1844 authorities in England stipulated that vessels of not less than 400 or 450 tons be engaged to convey female convicts from Ireland to Van Diemen's Land. Mr Lucas of Dublin Castle responded that there were only 140 female convicts in the country awaiting transportation at that time and the average number of children allowed to accompany their parents was 30. The number due to be transported was likely to diminish prior to the arrival of the ship; reconsideration of the sentence and

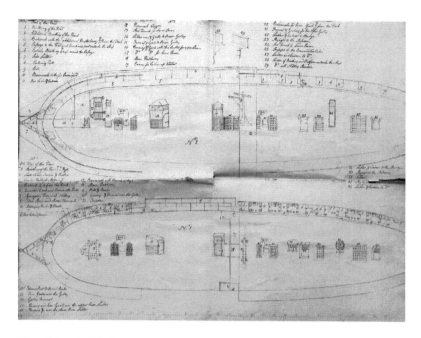

Plan of Convict Ship Part I. (NAI, OP/MA/187, reproduced with permission of the National Archives of Ireland)

unfitness to travel owing to ill health would account for this reduction in numbers. He felt it was not advisable to charter a vessel for a larger number than 150.[11]

The vessel selected by the Admiralty was the *Tasmania*, a 502-ton barque built in Sunderland in the north of England in 1841.[12] It had made a previous voyage to Van Diemen's Land in September 1844, transporting 191 female convicts from London. The ship's master on both voyages was William Black.

## SELECTION OF THE SURGEON SUPERINTENDENT

Part of the contract stated that a Surgeon Superintendent must be employed to oversee the prisoners' health during the voyage.[13] Mortality was high on early voyages, but in 1814 Royal Navy Surgeons Superintendent were selected to oversee convict health and from this time conditions improved. The authority of the Surgeon Superintendent was considerable not only in medical matters but also in decisions relating to discipline, education and religious instruction.

Moreover, the threat of infectious diseases on board was ever-present and cleanliness was paramount.[14]

The Surgeon Superintendent selected for the 1845 voyage of the *Tasmania* was Dr Jason Shepperd Lardner, appointed naval surgeon in 1838.[15] This was his second voyage to Van Diemen's Land; he sailed on the *Woodbridge* in 1843 with 204 female convicts. He later sailed on the *Asia* (with 169 female convicts) in 1847. Both these voyages departed from England. Surgeon Superintendent Lardner's report reveals him to be thoroughly professional in his treatment of the women and children in his care.

Once the Surgeon Superintendent boarded the ship, he had to remain there and make sure that the conditions of the contract were adhered to. Breaches were to be reported to the Office of the Admiralty and to the colonial governor and recorded in his journal. There were many rules relating to the role and behaviour of the Surgeon Superintendent; it was a position of responsibility.[16]

Similar instructions were issued to the masters of convict ships, but the list was much shorter than those issued to the Surgeon Superintendent. The master was also required to submit documentation at the end of the journey before he could be paid; a gratuity of £50 was payable if all reports of conduct were deemed satisfactory. It was one way of ensuring that the ship's human cargo was cared for during the voyage.[17]

For ships carrying female convicts, both the Surgeon Superintendent and the master were pressured to use their 'utmost endeavour to prevent their prostitution with any Person on Board'. This was a leftover from the early voyages, such as the *Lady Juliana,* where relationships between the crew and convict women were so loose that the ship was dubbed the 'floating brothel'.[18] The Surgeon Superintendent and the master were expected to set a good example. In the case of the master, he would forfeit his gratuity unless the colonial governor was satisfied that all means had been taken to prevent prostitution. To assist the master in preventing fraternisation with the female convicts, the chief mate was to be paid a gratuity of £20 and the second and third mates £15 each at the end of the voyage.[19]

## PREPARATION OF THE SHIP

Part of the fitting-out of the ship included the construction of convict quarters. An account in a Dublin newspaper in 1845 described the details of prison quarters on the *Tasmania* (2):

The visitors descended one of the two ladders which lead to 'the prison', as the place in which the convicts eat their meals, and sleep … [it is] entered by stooping, through a grated door-way, very much resembling that of an ordinary cell. This prison is situated under decks, and the mess-tables, which are constructed at each side, extend about two-thirds of the ship's length. Each table is sufficiently large to accommodate eight persons with ease; and at night can be converted into a bedstead, or receptacle for a mattress; it is railed or boarded-in like a sheep-pen, and separated from similar tables which at either side adjoin it. To reach these tables or leave them it is therefore necessary to climb over the wooden railings. At the time to which we allude all the convicts were penned-in.[20]

Major Cottingham, Superintendent of Convicts, was advised on 14 August that Dublin Castle had received the charter party for the ship *Tasmania* (2), together with a list of the stores shipped on board.[21] The *Tasmania* (2) arrived in Kingstown Harbour on 18 August. Major Cottingham then inspected the ship and 'found everything in clean and most perfect order, fitted out in a very superior manner and quite prepared to receive the convicts on board'. He then instructed the medical officer to inspect the convicts at Grangegorman Depot – this was the selection process.[22]

## TRANSMISSION OF CONVICTS TO GRANGEGORMAN

Once a ship was engaged, the governors of the county gaols compiled a return of those prisoners waiting to be transported who were fit and healthy and ready for immediate embarkation. A medical certificate was required and was attached to the return. On 28 June 1845, the Convict Department instructed the Superintendent of Constabulary to transmit a return of all female convicts under sentence of transportation and to take the necessary steps to remove them from the specified gaols to 'the Depot in Grange Gorman previous to their being embarked for Van Diemen's Land'.[23] The officer in charge of the escort was ordered to remove only those convicts included on the list and for whom medical certificates were completed by the medical officers in the gaols, confirming fitness of each convict to undergo the voyage. Once this paperwork was done, the prisoners were sent to Grangegorman in Dublin under the charge of the constabulary.[24]

When they reached Dublin, the constabulary handed over the convicts and their medical certificates to the governor of the depot. The medical

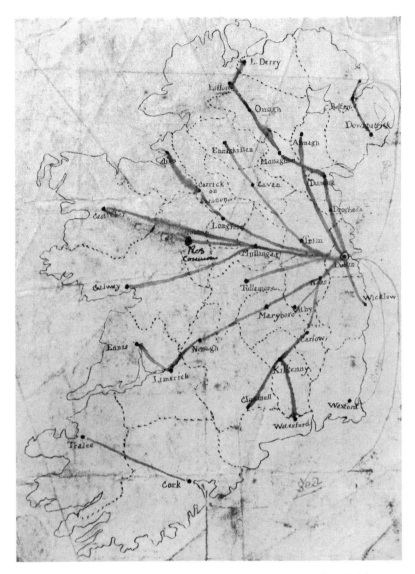

Convict Routes from the Gaols to Dublin. (NAI, CON LB1, reproduced with permission of the National Archives of Ireland)

returns were checked by the depot's medical officer to see that they matched the actual state of the health of the prisoners.

The majority of the *Tasmania* (2) women – ninety-one – arrived at Grangegorman in June 1845. A further thirty-three arrived in July and August; eight were received into Grangegorman between January and May while six had already arrived from their county gaols in the autumn of 1844.[25]

Convicts continued to be sent to Grangegorman almost up to the time of embarkation: eight convicts from Waterford, Clonmel (Tipperary), Kilkenny and Carlow were 'transmitted to Naas' (Kildare) and on 15 August were admitted to Grangegorman.[26] Another three arrived from Tipperary and four from Waterford.[27]

The convicts were usually conveyed by coach from their county gaol to Grangegorman, stopping at other gaols en route. Major Cottingham knew from experience that convict ships should not sail from September to April. Apart from the tempestuous weather conditions during this time, leading to early seasickness 'most detrimental', the removal of the women from the county gaols at this time was also likely to be injurious to their health as they travelled from their county gaols on open jaunting cars without any additional covering to protect them.[28]

At least one county gaol complained about the expense incurred through the maintenance of 'Government Convicts': in May 1845, Horatio Townsend, chairman of the Board of Superintendence of Cork County Gaol, wrote to Edward Lucas in the Convict Department, Dublin Castle. Townsend argued that one month from trial to their removal to the depot in Dublin was reasonable but any additional expense should be borne by the government. According to the accounts, ten women and five children spent a total of 2,595 days waiting to be sent to Dublin at a rate of 6d per day per woman and 3d per child. The total cost came to £53.11.6. The notes written in response, dated 21 May, were conciliatory and explanatory in tone, yet forceful in rejecting reimbursement of the expenses.[29] The eight women from Cork were not received into Grangegorman until 4 June – another twenty-three days.

## EXAMINATION AND SELECTION OF THE WOMEN

By 1845, the Convict Department had a clearly stated process for 'carrying into execution the sentence of transportation'.[30]

At the depot Surgeon Superintendent Lardner examined those convicts who were nominated for transportation.[31] In theory, this was a rigorous and thorough process but many slipped through who were elderly, infirm, pregnant, mentally ill, like Mary Griffen, or experienced chronic and life-threatening conditions, like Eliza Davis, who suffered from epilepsy.[32] The rules stipulated that the Surgeon Superintendent was not to permit anyone to sail whose life might be endangered by the voyage or who posed a possible threat of infection. He was to examine the prisoners in the presence of the medical officer of the prison where the prisoners were being held. However, it was considered that 'old age or bodily infirmity alone' should not prevent embarkation.[33]

In his final report, Surgeon Superintendent Lardner noted that there were ten convicts on board over the age of 50, most of whom were unable to gain a livelihood by working.[34] McMahon comments that aged women were transported before and during the Great Famine and cites Marian Rawlins, head matron at Grangegorman, who reported that a large number of 'old and useless women' had been sentenced to transportation; Rawlins considered it to be the duty of the prison to have their 'shipment' effected as much as practicable. The burden of care of these 'worn out' subjects was transferred to the colony of Van Diemen's Land.[35] The impact of this bureaucratic process on the lives of individual aged women was not a consideration.

Surgeon Superintendent Lardner examined 144 female convicts in Grangegorman Female Convict Depot and certified that he found all but six fit for embarkation. Another convict, Anne Kelly, was not examined as she had been pardoned by this time.

## REJECTION OF CONVICTS

Six women, aged between 30 and 70, were rejected for transportation by Surgeon Superintendent Lardner.[36] The women were also examined by William Harty MD, medical officer to the depot.

Two of the women were rejected because they suffered from some form of prolapsed uterus, or 'falling down of the womb'. Bessy Bogan, aged 35, was tried in Fermanagh in July 1845 and sentenced to transportation for seven years, but she was rejected because she had a prolapsed uterus. Ellen O'Brien, a vagrant, had the same complaint and was described as 'utterly unfit for transportation … having falling down of [the] womb between the thighs'. Ellen, tried in County Cork in March 1845, was 30. She was offered bail 'in six months' or seven years transportation. 'Commuted' was scrawled across her record.

Mary Jones, aged 40 and tried in Galway town in November 1844, was rejected because she had chronic asthma. In her petition, Mary described herself as a 'poor afflicted Petitioner, being of an advanced age, and precarious state of health' and 'poor, infirm and weak'. She claimed that her sentence had been commuted to two years' imprisonment, a great part of which had expired.

Ann Devlin, who was 30, was from Monaghan and was tried in October 1844. She was rejected because she had a 'deep abscess of leg and sinuses under treatment and [was unlikely] to recover'.

Catherine Ryan, aged 70 and tried in Westmeath in October 1844, was rejected because of her 'old age & infirmities with loss of teeth'.

Petitions on behalf of Bessy Bogan, Mary Jones, Catherine Ryan and Bridget Lawler. (NAI, CRF 1845 R31, reproduced with permission of the National Archives of Ireland)

Bridget Lawler, aged 31, was tried in Kilkenny in April 1844. Although she was in good health, her young child, aged 3½, was so 'desperately affected with scrofula that no one but its mother could pay it the attention required by the state of its disease'.[37] Bridget's daughter was so diseased that she prevented her mother from being transported.

## TO THE SHIP

The *Tasmania* (2) landed at Kingstown, a harbour south of Dublin, on 20 August 1845 to wait for its cargo of convict women and their children.[38]

Along with Cove in Cork, Kingstown was the departure point for Irish convict ships from 1825.[39] From 1840, all female convict ships left Ireland from Kingstown.

On 27 August 1845, a request was made to the Convict Office for 'an escort of Dragoons consisting of 36 men to be at the Female Convict Depot Grange Gorman Lane on Thursday 28 … to proceed to the end of the North Wall' in Dublin.'[40] In April of that year the Convict Office had suggested using vans similar to those in operation by the police in Dublin rather than 'the inconvenient mode of removing the convicts from the Depot in cars for embarkation'. The suggestion was approved but the vans were to be cheaper and larger. Vans were also considered more secure.[41] At this time, too, convicts were carried in 'cars' from both the Female Depot at Grangegorman and the Male Depot at Smithfield to the North Wall and placed on board a steam tug to travel to their ship at Kingstown. The vans in use by the Metropolitan Police carried only twenty to twenty-two prisoners.[42] Getting the convict women and their children to the ship was quite a rigmarole.

A large military escort was needed to guard the transport carrying the convicts because of rowdiness and frequent drunkenness during the journey.[43] How the women managed to acquire alcohol remains a matter of conjecture.

In January 1845, Major Cottingham, Superintendent of Convicts, considered the wellbeing of nursing mothers, suggesting that September to April be avoided for sailings because it was dangerous for nursing mothers to travel in jaunting cars in bad weather. He also complained about accommodation for mothers in convict ships, saying that the berths were inconvenient, if not dangerous: 'each woman being allowed a berth separated by planks and so narrow that a woman with an infant could not sleep in one without danger'.[44]

## EMBARKATION, 28 AUGUST 1845

On 22 August, Major Cottingham was placed in charge of loading the female convicts onto the *Tasmania* (2), then lying in Kingstown Harbour. The warrant for the governor of the colony containing the names of the convicts was forwarded to him. He was to take care not to incur any unnecessary expenses, including a charge for demurrage (the failure to load within an agreed time).[45] Under the terms of the charters, thirty days were allowed for the construction of the prison quarters on board ship and for the embarkation of the convicts.[46] In all of these arrangements, the convict women were depersonalised; their children were ignored. They were simply cargo.

On 28 August 1845, 138 convicts and 35 children embarked. Another woman was placed on board two days later. The Surgeon Superintendent reported a shortage of beds and requested an additional eight.[47]

On Saturday 30 August, a group of spectators gathered on the pier at Kingstown. The master and the Surgeon Superintendent gave permission for some of the visitors to board the vessel. Among them was Revd Bernard Kirby, chaplain of the Grangegorman Depot, who wished 'to give his parting and prayerful admonitions to the unfortunate prisoners to conduct themselves peaceably during the voyage, and respectfully for the remainder of their lives'.[48] Even at this traumatic and emotional time, the convict women were allowed no dignity. The visitors were allowed to view the women below decks in the prison quarters; some were:

Kingstown Harbour by P. Ward. (NLI, ET A368, image courtesy of the National Library of Ireland)

sewing, some winding thread or cotton into balls; some reading prayers from small time and thumb-worn books; some endeavouring "to make out" the last letter from home, while others were lulling their sickly-looking infants to slumber, or sitting silently and motionless in a state of morbid, moping melancholy.[49]

The visitors descended one of two ladders providing access to the prison quarters where the women slept and ate.

## THE ANTICS OF MARY KELLY

During the visit, the convicts were allowed on deck for recreation and it was during this time that the visitors witnessed the antics of Mary Kelly, 'who was mad or feigned madness … pursuing all who were within her reach'.[50] Mary was 'running about the deck, chasing and beating every person whom she met'.[51] Mary had exhibited symptoms of 'violent insanity', real or assumed, since boarding the ship. Following her outburst, her hands were fastened behind her back and her feet were tied with leather rings to prevent her hurting anyone. It was clear that the Surgeon Superintendent was not prepared to keep her on board as he feared she would disturb the peace and order of the vessel. He objected to leaving port until he heard further from Dublin Castle about her condition. Once he was reassured that there would be a medical investigation 'to test the state of the convict's mind', Mary was unfettered. However, she then carried out a frenzied attack on some of the women: she 'rushed furiously upon all whom she met, tearing the clothes, caps and hair of the women, striking the commander, surgeon, and sailors, and creating … consternation and dismay'.[52]

Following this second attack, Revd Kirby succeeded in calming Mary by gathering together all the Roman Catholic women – over 100 – on both sides of the vessel to kneel and pray:

The scene at this period was very imposing. Here were a number of human beings, varying from ten years to seventy – the black glossy curls of girlhood, contrasting with the hoary locks of wintry age; the bright beaming eye and rosy cheek of dawning womanhood, with the sunken tearful eye and withered cheek of 'three score years and ten' – all kneeling to supplicate mercy from an offended God for crimes different in complexion and kind ... near them sported, in happy innocence, unconscious of their degradation unobservant of the misery around them, happy and playful as if they were gathering flowers in the field, two little girls, the children of convict-mothers.[53]

The calm was short-lived respite. Mary again became violent, and 'with a heavy blow laid [a] poor penitent prostrate upon the deck'. Panic ensued with some of the women running towards the front of the ship and tripping over wet coils of rope. Mary was handcuffed a second time.[54]

Mary was then removed from the ship and taken back to Grangegorman, 'to enable the Medical Officer to ascertain whether she be sane or insane'.[55] It was decided not to further delay sailing. Major Cottingham completed the muster of the convicts and, in a tin box to be presented to the Lieutenant Governor of Van Diemen's Land on arrival, enclosed the Lord Lieutenant's warrant, along with a list of the names of the prisoners.[56]

Mary, aged 30, was originally admitted to Grangegorman on 22 August 1845; she was convicted in Dublin City of stealing geese.[57] In January 1846, Mr Pennefather summarised Mary Kelly's case. She arrived in Grangegorman in 'a perfectly sound state of health' but on hearing she was to be sent on a convict ship she feigned insanity. Once the other women had left for Kingstown, she called for the matron, apologised for her conduct and promised to be of good conduct in the future. She was taken to the ship, perfectly quiet, but once she was about to go on board 'she became furious disclosing she would never go out alive'.[58] With difficulty, she was put on board and was restrained until 1 September when she was returned to Grangegorman where she was restrained with handcuffs and straps. Her behaviour was threatening and she used blasphemous and abusive language to the staff. Mary's treatment did not conform to the depot's rules and it was decided that if she was really insane, she 'should be removed to a lunatic asylum where proper treatment for treating insanity can be applied'.[59]

The debate about Mary Kelly's sanity continued. Since being brought on shore on 1 September, she had been under medical treatment and observation in the depot.[60] In March 1846, she was removed to the Richmond Lunatic Asylum, where she remained until 24 June 1846. The last entry in this register noted that she was again removed to the asylum on 16 January 1847.[61]

Mary Kelly's chaotic antics no doubt contributed to an unsettled start to the voyage, which relied so much on order and discipline. Mary certainly delayed sailing by several days, during which time the women and their children remained on board in Kingstown Harbour. It must have been a relief to all to finally set sail.

At last, on 2 September 1845, the *Tasmania* (2) with its cargo of women and children was on its way to Van Diemen's Land. On 3 December, after a journey of ninety-three days, it arrived at the River Derwent near Hobart Town, where the convict women and children would begin the next stage in their lives, in an unfamiliar land at the other end of the world.

# 5

# The Floating Dungeon[1]

The *Tasmania* (2) was expected to sail on 30 August 1845. However, departure was delayed until Tuesday 2 September at 6.30 a.m. as a result of Mary Kelly's behaviour.[2] The weather on the day of departure was hazy and thick at 9 a.m. and by the end of the day, perhaps appropriately, the weather had turned gloomy.[3]

Dublin Bay and Kingstown Harbour by J. Newman & Co., engravers. (NLI, ET A363, image courtesy of the National Library of Ireland)

## LEAVING IRELAND

There is no way of knowing what the women of the *Tasmania* (2) thought as they left Ireland, but another convict, Young Irelander John Mitchel, transported for high treason, captured some of the emotions of those exiled in his book *Jail Journal*.[4] A lawyer and newspaper editor from a privileged background, Mitchel worried about how his family would fare once he was no longer there to support them:

> There was a huge lump in my throat all the time … At Charlemont Bridge, in Dublin, this evening, there is a desolate house – my mother and sisters, who came up to town to see me (for the last time in case of the worst) – five little children, very dear to me; none of them old enough to understand the cruel blow that has fallen on them this day, and above all – above all – my wife … What will they do? What is to become of them?[5]

Yet Mitchel knew his 'wife and little ones' would be cared for. The same could not be said for the women on board the *Tasmania* (2) who had left children behind. Although Margaret Butler brought two children with her, William and Mary Ann, she left four children in Carlow. She must have agonised over what was to 'become of them'. Thirty-five children sailed with their mothers but twenty-six women left at least eighty-one children behind.[6] According to Elizabeth Wright's petition, she had six children ranging in age from 6 to 19.[7] Mary McVeagh claimed she was the mother of ten children, eight of whom were living.[8] The reality is that many of those left behind probably died in the famine.

Mitchel poetically expressed his feelings on leaving his beloved Ireland:

> Dublin City, with its bay and pleasant villas – city of bellowing slaves – villas of genteel dastards – lies now behind us, and the sun has set behind the blue peaks of Wicklow, as we steam past Bray Head, where the Vale of Shanganagh, sloping softly from the Golden Spears, sends its bright river murmuring to the sea. And I am on the first stage of my way, faring to what regions of unknown horror? And may never – never more, O, Ireland! – my mother and queen! – see vale, or hill, or murmuring stream of thine.[9]

It must have been heartbreaking for the women as they travelled down the east coast of Ireland, past Wicklow and Wexford and south of Waterford and Cork. Did the seventeen convict women from those counties realise as they were held below deck that they were passing their home counties for the last time?[10] A rare glimpse of Ireland remembered comes from the obituary of one of the children on board, Alicia Burgess, who always 'cherished a love for Ireland' and 'followed the happenings of that unhappy country with the keenest interest'.[11]

Records of the voyage give some idea of the conditions faced by the women and their children on board. The ship's log for the second voyage of the *Tasmania* has not been uncovered. However, its master, William Black, made the same voyage (although from Woolwich, London) on the same vessel at approximately the same time of year in 1844, departing on 8 September and arriving in Hobart on 20 December.[12] The management of the convicts on board and some of the events that occurred and were recorded by Black on the first voyage of the *Tasmania* may well have been similar to his experiences on the second voyage.

The log for the first voyage of the *Tasmania* in 1844 described preparations undertaken before the convict women came on board, including building the prison below decks and storing provisions. Black recorded the day-to-day work of the sailors on board – washing the decks, loosening the sails to dry, cleaning and ventilating the prison and stowing

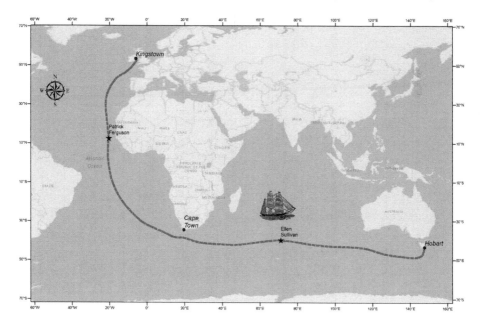

Map of the voyage. (Courtesy of Martin Critchley)

provisions. The names of his crew of thirty-two are listed, as are the 191 convicts. Unlike in the Irish voyage, there were two matrons on board. It was the role of the matrons to supervise the convicts, arranging them into messes before embarkation.[13] Matrons were not appointed to Irish ships until 1846.[14]

For the second voyage of the *Tasmania* in 1845, according to Major Cottingham, Mrs Rawlins, the matron of Grangegorman Penitentiary, played a role in the selection of the mess women: 'The assiduity and anxiety evinced by Mrs. Rawlins, the matron of the Grangegorman prison, in preparing each convict for the voyage, and seeing that everything was provided for her which necessity required, is beyond all praise.'[15]

Ensuring adequate supplies of food was an important part of the preparation for a long sea voyage. For the *Tasmania* (2):

A plentiful supply of provisions has been laid in, comprising pigs, sheep, and all descriptions of fowl, and this fine vessel, one of the largest, most cleanly, and most expeditious in the service of the government, intended for the transmission of the convicts, has been fitted up in every way that could ensure the comfort of those women who it is intended to convey to exile.[16]

Regulation of life below decks was by organisation into 'messes', with usually one woman in charge of eight to twelve others.

A number of attendants have been appointed from amongst the convicts themselves, the most active and intelligent being selected to wait upon the rest during the meals; and to prevent confusion, all the items belonging to each convict have been numbered, the number of which they bear corresponding with that affixed to a plate worn by her.[17]

The mess woman was responsible for cooking and the cleanliness and good order of her group. Catherine Foy was the only woman identified as a mess woman; following her stay in the ship's hospital she was not permitted to return to this post.

The women and their children spent a considerable amount of time in the cramped 'prison', sleeping and eating and remaining there during heavy swells and riding seas.

While Mr Lardner's journal is detailed in relation to the care and attention given to the women on board, he does not mention the daily routine during the voyage. As William Black was the master of both the 1844 and 1845 voyages, it is likely that the 'established daily routine' was similar for both: 'At 6am up prisoners beds & cleaned the prison & hospital. At 6 pm down prisoners & locked the prisons. At 5am Starboard prisoners up washing clothes. At 7 am up beds. At 8 am up prisoners & cleaned the prison & hospital.'[18] Cleanliness, hygiene and ventilation were seen as crucial to curtailing disease.

On the *Tasmania* (2), the women 'retire to rest and rise, and eat their meals and amuse themselves upon deck at certain hours, the rules in these respects being very rigid'.[19]

By the 1840s, voyages on convict ships were relatively safe and conditions were improved compared with earlier voyages such as those of the second fleet, which had a high death rate, and the voyage of the infamous *Lady Juliana*, 'the floating brothel'.[20]

A young midshipman writing in 1866 of his journey on the *Gilbert Henderson* in 1839 described an almost cruise-like atmosphere on board, with convicts allowed freely on deck:

A great deal of freedom was permitted to all, so long as they conducted themselves properly. They were permitted to choose their own companions, with whom they could sit and chat, and work or read, and were allowed to roam about the decks, as they pleased, so long as they kept off the quarter-deck, and refrained from encroaching beyond the limit of the foremast, where the sailors had their quarters; and the sailors were forbidden to come amongst them on that part of the deck appropriated for their use, unless to attend to their necessary duties of the ship. Conversation with the sailors was also strictly forbidden; but it was found impossible to prevent this, and so long as the conversation was carried on in quiet tones, and without any attempt at improper familiarities, it was winked at by the doctor and the officers of the ship. Indeed, the officers and passengers occasionally conversed familiarly with the best-conducted and best-looking of the females, and passed harmless jokes with them, for a long sea voyage often proves a great leveller of social distinctions.[21]

It is unlikely that the master, William Black, 'winked' at any fraternisation between the convicts and the crew because such behaviour was strictly forbidden under the instructions given to both the Surgeon

Superintendent and the master. Contact could have jeopardised the payments to the Surgeon Superintendent and the master on the completion of the voyage.

Mr Lardner in his general remarks on the *Woodbridge* wrote:

> The employment of the prisoners during the voyage had the best effects on health and discipline. The surgeon recommends all female convict vessels to be provided with means of employing the prisoners, such as shirt making, with women appointed to cutting out and supervising to prevent wanton waste and destruction of the materials. More than 1100 shirts were made on board during the voyage, the women making on average one shirt a day. Those employed at needlework in the morning read in the afternoons and vice versa.[22]

Control of the convict women, through occupation and useful labour, was an important part of shipboard discipline. The *Tasmania* (2) women were 'usefully employed during the voyage in making shirts, stockings, and other articles of clothing' while up on the deck.[23]

Divine service and schooling were also an integral part of the voyage.[24] Bibles for those of the established Church and rosary beads for the Roman Catholic convicts were distributed. Mr Lardner noted that the women were 'very ignorant'; none were 'capable of teaching and but few were inclined to learn'.[25] Communication, for women from the Irish-speaking areas in the west of Ireland, such as Donegal, Clare and Kerry, may have posed some difficulties, though it is unclear if any of the women spoke only their native language.

Only snippets of information survive about life for the women and their children on board the *Tasmania* (2). The children, many of whom were only infants and toddlers, were largely invisible in the records and it has not been possible to determine whether special arrangements were made for their care and hygiene. Nor has it been possible to ascertain how the older children were occupied. Thomas Seaton, Surgeon Superintendent on the first voyage of the *Tasmania* (2) in 1844, recorded in the sick book two boys and a girl who required attention; one 5-year-old boy had a contused finger, a 10-year-old boy fell down the hatch and was slightly bruised and a 10-year-old girl had a head wound.[26] Mr Lardner recorded a 4-year-old boy on the *Woodbridge* as 'severely scalded on the right arm'.[27] On the *Tasmania* (2), he treated Sarah Brennan's son, Joseph, aged 18 months, for a wound.[28] Indeed, given the confined spaces and constant movement of the ship, it is a wonder more accidents were not recorded.

Of the twelve women who were treated in the hospital on board, four had children – eight in total. Little information has been found about the care of the children while their mothers were being treated in the ship's hospital or undergoing punishment. When Ellen Sullivan became ill, her 6-month-old baby was 'taken from her and given in charge to another woman'. Mary Connell spent sixty-eight days in hospital but there was no mention of her three children, aged from 3 to 8. Similarly, Mary Griffen was in the hospital for a fortnight; she had three children on board, aged from 2 to 9. Mary was also placed in the solitary box three times and again, no mention was made of her children during this time.[29]

## PUNISHMENT ON BOARD

On board, bad behaviour and contravention of rules were not tolerated. Keeping order was paramount, so squabbling, quarrelling, fighting, using bad language and stealing were punishable.[30] At the end of the second voyage of the *Tasmania*, Surgeon Superintendent Lardner remarked that the behaviour of the convicts en route was generally good: 'Their principal offences were against discipline. Strict attention was enforced to the established daily routine which not only induced regularity, but was also conducive to their health.'[31]

At the time the *Tasmania* sailed, a common punishment was the solitary box, a narrow box placed on the deck in which the prisoner was held standing upright.[32]

The memoirs of the young midshipman on the *Gilbert Henderson* recorded an account of this shipboard punishment:

The punishments were few and far from severe, and, as a general rule, after the first month at sea were seldom called for. Stopping the allowance of tea at supper time or the allowance of plum pudding on Sundays and Thursdays, were the mildest and the most frequent punishments. Next to these was the sending of the culprit below in fine weather and compelling her to work while her companions were enjoying themselves on deck. For the more refractory, a wooden box, something like a sentry box was provided. The culprit was placed in

this box, where she was compelled either
to stand upright, or to stoop in an uneasy
posture for an hour, or two, or three,
according to the nature of the offence;
and when the door of this prison was
closed the only light and air came from a
hole in the top.[33]

Another account of shipboard punishment
was recorded by Charles Wilkes:

> The usual, and most effectual, punishment
> for misbehaviour is to place the culprit
> in a narrow box on deck, in which he
> is compelled to stand erect. This punish-
> ment is said to be effectual in reducing
> the most refractory convicts to order, but
> it was not found so efficacious in the
> female convict-ship; for, when put in the
> box, they would bawl so loudly, and use
> their tongues so freely, that it was found
> necessary to increase the punishment by

Solitary box. (Reproduced with
permission of the Tasmanian
Museum and Art Gallery)

> placing a cistern of water on the top of the box. This was turned over
> upon those who persisted in using their tongues, and acted upon the
> occupant as a shower-bath, the cooling effect of which was always and
> quickly efficacious in quieting them. I was informed that more than two
> such showers were never required to subdue the most turbulent.[34]

Refractory women were generally held in the box for up to twelve hours
on bread and water.[35] As noted already, Mary Griffen was placed three
times in the solitary box.[36]

## SURGEON SUPERINTENDENT LARDNER'S JOURNAL: THE SICK LIST

Surgeon Superintendent Lardner commenced his journal on
28 August 1845.[37] Although he was well qualified for the position, as with
all Royal Navy medical personnel, his medical experience was primarily

with male patients. Of the 138 women and thirty-five children on board, Surgeon Superintendent Lardner attended fifty-nine women and four children. He kept detailed medical records throughout the voyage.

Eliza Davis, healthy during the voyage, did not appear in Lardner's journal, and apparently did not display any symptoms of her epilepsy.[38]

Margaret Butler 2nd was one of nineteen women treated for diarrhoea.[39] Mary Meagher, who was 46, suffered from the complaint for seventeen days – it is a wonder she survived! Lardner attributed the frequency of the complaint to cold and damp conditions and changes in the weather: 'When the weather would permit, lighted stoves were placed in the prison and every practicable precaution taken to prevent dampness.' Extra clothing was also issued. The water closets were cleaned using a solution of chloride of lime but the conditions on board during outbreaks of diarrhoea must have been extremely unpleasant. In so confined a space, the stench was no doubt overwhelming.[40]

One of the most severe cases of diarrhoea was that of a Kildare woman, 17-year-old Ann Delany, who was transported for the seemingly innocuous offence of stealing potatoes. In total, she spent at least 242 days in prison waiting to embark. Whether this contributed to her ill-health on board ship is difficult to say. In mid-November, Ann was seized suddenly by violent vomiting and purging. She was treated with a mixture and arrowroot and a flannel bandage was applied around her abdomen to relieve the gripping pains. By the end of November, she was discharged from the sick list. The surgeon commented that Ann had been particularly healthy during the voyage; he attributed her ailment to the change in weather.[41]

Roscommon arsonist, 25-year-old Ann Flannery, had been over 180 days in gaol and entered the ship's hospital after only three weeks at sea. Her pulse was weak, her skin was cold and she had a 'pain in the region of her stomach'. Lardner diagnosed 'hæmetemosis' (vomiting blood). She was given a mixture, put in a hipbath and allowed some gruel. By 30 September, she was well enough to be discharged and was back on a full diet.[42] Ann fully recovered; she married in the colony and the last record of her was in December 1854 when her conditional pardon was approved.[43]

Mary McManus from Antrim also spent over 300 days incarcerated before boarding the *Tasmania* (2). She presented herself to Mr Lardner at the end of October with ulcers on both legs. She was confined to bed with very painful legs; one ulcer measured two inches in circumference. Her salt provisions were stopped; she was given a double allowance of lime juice and the ulcers were continuously strapped. On 9 December, she was discharged to the *Anson* prison hulk, which was moored on the River Derwent.[44] Mary died on New Year's Eve 1850, a year after marrying and while she was still under sentence.[45]

At the beginning of November, Derry woman Fanny Doherty was diagnosed with pleurisy. She had severe pain in her side, which made it difficult for her to breathe; her skin was hot, with a pulse of 100; and she was coughing and vomiting. She attributed her condition to the fact that she had got wet the day before when washing. She was given a mixture, allowed barley water, put on a low diet, washed in tepid water and given clean clothes. After nearly a month in the hospital she was discharged.[46] Fanny, who admitted to having been '8 months on the town', did not survive long in the colony; she died in Hobart in March 1846, aged 26.[47]

Four women began their new life in the Colonial Hospital, having failed to make a complete recovery before disembarking. Ellen Neill and Catherine Foy suffered from chronic rheumatism; Mary Griffen from 'dyspepsia' (abdominal pain or discomfort) and mental illness; and Mary McCarthy from venereal disease (she had been 'on the town' for nine months).

Carlow woman Ellen Neill, aged 22, was transported for seven years for larceny. She had been in the hospital of Grangegorman Depot for nearly a year and had not been transported on previous ships bound for Van Diemen's Land, probably because she was rejected by the Surgeons Superintendent.[48] Mr Lardner reported that Ellen had led a most debauched life; she had been 'on the town' for two years. He found 'her pulse to be quick, her tongue foul, skin hot', and she suffered occasional hysterical fits. Her condition was diagnosed as rheumatism, or joint pain. Her right knee was swollen; the pain was much worse at night. Her other knee was slightly affected, as was her right hip. Poultices and flannel bandages were applied to the swollen knee. She was allowed a nourishing diet and was sent on deck for two hours each day. By the time the ship arrived, Ellen was still unable to walk without assistance and she was sent to the Colonial Hospital on landing.[49] There was no further record of poor health. From the hospital, she was sent to the *Anson*. She had two colonial offences (neglect of duty and insolence; absconding) and was granted a free certificate in August 1851. The following April she left the colony for Melbourne.[50]

Catherine Foy, aged 22, from Fermanagh, was treated for syphilis four months before embarkation. Catherine was employed on board ship as a mess woman, a position of some responsibility. Towards the end of September she complained to the surgeon of a severe headache, pain in the loins, thirst, flushed face and hot skin and shivering. She believed she 'took cold going on deck when much heated'. She was confined to bed in the hospital and washed; her hair was cut short and she was dressed in clean clothes, with cold applied to her forehead. She was discharged from the sick list in mid-October but was not returned to her mess duties. She returned to the hospital in late October, complaining of severe pains in her arms and legs and swelling in her ankles. Lardner diagnosed this as rheumatism. She was placed in the hospital, where she was given barley water and warm wine. She gradually improved and was allowed up on deck for an hour daily. However, by the time the ship landed, the pains had returned and she was removed to the Colonial Hospital.[51] She died in the General Hospital in March 1851.[52] She left behind her father Bernard and her two brothers Thomas and James in Enniskillen, her native place in Ireland.[53]

Cork woman Mary McCarthy was another treated for venereal disease; she had received treatment for this in Grangegorman Hospital. Mary had only one eye and she admitted to being 'on the town' for nine months. She received treatment twice during the voyage, for 'verruca' (a wart) and then 'vulneris' (a wound). Mr Lardner applied ointment, carried out a surgical procedure and confined Mary to bed. He required her to pay strict attention to cleanliness. Mary was discharged on 31 October, 'nearly well'. However, she was back again on 4 December as her symptoms had returned. She was discharged from Mr Lardner's care to the Colonial Hospital on 9 December.[54]

Within days of sailing, Mary Griffen, from Tullow, was admitted to the sick list.[55] The surgeon diagnosed her case as one of 'dyspepsia' and 'moral insanity'. On 10 September 1845, at sea, he reported that she had been in the hospital of the Carlow County Gaol for two months with fever.[56] The youngest of her three children, Edward, was weaned the week before embarking. Mary suffered extreme seasickness and had been confined to bed from the time the ship sailed; she was unable to keep anything in her stomach, her bowels had not opened since being on board, her tongue was foul and she had severe headaches. She was prescribed medicine and it was recommended that she be 'well-washed' and that her bedding be sent on deck to air. The following day she was admitted to the ship's hospital, as she was weak; she was given gruel or arrowroot. After an enema, Mary Griffen's bowels opened and according to the surgeon, she felt much relieved. He continued to treat her in the ship's hospital but the constipation and headaches continued. By the end of September, Mary's health had improved but her conduct had become difficult: 'she is morose, vindictive, and had secreted in her bed an iron bar, threatening everybody.' She occasionally displayed 'a paroxysm of rage without cause'.[57]

Mary was discharged from the sick list but only for a short time. She complained of severe griping pain in her bowels and she was not sleeping properly because she was suspicious of her messmates. She was placed in bed, prescribed medicine and allowed gruel and some preserved meat. Mary was occasionally in a very excited state, quarrelling and fighting. She was separated from the others and confined in the solitary box. By the time the ship arrived in Van Diemen's Land on 3 December, Mary was unable to pass urine and was in great pain.[58] Shortly before she was due to disembark, she was overwrought, irritable and her behaviour was very suspicious and vindictive. Consequently, she was again separated from the others 'as well as circumstances will admit'. Mary was admitted to the Colonial Hospital on 9 December. Mr Lardner saw her a month later and wrote that before he left the colony, she appeared to have quite recovered and was sorry for her former behaviour.

As well as its cargo of convict women, the *Tasmania* (2) brought thirty-five of their children.[59] In all, there were twenty-three women who brought their children with them. These children had been with their mothers in Grangegorman and may have been with them in the county gaols as well.

Children were admitted to the ship's hospital with a variety of complaints. The age of the children ranged from 6 months to 14 years.[60] They were usually named in reference to their mothers: for example, 'Sarah Kelly's child', aged 8, was admitted to the sick list with 'opthamalia' (inflammation of the eye); 'Mary Griffin's child', aged 10, with 'cynanche' (throat infection or tonsillitis); and 'Sarah Brennan's child', aged 18 months, with 'vulnus' (wound).[61]

There was one birth during the voyage. Sarah McArdle, a frequently convicted vagrant, gave birth to a son. His birth was registered by 'Jason Lardner, *Tasmania* SS', on 22 December 1845; his mother was recorded as Sarah McArdle, 'Prisoner of the Crown'.[62] The child was not named at the time his birth was registered and no baptism has been located. However, he lived only 2½ months and his name, James, was recorded on his death certificate. He died of gastroenteritis on 31 January 1846.[63]

On completion of the voyage, Surgeon Lardner was required to complete a 'Nosological Synopsis of the Sick List', a classification of the diseases which occurred during the voyage. As already noted, the most common complaint suffered by the women was diarrhoea, followed by 'dyspepsia' (abdominal pain). Unlike in other voyages, Mr Lardner had no cases of scurvy, the scourge of long sea travels.

## DEATHS ON BOARD

Two deaths occurred during the voyage.[64] The first was that of Patrick Ferguson, aged 6 months, the son of Mary Magowan. Patrick was Mr Lardner's first patient; he was entered in the sick book with 'phthisis' (tuberculosis) on 30 August, before the ship had even left Kingstown. He died only eighteen days out of port.[65] His mother, aged 29, had been transported for seven years for larceny. She had another child with her, Ann Ferguson, aged 8. According to the notes in the sick book, Patrick had been very sickly from birth. Much emaciated, he occasionally coughed up 'purulent matter'. He was given arrowroot and, as his mother was still feeding him, she was allowed extra gruel. Patrick's death was drawn out. By 6 September, he was nearly 'acutely suffocated', with laboured breathing and purple lips. He was placed in a warm bath and given a mixture which seemed to relieve the urgent symptoms. By 18 September, Patrick was 'evidently sinking' and could scarcely swallow a little warm wine. He died two days later. He was buried at sea south of the Canary Islands, off the coast of West Africa.[66] Patrick had been given 'farinaceous food or arrowroot' which are starchy foods; arrowroot is also a nutritional food. Today Patrick Ferguson would be given fluids intravenously and antibiotics. The 'emetic', medicine given to Patrick to induce vomiting, would probably have dehydrated him.

The second death was that of Ellen Sullivan, aged 20, who had been sentenced to transportation for ten years in March 1844 for housebreaking.[67] She had been in the county gaol in Tralee since her arrest in January 1844 and was not removed to Grangegorman Depot until 4 June 1845. Ellen spent over 530 days in gaol before boarding the ship. According to Lardner's entry, dated 20 October, Ellen suffered from dysentery, while at the same time suckling a baby. She was given extra gruel but seldom ate it. As the gripping pains got worse, her baby girl, Mary Reardon, aged 9 months, was taken from her and placed in the care of an unknown woman. Ellen had been in a despondent state since embarking. She refused her food, seldom spoke to anyone and expressed a wish to die. Daily, she appeared to get weaker. She was given rice water and arrowroot and was confined to bed. An entry in the book records the fact that it was 'blowing hard' and somehow Ellen's bedclothes were completely saturated 'and from the fright and immersion she is in a most depressed state'. She was removed to the hospital and given warm drinks and warm baths. Her skin was cold and she was in continuous pain, though the 'warm formulations appeared to give her much relief'. By 24 November, Ellen's stomach rejected everything, even the warm wine and water. At 2.30 p.m. on 28 November, Ellen 'died without a struggle'.[68]

It is likely that Ellen was about three months pregnant at the time of her trial in March 1844. In her petition to the Lord Lieutenant in July 1844 she stated she was within two months of her confinement and was 'in bad health confined in the [gaol] Hospital'.[69] It is no wonder Ellen was 'despondent' having spent such a long period incarcerated before embarking; she may have suffered from what is now widely acknowledged as post-natal depression.

## BURIAL AT SEA

In *Life on Board a Female Convict Ship*, the writer described the burial of a young convict woman, Mary Connor, afflicted with consumption:

All on board felt for her, all on board pitied her fate. She was buried at midnight, on a calm moonlit night, when the surface of the ocean was smooth and glittering as that of a mirror. Sewn up in a white sheet, and strapped to a board loaded with shot at one end, the lifeless form was laid across the bulwarks near the gangway. The sailors of the watch below and all the convicts were summoned to the deck by the slow tolling of the ship's bell. The passengers came forth from the cabin. Sir John Hammett read aloud the prayers appointed by the Church to be read at the funeral of those buried at sea, and when he spoke the solemn words – "We therefore commit the body of our beloved sister to the deep etc etc" – the board was loosened, it slid swiftly over the side, a splash was heard, and the corpse sank deep beneath the parting waters, there to abide until the Great Day when the sea shall give up her dead. The splash was heard amidst solemn silence, but immediately there arose from the assembled females a wild 'keene' of lament, which rang in the ears of the listeners for long afterwards and, many among them sobbing hysterically, the females retired to the deck below.[70]

Traditionally, the deceased was sewn into a shroud generally made of burlap and weighed down with weights to prevent the body floating.[71] It was usual for the ship's master to perform the official burial service on deck before the body was thrown overboard. As Mr Lardner did not record events in his journal other than those related to his role as Surgeon Superintendent, the details of the burials were not recorded and it is not known whether the *mná caointe*, the keening women, followed the traditional lamentation and weeping for Patrick or Ellen.

## ARRIVAL IN VAN DIEMEN'S LAND

When the ship was leaving Ireland, it was reported that: 'The authorities of the vessel stated that they had never had a better conducted class of convicts entrusted to their care, or persons more disposed to submit to discipline and observe the regulations which they had made.'[72]

When he arrived in the Derwent, Mr Lardner compiled general remarks in his journal.[73] He recorded that the health of the convicts and the children was generally much improved during the voyage and some who were weighed at the beginning of the passage and again at its end were found to have averaged an increase of 7.5lbs. He also remarked that fresh potatoes sent on board for the use of the convicts were issued daily, in lieu of flour, and contributed to the gradual change of their diet. Ironically, the first sightings of the potato blight were occurring in Ireland at this time.

Mr Lardner's general remarks concluded by giving 'testimony to the very liberal manner in which everything was furnished for the use of these unfortunate females'.[74] The women were discharged from the *Tasmania* (2) to the prison hulk *Anson* on 9 December.

The entrance to the River Derwent, *c.* 1840. (Reproduced with permission of the Tasmanian Archive and Heritage Office)

Mr Lardner also noted that one convict was 'idiotic'.[75] Another displayed symptoms of insanity, but she appeared to have recovered before he left the colony.[76] For the majority of the women, however, a new life beckoned.

After a voyage of ninety-three days, the human cargo of the *Tasmania* (2) arrived in the River Derwent on 3 December 1845.

No doubt the blue-and-gold flag denoting a convict ship and a red-and-white flag signalling that she was carrying female convicts were hoisted.[77] It was the beginning of the Tasmanian summer and conditions were hot and windy:

> On Sunday the mercury slowly fell to 29.3, with a hot wind from the north-east, which rose the temperature to 85 in the shade. Yesterday the mercury had fallen to 28.9 followed by a very heavy hot gale from the north-west which did much damage to the fruit, and gardens in general. These heavy gales, consequent on a low barometer, and not followed by rain, are only of recent habitude here. During the first thirty years of the settlement, hot winds were invariably followed by heavy rains. The mercury rose to 29.3 in the course of the day, and this morning it has risen to 29.5.[78]

Except for Ellen Sullivan and Patrick Ferguson, the women and their children had survived an arduous journey, long and often monotonous, at times fraught and fearful, to begin a new life 'o'er the seas', far from the familiarity of home.

# 6

# A New Life in
# a Strange Land

It is hard to imagine what Eliza Davis, Margaret Butler and their shipmates felt on their arrival in the colony of Van Diemen's Land, so far from home. It must have been a strange experience: summer in December – nearly 30 degrees, hot and windy[1] – and no chance of snow for Christmas; there were oddly shaped trees, strange light, an overwhelming brownness to the landscape and a sparsely spread population.

Like all convicts, the women of the *Tasmania* (2) were interviewed on arrival in the colony. Each woman was asked to state her offence. Often, additional information about the offence was provided, giving a rare

Hobart Town and the Derwent River, Van Diemen's Land. From a sketch by Captain Hext, 4th King's Own Regiment, Charles Hutchins. Lithographer [c.1845] (Reproduced with permission of the Tasmanian Archive and Heritage Office)

glimpse of the woman's understanding of her crime expressed in her own words. When asked to state her offence, Eliza Davis stated that she was transported for 'Strangling my child, it was a fortnight old, [I was] sentenced to be executed & reprieved'.[2] Margaret Butler 2nd admitted to stealing twelve potatoes, adding that she was tried with Esther and Mary Burgess, and Mary Griffen.[3]

## THE PROBATION SYSTEM

The women of the *Tasmania* (2) arrived shortly after the introduction of a new system of convict management known as the probation system.[4] In this period, from 1843 to 1853, just over 7,000 convict women arrived in Van Diemen's Land. A significant number – 42 per cent – were Irish.[5]

In all, there were three phases of female transportation to Van Diemen's Land: exile or open prison (1803–1813), the period of the assignment system (1814–1842) and the period of the probation system (1843–1853).[6] In each phase, the numbers of convict women arriving in Van Diemen's Land increased and they were subjected to more severe penal conditions. In 1840, the number grew significantly when transportation to New South Wales ceased and all female convicts were shipped to Van Diemen's Land.[7]

According to Sprod, the probation system was an experiment in penal discipline unique to Van Diemen's Land, and was based on 'key principles [of] punishment and reform [which] could be achieved by separate confinement and a regime of hard labour, religious instruction and education'.[8] It offered male and female convicts under sentence incentives for good behaviour and hard work. As Sprod explains:

> All convicts were to be subjected to successive stages of punishment, commencing with a period of confinement and labour ... If they progressed satisfactorily through several stages of decreasing severity, they received a probation pass and became available for hire to the settlers ... Sustained good conduct eventually led to a ticket-of-leave or a pardon.[9]

The probation system for male convicts, introduced in 1839, was based on the recommendation of the 1838 Molesworth Report for a standard period of incarceration followed by a period of labour which could be decreased with good behaviour.[10]

For female convicts under the probation system, the system of control was tighter than under the assignment system and there was an increased focus on classification, surveillance and isolation, and punishment and rehabilitation rather than humiliation. Work-related discipline was an integral crucial part of reform.[11]

Newly arrived convicts were separated as much as possible from earlier arrivals. Many of these ideas reflect the influence of prison reformer, Elizabeth Fry.[12] From 1843–1847, on arrival, female convicts were sent to the *Anson*, a penitentiary housed in a converted naval ship moored in the River Derwent, for a six-month training period in domestic skills. This first stage of their probation incorporated a daily routine of early rising, sweeping, cleaning, sewing and scripture reading.[13]

At the end of six months, the women were eligible to become probation pass-holders and were sent to the female hiring depots to be engaged in private or government employment, usually as domestic servants. During the first year, the convict woman was entitled to half her wages; the other half was paid by her employer into a savings bank, for reclaiming when she was granted a ticket of leave, usually after three years for a seven-year sentence. The probation pass was linked to conduct and could be revoked for serious breaches of behaviour. Those women found guilty of misconduct were sent to a house of correction for a period of punishment, employment and reformation. A ticket of leave was granted at the satisfactory completion of the probation pass-holder stage. This allowed the women to choose an employer, but it also often restricted them to a particular police district. It was the first step towards freedom.

The ticket of leave was followed by the final stage, the granting of a pardon, either a conditional pardon or, more rarely, an absolute pardon.[14]

Risdon Ferry (Derwent) with the prison ship, *Anson*. (SLNSW A1192067 PXB834, reproduced with permission of the State Library of New South Wales)

## THE ANSON

Once the women had disembarked and after their details were recorded,
they were removed to the *Anson*. By the time the women of the
*Tasmania* (2) arrived in Van Diemen's Land, they had already experienced
institutional life in Irish gaols and at Grangegorman, as well as on board
the convict ship. For most, their first experience of a colonial institution
was on the *Anson*. Did they know that when they arrived in Van Diemen's
Land they would spend another six months on board a prison ship?

By 1842, the female factories (or female prisons) in Van Diemen's Land
were overcrowded. A new female house of correction was proposed near
Hobart but was never built.[15] In 1843, it was decided to use the *Anson*,
a converted naval ship moored in the River Derwent, to house female
convicts.[16] The HMS *Anson* was originally built as a warship but according
to archaeologist Brad Williams, it was considered third-rate and never saw
active service.[17] It was used as a quarantine ship from 1827 until 1843,
when it was converted to a transport ship in England and then converted
for use as a convict hulk.[18] In 1844, it delivered 499 English male convicts
to Hobart Town – the largest single shipload of convicts to that date.[19]
The *Colonial Times* reported its arrival:

> THE Anson, 72 guns (now fitted as a prison Hulk, her ports iron-barred,
> &c) ... arrived on Sunday. She has on board 500 prisoners, 150 soldiers,
> about 150 women and children, and the same number of sailors.[20]

It was originally proposed that the hulk be located at Eardley Inlet, Oyster
Cove, but this did not happen.[21] On 25 April 1844, it loaded female
prisoners from the *Woodbridge* and *Angelina* and was then towed to New
Town Bay and soon after to Prince of Wales Bay. It was used as a prison
hulk until 1850 and held from 250 to 519 women at any one time.[22]

The *Anson* allowed the implementation of Elizabeth Fry's philosophy
that newly arrived female convicts should be separated from the 'old hands':

> A large staff of officers, male and female, was sent out, and Dr. and
> Mrs. Bowden were placed at the head of the establishment. In this ship
> (the "Anson"), all females transported from the United Kingdom are
> received on their arrival in the colony. They remain under systematic
> instruction for six months, and are then placed in the service of the
> colonist. An opportunity of testing their characters is thus afforded.

If they are well disposed, they are recommended to situations where they are not exposed to temptations, too strong, for their newly-formed resolutions of amendment to resist.[23]

In the words of a local newspaper, the *Anson* prevented the contamination of the new arrival by 'the worst of her sex'.[24]

In April 1845, a few months before the arrival of the *Tasmania* (2), the *Launceston Examiner* introduced the *Anson* to its readers:

THE "ANSON" PENITENTIARY.

MANY of our northern readers are scarcely aware, that an interesting and highly important experiment is now in progress on board the Anson. This vessel is moored in the Derwent, near Risdon, and contains accommodation for about six hundred prisoners. All the females transported to this country are, on their arrival, transferred to this ship. Upon passing through a prescribed course of probation, they are discharged to private service; but whatever their subsequent conduct, they are never returned to the Anson. The discipline adopted is calculated to

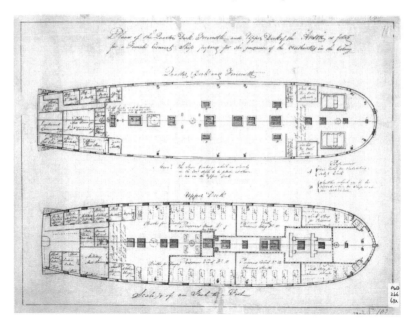

The conversion plans for the *Anson* from a transport ship to a hulk for female prisoners – the Quarter-Deck and Upper Deck (top) and profile (bottom). (TAHO PWD 266/682, reproduced with permission of the Tasmanian Archive and Heritage Office)

subdue the passions, to instruct in the practice of self government, and to form and perpetuate habits of industry. The results, so far as known, are satisfactory. That women of weak principle, surrounded by innumerable temptations, should sometimes relapse into crime, cannot astonish any person. When we recollect the peculiar circumstances of the colony, and the degrading association into which female prisoners are sometimes thrown, it is rather surprising that so many have been really reformed.

Management of the women on the *Anson* was entrusted to Dr and Mrs Bowden. In October 1844, the *Hobart Town Courier* reported:

> We had the pleasure a few days since to pay a visit, too long deferred, to the female penitentiary on board the *Anson*, under the superintendence of Dr. and Mrs. Bowden. As we ascended the ship ladder we were agreeably saluted by the singing of the prisoners, who are assembled on Wednesdays for afternoon service. The singing, as well as the general service, is conducted by the Rev. Mr. Giles, and with very great effect, his congregation appearing to unite with him throughout.[25]

A tour of the *Anson* was conducted by Mrs Bowden:

> We found that besides the necessary duties of the establishment in washing and cooking, the women were employed in various descriptions of needlework, in the manufacture of shoes, straw-hats, door mats, &c., as far as the very limited means at Mrs. Bowden's command will allow. Every part of the ship exhibited remarkable cleanliness, and we could not have expected to witness such general health, and to find the ventilation so good, where so large a number are collected together in a limited space.

The newspaper report provided not only description of the physical appearance of the *Anson* but also an explanation of the management of the women:

> We remarked with great satisfaction the subdued, respectful, and throughout proper deportment of the women, exhibiting a very striking contrast with what we have been too long accustomed to in similar establishments in this country. No one who is acquainted with the trying circumstances in which the best disposed are placed in

service in this colony, will expect too much from the subjects of Mrs. Bowden's management when they are again turned into society; but this reflects nothing upon that lady's management, from which, in more favourable circumstances, the best results could not fail to arise.[26]

The three decks of the vessel were subdivided by iron railings into suitable compartments and thoroughly ventilated. 'Personal cleanliness and submissive deportment' were strictly enforced.[27]

A chaplain regularly performed divine service. The prisoners, according to the newspaper, were satisfied with life on board. Compassion was expressed for the elderly convicts:

> Among the prisoners now on board the *Anson*, are several old and infirm women, who never ought to have been transported. They are suitable for a poor-house, but ought not to have been subjected to so long a voyage in their declining years.[28]

In the opinion of the reporter, the elderly convicts could make no economic contribution to the colony:

> They are incapable of performing the most simple domestic duties, and could have been sustained in England at far less cost to the crown than in this country. This subject deserves the notice of the local executive; and a remonstrance addressed to the authorities at home, would doubtless prevent the transit of superannuated paupers.[29]

The *Anson* was the subject of numerous detailed newspaper reports, most of which highly commended the work of Dr and Mrs Bowden.[30] John West described Phillipa Bowden as 'a lady of majestic presence and enlightened mind', well suited to the position of matron.[31] He attributed the failure of the *Anson* experiment to government negligence and lack of employment.[32] Furthermore, the women 'discharged from the ship ignorant of the colony, were at once thrown into every temptation of convict associations' that not even instruction in the principles of religion, reading and needlework could moderate.[33]

The *Anson* was kept in use until late 1850. Dr Bowden died in 1847 and Mrs Bowden continued as sole superintendent. Brand commented that the establishment 'all but collapsed after her departure, though it lingered on until late 1850'.[34]

## HIRING OUT

Pass-holders, having passed through the early stages of probation, could be hired by settlers at a stated wage. Contracts were made by the Convict Department with individuals. The name of the employer, the date of contract, the name and ship of the pass-holder, the rate of wages and period of employment were included in a Convict Department register.[35]

Having completed their time on the *Anson*, the women were taken to a hiring depot. The Brickfields Hiring Depot at New Town was the main depot but other depots operated throughout the colony, sometimes in female factories. In November 1846, the *Launceston Examiner* inspected the female factory and hiring depot in Launceston:

> The cleanliness, order and decorum that prevailed were highly credit-
> able to the officers in charge. But although washing and other kinds of
> work are performed in the Factory, there appeared to be a lack of active
> employment [in the hiring depot].[36]

At least two of the women did not complete their probation period on the *Anson* until 1847 but it is not clear why. Forty-year-old Carlow widow and mother of seven Esther Burgess was not admitted to the third class until 12 January 1847. Mary McCarthy, a 20-year-old farm servant from Cork, was released two days after Esther Burgess, on 14 February 1847.

Louisa Ann Meredith, who wrote *My Home in Tasmania* and lived on the East Coast, received servants from the *Anson*.[37] Her first *Anson* servant, unaccustomed to bush life, proved unsuitable:

> My nursemaid had become far too much enamoured of the charms
> and gaieties of the city to think with any composure of a return to
> the solitude of bush life, and I found it requisite to supply her place.
> She had been my first trial of the effects of Mrs. Bowden's system of
> female discipline on board the "Anson" and for a year and a half had
> been all I could desire in a servant, irreproachable in her conduct,
> clean, cheerful and industrious, until the visit to town, and the greater
> opportunities of showing her pretty face, caused neglect of her duty,
> and an alarming exhibition of pink silk stockings, thin muslin dresses,
> and other town vanities. I again applied to Mrs. Bowden, and again
> had cause to appreciate the value of her influence, not so much in the

fitness of the woman I selected for the situation she was to fill (for at first she was awkward and uncouth in the extreme), as in the almost miraculous change which must have been wrought in her to fit her for any decent occupation whatever. She had, as I afterwards discovered, been reared amidst the worst of the bad – been imprisoned in some dozen different gaols, and no sooner liberated than, partly from destitution, partly from inveterate habit, she had sinned again, to again be punished. At last she was transported, and after remaining the usual period (six months, I believe) under Mrs. Bowden's government, she came to me a willing, orderly, thankful creature, and remained with us a year and a quarter, when she married comfortably. How different to her former wretched lost condition!

Meredith added:

Simply judging from the superior usefulness, willingness, and orderly, decent, sober demeanour of the women I have taken from the "Anson", over all others of their unfortunate class that I have known, I must believe the system pursued there by Mrs. Bowden to be an excellent and effective one, and rendering the greatest possible benefit to the colony generally.

The women always seem to feel gratitude and reverence for Mrs. Bowden, which her earnest solicitude for their well-doing, and also her own exalted character and endowments, well deserve; they also express much attachment to her female assistants, or "officers", as they are termed.[38]

A correspondent to the *Launceston Examiner* wrote in November 1846 that:

Nothing requires so much reform as the management of female prisoners. As servants they are utterly reckless in their behaviour; for if dismissed they always have abundant board and comfortable lodging to fall back on. If hard labour and bread and water were the factory fare, they would behave very differently.[39]

The newspaper disagreed with its correspondent on the grounds that 'prolonged incarceration on such subsistence would be ... pernicious to the health and constitution':

The treatment of female prisoners is certainly the most perplexing part of penal discipline; and had we not witnessed the salutary effects produced on board the *Anson*, we should have been tempted to despair of success. But the experience of Dr. and Mrs. Bowden has established the fact that even the most vicious and degraded may be reclaimed by proper management ... This lady and gentleman carry on the work of reformation in the spirit of Christian philanthropists rather than paid functionaries, and the result of their labours is sufficient to show that personal instruction, judiciously mingled with kindness or severity, according to circumstances, is a system from which more may be expected than any other scheme.[40]

Some of the *Tasmania* (2) women were punished while incarcerated on the *Anson*. Ellen Cummane, a farm servant from Kerry, received six weeks' hard labour for being insolent. This was her only colonial offence.

Mary O'Brien 2nd had almost completed her period of probation on the *Anson* when she was charged with misconduct for having five carrots in her possession. As punishment, her probation period was extended two months.[41]

By mid-June 1846, the first group of *Tasmania* (2) women had completed their six months' probation on the *Anson* and were available for hire. Some, like Mary Scallon, transported at the age of 60, had no colonial offences; little is known of her after she left the *Anson*. Others became part of a vibrant colonial tapestry, at times a source of great amusement to local newspapers, spending time in the facetiously named 'Cascades Convent' or one of the two other female factories that existed at the time.

Two women of the *Tasmania* (2) died on board the *Anson*, Mary Murphy on 9 January 1846 and Fanny Doherty on 26 March 1846. Their inquests were held on board. In Mary Murphy's case, the inquest concluded that she died due to a 'visitation of God in a natural way to wit, from inflammation of the lungs'.[42] An inquest into Fanny Doherty's death also determined that she died 'by the Visitation of God in a natural way'.[43]

## TRADES: IRELAND AND VAN DIEMEN'S LAND

Trades were routinely noted on convict records. In the period when the *Tasmania* (2) arrived, trades were recorded on all three main convict documents: the conduct record, the indent and the description list. Margaret Butler, who had no trade in Ireland, was described as a farm servant or a country servant.[44] Eliza Davis, a servant in Ireland, was a housemaid.[45]

As can be seen from Table 4 and Table 5, 70 per cent of the
*Tasmania* (2) women did not have a trade when they were admitted to
the Grangegorman Female Convict Depot in Dublin but by the time
they arrived in Van Diemen's Land, they all had a trade. Table 6 lists some
of the employers who hired women from the *Tasmania* (2). Some Irish
trades – millworker and piece worker, for example – were not needed in
the colony.

When Margaret Randall entered Grangegorman, she was recorded as
a servant. Her colonial records described her as a midwife. At the time of
her trial, Margaret was married (to Edward Randall, an auctioneer) and
had four children.[46]

As always, there are discrepancies on some of the convict records. Two
women, Bell Amos and Maria Brien, had no trade recorded on their indent
but a trade was recorded on their conduct record.[47] Bell Amos, recorded
as a 'spinster' in Grangegorman, was later recorded as a farm servant in
Van Diemen's Land. Maria Brien had no trade in Grangegorman but on
her conduct record was a housemaid.

| | |
|---|---|
| Bonnet maker | 2 |
| Dress maker | 1 |
| Milliner | 1 |
| Millworker | 3[48] |
| Pieceworker | 5[49] |
| Servant | 20 |
| Spinster | 5 |
| No trade recorded | 97 |
| Total | 138 |

Table 4: Trades of the *Tasmania* (2) convicts at Grangegorman [n=138],
NAI, Registry of Female Convicts, Grangegorman Depot.

| | |
|---|---|
| Bonnet maker | 1 |
| Country servant | 21 |
| Country servant & housemaid | 1 |
| Country servant & laundress | 1 |
| Dairymaid & housemaid | 1 |
| Dairywoman | 6 |
| Dressmaker | 1 |
| Dressmaker, country servant, can make butter | 1 |
| Farm servant | 4 |

| | |
|---|---|
| Housemaid | 38 |
| Housemaid & dairy woman | 1 |
| Housemaid & plain laundress | 3 |
| Housemaid – can wash | 8 |
| Housemaid, laundress, can milk | 1 |
| Housemaid – can wash & iron | 2 |
| Housemaid & country servant | 1 |
| Housemaid & laundress | 1 |
| Kitchen maid | 2 |
| Laundress | 8 |
| Laundress & knitter | 1 |
| Laundress & dairymaid | 1 |
| Laundress & plain cook | 3 |
| Midwife | 1 |
| Needlewoman, laundress | 1 |
| Needlewoman, laundress, housemaid | 1 |
| Needlewoman, nursemaid, laundress | 1 |
| Needlewoman, housemaid, can wash | 1 |
| Nurse & needlewoman | 1 |
| Nursemaid | 11 |
| Nursemaid & laundress | 1 |
| Plain cook | 3 |
| Plain cook & dairymaid | 1 |
| Plain laundress | 4 |
| Professed cook | 1 |
| Staymaker & shirt maker | 1 |
| Washerwoman | 1 |
| Washerwoman, housemaid & dairywoman | 1 |
| Total | 137 |

Table 5: Trades recorded on arrival in Van Diemen's Land TAHO, CON15/1/3 Indent *Tasmania* (2).[50]

| Convict | Date of Contract | Employer | Wage | Period in Months | Source |
|---|---|---|---|---|---|
| Isabella Amos | 19 Sep 1848 | John Lookin, Elizabeth St | £7 | 3m | CON30/1 p. 60 |
| Jane Bradshaw | 13 Sep 1849 | Elizabeth Clayton, Collins St | £8 | 1m | CON30/2 p. 123 |
| Mary Barry | 9 Jun 1849 | Samuel Loring, Liverpool Street | £8 | 3m | CON30/1 p. 32 |
| Mary Byrne | 19 Mar 1850 | Thomas Ball, Macquarie St | £7 | 12m | CON30/1 p. 151 |
| Ellen Callaghan | 12 Sep 1848 | William Heywood, Elizabeth St | £9 | 1m | CON30/1 p. 80 |
| Anne Dougherty | 20 Jun 1849 | Samuel Gunn, Park St | £8 | 1m | CON30 /1 p. 92 |
| Mary Dogherty | 15 Jul 1850 | Robt Wm Carns, New Town | £9 | 12m | CON30/2 p. 124 |
| Eliza Dwyer | 2 May 1849 | James Callon, Murray St | £7 | 1m | CON30/2 p. 77 |
| Bridget Fanning | 14 Aug 1849 | William Flack, Cocked Hat Hill | £9 | 1m | CON30/1 p. 123 |
| Bridget Fanning | 18 Jan 1851 | Geo Byworth, Pattersons Plains | £9 | 12m | CON30 /2 p. 261 |
| Bridget Fanning | 8 April 1853 | George Coulson, East Tamar | £10 | 12m | CON30/2 p. 283 |
| Anne Flannery | 3 Jan 1849 | Thomas Jones, Elizabeth St | £10 | 3m | CON30/1 p. 81 |
| Margt Gallagher | 27 Dec 1848 | Walter Cleary, Liverpool St | £7 | 1m | CON30/2 p. 75 |
| Anne Gardner | 1 Jun 1848 | William Duke, Argyle St | £7 | 1m | CON30/2 p. 79 |
| Mary Gillespie | 27 Jun 1849 | Charles Lovett, Collins St | £9 | 1m | CON30/1 p. 131 |
| Mary Gillespie | 1 Aug 1849 | Michael Arkwright, Collins St | £7 | 1m | CON30/1 p. 157 |
| Mary Gillespie | 29 Nov 1849 | Rchd Frederick, Restdown Rd | £8 | 1m | CON30/1 p. 157 |
| Margaret Grady | 29 Jun 1849 | Rchd Frederick, Restdown Rd | £8 | 1m | CON30/1 p. 157 |
| Margaret Henry | 14 May 1849 | James Eckford, Ross | £9 | 12m | CON30/2 p. 115 |
| Catherine Hughes | 6 June 1841 | Richard Drury, Liverpool St | £8 | 12m | CON30/2 p. 224 |
| Eliza Hunter | 23 Jun 1849 | Revd Jas Bell, St John's Manse | £10 | 12m | CON30/1 p. 155 |
| Eliza Hunter | 18 Feb 1850 | Benjn Hurst, Elizabeth St | £7 | 1m | CON30/1 p. 182 |
| Bridget Hurley | 22 Feb 1851 | George Jones, Launceston | £9 | 12m | CON30 /1 p. 195 |
| Margaret Kelly | 1 May 1849 | Mary A Gormley, Murray St | £6 | 1m | CON30/1 p. 142 |
| Margaret Lee | 3 July 1849 | Michael Arkwright, Collins St | £9 | 1m | CON30/2 p. 157 |
| Margaret Lee | 21 July 1849 | Chas Billings, Collins St | £7 | 1m | CON30/2 p. 165 |
| Sarah McArdle | 13 Jan 1851 | Clement Buesnell | £9 | 12m | CON30/2 p. 304 |
| Ann McCormack | 14 Sep 1850 | John Brent, Roseneath | £10 | 12m | CON30/2 p. 174 |
| Sarah McGinley | 9 April 1849 | Samuel Hickling, Liverpool St | £7 | 1m | CON30/1 p. 120 |
| Sarah McGinley | 25 Jun 1850 | John C Cuff Launceston | £9 | 12m | CON30/2 p. 210 |
| Martha Martin | 7 May 1850 | George Barnes, Barrack St | £9 | 12m | CON30/2 p. 242 |
| Catherine Meaney | 15 Oct 1849 | John Coverdale, Richmond | £9 | 2m | CON30/2 p. 116 |
| Mary Meehan | 23 Sep 1850 | John Brooks, Launceston | £10 | 12m | CON30/2 p. 208 |
| Joanna Murray | 7 Mar 1850 | James Lord, Campbell Town | £9 | 12m | CON30/1 p. 202 |
| Margaret Sloane | 6 Jun 1849 | Charles Farrell, Argyle St | £9 | 1m | CON30/1 p. 88 |
| Margaret Sloane | 27 Jun 1849 | James Costin, Goulburn St | £7 | 3m | CON30/2 p. 109 |
| Mary Sullivan | 16 May 1849 | Bernard Conolan, Macquarie St | £7 | 3m | CON30/2 p. 106 |
| Mary Sullivan | 16 Jun 1849 | Thomas Ball, Macquarie St | £6 | 1m | CON30/2 p. 151 |

Table 6: TAHO, CON30/1/1-2 Register of Employment of Peobation Passholders.[51]

Increasing numbers of convict women arriving in Van Diemen's Land and
the depressed local economy reduced the demand for domestic labour
and consequently the bargaining power of the convict women. By 1846,
more women were housed on the *Anson*, in the hiring depots and in the
female houses of correction than were in domestic employment.[52]

It is not clear where the infant children who remained with their convict
mothers in the period immediately after arrival were housed. No evidence
of children on the *Anson* has been found but given the invisibility of very
young children in the convict records this is not surprising. At least one of
the Irish children was at the Brickfields nursery: on Christmas Day 1846,
Jane Lynam, daughter of Mary Lynam or Egan, died at the Brickfields Hiring
Depot. Jane was born while her mother was in Grangegorman in Dublin.[53]

Because of the existence of the *Anson*, some of the *Tasmania* (2)
women had no experience of the female factories. There is no evidence,
for example, that either Eliza Davis or Margaret Butler 2nd were ever
confined in a female factory.

For the women of the *Tasmania* (2), a new life began on the *Anson*
and in the hiring depots. It was a life constrained by a mass of rules and
regulations. Some women adjusted quickly and quietly while others were
constantly in trouble.

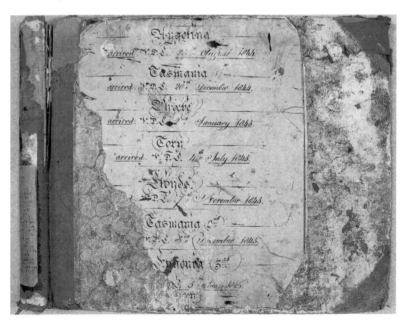

Indent of the *Tasmania* (2). (TAHO, CON15/1/3, reproduced with permission of the
Tasmanian Archive and Heritage Office)

# Behind Stone Walls

By 1845, when the *Tasmania* (2) arrived, there were a number of convict institutions that were an integral component of the penal system in Van Diemen's Land, as well as others that were an important part of the colonial welfare system generally.

## HOUSES OF CORRECTION AND FEMALE FACTORIES

Female factories were also known as houses of correction. In Van Diemen's Land, there were five female factories: Hobart Town (*c.* 1821–1828); George Town (*c.* 1822–*c.* 1824); Cascades (1828–1856); Launceston (1834–1855); and Ross (1848–1854).

When transportation finished in 1853, the female factories became houses of correction, operating as gaols. Even after this, the institutions were still sometimes referred to as 'factories' in the colonial press and in official documents. Other establishments, such as the Brickfields and Campbell Street Gaol, were at times referred to as houses of correction. Brickfields was also sometimes designated a branch factory of Cascades Female Factory.

After the end of transportation to Van Diemen's Land in 1853, administration and funding of the houses of correction in the colony, including the female factories, transferred from the British government (through the Comptroller General's Department) to the local authorities (through the Sheriff's Office). This marked the end of female factories as institutions; they either closed altogether (for example, Ross) or operated as gaols (Cascades and Launceston).

There were also associated convict institutions, such as separate hiring depots, convict nurseries and, to a lesser extent, the New Norfolk Insane Asylum and the Orphan Schools.[1]

Cascades Female Factory by J.C. Goodhart, *c.* 1927. (AUTAS001131822066, reproduced with permission of the Tasmanian Archive and Heritage Office)

## THE FEMALE FACTORY

Female factories confined women who were undergoing punishment, or were waiting to be assigned (in the assignment period) or hired out (in the probation period), or were pregnant or weaning infants. Towards the end of the convict period, those factories still operating accommodated some colonially convicted prisoners as well as transported convicts.[2]

When a woman arrived at a female factory to be punished, her hair was cut short and it continued to be cut regularly while she was there.[3] This was for reasons of hygiene, not punishment, and it was a standard practice in English institutions, such as Millbank Penitentiary.[4] It was a practice dreaded by the women: James Montague Smith, who arrived as a seaman on the *Sir Robert Seppings* in 1852, noted in his memoirs: 'I believe that this punishment is feared next to death by the young ones, but they get used to it after a little colonial experience.'[5]

Women who committed offences were sentenced to serve periods of hard labour (including at the washtub), solitary confinement or time in the separate apartments at the Cascades Factory. If they were tried for further offences while imprisoned – mostly against the rules and regulations of the factory – they were sentenced to solitary confinement, bread and water rations, hard labour at the washtub and cleaning the yards.

Neither Eliza Davis nor Margaret Butler 2nd were confined in a female factory. In all, there were thirty-four *Tasmania* (2) women – 25 per cent – who did not spend time there.

Martha Merryfield was admitted to all three female factories. A house servant from Belfast, Martha had several previous convictions and had been 'on the town' for two years when she was transported. Her first colonial offence was in August 1846 when she was sent to the Cascades Female Factory for being absent without leave. She went on to commit at least twenty colonial offences. Martha was sent to the Ross Female Factory in 1848 and Launceston Female Factory in 1851, not long after she married Elias Norton in Fingal. She had several more offences for absconding, as well as minor offences, before being granted a certificate of freedom in June 1854.[6]

Isabella Warnock was in two female factories: Cascades and Launceston. Isabella, a thief tried in Antrim, had a colourful colonial history. After several short spells in the Cascades Female Factory, mostly for being drunk, out after hours or disturbing the peace, Isabella appeared in the Launceston Female Factory in January 1853, most likely to be hired. Shortly afterwards, in February 1853, she was charged with being drunk and was sentenced to three months' hard labour. Over the next two years, she was in and out of the factory, mostly for being drunk or disorderly, and each time she was returned to her husband.[7]

Others who were in both Hobart and Launceston female factories included Margaret Daley, Elizabeth Dwyer, Bridget Fanning and Mary Francis.[8]

## CASCADES FEMALE FACTORY 1828–1856

The Cascades Female Factory was Van Diemen Land's largest institution for the punishment and reform of convict women. At its peak in 1851, it comprised five large yards. By the mid-1840s, conditions in the Cascades Female Factory were austere, damp and miserable. Overcrowding was common: at one stage, the institution housed more than 1,200 women and children.[9]

At least eighty-two *Tasmania* (2) women – 60 per cent – were incarcerated in the Cascades Female Factory at some stage.

Some of the *Tasmania* (2) women were sent to the Cascades Female Factory to give birth. Jane Bradshaw, whose Irish daughter was in the Female Orphan School, gave birth to a daughter, Ann, in September 1848. Ann died of 'catarrh' in the Dynnyrne Nursery in June 1849.[10]

Others were sent to the Cascades Factory to be punished after giving birth: in January 1849, Mary Byrne was charged with being absent without leave and for having given birth to an illegitimate child. She was sentenced to six months' imprisonment with hard labour.[11]

Other women were there to be punished for various offences. Between December 1846 and December 1850, Henrietta Beresford, a thief from Limerick, was in and out of the Cascades Female Factory at least nine times. She was first sent there to serve one month with hard labour for being absent without leave. Five months later she was back to serve three months' imprisonment with hard labour, again for being absent without leave. This pattern continued over the next four years. Her longest sentence was six months for absconding.[12]

## LAUNCESTON FEMALE FACTORY 1834–1855[13]

The Launceston Female Factory was first occupied in November 1834.[14] At least twenty-seven *Tasmania* (2) women are known to have spent some time there.

The first of the *Tasmania* (2) women to be sent there was Johannah Murray, sentenced to imprisonment for three months for 'misconduct in having a man concealed in her master's kitchen for an improper purpose'.[15]

Most of the *Tasmania* (2) women sent to the Launceston Female Factory (including Johannah Murray) were sent there for alcohol-related and public-order offences as well as breaches of convict discipline, such as being absent without leave and absconding. Nearly all Mary Lynam's spells in the factory were caused by her drinking, as were Ellen Maguire's.[16]

A more unusual instance was that of Anne Mallon, a thief from Antrim, who in October 1849 was charged with being in a public house 'with a male passholder and with improperly administering to him ale with snuff in it for the purpose of stupefying him'. For this, she received nine months' hard labour. Before she had served this sentence, she was charged with removing documents (fourteen days in the cells) then assaulting a constable in the execution of his duty (six months' hard labour) and refusing to go to her ward in the factory (seven days in the cells). She was still being charged in Launceston as late as 1875 (for larceny and being idle and disorderly).[17]

Of all the women on the *Tasmania* (2), Mary Salmon was perhaps best acquainted with the Launceston Female Factory. Her story is told in Chapter 8.

Not all the *Tasmania* (2) women had long records like Mary Salmon. Ellen Neill was charged with absconding in August 1848 and was sentenced to two months' imprisonment in the Launceston Female Factory. This was her last recorded offence: she married in 1848, received a ticket of leave in December 1849 and a free certificate in August 1851.[18]

Bridget Hurley had several spells in the Launceston Female Factory between June 1849 and June 1851. Her son Dennis was born there in June 1849 but died there in December 1851.[19]

## ROSS FEMALE FACTORY 1848–1854

As with the female factories in Hobart Town and Launceston, the Ross Female Factory served as a place to hire convict women; a place of secondary punishment; and a place for convict women to give birth. It opened in a recycled male convict station.[20]

The Ross Female Factory was smaller than the ones in Hobart and Launceston but provided the same services: a hiring yard, punishment blocks, solitary cells, a chapel, a hospital, a lying-in hospital and a nursery for infants until they were weaned and could go to the Orphan Schools.[21] It also provided an overnight station for female convicts travelling between settlements.

In March 1848, the *Hobart Town Gazette* reported the opening of the institution:

CONVICT DEPARTMENT
*Comptroller-General's Office, 28th March, 1848*

A DEPOT for the reception and hire of Female Passholders has been established at the Ross Station; and Female Passholders can therefore be forwarded to that Depot in all cases where it may be nearer to the employer's residence than Hobart Town or Launceston.[22]

J.S. HAMPTON, *Comptroller-General*

The remains of Ross Female Factory. (Courtesy of Trudy Cowley)

At this time, convict arrivals were increasing; 40 per cent of arrivals were women. Many of the women were from Ireland, convicted during the Great Famine and its aftermath. The existing female factories were over-crowded. Some convict women were hired in 'the interior' at a distance from both Hobart and Launceston, often as a deterrent to misconduct in the towns. A number were in the Campbell Town district, where the Ross Female Factory was also located.

The reformatory principles of the probation system were adapted for the Ross Female Factory, particularly the system of punishment and reward through labour known as 'task work':

> Women were to work for a set number of hours per day, ten in summer, reducing to seven and a quarter in winter with intermediate hours in spring and autumn. Within those hours a certain amount of work must be done. Over eighty different tasks in various categories were listed, ranging from picking old rope apart to stitching ladies' night-caps, with prisoners being graded 'to prevent the active, the intelligent and the healthy being placed in a better position than the weak, the ignorant and the sickly'.[23]

As Parker explains, to even qualify for 'the privilege of Task Work', a prisoner was required to 'attend school regularly'. Parker adds: 'As the Factory at Ross was both a hiring depot and a house of correction, it … supplied the labour-force *and* the means of disciplining that labour force'.[24]

Conditions for babies and infants were significantly improved at the Ross Female Factory and the child mortality rate was much lower than at the Cascades and Launceston female factories.[25]

At least seven of the women who arrived on the *Tasmania* (2) spent time in the Ross Female Factory: Sarah Brennan; Catherine Burnet; Margaret Meara; Mary Meehan; Martha Merryfield; Margaret Randall; and Mary Russell.[26]

In all, four of the women from the *Tasmania* (2) either gave birth in the Ross Female Factory or brought a child with them when admitted.[27]

It is not clear why Mary Meehan was admitted to the Ross Female Factory but she was there by mid-February 1849, when she was reprimanded for insolence. Mary, a 30-year-old housemaid from Clare, had been 'on the town' for eight years when she was transported for stealing. She had two minor colonial offences before giving birth to a son, John, in April 1848; no further details about the child have been found. Mary was punished three times while she was in the Ross Factory. Besides being punished for the insolence charge already mentioned, she was also sentenced to one month's hard labour for obscene language and fourteen days' hard labour for abusive language. In November 1849, Mary was granted a ticket of leave. From this time, Mary regularly appeared in court on various charges, including 'being a common prostitute and indecent conduct', for which she received three months' hard labour in the Launceston Female Factory. She was also sentenced to three months' hard labour for representing herself to be free and four months' hard labour for absconding, both to be served in the Launceston Factory. She received her free certificate in March 1852.[28]

Similarly, it is not obvious why Margaret Randall was admitted to the Ross Female Factory, but she was there by March 1851, when she was charged with causing a disturbance in the cells. In November 1850, Margaret was sentenced to three months' hard labour in an unspecified factory, for being drunk and neglect of her duty. She was later punished for fighting (one month's hard labour); talking at prayers (reprimanded) and disobedience of orders (one month's hard labour). Margaret and William Cook applied for permission to marry before she was admitted to Ross and twice after she had been discharged, but no marriage appears to have taken place. Margaret was married with four children when she was transported; she was a midwife aged 31.[29]

All seven of the women from the *Tasmania* (2) were punished while they were in the Ross Factory. Generally, the offences were typical of convict women in and out of the factories – offences against convict discipline such as disobedience of orders; neglect of duty; insolence; and obscene language. It is tempting to dismiss them because they are such common offences, but occasionally additional information provides context for the offence: Margaret Meara, for example, was sentenced to two months' hard labour for neglect of duty only days before she gave birth in the factory.[30] This charge also highlights the fact that there was no special treatment for those convicts who were pregnant.

Within days of being sent to the factory, Sarah Brennan received the first of the seven punishments she was to undergo there: in April 1849, she was sentenced to one month's hard labour for bringing in tobacco. The following year in March, she was again sentenced to one month's hard labour, for allowing smoking.[31] This implies that she had a responsible position at the factory.

Sarah was also one of the women charged with food-related offences while there. Pregnant at the time, she was punished for taking a ration of bread away from a fellow prisoner; she received two months' hard labour. A fortnight later, she was accused of having 'white bread improperly in her possession'; she was sentenced to one month's hard labour.[32]

There seems to have been a great deal of inconsistency in sentencing. Sarah Brennan, for example, was sentenced to ten days' hard labour for washing in the nursery yard – a seemingly innocuous offence – and yet Mary Russell was merely admonished for cruelly beating her child. Interestingly, Mary received greater punishment for her other two factory offences: fourteen days' hard labour for using obscene language and four days in the cells for profane and obscene language.[33]

Punishment was a means of social control in the confined conditions at the factory. Quelling behaviour likely to cause disruption was essential. Margaret Randall was sentenced to three months' imprisonment with hard labour for creating a disturbance in the cells and one month's hard labour for fighting. She also received one month's hard labour for disobedience of orders: a total of five months' hard labour in the short period she was in the factory.[34] Mary Meara received seven days in the cells for causing a disturbance in the yard. Martha Merryfield received eight days in the cells for fighting and fifteen days in the cells for violent assault. The longest sentence meted out to a *Tasmania* (2) woman in the Ross Female Factory was four months' imprisonment with hard labour, which Sarah Brennan received for wilfully making a false statement.[35]

## HIRING DEPOTS

Female probation pass-holders were housed at hiring depots while waiting to be hired into service. Hiring depots were located at the Brickfields and in the female factories. For a time in Launceston, the hiring depot operated from a rented house in St John's Square (now Princes Square).[36] The growth of the colony increased the demand for female labour. Those requiring labour (or their agents) attended the hiring depot to select a convict employee, who was returned to the depot when no longer needed.

## BRICKFIELDS HOBART

The Brickfields Hiring Depot was located on the old brickfields site at the top end of Argyle Street, in what was then called New Town but is now North Hobart. The building was completed at the beginning of October 1842 but housed convicts for hire from February 1842.[37]

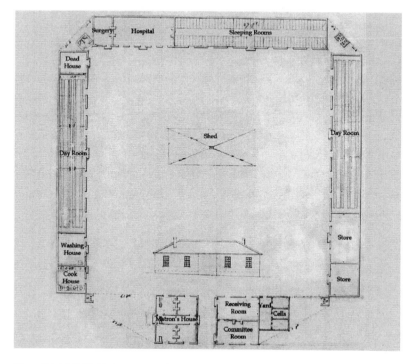

Plan of Brickfields Hiring Depot. (TAHO, PWD266/1/748 (edited by Trudy Cowley), reproduced with permission of the Tasmanian Archive and Heritage Office)

At least thirteen of the women from the *Tasmania* (2) were at the Brickfields; they were there for various reasons but mostly waiting to be hired. Those who transgressed in the Brickfields or other hiring depots were usually sent to the factory.

Bell Amos, a young farm servant from Fermanagh, was part of the first group to complete probation and to be admitted to the Third Class (or hiring class) on 16 June 1846. She was at the Brickfields Hiring Depot in August 1846, possibly waiting to be hired. While there, she was charged with misconduct for striking her officer. For this, she received six months' imprisonment with hard labour; this was added to her probation period. This was her first colonial offence and it was a serious one. She committed four other offences, mostly minor but no more for assault. Bell gave birth to a son, Joseph Amos, in February 1849 at the Cascades Female Factory. Joseph died on 14 March and, by December that year, Bell was back in the Brickfields Depot, where the remainder of her probation sentence was remitted.[38]

Jane Bradshaw was probably at the Brickfields waiting to be rehired after serving a sentence of seven days for being absent without leave. While she was there, in November 1846, she was charged with misconduct, earning a sentence of one month's hard labour in the Cascades Female Factory.[39]

Two of the *Tasmania* (2) women lost children while they were incarcerated in the Brickfields. In December 1846, Mary Lynam's Irish-born daughter Jane died and in June 1848, Mary Ryan gave birth to a stillborn child.[40]

The Brickfields had an extremely poor reputation:

FEMALE PENITENTIARY.—We have received numerous communications relative to the discipline of this establishment, which is represented as very defective. The women hired from this depot are, generally speaking, of the most troublesome character; drunken, impudent, and setting all restraint at defiance. In one family four servants have been tried in the short space of a month. The first two were incorrigibles, taking day about to absent themselves from their service, and returning home drunk. One of the second two was of the same character, and each of the three asserted that she would 'sooner be at the brickfields than in any service where she was not allowed to have her own fling'.[41]

Some of the *Tasmania* (2) women fitted the *Observer's* categorisation of the Brickfields' inmates as 'troublesome'. Honor Mugan certainly did: while there in April 1847, Honor was charged with misconduct for behaving in a riotous and disorderly manner. She was sentenced to six months' hard labour at the Cascades Female Factory.[42] Bridget Stankard was reprimanded for disorderly conduct.[43] Maria Brien, Mary Meehan, Mary Hurley and Mary Lynam were charged with drunkenness while they were there.[44]

The women were subject to strict regulations while at the Brickfields: breaches such as not returning to the depot on time or being absent were severely regarded. Deborah Connor was sentenced to four months' imprisonment with hard labour for overstaying her pass while she was at the Brickfields. She received another three months' imprisonment with hard labour for disobedience of orders the following year and on the same day was reprimanded for disorderly conduct.[45] Annie McCarmack, from Wexford, transported at the age of 30 for receiving stolen goods, was twice charged with not returning to the depot according to her pass: in February 1849, she was sentenced to six months' hard labour in the Cascades Female Factory and again in December 1849, when she was found in a disorderly house.[46] Bridget Kelly was charged with being absent and was sentenced to seven months' imprisonment with hard labour at the Cascades Factory. She was also not allowed to enter service in Hobart Town, a punishment unique to the penal settlement, designed to keep the women away from the contamination of Hobart Town.[47]

The *Observer* queried why the women behaved so badly and answered its own question:

> It is asserted by the women themselves they can get supplied with every luxury they require in the depot, and to secure these they get hired for a few weeks until they get a supply and then away to the Brickfields to enjoy the *otium*,[48] until their means are expended. To make use of the exact expression of one of those ladies 'they can fence (sell) anything in the Brickfields from a needle to an anchor'. No matter how they came by the property, a ready sale is afforded at the depot, and the privileged reap the benefit of all the petty robberies committed in the families of these worthies.

Not only was a black market allegedly operating, but the women were:

> principally occupied in smoking and dancing, varied by an occasional 'set too'. Their language is disgusting, and they appear to give loose to all the wildest and worst passions without control. We understand that the superintendent has endeavoured lately to put a stop to these proceedings by dismissing one of the female officers, for accepting goods from the

women. When leaving, it is said that she had three trunks filled with all descriptions including wearing apparel and jewellery, which she obtained from her mates as they returned from their experimental visits to families in the town. The whole system is rotten, and requires immediate revision.[49]

In October 1852, the Brickfields Hiring Depot was designated a house of correction; the hiring depot was closed and relocated to the Cascades Female Factory:

NEW GAOL.—The buildings at the upper end of Argyle-street, known as the Brickfields Depôt, are proclaimed to be a house of correction for the reception and punishment of male and female offenders.[50]

In November 1852, the *Colonial Times* reported the closure of the Brickfields as a hiring depot:

THE BRICKFIELDS DEPOT.—This establishment has been closed and for the future female passholders must be hired from and returned to the Cascade Factory, between the hours of 9 and 4.[51]

As well as a hiring depot and house of correction, the Brickfields establishment operated a nursery at three different times: from 1849 to 1851; from September 1852 to 1854; and from 1855 to *c.* 1859.[52] In 1849, thirty-seven women and sixty-five children were moved to the Brickfields nursery.[53]

## CASCADES HOUSE OF CORRECTION (GAOL) 1856-1877

When transportation finished, the Cascades Female Factory became the Cascades House of Correction or Gaol. At least one *Tasmania* (2) woman was sent to the Cascade Gaol. In September 1860, Mary McCarthy, who was free by servitude in 1852, was sentenced to three months there when she was found guilty of larceny. Mary's 5-year-old daughter accompanied her to gaol. Mary was again sent to gaol for three months in 1863 for being idle and disorderly.[54] In 1873, as Mary Rourke alias Kent, she was again charged with larceny and was imprisoned for three months with hard labour.[55] Even though this was nearly thirty years after she arrived in the colony and she had been free for twenty-one years, this offence was recorded on her convict conduct record.

## LAUNCESTON GAOL (1855) AND COUNTRY GAOLS

Launceston Female Factory was handed over to local authorities in 1855 and then operated as a house of correction or gaol. As Agnes Leach, in 1875, Ann Mallon was sentenced to two months in the Launceston Gaol for larceny (stealing a shawl). The crime report noted she was 49, 5ft 4in with grey eyes and 'W.M.' on her left arm.[56]

At least from 1862, Mary Salmon, a notorious recidivist, was in and out of Launceston Gaol (having been a frequent inmate of the Launceston Female Factory).[57] The last record of her being imprisoned in Launceston was in March 1885.[58] She also lived at Westbury and Deloraine and may have served time in local gaols there.

## CAMPBELL STREET GAOL

Campbell Street Gaol in Hobart began taking female prisoners in 1877 when the Cascades House of Correction (or gaol) closed.

Jane Brady (*née* Burgess) was the Irish-born daughter of Esther Burgess. She was a frequent inmate of the Campbell Street Gaol and died there in 1893.[59]

For many of the sentences to imprisonment or hard labour noted on convict conduct records, the place of incarceration is uncertain or unknown.

Campbell Street Gaol. (Courtesy of Brian Rieusset)

## HOSPITALS

There were several hospitals throughout the colony. At least nine *Tasmania* (2) women were treated in hospital when they were under sentence or when they were free. Some were admitted to hospital on arrival: these included Catherine Foy; she was readmitted in 1851 and died there.[60] Hobart Hospital, also known as Hobart Colonial Hospital and Hobart General Hospital, treated many of the women living in the Hobart area. Launceston General Hospital, otherwise known as the Cornwall Hospital, also treated several of the women.

In 1847, Margaret Sloane, transported as a 40-year-old widow, was charged with misconduct at the Colonial Hospital; her convict record indicates that she was probably working there.[61]

## THE ASYLUM AT NEW NORFOLK

Mentally ill patients were treated in the Asylum for the Insane at New Norfolk.[62] Some were admitted for 'amentia', which referred to mental retardation or intellectual disability and was sometimes recorded as 'idiocy'. Others were admitted for 'mania', a mental illness marked by periods of great excitement, euphoria, delusions, and overactivity. As with all government institutions at the time, space and resources were inadequate and overcrowding was a constant problem.

Six of the women who arrived on the *Tasmania* (2) are known to have spent some time in the New Norfolk Asylum and at least five died there – Margaret Kelly (d. 1856), Johanna Murray or Gillespie (d. 1876), Catherine Molloy (*née* Stewart, d. 1884); Martha Merryfield (d. 1891) and Mary White (*née* O'Brien, d. 1900).

Asylum for the Insane, New Norfolk, 1833. (AUTAS001126077064, reproduced with permission of the Tasmanian Archive and Heritage Office)

Mary Griffen, aged 32, had spent two months with fever in the hospital of Carlow County Gaol and it is surprising that she was allowed to embark.[63] Mary's youngest child was only weaned the week before embarkation.

Mary's time on board was challenging but she appeared to have recovered shortly after arrival.[64] Her recovery was short-lived:

Mary was admitted to the asylum on 16 May 1846 with 'mania'. In the asylum, Mary had trouble sleeping and was violent and troublesome. She quarrelled with the nurses and patients and 'disturbed the whole establishment with her loud voice'. She was confined in a padlocked cell but managed to break the wooden bars at the top of her cell door in August 1847. She escaped into the yard using two sheets and was out of the asylum for almost three weeks. She was found in the scrub near the asylum's gardens; there was no mention of how she survived during this time. She was 'very indignant at the treatment she has received but at the same time much subdued and very anxious to return to her ward and former occupations'.[65] Her submissiveness did not last long: in mid-September, she was again 'very troublesome and obstinate' and broke through panes of glass when in the yard. She stopped eating but was suspected of getting food from other patients. She continued to be violent and unmanageable, tearing her bedding and clothes, breaking glass. Her language was 'most obnoxious'. After one incident of breaking glass, she was handcuffed with her hands behind her back for twenty-two hours. In all, she absconded four times, once scaling the wall to do so. It was noted that 'nothing can be worse than her conduct'. She seems to have turned the corner by mid-1851 and was discharged on 31 July that year.[66]

In October 1852, Mary received her free certificate and this is one of the last records located for her. Her son Edward, who had been admitted to the Male Orphan School on arrival, was released to her in 1853.[67]

The other five women died in the asylum.[68] Mary O'Brien 2nd was admitted to the asylum as Mary White, aged 39, suffering from 'amentia'. A pauper, she had been living at the rural district of Cleveland. In the asylum, she gradually declined to the point where she was 'vacant' and not responsive.[69] She died in September 1900, suffering from dementia, having been 41 years in the asylum.[70]

Margaret Kelly, a pauper aged 55, was also admitted to the asylum with 'amentia' in May 1856. Described as 'a poor imbecilic helpless creature … dirty in her habits and tottering on her feet … and doubtless, the victim of intemperance', she died there five months later.[71]

Johannah Murray or Gillespie, a pauper aged 54 described as 'a very quite [sic] imbecile', was admitted with 'mania' in 1862 and spent fourteen years there before her death. She died of 'disease of the brain' in 1876.[72]

Catherine Molloy, described as 'a person of unsound mind', was admitted on 6 March 1884.[73] She was living at New Norfolk and the doctor noted:

I have known her for many years and have observed for some time past that her mind was failing. About three weeks ago I found her lying in bed where she had been for some days with a dislocation of the left shoulder joint but of which she knew nothing, she having received the injury while under the influence of drink, her habits being intemperate. She has since that time been in a more demented condition, sometimes very incoherent with a defective memory and is quite helpless in her bodily condition … Her husband states that she is at times unmanageable and inattentive to the calls of nature.[74]

Catherine, a housewife aged 72, died later that year, in early October, of paralysis.[75]

Martha Merryfield, a labourer's wife aged 40, was admitted to the asylum twice. When she was admitted in July 1873, she was described as 'given to drink and when under the influence of liquor and for days after she is violent and dangerous'. Furthermore, she was 'full of religious delusions of a rambling and incoherent character'. Recovered, she was discharged in May 1874 but was readmitted in September 1875 from Launceston Gaol; the cause of her insanity was drink.[76] She died of 'vascular disease of the heart' in the asylum sixteen years later.[77]

Eliza Davis' first husband, Joseph Roebuck, was also admitted to the asylum. He died there when he was 72.[78]

Two women, Maria Lynch and Mary Magrath, were labelled 'idiotic' but escaped being admitted to the asylum. Maria Lynch, transported for arson, died in the General Hospital less than a year after arriving

Asylum for the Insane, New Norfolk. (Courtesy of Mark Krause)

in the colony.[79] In January 1848, Mary Magrath, a Dublin vagrant, was sentenced to three months' imprisonment in the Cascades Female Factory when she was found guilty of idleness and insolence. Later that year, her master had her charged with disobedience of orders in refusing to work. Mary pleaded guilty and was returned to the depot. Her conduct record was marked 'idiotic'.[80]

## PAUPER ESTABLISHMENTS AND INVALID DEPOTS

Pauper establishments and invalid depots were established in Tasmania to accommodate the destitute, ill, disabled and elderly, many of whom were ex-convicts.

The first pauper establishment to house women, the Brickfields Pauper Establishment (originally known as the Brickfields Invalid Depot), opened in 1859 on the site of the Brickfields Hiring Depot.[81] As ex-convicts reached old age or were unable to work, the demand for these institutions increased. In 1867, Cascades Invalid Depot (also known as the Cascades Pauper Establishment) opened on the site of the Cascades Female Factory. The women from this invalid depot were transferred to New Town Pauper Establishment in 1874 in the former Infant Orphan School buildings.

The institutions were highly regimented. Superintendents had the power to punish residents for failure to carry out light duties, for destroying government property or for 'gambling, profane or obscene language, quarrelling, fighting' or using insulting language towards officers. Punishment varied from deprivation of tobacco, through solitary confinement within the institution, to a three-month gaol sentence.[82]

According to Brown:

> The chief faults of all the institutions were the separation of man and wife, the lack of provision for the retention of human dignity and the soul destroying monotony of life in the depots. The roughest and coarsest men and women lived crowded together with the quiet and the decent. Facilities for privacy were non-existent, the inmates slept in large dormitories, meals, eaten off tin-ware, were in crowded dining rooms and day room facilities were limited. There was room neither for individual possessions, nor individual tastes. Bathing and washing facilities were usually inadequate and occasionally repulsive.[83]

Only three of the *Tasmania* (2) women: Mary Salmon or Kewley, Ellen Gregory (*née* Maguire) and Mary McLeod (*née* McBride) are known to have been in a pauper establishment. All three died there.[84] Others may also have been admitted to these institutions but no evidence has yet been found.

Towards the end of the nineteenth century, the number of invalids and elderly provided with outdoor relief increased, paving the way for the introduction of the old-age pension in 1908.

Institutional life was an integral part of the convict experience. For the women of the *Tasmania* (2) and their children, institutional life began in Irish gaols and at the Grangegorman Female Convict Depot. It continued during the voyage to Van Diemen's Land, which culminated in a minimum of six months on the *Anson*. Once they had served their initial period of probation, most of the women were exposed to a range of convict and colonial institutions: female factories, houses of correction, gaols, hiring depots, hospitals and asylums and convict nurseries.

It was not much different for the Irish-born free children – children such as William and Mary Ann Butler – who accompanied their mothers. They had committed no crime but were nevertheless exposed to convict-related institutions such as the Orphan Schools, which were prison-like in design and administration.

# 8

# A Sad Spectacle of Humanity

Neither Eliza Davis nor Margaret Butler 2nd were convicted of offences in the colony. Margaret received her certificate of freedom (or free certificate) on 25 May 1852.[1] Eliza, whose life sentence did not entitle her to a certificate of freedom, received a conditional pardon on 30 May 1856.[2] They appear to have made a fresh start in the colony.

There were another fourteen women who, like Eliza Davis, were convicted on their first offence, but were not convicted while serving their sentence in Van Diemen's Land.

Cascades Female Factory. (TAHO, NS1013/1/1453, reproduced with permission of the Tasmanian Archive and Heritage Office)

Eliza Davis' convict conduct record. (TAHO, CON41/1/8, reproduced with permission of the Tasmanian Archive and Heritage Office)

Margaret Butler's second convict conduct record. (TAHO, CON41/1/8, reproduced with permission of the Tasmanian Archive and Heritage Office)

In all, there were thirty-three women – 24 per cent – for whom no colonial offence was recorded. These included two women who died on the *Anson*, Mary Murphy and Fanny Doherty.[3] No details were recorded on the conduct records of another woman, Mary Carroll, except for basic information, so it is difficult to say what happened to her.[4]

Like Eliza Davis and Margaret Butler 2nd, Rose Fitzpatrick, her daughter Bridget Gallagher, and sister Ann Fitzpatrick also settled down to their new life.

Some of the women were charged but not convicted. Esther Burgess was charged twice: in July 1847 she was reprimanded for drunkenness and in April 1848 she was discharged for being absent without leave and drunkenness.[5]

## COLONIAL OFFENCES UNDER SENTENCE

At least 76 per cent of the *Tasmania* (2) convicts were convicted of colonial offences while under sentence. Of these, seventeen women – 12.5 per cent – had only one colonial conviction while they were serving their transportation sentence. Punishment ranged from twenty-four hours of solitary confinement (for being drunk) to six months' imprisonment with hard labour and solitary confinement (for insubordination).[6]

Anne Mullan's only colonial offence was misconduct. While serving a two-month sentence for this, she died in the Cascades Female Factory.[7] Like Anne, many of the women were simply charged with 'misconduct', with no specific details of the offence being recorded.

Bridget Dignan had one major offence: in October 1846, she was charged with wilfully destroying the property of a fellow servant 'under aggravated circumstances' and received nine months' imprisonment with hard labour. Bridget also had a minor offence – she was sent to solitary confinement for three days for being drunk on the same day that a charge of felony against her was dismissed – perhaps she was celebrating![8]

Similarly, Eleanor Daley's only offence, in June 1847, was insubordination, but this was a serious charge and she received six months' imprisonment with hard labour in the Cascades Female Factory. A portion of her time was to be spent in solitary confinement.[9]

## REPEAT OFFENDERS

Almost twelve months after the *Tasmania* (2) women arrived, the *Launceston Examiner* warned of the likelihood of recidivism once the women were removed from the *Anson*:

It will not excite wonder if some of those who pass through probation
on board the Anson relapse into crime when restraint is removed.
A radical reform cannot be accomplished in every instance; and when it
is recollected that in this country a female is surrounded with numerous,
strong and peculiar temptations, it is rather surprising that numbers
have resisted than that many have been overcome.[10]

Despite determined efforts by the authorities in charge of the penal
system, some of the women showed no signs of rehabilitation or reform.
Only four women, however, committed twenty or more offences while
they were under sentence.

Bridget Fanning, only 16 when she was transported, was convicted
twenty-two times while she was serving her sentence. She was charged
for the first time just twelve months after arriving in the colony: her
master in Battery Point brought her before the court for neglect of duty.
For this, she was sent to the Cascades Female Factory for two months'
imprisonment with hard labour. Shortly after she was released, she was
again charged, this time with neglect of duty and disobedience; she was
sent back to the factory for another two months' imprisonment with
hard labour. In September 1847, while waiting to be assigned at the hiring
depot, she was punished with a fortnight in solitary confinement for
misconduct. In October and November, she was again sent to solitary
confinement for fourteen days, for misconduct and then for being absent.
In December, she was sent to the Launceston Female Factory for six weeks'
imprisonment with hard labour for being out after hours. No sooner had
she served this sentence than she was sent to the factory for six months'
imprisonment with hard labour for absconding: she was charged by a
man named Suitor and in a later record she was described as his mistress.[11]
She absconded for the second time in January 1849 and was sent to the
Launceston Female Factory for six months' imprisonment with hard
labour. In September that year, Bridget was charged with larceny under
the value of £5; her existing sentence of transportation was extended by
twelve months and she was sent to the Launceston Female Factory for six
months and was not allowed to enter service in Launceston.[12]

During one spell in the factory, in 1848, Bridget was charged with
smoking in the separate apartments, earning ten days in the cells. Another
time, in December 1849, she was charged with disobedience of orders
and sentenced to another ten days in the cells. She was pregnant at the
time: in January 1850, she gave birth to a stillborn child.

Bridget continued to offend on a regular basis: twice charged with disobedience of orders; being absent without leave; being under the influence of drink and disorderly conduct. In June 1851, she was charged with wilful destruction of government property, which resulted in eighteen months' imprisonment with hard labour in the Launceston Female Factory. While she was there, she was sentenced to fourteen days in the cells for attempting to break out of the separate apartments. She received her certificate of freedom in November 1853; no further convictions after that time could be located.[13]

Catherine Burnet and Sarah McArdle both had twenty-one offences and Martha Merryfield had twenty (and may have had more if she had not been locked away in the New Norfolk Asylum for nearly twenty years!)

## CLASSIFICATION OF COLONIAL OFFENCES

Colonial magistrates' courts classified offences into five primary classes with sub-classes. The five categories were:

Class I:    Offences against the Person
Class II:   Offences against Property
Class III:  Forgery and Offences against the Currency
Class IV:   Offences against Good Order
Class V:    Offences not included in Preceding Classes

This classification system provides a useful way of considering colonial offences. Many of the women committed a range of crimes while under sentence; many were offences against convict discipline.

### Class I: Offences against the Person

In August 1846, Bell Amos was charged with misconduct for striking her officer. For this, she received six months' imprisonment with hard labour; this was added to her probation period. It was her first colonial offence and it was a serious one. She committed four other offences, mostly minor but no more for assault.[14] Three other women – Maria Brien, Ann Collins and Anne Mallon – were convicted of assault.[15]

## Class II: Offences against Property

At least thirteen women were tried for property offences. Most of the offences against property were for stealing. Larceny was considered a serious offence. Sentences ranged from three months to an extension of the original transportation sentence.

In October 1846, Bridget Dignan, tried in Co. Longford for stealing, was charged in Van Diemen's Land for wilfully destroying the property of a fellow servant under aggravated circumstances. She was sentenced to nine months' hard labour.[16]

Jane Bradshaw was charged with feloniously stealing a silk handkerchief in April 1847.[17] She was sentenced to six months' imprisonment with hard labour. Handkerchiefs, easily stolen and readily disposable, were a popular item to steal: Mary Liston was also charged with this offence and Mary Ann Smyth or Swan was charged with having a handkerchief in her possession 'for which she could not properly account'.[18] The former received a sentence of eight months' hard labour in the Cascades Female Factory and the latter a sentence of three months' hard labour, also in Cascades Female Factory.

## Class III: Forgery and Offences against the Currency

Two *Tasmania* (2) women, Margaret Gallagher or Toland and Bridget Hurley, were charged with currency offences. Margaret was charged with uttering a counterfeit shilling in 1849 and Bridget with 'passing bad florins' in a public house in Launceston in 1879. Neither were convicted. However, Bridget, free by servitude in 1852, was described as 'a bad character'.[19]

## Class IV: Offences against Good Order

Some of the women appeared in the lower courts charged with a range of misdemeanours but mostly for drunkenness and bad language.

Offences against good order included drunkenness; drunk and disorderly conduct; habitual drunkenness; obscene, threatening or abusive language; vagrancy; begging; and indecent, riotous, or offensive conduct. Sentences ranged from twenty-four hours in the cells to six months in the factory (usually for drunkenness combined with another offence). Some were merely admonished. Those holding a ticket of leave were fined 5/-.

## Alcohol-related offences

Many convict women, including those from the *Tasmania* (2), were frequently convicted of alcohol-related offences. At least forty-two women – 30 per cent – had an alcohol-related conviction.

Isabella Warnock was a repeat offender, convicted eleven times for drink-related offences.[20] Ellen Maguire was convicted eight times between 1848 and 1852, for being drunk, being drunk and out after hours, and being in a public house after hours.[21] Sarah McArdle was also convicted eight times for being drunk, and being drunk and insolent.[22]

Anne Daley, who had been convicted of drunkenness six or seven times in Ireland, was convicted at least six times for drink-related offences, the first only ten months after arriving in the colony.[23] Not long after her marriage in 1846, Anne Daley or Fryer was charged with being drunk and disorderly:

> Upon complaint of Constable Edward Griffiths with being drunk and disorderly at New Town on the 21st instant about a quarter before 12 pm with using indecent language and also with having struck Mr Frederick and two other persons there.[24]

Anne was sentenced to three months' imprisonment with hard labour in the Cascades Female Factory. Her last known offence was in 1852, when, as a ticket of leave holder, she was fined 5/- for being drunk.[25] Like Anne Daley, Maria Johnson also had six offences for being drunk.[26]

## Obscene, threatening or abusive language

At least nine women were charged with language offences. In rare instances, the language used by the women was recorded. In 1849, Catherine McNally or Shaw was charged with being out after hours and using indecent language in a public street. She pleaded not guilty but Constable Topham's evidence was convincing:

> William Topham upon his oath saith at about ½ past 9 o'clock last night I saw the prisoner and another woman and two men in Campbell Street. One of the men said he would stop with her the night, she said you be buggered, have you any money, you go and bugger yourself. I then took her into custody. She was not with her husband nor did I take her from her own house.[27]

Catherine was sentenced to ten days in solitary confinement: 'John [Brent?] upon his oath saith last night I heard the defendant say to a man with whom she was and who said he would stop the night, 'go to hell, you bloody bugger'.[28]

## Disorderly house or brothel and disorderly conduct

Generally speaking, disorderly conduct was a minor offence and referred to unruly behaviour. Being in a disorderly house was a reasonably common colonial offence for convict women and disorderly conduct even more so. In some instances, a disorderly house was synonymous with brothel.

In January 1851, Bridget Stankard, a ticket of leave holder, was convicted of living in a disorderly house and was ordered not to live in Hobart Town. Bridget ignored this and ten days later was found in 'a common brothel'. She was sent to prison for six months and again ordered to move from Hobart Town. However, she was still there in October when she gave birth to her daughter Jane in the Cascades Female Factory.[29]

Three other women were found in a brothel: Margaret Grady in 1848; Annie McCarmack in 1852; and Johannah Murray, who was found in a disorderly house in 1849.[30]

Generally speaking, disorderly conduct referred to being drunk in public, disturbing the peace or loitering. At least six women were found guilty of disorderly conduct; they received sentences ranging from ten days in the cells to six months' imprisonment with hard labour.

At least eight women were convicted of disturbing the peace, a common offence for women once they were free. Anne Daley was convicted of this offence three times, all in 1851.[31] Ann Flood's convictions were just over ten years apart, in 1851 and 1862.[32]

Mary McCarthy, transported at the age of 20 from Cork and blind in one eye, was charged with fighting in a public street in Hobart in 1848. She was sentenced to the Cascades Female Factory for four months' imprisonment with hard labour, half of that time to be spent in the separate apartments.[33]

## Class V: Offences not included in Preceding Classes

Many of the women were charged with committing offences against convict discipline. A number of these offences were similar but were differentiated by degree of seriousness. For example, absconding was regarded more severely than being absent without leave. Similarly, insolence and insubordination were closely related but insubordination – disobedience to authority – was the more serious offence.

## Absconding

Absconding was a serious offence against convict discipline. It was a more serious charge than being absent without leave. At least twenty-one of the women were charged with absconding.

Henrietta Beresford absconded from her employer in February 1848. For this, she received six months' hard labour in the Cascades Female Factory.[34] She also had several offences for being absent without leave.

Margaret Daley absconded for the first time one month after she married. She also had offences for being absent and for being absent from her authorised place of residence.[35]

Martha Merryfield was obviously a restless soul: she absconded six times and was convicted of being absent without leave six times.[36]

## Absent without leave

The convict system was tightly regulated and those under sentence did not have the freedom to go where they pleased. Nearly fifty of the *Tasmania* (2) women were charged with this offence, and were sentenced from a few days in the cells to nine months' imprisonment. Catherine McNally was sentenced to nine months' imprisonment with hard labour at the Cascades Female Factory; she was found in a brothel.[37]

## Absent from authorised residence

At least eleven women were convicted of being absent from their authorised residence and received sentences ranging from three days in the cells to six months' imprisonment with hard labour in a female factory.

In some instances, the authorised place of residence was the marital home.

## Out after hours

At least twenty of the women were convicted of being out after hours. In March 1850, ticket of leave holder Margaret Sawyer was charged with this; she was sentenced to fourteen days' hard labour. It was her only colonial offence.[38] Ann Williams was convicted five times with being out after hours.[39]

## Work-related offences

Mary Magrath had a hard time of it in the colony. A Dublin servant transported for vagrancy, Mary was considered 'idiotic' by the colonial authorities. In January 1848, she was charged with idleness and insolence. In July 1848, Mary was charged with disobedience of orders in refusing to work but was discharged and returned to the hiring depot; it was 'recommended that she may not be allowed to hire in private service being deficient in intellect'.[40] Mary then disappears from the records.

As well as Mary, four other women were sentenced to imprisonment with hard labour for refusing to work. Their sentences ranged from one month to eight months.

At least twelve of the women were charged with neglect of duty. Their punishments ranged from three days in the cells to three months' imprisonment with hard labour.[41]

Mary Burgess had only one colonial conviction. In July 1847, she was sentenced to the three months' imprisonment in the Cascades Female Factory with hard labour for disobedience of orders.[42] She was one of fourteen of her shipmates to be convicted of this offence. They received sentences between seven days' solitary confinement and six months' with hard labour.

At least twelve of the women were charged with insolence. Ellen Cahil had been in the colony less than a year when she was charged by her mistress, Sarah Ann Wilkinson, with insolence. Mrs Wilkinson testified:

> yesterday the prisoner did not eat anything all day and I spoke to her about it and she said she would not eat any more, in consequence of her having used more than she ought to have used. I said I would weigh [illegible]. She said she would not remain in a place where things were weighed out to her.[43]

Although she pleaded not guilty, Ellen was sentenced to one month's imprisonment with hard labour in the Cascades Female Factory.

Catherine Heenan, charged with insolence to her master, was sentenced to six days in solitary confinement. Her master, Charles Flegg of Liverpool Street, gave evidence:

Mr Charles Flegg upon his oath saith this morning the prisoner's mistress told her in my hearing to light the parlour fire, she said that the wood was too much trouble, that it was green, and she then told her mistress that she had better turn her in, that she was then quite ready to be off. The mistress told her she would take her before Mr Mason [the magistrate]. The prisoner said the sooner the better.[44]

Catherine pleaded not guilty but was sentenced to six days' solitary confinement.

Eliza Hunter was in the service of Revd Bell when she was charged with gross insolence to her mistress and being drunk. The arresting constable testified that he was called to the Bell residence about five o'clock to take Eliza into custody. Mrs Bell was attempting to send Eliza to bed: 'the prisoner said she would see her buggered first and she afterwards said Mrs. Bell was no lady or she would not give her into custody'. Eliza pleaded guilty only to the charge of being drunk but was found guilty of both charges and was sent to the Cascades Female Factory for six months.[45]

## Insubordination

In October 1846, Mary Russell was sentenced to two months' imprisonment with hard labour in the Cascades Female Factory for insubordination and general bad conduct.[46]

## Misconduct (not specified)

At least nineteen women were charged with misconduct. In most cases, details were not specified. Punishments ranged from being admonished or reprimanded to four months' imprisonment with hard labour in a female factory. Bridget Egan was charged three times with misconduct in 1847 and 1848.[47]

In some instances, lower-court records provide additional information to the non-specified misconduct charges. Isabella Warnock's conduct record simply states that she was charged with misconduct but when she appeared before the magistrate the following was recorded:

Mr [Grouber] Prosser's Plains

Upon complaint of Constable John Smith with misconduct in being in a public shed on the night of the 2nd instant after hours in an indecent state having been forced out of a public house where she had entered without authority.

Plea: Guilty
Sentence: 2 calendar months' imprisonment & hard labour.[48]

## Convict system offences

There were specific offences relating to the convict system and the control of the women's movements and freedom: representing herself to be free; not proceeding according to her pass; overstaying her pass and so on. In all, at least eighteen of the women were convicted of this offence.

In 1849, Mary Brown was convicted of not proceeding to the depot according to her pass. This earned her three months' imprisonment with hard labour in the Cascades Female Factory and she was not allowed to live in Hobart Town once she was released.[49]

Anne Dogherty, a young mother from County Longford, was sentenced to one month's hard labour in the Cascades Female Factory for dancing in the taproom at her master's house and representing herself to be free in March 1848. (Her master was Drinkwater, a great name for a publican!) Somehow, from 1850 to 1851, Anne managed to live in the district of Pontville for three or four months without reporting herself and was consequently charged with representing herself to be free. She was sentenced to nine months' imprisonment with hard labour in the Cascades Female Factory and her ticket of leave was cancelled.[50]

Catherine Riley, who had a history of dressing in male clothing, directly challenged convict authority. In July 1851, Catherine was found 'in the enclosed yard of Richard Filbee without authority and dressed in man's clothing'.[51] She was sentenced to nine months' imprisonment with hard labour in the Cascades Female Factory, every alternate month to be spent in the separate apartments. While she was there, she was charged with 'purloining one pound of bread from a fellow prisoner' and her existing sentence of hard labour was extended.[52]

## Pregnancy offences

Pregnancy interfered with a convict woman's capacity to work and she could be punished after the birth of her child, usually with a sentence of six months in a female factory. In 1849, Mary Byrne was charged with being absent without leave and for having given birth to an illegitimate child, James. For this, she received six months' hard labour in the Cascades Female Factory.[53] While she was serving this sentence, Ann, the daughter that she brought with her from Carlow, died in the Female Orphan School.[54]

Sadly, even women who gave birth to stillborn children were punished. This was the case for Ann Flood, whose child was stillborn in July 1847. She was ordered to serve six months' probation in the Cascades Female Factory.[55] Ann had more children after she married in 1848, at least two of whom died in infancy. Four survived.

## Sexual offences

A convict woman's sexual behaviour was subjected to close scrutiny by the authorities and a woman could be punished for a range of offences, which would not have been the case had she been free. Sentences ranged from one to six months' hard labour in one of the female factories. At least nine of the women were convicted of offences in this category.

Anne Daley was 37 and married eight years when she was charged with sleeping in a hut with three men. She was absent from her 'authorised place of abode' (presumably her husband's house) and received one month in the Launceston Female Factory. Just over two months' later, Anne received her free certificate and no evidence of further offences has been found.

Two other women, Martha Martin and Mary Leonard, were also married when convicted of similar offences. Martha Martin had been married just over three years when she was found in bed with a man on her master's premises. She was sent to the Cascades Female Factory for four months. Mary Leonard had only been married a matter of weeks when one night she admitted a man 'into her premises … in the absence of her husband for an immoral purpose'. She was sentenced to six months' hard labour in the Cascades Female Factory. It is not clear whether her marriage lasted. Not long after she was released from serving this sentence, Mary was charged with being drunk and 'found laying with George Sharrocks in her master's paddock'. She was sentenced to three months' imprisonment with hard labour at Cascades Female Factory.[56]

The most common sexual offence was being found with a man (or men) in a bedroom. In 1851, Catherine Burnet, during a brief spell out of the female factory, was charged with being absent from her authorised place of residence and found in bed with two men. For this, she was sentenced to four months' imprisonment with hard labour in the Launceston Female Factory.

Annie McCarmack and Mary Smyth (or Smith) had been in the colony less than a year when they were charged with admitting two men into the coal shed of their master's house in Battery Point in 1846. Their master, Charles Babbington Brewer, gave evidence that the women had opened a locked door to let the men in:

> last night about seven o'clock I heard voices and on going out I found two men in the Coal Shed and the two prisoners with them. The door of the shed had been locked all day and was unlocked when I found the men and the prisoners there. There is the key of another door which will unlock the Coal Shed door. The key of the Coal Shed door is usually kept in the house.[57]

Both women received three months' hard labour in the Cascades Female Factory. It is not known whether the men were also charged.

Johannah Murray was twice charged with concealing a man on her master's premises 'for an improper purpose' in 1847 and 1850. She received three month sentences for each, in the Cascades Female Factory and the Launceston Female Factory.

Catherine McNally or Shaw took advantage of her mistress having gone to church to bring a man into the house in January 1847. She was sentenced to two months' imprisonment with hard labour.[58]

Anne Agnew's only colonial offence while under sentence was in August 1846, when she was sentenced to fourteen days' hard labour in the Cascades Female Factory for 'misconduct in having slept with Mary Swain'.[59]

## Prostitution

As already noted, several of the women were found in brothels and disorderly houses, but rarely were they labelled prostitutes. When she died in 1855, Esther Burgess was described as a prostitute on her death certificate but there is no evidence to suggest she was actually a prostitute.[60] It is a puzzling and unwarranted label.

Only two women were convicted of 'being a common prostitute', both in April 1850: Mary Meehan was convicted of this offence in conjunction with indecent conduct and Ann Williams in conjunction with being a drunkard. Mary was sentenced to three months' imprisonment with hard labour in the Launceston Female Factory; Ann to six months' with hard labour in the Cascades Female Factory.

## COLONIAL OFFENCES ONCE FREE

Tracing the offences of the women once they were free is difficult. It is possible that they were convicted, but the information hasn't been located. For a significant number of the *Tasmania* (2) convicts, we simply do not know what happened to them after they gained their freedom.

Destitution, drunkenness and mental instability all made surviving difficult; many of the women lived hand-to-mouth.

Catherine Grace's only offence was in 1873 – twenty-eight years after she arrived in the colony! Catherine's husband was also transported and she brought her three young daughters with her. In August 1873, Catherine was charged with perjury at the police office in Franklin. She was committed for trial:

FRANKLIN POLICE COURT.
Monday, August 4th, 1873.
Before E. A. Walpole, Esq., Stipendiary Magistrate.

Perjury.—Catherine Grace was charged, on the information of C.D.C. Lambert, with having, at a Court of Petty Sessions, held at Franklin, on the 31 July ult., committed wilful and corrupt perjury. It appeared from the evidence that on the day named, one Patrick Calder charged John Stephens and five other persons with having violently assaulted him at Glazier's Bay. The accused, Catherine Grace, gave evidence on behalf of the defendants on that occasion, to the whole of whom she is related, in which she directly negatived some of the more important statements of the complainant. After a full and patient hearing, the accused was fully committed for trial, but admitted to bail on finding two sureties in £150 each.[61]

Members of Catherine's family were often before the court: in 1858, her husband, Pierce 'Cantrill' or Grace, transported for stealing sheep, was sentenced to 'penal servitude' at Port Arthur for eight years for stealing calves. Catherine's son-in-law Michael Hassett, transported for killing a cow, was sentenced with him.[62] Catherine, though, does not appear to have committed any further offences.

Mary Barry was first in the Cascades Female Factory in October 1850, charged with indecent language. The following year, Mary was sentenced to twelve months' imprisonment with hard labour for larceny under £5.

Her ticket of leave was revoked as a result of the offence. Mary received her free certificate in July 1852. In December 1854, she was reconvicted as Mary Bateman.[63] She had earlier applied to marry William Bateman, free.[64] Although the application to marry was approved, no record of a marriage has been located. Tried with Mary Doyle in the Hobart Quarter Sessions for housebreaking and stealing, she was sentenced to two years' imprisonment with hard labour in the house of correction for females. The newspaper report of the trial stated:

> Mary Doyle and Mary Bateman, indicted for stealing one dress of the value of £1, two children's frocks, and four yards print, value £1 1s. the property of Benjamin Marsh of New Town were then put on their trial; a second count charged these parties with receiving the above articles, knowing them to have been stolen.[65]

The women had pledged the property with a pawnbroker.[66]

Bridget Stankard had several colonial offences while she was serving her sentence, mostly for being idle and disorderly but also for being in a common brothel. She received her free certificate on 31 December 1851 and was granted a conditional pardon early in 1852.[67] In October 1859, a local newspaper reported:

> Bridget Stankard was charged by ... Constable [Walker] with [being a common disturber of the peace] in Liverpool street.
>
> The case having been proved, Mr. Superintendent Hamilton informed His Worship that the defendant was one of the worst characters in Hobart Town. She was bound over to keep the peace for three months.[68]

It is not clear why Bridget deserved her reputation as 'one of the worst characters in Hobart Town' as there is no evidence that she appeared in court in the eight years after she received her free certificate.[69]

Anne Mallon, a thief from Antrim, arrived in the colony with four previous convictions for stealing. While she was serving her sentence, she appeared in the police court at least ten times for a range of offences, including being drunk and disorderly and assault. She continued to offend and in September 1875, as Agnes Leach, she was sent to prison for two months for stealing:

From the evidence of the complainant and Kate Hill, a girl in the employ of Mr Pettard of the Terminus Hotel, it appeared that the complainant came into the bar of the hotel with two bundles, which she lay down on a form, throwing her shawl over them. The two prisoners were in the bar, and while complainant was at the counter getting a drink Lake stole the shawl and passed it to the woman Leach, who then went out and came back shortly afterwards without it.[70]

Anne was again convicted on 31 December 1875, at Longford, for being idle and disorderly, and was sentenced to imprisonment for two months, possibly in the Longford Gaol.[71] A newspaper report stated:

A Foul Tongue—Agnes Leach, charged by Constable Carey with having used obscene language in a public street was sentenced to 7 days' imprisonment.[72]

In August the following year, she was back in Launceston, at the police court, where she was fined 5 shillings for again using obscene language in a public street.[73] A month later, she was sent to prison for seven days for the same.[74] This was the last recorded offence for which evidence has been found up to the time of her death in 1891.[75]

Information about Mary McCarthy's criminal activities came to light in September 1860 when Mr Atkins, keeper of the Cascade Factory, applied for admission to the Female Orphan School of Mary's daughter, Esther, aged 5. Mary was free by servitude in March 1852 and in 1860 was serving a sentence of three months at the female factory for larceny. Esther's father, James Rourke, was a tinker, also free by servitude.[76] Rather than going to the Female Orphan Schools, the authorities decided that Esther could remain with her mother at the female factory.[77]

## EXTENSION OF TRANSPORTATION SENTENCE

For serious offences, the women had their original transportation sentence extended. This could be anywhere from one month, in the case of Margaret Randall, for having a forged pass, to eighteen months, in the case of Catherine Coleman, who was convicted of larceny under £5 when she was in the house of correction, Launceston, in 1847.[78] Martha Merryfield had her original sentence extended twice: in August 1848 for six months for absconding and in November 1850 for eighteen months for larceny under £5.[79]

## MARY SALMON, 'A SAD SPECTACLE OF HUMANITY'[80]

Mary Salmon or Lyons was a notorious recidivist and was known by several names in Van Diemen's Land, including Kewley, Johnson, Salman, Marr, White and Payne. In September 1846, charged with being drunk, Mary was

Mary Salmon's record. (TAHO, CON41/1/8, reproduced with permission of the Tasmanian Archive and Heritage Office)

initiated into female-factory life when she was sent there for one month. She had three more stints in the factory (for being absent without leave, disobedience of orders and stealing a petticoat) and then in October 1848, charged with being drunk and disorderly, she was sent north to the Launceston Female Factory. No sooner had she served this two-month sentence than she was back inside, charged with absconding.

Between December 1848 and July 1849, she was barely out of the factory. Yet at the end of July 1849, permission to marry John Kewley was approved. John was a tailor transported from the Isle of Man; he had served his sentence by 1844.[81] Unusually for a convict couple, a marriage notice was published in the local newspaper:

MARRIED.—At Perth, on the 1st September, by the Rev. A. Stackhouse, Mr. John Kewley, master tailor, of the Blue Cottage, Perth, and eldest son of Mr. Philip Kewley of the Isle of Man, to Miss Mary Salmon, late of Vron.—They both signed the Teetotal Pledge before they left the Church.[82]

Mary's pledge may have been well intentioned, but it was short-lived: in September 1849, she was charged with being drunk and sent once again to the Launceston Female Factory, this time for two months' hard labour. It was by no means an isolated offence.

A Degraded Female.—Mary Ann Salmon, a woman aged twenty-seven, but whose personal appearance indicated her to be at least forty years of age, arising from habitual intemperance and vice, appeared before the Police Magistrate, on Wednesday, to answer the charge of being an idle and disorderly person. This wretched creature had an infant at the breast in her arms, whose hollow cough and hectic flush of countenance most affectingly proclaimed that consumption in its incipient stage had commenced its deadly work. Such a sad spectacle of so fallen a specimen of humanity was calculated to excite the intensest pity and commiseration in every beholder. The Police Magistrate expostulated with the unfortunate woman, and pointed out to her the consequences of her career, adding, "it is dreadful to see such a creature with a child; how can an infant live whose mother is an habitual drunkard? You can go, but leave town directly, otherwise I shall be obliged to send you to the factory, for three months". Defendant, not being altogether devoid of shame coloured up occasionally; and quickly left the Court.[83]

Mary lived with John Kewley until she obtained her freedom, stating 'in consequence of Kewley being a great drunkard and never bringing home any money for her support', she left his house and took up with James Johnson, the father of her children.[84]

Perth, Tasmania. (AUTAS001125644393, reproduced with permission of the Tasmanian Archive and Heritage Office)

In August 1862, Mary was sentenced to twelve months' imprisonment with hard labour in the female house of correction, Launceston. In May 1863, as Mary Johnson, she applied to have her two oldest sons, James and Thomas Johnson, admitted to the Orphan Schools.[85] According to the application, their father, James Johnson, was a sawyer who had deserted his family and was 'never heard of since'. The application stated:

> The mother is a drunkard and a thief, during the twelve months she has been in this town she has been three times charged with larceny, and convicted twice. In August 1862, she was sent to the House of Correction 'where I also have been forced to send these children'. She had served three months 'as an idle and disorderly person' and had several sentences for drunkenness.

Evidence taken during her last conviction suggested that Mary had employed one of the children to dispose of stolen property. The application noted:

> To admit them into the Asylum may preserve them from a life of crime. I have no hope that it will induce the mother to abandon her vicious habits and strive to maintain herself by the pursuits of honest industry.[86]

In a later application for the admission of another two children to the Orphan Schools in December 1868, the application stated that 'This woman is also known by the name of Marr'. The application was made by Mary Ann Salman, wife of James Johnson, Mangana, for John Johnson (7 years 2 months) and Ellen Johnson (4 years 3 months). The children's father, who arrived on the *Joseph Somes* and was free by servitude, was in gaol in Launceston. At the time of the application, Mary had no work and had three other children to support: James Johnson, aged 12; Thomas Johnson, aged 11; and Mary Ann Johnson, aged 2. The warden of Fingal reported: 'The applicant is a woman of disreputable character and her children are at present starving. She is not likely to obtain work sufficient to obtain bread.'[87]

From 1869 to at least 1884 Mary was before the court frequently, mostly for being idle and disorderly.[88] In September 1873, the *Mercury* reported:

INSULTING PASSERS-BY.—Mary Ann Salmon, a woman from the country, who was fined on Saturday for drunkenness, was charged with insulting passers-by in Elizabeth-street on Saturday night. She was fined 10s, or seven days' imprisonment.[89]

In 1877, the *Cornwall Chronicle* noted:

USING BAD LANGUAGE.—Mary Ann Salmon, aged 44 years, was charged by Sub Inspector Sullivan with using obscene language in Wellington street that morning. The woman pleaded guilty, and said that she only used one obscene word, and that was used 'promiscusley'. Mr. Sullivan stated that the obscene word was used by the defendant several times to boys.[90]

The last offence located for Mary was in November 1884, when she was sentenced to three months' imprisonment, convicted of being an idle and disorderly person without lawful means of support. She died as Mary Salmon or Kewley in the Launceston Benevolent Asylum two days before Christmas 1896. She was only 66.[91] Mary may have escaped the poverty of the Great Famine, but her colonial experience was fraught and troubled; her life was lived on the edge and she never quite shook off her entanglement with the law.

# 9

# All Are Certain of Marrying, if They Please

*All* are certain of marrying, if they please; *Proposals* are plentiful.[1]

Not long after the *Tasmania* (2) arrived in Van Diemen's Land, the *Launceston Examiner* highlighted the link between marriage and behaviour:

> The best feature of the existing system [of the management of female convicts] is the facilities afforded for marriage ... No unnecessary obstacles were presented to the union of prisoners, and in numerous instances women have by this means been separated from evil companions of their own sex, and become industrious, and well-conducted members of society.[2]

Marriage was an important aspect of colonial life. For many convict women it provided an opportunity to recreate the family life they left behind and to remove themselves from the scrutiny of those in authority. Convict marriage was encouraged by successive colonial administrations, as a form of control or means of reform.[3] It was a reward or indulgence for good behaviour.[4] Marriage was promoted by the colonial authorities because they believed that it was a civilising influence in a society where men greatly outnumbered women.[5] As late as 1847, women accounted for only 32 per cent of Tasmania's population.[6] The transportation of convict women helped redress this imbalance.

## ELIZA'S STORY

Eliza Davis, transported from Wicklow for infanticide, married twice in Van Diemen's Land, both times to men who had been transported.[7] Eliza's first husband was Joseph Roebuck; they married in 1847 and had three children. She married her second husband, Amos Eastwood, in 1898, a week before she died.

Joseph Roebuck, a widower, arrived in Van Diemen's Land on the *David Clarke* in October 1841 when he was 36.[8] According to his convict description, Joseph was 5ft 6¾in tall, with brown hair and whiskers, and brown eyes. He was 'pockpitted' with a hair mole on his left arm and had two rings tattooed on the fingers of his left hand. A native of Pennington, Yorkshire, and a groom, Joseph was tried at York in July 1840 for stealing wearing apparel; he was transported for ten years. He had already been convicted twice: once for poaching and once for having skeleton keys in his possession.[9] He served three months in prison for each offence. He behaved badly in gaol in England and was idle, but his behaviour improved once he was on board the ship.

Joseph served his probation period at Brown's River Probation Station (now Kingston). In April 1843 he was charged with 'misconduct in improperly receiving a half loaf from the bakehouse' and was sentenced to three months' imprisonment. By September 1843, Joseph was in the north of the colony at Campbell Town. He was granted a ticket of leave in 1847 and was recommended for a conditional pardon in April 1848; this was approved in July 1849. Joseph Roebuck was a servant at the Leake property Rosedale from 1843 to about 1853.[10]

Rosedale Campbell Town, where Joseph Roebuck was a servant. (Leake Collection L1/B (287), courtesy of the University of Tasmania Library Special & Rare Collections)

It is a matter of conjecture how Eliza and Joseph met. Eliza, having served her probationary period, left the *Anson* on 16 June 1846. Approximately three months later, she was pregnant with twins.

As both Eliza and Joseph were still under sentence, they were required to apply for permission to marry. Application was successfully made in June 1847.[11] Banns for the marriage of

St Luke's Church of England, Campbell Town. (QVM:1986:P:0591 c1900–1909, reproduced with permission of the Queen Victoria Museum and Art Gallery)

Elizabeth Davis, a convict, and Joseph Roebuck of Campbell Town, holding a ticket of leave, were called on 11 June, 18 June and 25 June.[12] The couple were married on 26 June 1847 in St Luke's Church of England, Campbell Town, 'according to the rites and ceremonies of the United Church of England and Ireland'. Joseph, aged 43, signed his name; Eliza, aged 23, signed with an [x].[13]

Two months before the marriage, on 20 May 1847, Eliza had given birth to twin daughters at St John's Hospital, Launceston.[14] The children, Amelia Eleanor and Elizabeth, were baptised in Campbell Town under the name of Davis on 27 June 1847.[15] They were baptised by Revd William Bedford, who added to the register, 'now wife of Joseph Roebuck'.

By 1855, Joseph had developed a mental illness. In November 1855, the *Hobarton Mercury* reported:

MANIAC.—Joseph Roebuck, who had formerly been in the service of Mr. Burnett, the Sheriff, and is well-known in Hobart Town, was brought before the Bench … charged with being of unsound mind; he was remanded for the necessary Medical certificate. From the appearance of the poor man, there can be little doubt of his unhappy condition.[16]

In November 1855, the *Mercury* reported, in the language of the day:

A Lunatic.—Joseph Roebuck, who had been remanded for the certificate of a medical man, was again brought up, and the statement of Dr. Benson was taken; he deposed to the effect, that he had examined the Lunatic, whom he had known for about 3 months; he was of unsound mind, unfit to be at large, and incapable of taking care of himself. On being asked if he had anything to say, or any questions to put to Dr. Benson, the poor fellow replied: 'no; I have nothing to say; I am dying as fast as I can.'[17]

The Bench, being of the opinion, that the man was insane, the necessary order was made for his committal to Her Majesty's gaol, to await His Excellency's warrant for his admission to the Lunatic Asylum.[18]

There is a gap of several months in Joseph's story and it is not clear where he was during this time. In September 1856, the *Colonial Times* reported:

INSANITY.—Joseph Roebuck, a man of unsound mind, subject to epileptic fits, and unable to maintain himself, was yesterday committed to H.M. General Hospital, pending the order of the Governor-in-Chief for his disposal, on the information of Dr. Bedford and Elizabeth Roebuck, the unfortunate man's wife.[19]

The following day, the *Mercury* described Joseph's circumstances in greater detail:

LUNACY.—Joseph Roebuck who, we stated, had been declared by Dr. Bedford to be of an unsound mind, was on Wednesday ordered to the New Norfolk Asylum. Dr. Bedford stated that he was quite unfit either to maintain or take care of himself. Mrs. Roebuck (who has three children) stated that she had supported him by her labor for some time—he had threatened her once or twice last week. Roebuck said he had no desire to do his wife an injury. He thought that if they bled him and applied blisters to his head he should recover.[20]

Joseph was committed to the General Hospital while his 'disposal' was decided upon.[21] Evidence as to Joseph's condition was taken by Mr Duncan McPherson and the Chief Superintendent of Police, Mr J. Burgess. Eliza's ability to contribute to his maintenance while he was in the asylum was also considered. Dr Bedford had stated that he had seen Joseph on a number of occasions, once two years previously and again some months before the hearing. He found him to be 'subject to epileptic fits and temporary insanity'.[22] Ironically, as already noted, Eliza too suffered from epilepsy. It was this condition which many believed led Eliza to drown her baby. Its revelation after her trial was considered a mitigating circumstance and led to the commutation of her death sentence to transportation for life.

Eliza's evidence provided an insight into her life with Joseph. She stated that he had been unable to work for almost four years and it was only through her labour that their family survived:

> Sometimes I earn thirty shillings a week and sometimes less by taking in washing and mangling. I have no other means of procuring support for myself and family. And I am not able to pay for my husband's treatment in hospital.

As Joseph's condition deteriorated and his behaviour became more erratic, life with him became more difficult:

> My husband threatened me last week. He said he would kill me. He was in a worse state of mind than he is at present. He was more violent. He threatened me on last Friday and Saturday—I am afraid that he will do me some bodily injury unless he is placed under restraint.[23]

Joseph was committed to the New Norfolk Asylum on 30 September 1856 and remained there until his death on 24 September 1873. The cause of his death was recorded as 'disease of the brain and natural decay'. He was 72.[24]

When Joseph was admitted to the Asylum in 1856, Eliza had three children: the twins, born in 1847, and Joseph Henry Roebuck, born in 1850.[25]

By May 1860, when her daughter Alice Eastwood was born, Eliza was living in the northern town of Evandale with Amos Eastwood, a wheelwright.[26] Eliza and Amos had six children in all; Sarah Eastwood born about 1859,[27] Alice Eastwood in 1860, Harriet Eastwood in 1862, Hannah Eastwood in 1864, Amos Eastwood in 1865 and James Eastwood in 1869. The family eventually settled in Burnie, where Amos worked as a wheelwright and Eliza was a respected midwife.

When the Eastwood children were born, their mother was still married to Joseph Roebuck. Eliza and Amos appear to have lived quite openly together and their children were registered under the name of Eastwood, not Davis.

Amos Eastwood was serving in the 78th Regiment when he was court martialled at Colaba (near Bombay, India) for striking his superior officer in December 1850. For this, he was sentenced to transportation for seven years; he arrived on the *Royal Saxon* in 1851 when he was 26. Like Joseph Roebuck,

Amos was a Yorkshire man. A wheelwright from Doncaster, Amos was single, belonged to the Church of England and could read and write a little when he arrived. His probationary period was three and a half years. He was stationed firstly in the prison barracks (presumably Hobart) and then in 1852 at Impression Bay on the Tasman Peninsula. By October of that year he was 'a pass holder'.

Impression Bay Probation Station, c. 1850. Amos Eastwood was stationed here. (AUTAS001125298521, reproduced with permission of the Tasmanian Archive and Heritage Office)

From 1853 to 1855, Amos committed a number of offences. He was punished five times for being drunk and disorderly. Each offence occurred in Hobart; the first in November 1853 when he was sentenced to ten days' solitary confinement in the prison barracks for 'misconduct in being in a Public House on the Lord's day & drunk'. On the second occasion, in April 1854, he received fourteen days' solitary confinement. By June of that year, as well as being drunk and disorderly, he was also out after hours and was sentenced to two months' hard labour, after which time he was returned to his service. In September he was again in the prison barracks, this

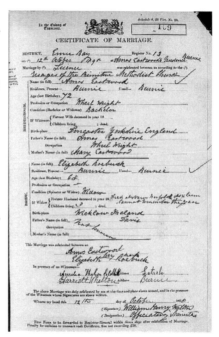

Marriage certificate Elizabeth and Amos Eastwood 1898. (Courtesy of Bryan Lucas)

time to serve six months' hard labour for being drunk and misconduct in resisting a constable. He was not to return to service in Hobart. This pattern of behaviour continued: in February 1855, he was charged with 'misconduct in returning late under the influence of liquor and assaulting a constable'. He received six months' hard labour on 17 February. By 21 February, he had absconded. Nothing more is known of this episode.[28]

By 1858, Amos had served his transportation sentence, and was entitled to a certificate of freedom. It is possible that he met Eliza Davis Roebuck around this time.

Almost forty years after the birth of their first child, Eliza and Amos married. On 12 October 1898 at Amos Eastwood's residence in Burnie, in a Primitive Methodist service, Eliza married as Elizabeth Roebuck, a widow aged 68. The marriage record noted that her first husband died at the New Norfolk Asylum and included the telling phrase – 'cannot remember when'. It also stated that she had three children living (presum-

Elizabeth and Amos Eastwood on their wedding day. (Courtesy of Bryan Lucas)

ably the Roebuck children) and that she was born in Wicklow, Ireland, as Davis. Her parents' details were 'not known', which was only to be expected as she was a foundling. Amos Eastwood was a bachelor and wheelwright aged 72. He was born in Doncaster, Yorkshire, to Amos Eastwood, a wheelwright, and Mary Eastwood. Witnesses were Amelia Helen Coldhill, of Latrobe, and Harriet Whitton, of Burnie – a daughter from each of Eliza's marriages.[29] Eliza signed the certificate with 'her mark', [x]. On her convict conduct record in 1845, she had been able to read only and this appears to have been the case 53 years later.[30]

One week after the marriage, on 19 October, Eliza died in Burnie of 'cerebral apoplexy'. She was 69.[31]


## MARGARET'S STORY

Unlike for Eliza Davis, there was no happy marriage for Margaret Butler 2nd. Margaret also married a Yorkshireman who had been transported. John Shakleton, a 42-year-old drover and waggoner, was from Todmington. He arrived on the *Marquis of Hastings* in November 1842. He was tried in Lancaster Salford Quarter Sessions in April 1842 and sentenced to transportation for ten years for larceny. He stated his offence to be stealing about

400 yards of cotton cloth. He had been convicted before, for seven years, for stealing potatoes, and had served three years at the penitentiary. His conduct, according to the surgeon's report, was 'good'.

John was a Protestant who could read. Just over 5ft 9in tall, he had a fresh complexion, light hazel eyes, brown hair and eyebrows, reddish whiskers, a long nose, and a long chin. Part of his little finger on his left hand was missing and he had a scar on the third finger of his left hand. He was 'stout made'.

After his arrival in Van Diemen's Land, John progressed through the various stages of the convict system, firstly serving a two-and-a-half-year period of primary labour. Another two months was added to this in April 1842, when he was found absent without leave during the dinner hour. He emerged from the probation gang while he was stationed at Southport in August 1845. In September 1846, he was found guilty of larceny under £5 and was sentenced to two months' imprisonment and hard labour at Broadmarsh. In May 1848, John was granted his ticket of leave and, almost a year later, in June 1849, he was recommended for a conditional pardon. This was approved in October 1850. In June 1852, he was awarded his free certificate.[32]

St Joseph's Catholic Church, Macquarie Street, Hobart Town, 1844.
(AUTAS001139593875, reproduced with permission of the Tasmanian Archive and Heritage Office)

It is not clear how Margaret and John met. They successfully applied for permission to marry on 16 April 1850.[33] On 24 May 1850, Margaret, a servant aged 35, and John, a labourer aged 42, were married in St Joseph's Catholic Church, Hobart by Revd Hall. Both signed their mark [x]. Witnesses were Robert Becket [x] and Anne Cully [x].[34] There were no children of the marriage.[35]

After a little more than five years of marriage, on 4 November 1855, Margaret Butler died in the Colonial Hospital as the result of injuries inflicted by her husband.[36]

## MARITAL STATUS

Of 138 women on board the *Tasmania* (2), two thirds stated that they were single when they arrived in Van Diemen's Land. There were more widows than married women: twenty-three were widowed and fifteen were married.

Ann Williams, a Dublin thief in her late 20s, stated that she was single: 'I never was married. William Delap passed as my husband at the Gaol'.[37] No doubt Ann perceived that there was some benefit to pretending to be married in gaol or single in the colony.

Several of the married women had been deserted by their husbands for some time. In some instances, additional information about husbands was provided on the convict indent: Mary Griffen's husband, Samuel, was in America.[38] Margaret Connor, in her mid-20s, was married but she stated that her husband, Richard Carey, left her ten years ago. She had also been ten years 'on the town' and there was possibly a link between this and her husband's desertion.[39]

Deserted and widowed women were particularly vulnerable economically, as the case of Judith Dooling or Dowling demonstrates. Her petition from gaol in Ireland stated that she was 'upwards of twelve years a poor Widow and has endeavoured by her hard labour and industry to rear four fatherless children the youngest of who is only about twelve years of age'.[40]

In some instances, contradictory information was recorded: Bridget Dignan was recorded as single on her conduct record and widowed on her indent.[41] Margaret Gibson, aged 24, was recorded as both single and married.[42] Catherine Hughes, who was 20, was either single or married.[43] There is no apparent reason for these anomalies in the records.

## HUSBANDS TRANSPORTED

The husbands of at least four of the women – Catherine McNally or Shaw; Elizabeth Wright; Catherine Hughes and Catherine Grace – were transported. Catherine McNally or Shaw was tried with her husband; the others were tried separately. Catherine Grace and her husband were reunited in the colony.

Catherine McNally or Shaw's husband, Stephen Shaw, a seaman from Drogheda, arrived on the *Samuel Boddington* in January 1846, just over a month after Catherine. Stephen admitted to stealing a petticoat, adding that his wife was transported with him. He drowned in the Carlton River in November 1847. His inquest recorded that he was employed conveying firewood on board the *Jane*, a cutter, lying near Primrose Point at the Carlton River. The loaded boat sank and Stephen drowned.[44] It is not clear whether the couple reunited before Stephen's tragic death; certainly Catherine made no mention of him when she arrived and her colonial offences revealed that she frequently was found with men, including in a Hobart brothel. She later married Thomas Stokes, in 1849, and had three sons (including twins) to him. She died as Catherine Stokes in Launceston when she was only 28.[45]

Elizabeth Wright's husband, John Wright, was transported three years before her, arriving on the *North Briton* in 1843. John was tried in Londonderry in July 1842 for passing base coin and admitted to having lived for two years doing this. John was from County Tyrone and was Protestant and illiterate. On arrival, he stated that his wife Betty was living at Armagh. John bore the following tattoos and marks: 'ORANGE coat of arms the Royal Arch purple on left arm [and] scar over left eye'. John's indent recorded that he had six children.[46] His wife Elizabeth (or Betty) was tried in Londonderry on 17 March 1845 for having instruments (a mould) for coining in her possession. She had been previously discharged for a similar offence.[47] None of Elizabeth and John's six children came to Van Diemen's Land. It is not known whether the couple were reunited in the colony.

Catherine Hughes, convicted on her first offence for 'taking a few shillings', stated that her husband James was transported 'about two years' previous under the name of James McMahon on the *Cadet*.[48] Again, there is no evidence that the couple reunited in the colony.

Catherine Grace was from Tipperary but was tried in Carlow. According to her indent, her husband 'Pearce' was transported in the

name of Cantwell to Van Diemen's Land.[49] Catherine was accompanied
by three children, Bridget, Catherine and Mary Grace, all admitted
to the Orphan Schools on 9 December 1845, with other *Tasmania* (2)
children. Catherine's husband, Pierce 'Cantrill', arrived on the *Cadet* (1)
in August 1844, sixteen months before Catherine. He was tried in
Queen's County in March 1844 and was sentenced to transportation
for fifteen years for killing fourteen or fifteen sheep. Pierce, a farm
labourer and ploughman from Kilkenny, aged 35, was Roman Catholic
and literate. He was 5ft 6in, with a sallow complexion, brown hair and
whiskers, dark blue eyes and crooked nose. Ironically, not long after he
arrived, in May 1846, Pierce falsely accused his master at Richmond
with stealing sheep. For this accusation, he received six weeks' imprisonment with hard labour. Catherine and Pierce had reunited by late
1846. Catherine gave birth to a son in the Cascades Female Factory
in May 1847.[50] In January 1851, a daughter, Eliza Cantrell, was born
in Hobart.[51] Pierce was often in trouble, but received his ticket of
leave in November 1852, eight months after Catherine was granted a
free certificate. By December 1854, Pierce had received a conditional
pardon but in July 1858, he was charged, as Pierre Grace, with having
stolen bull calves.[52]

## COMMON-LAW MARRIAGE

Some of the *Tasmania* (2) women lived in common-law marriages
before transportation. For many in the nineteenth century, common-law
marriage was accepted as a customary and binding form of marriage.[53]
Robinson suggested that, among the high number of single men and
women arriving in New South Wales in the period of her study, there
may have been many couples who were married according to common
law and would therefore have been considered single by the authorities.[54] Robinson's study accentuated the existence of different, socially
acceptable types of marriage and family structures. Discussion of colonial
marriage has been distorted to a large extent by terminology and the
failure to recognise common-law marriages, or cohabitation, as an
accepted form of marriage.

There is some evidence that the *Tasmania* (2) women lived in
common-law or *de facto* relationships before they were transported.
Information about this was recorded on the convict indent. Mary Byrne

stated that the father of her child was Martin Murphy and that she had lived with him for two years.[55] Anne Agnew, who was single and 27 when she arrived, confessed to having lived with a man named Curtin for five years before she was transported.[56] Sarah Brennan, who brought her young son Joseph Rutherford with her, stated that the father of her child was Frederick Rutherford, and that she had lived with him for four years.[57] Eleanor Daley lived with John Brennan for four and a half years.[58] Annie McNeil, transported when she was 30, stated that she had lived with James Moran in Athlone for eleven and a half years. She brought her son, William Moran, with her.[59]

In some instances the information is ambiguous: Ann Burns stated that her husband John was a soldier in the 15th Regiment and that she had lived with Mr Hart, a farmer, for four years.[60] Was she employed by Mr Hart or were they cohabiting?

While some of the *Tasmania* (2) women named the fathers of their children, it is not clear whether they lived with the men. Jane Bradshaw, for example, stated that the father of her child, Mary Jane Connor, was Barnard Connor, a cabinetmaker.[61] Margaret Grady admitted that the father of her child was Josh [Joseph?] Austin who lived at her native place.[62]

Cohabitation, in colonial society, was not limited to convict couples. In her study of immigrant women, Rushen found strong evidence that some of the immigrant women found security through living with a partner who they did not marry, following the prevailing working-class tendency to delay formal marriage.[63] In colonial Van Diemen's Land in the second half of the nineteenth century, cohabitation continued to be accepted, at least among some groups. Cohabitation may also explain why marriages cannot be located for some of the women.

Despite having married James Rourke in 1847 – a man more than twice her age – Mary McCarthy later left her husband and lived with a man named Kent, 'a most disputable character, in short, a thief'.[64] She seems to have lived with Kent until her death in 1884.[65]

When Mary Russell died in Launceston in 1868, an inquest was held into her death, which revealed that she had been cohabiting for several years:

Samuel Leonard deposed—I am a carpenter, and reside on the Swamp. The body of the woman shown to the jury in my presence is that of Mary Russell, who lived with me as my wife for the last 15 or 16 years. She was a single woman and I am a single man.[66]

## MARRIAGE BEFORE TRANSPORTATION

In theory, those women who were married when they were transported should have found it difficult to marry in the colony. In practice, like most colonial regulations, the rules were applied inconsistently.

## APPLICATION FOR PERMISSION TO MARRY

In colonial Van Diemen's Land, marriage was not a straightforward arrangement but one that took place in the context of a penal society. Colonial regulations not only determined when a woman under sentence could marry but also whom she could marry. From 1829, convicts under sentence or holding a ticket of leave were required to obtain permission from the Lieutenant Governor before they could marry.[67] Administration of the regulations surrounding applications for permission to marry was not always clear-cut and there are many anomalies and apparent clerical errors.

Author Louisa Ann Meredith commented that 'a suitable marriage is so probable and legitimate a means of reformation, that we never place obstacles in the way of good intentions'.[68] Nevertheless, applicants had to demonstrate that they were worthy of receiving permission to marry, which was considered an indulgence rather than a right. Applications could be refused if the male applicant was not able to support a wife or if either party was already married, had not been free from offences for six months before the application or had not served a sufficient amount of their sentence.[69]

The *Tasmania* (2) women were required to complete their period of probation on the *Anson* before they could apply for permission to marry (and presumably meet any eligible men!)

Most of the women – 69 per cent – were party to at least one application for permission to marry. Generally, the first applications began to appear within a few months of completion of the probation period on the *Anson*. One of the first applications, in July 1846, was for Anne Daley, a widowed farm servant from Tipperary who was transported at the age of 30.[70] The application was approved on 20 July 1846 and Anne married William Friar, a stonemason, the following month.[71] Other applications in 1846 were for Bell Rooney and Edward Frost (September 1846); Martha Martin and William Blackmore (October 1846); and Harriet Madine and

John Vernon (November 1846).[72] All these applications were successful.

As well as length of time in the colony, behaviour was a critical determinant in gaining permission to marry. Behaving well was crucial right up to the time when the marriage took place. Maria Johnson and fellow convict James Derbyshire were granted permission to marry in December 1847, but before the marriage took place Maria was charged with being drunk and creating a disturbance and was sentenced to three months' hard labour in the Cascades Female Factory.[73] The couple did not marry until April 1848, after Maria had served her sentence at the factory.[74]

Margaret Randall was 31 and married with four children when she was transported. In the colony, she was party to four applications for permission to marry: in October 1848 to John Baker; and November 1850, September 1851 and February 1852, all to William Cook.[75] Margaret was a persistent applicant: her 1852 application was the latest found for the *Tasmania* (2) women. No evidence for a marriage to William Cook has been located.

Like Margaret Randall, Anne McAvine had four applications for permission to marry, between April 1847 and October 1850, two of which were to the man who was to become her husband, Aaron Patient.[76] The first and second applications were both approved but no marriage took place. Her first application to marry Aaron Patient was refused but no reason was stated. Finally, on 9 November 1850, Anne, aged 26, and Aaron, aged 32, married in Bothwell.[77]

Elizabeth Hearns was a widow on arrival. Elizabeth and Charles Thompson applied for permission to marry three times between 8 May 1849 and 8 January 1850 before finally marrying in Hobart in January 1850.[78]

James Lines, a convict who arrived on the *Coromandel*, must have been a good catch: in July 1847, he applied to marry Mary Watt; the application was approved but no marriage took place.[79] A year later, James married Mary's shipmate, Honora Cullen.[80]

Not all of the *Tasmania* (2) women were party to a permission-to-marry application. It is not always possible to tell why this was the case. In some instances, it may have been age, infirmity or early death; in others it was simply an unwillingness or inability to meet the standards of good behaviour required for permission to marry.

Henrietta Beresford married John Lenny the year after she was freed. She had no applications for marriage. She was 30 when she married John, a widower aged 46. They married in the Church of Scotland manse at Evandale in June 1853.[81] It is not clear what happened to John, but in

October 1857, as Henrietta 'Linie', widow aged 27, she married Elijah Harvey, a shepherd aged 36, in Swansea on Tasmania's east coast.[82] Two years later, Henrietta – as 'Henrietta Lenny alias Harvey alias Richardson' – appeared in the Supreme Court in Hobart, indicted for having married at Avoca, in August 1859, Keeling Richardson when her husband Elijah Harvey was still alive. It was a complex case. The first marriage (to Elijah Harvey) was proved by a witness who was present at the ceremony; extracts from the marriage register were submitted:

> The Defendant admitted having gone to the Church with Elijah Harvey, but denied that she had married him as he had treated her so badly, tearing the clothes off her back, and she therefore refused to put the ring on or answer the clergyman. She had been married previously but her first husband had died at Mr Donald Cameron's. She had never married Elijah Harvey at all, and she dared him to come there and prove such a thing.

> His Honor said the law as it stood might appear inconsistent for it did not admit the testimony of the first wife or first husband in cases of bigamy.[83]

Mary Jones *née* Burgess and Thomas Jones. (Courtesy of Kevin Reed)

The jury decided that Henrietta was not guilty.

Age was not a barrier to marriage. Anne Gardiner or Harrison was a 64-year-old Fermanagh widow (with six children) when she arrived. Five years later in June 1850, she married fellow convict Peter Kelly, aged 40, at Green Ponds (now Kempton).[84] Ann gave her age as 50. The marriage, however, was brief as Ann died at Brighton ten days later.[85]

Another short-lived marriage was that of Mary McManus, a 27-year-old Belfast housemaid when she was transported. In November 1850, Mary and Moses Norcut, who had been transported on the *William Jardine*, married. As with her shipmate Anne Gardiner, Mary was married in the house of Congregational Minister Revd William Waterfield at Green Ponds. Anne's husband Peter Kelly was a witness. Mary was a house servant aged 32 and Moses was a labourer aged 33.[86] Mary died on the last day of 1850.[87]

In contrast, some marriages lasted a considerable time: Mary Burgess, one of the Tullow women, married Thomas Jones, a convict who arrived on the *London*. Mary was 19 when she married; her husband, Thomas, a cabinetmaker, was 32.[88] Witnesses to the marriage were William Briggs, a carver, and Mary's shipmate Bridget Briggs (*née* Gallagher). Mary and Thomas had ten children. They had been married 37 years when Thomas, aged 75, died in Launceston. Mary died in 1898, aged 68.[89]

## MARRIED LIFE

Not every marriage was a bed of roses. Mary Leonard, a widow, was 38 when she married 48-year-old widower John Press in Hobart in April 1849.[90] It does not seem to have been a successful marriage. Mary was twice found in a compromising situation with another man, the first time only six weeks after her marriage.[91]

In some instances, husbands brought their errant wives before a magistrate. It was a way of controlling them. Annie McNeill, aged 30 from Westmeath, brought her young son, William Moran, with her to the colony and he was admitted to the Male Orphan School. In 1847, Annie and John Spong married.[92] In February 1849, Annie was charged by her husband with using obscene language and was sentenced to one month's hard labour in the Cascades Female Factory. John, who seems to have had second thoughts, petitioned for her release days later and Annie's sentence was remitted. A son, John, was born in Hobart in February 1850, so it seems that the marriage was not beyond repair.[93]

In 1849, Margaret Wilson 'now Heelan' was found guilty of being absent from her husband's residence for three days. She pleaded not guilty, stating 'my husband put me out'. She was discharged and returned to her husband.[94]

Ann Flannery, an arsonist from Roscommon, married fellow convict John Brown in 1848. In May of the following year, John had Ann charged with being drunk; she was sentenced to fourteen days in the cells. Later that year, towards the end of November, Ann absconded but was returned to her husband when she was found. In May 1850, Ann was again brought before the magistrate 'upon complaint of her husband with being drunk'.[95] She pleaded not guilty and was discharged. In June 1851, she was charged with being absent without leave from her husband's residence. She was sentenced to one month's imprisonment with hard labour in the Cascades Female Factory.[96]

Lower-court records and newspapers also provide glimpses of married life. In March 1849, Isabella Warnock was sentenced to six months' hard labour in the Cascades Female Factory. Calling her 'Clementina Wharnick', the *Colonial Times* detailed the story with great relish:

Clementina Wharnick, the wife of James Peters, better known in this place by the cognomen of Sheepy, was charged by her husband with being drunk and disorderly, and leaving her residence. It appeared that on his return home, expecting to find it in order, he was compelled to make a forcible entry into his own mansion, which led to high words between him and his spouse, and after disturbing the whole neighbourhood they attracted the constables' notice, and on Mr. Peters' charge she was conveyed to the watch-house—her old place of retreat. Mr. Peters addressed a letter to the magistrate, stating his determination never to take her to his bosom again, but return her to the place from whence she came—Government. The fair one with a large bunch of black bushy hair in her hand, which she said Sheepy had torn from her head, implored pity and forgiveness. Sheepy was obdurate; he was resolved to part for ever. The magistrates threatened, as they had so very frequently appeared on the police-office boards, to sentence her to condign punishment forthwith, when Mr. Peters craved a hearing, and acknowledged himself in fault. Here a series of riotous crimination ensued, which to end, and for the peace of the neighbours who had repeatedly complained of riotous conduct of the pair, their Worships sentenced the fair one to 6 months' hard labor, and at the end of that period to be disposed of by the Government. This was a death-blow to poor Sheepy, who cried out, "must I lose her; I'll take her back, your worships," and a most affecting scene ensued, to end which the fair one was banded to durance vile, to prepare for her journey to the Cascade Convent. Peters begged that his wife might be indulged with a ride to town, to which their Worships paid no attention.[97]

Convict marriage was complex:

> From the time of embarkation, details about marital status were recorded, an indication that it was important to colonial authorities but not necessarily why it was important. Convict marriage, because it was a reward for good behaviour, was a means of control … Convict marriage was seen as a reward for reformation as well as a means to reformation. It was not simply an agreement between two people, or their families. Despite the rigorous permission to marry regulations, most … women married in the colony. They worked within established government process to achieve what they wanted.[98]

For some, marriage was a long-term partnership, promising stability and security. For others, death or desertion of a spouse brought economic and social vulnerability and hardship. Above all, marriage was a survival strategy. For many of the women of the *Tasmania* (2), as for convict women generally, finding a male provider helped avoid poverty and guaranteed a degree of protection in a colony where there were many more men than women.

Only fragmentary evidence about married life survives. Private lives only became public if they came to the attention of the authorities, as in cases of domestic violence and brutality. A woman under sentence was subject not only to the authority of the convict system but also to that of her husband, who was able to control her behaviour by bringing her before the police court if, in his eyes, she transgressed. What was private for the general population was subject to scrutiny for convict women.

# A Mere Accident of Birth[1]

Children have always been a part of the convict story, if not always a visible one. As Casella comments, 'For the children of convict women, their exile and incarceration did not reflect any enlightened European mode of punishment. It was a mere accident of birth.'[2]

The children of the *Tasmania* (2) experienced institutional life even before arriving in Van Diemen's Land. Some were in county gaols with their mothers, where conditions were often wretched and bleak. All were in the Grangegorman Female Depot in Dublin.[3]

Admission Register Grangegorman Female Convict Depot, showing the children's names. (NAI, Grangegorman Prison PRIS 1/69/7, reproduced with the permission of the National Archives of Ireland)

The Grangegorman Female Depot register contains details of name, age, crime, sentence, location of conviction, marital status, literacy level, trade or occupation and number of previous convictions.[4] It gives a unique picture of nineteenth-century Irish institutional life.

Grangegorman Female Convict Depot, 2013. (Courtesy of Bob Gordon)

Between 31 March and 15 August 1845, thirty-four children were admitted to the Grangegorman Female Depot. Their ages ranged from 4 months to 11 years.[5] Another child, Jane Lynam, was born there in early July. Many of the children, including Margaret Butler's son and daughter, were admitted in June 1845 and so had about three months in the prison before embarking.

Sarah Brennan and her young son Joseph Carroll or Rutherford, admitted in March 1845, were the first of the *Tasmania* (2) women and children to arrive at Grangegorman. Sarah was tried in Dublin City on 29 March 1845 and two days later was admitted with Joseph, who was nearly 2.

Two of the last to be admitted, in mid-August 1845, were Elizabeth Hearns and her 14-month-old child[6] and Mary O'Brien and her daughter Margaret, who was 6½ years old. Elizabeth was tried in Kilkenny City on 26 July 1845. Mary was tried in Limerick City on 18 July 1845.

Two women were pregnant when admitted to Grangegorman. Mary Lynam or Egan was admitted on 3 June 1845, having been tried in Longford in early April 1845. Her daughter Jane was born in the depot in early July. Jane died not long after arriving in Van Diemen's Land.[7] Sarah McArdle was also pregnant when she was admitted to Grangegorman. Her son James was born during the voyage.[8] Like Jane Lynam, James McArdle died not long after arriving in the colony.[9]

All thirty-five children from Grangegorman embarked. Margaret Butler was accompanied by two of her six children, William and Mary Ann.[10] Esther Burgess brought four children and Mary Griffin three.

As well as the Tullow women, some of the other women brought several children with them. Catherine Grace was accompanied by three of her children, as was Mary Connell.[11] Margaret Kelly and Mary Wall both brought two.[12]

## ORPHAN SCHOOLS

The King's Orphan Schools were established in 1828 on separate sites in Hobart Town. In the early 1830s, the schools relocated to New Town, 7km from Hobart Town, in a purpose-built complex which operated under various names. By the time the *Tasmania* (2) children arrived, the institution was known as the Queen's Orphan Schools. The building had two wings, one for the girls – the Female Orphan School – and one for the boys – the Male Orphan School. Very young children were admitted to the Female Orphan School; boys later transferred to the Male Orphan

School. In 1862, an Infant Orphan School was built for the youngest weaned children. Most of those admitted to the Orphan Schools were the children of convicts.[13] Conditions at the Orphan Schools were strict and harsh and the infant mortality rate was high.[14]

The majority of the *Tasmania* (2) children were separated from their mothers, most of whom were taken to the *Anson* on arrival.[15] How heartbreaking it must have been for Margaret Butler and her shipmates to come to the other side of the world only to have their children taken from them and admitted to this bleak institution. A few days after arriving in Hobart Town, on 9 December 1845, twenty-four children were admitted to the Orphan Schools. Esther Burgess fought determinedly to bring her children with her.[16] Esther was tried with her daughter Mary. Five of her younger children, aged between 2 and 14, came with her.[17] The four oldest – Elizabeth, Alicia, Jane and William – were admitted to the Orphan Schools on 9 December 1845.[18] The youngest, Robert Burgess, aged 2, was admitted in May 1846; he died there in November 1846.[19] Another daughter, Ann or Mary Ann Burgess, travelled to NSW as a free migrant in 1849.[20]

Mary Griffen's colonial convict records reveal a discrepancy in the number of children who accompanied her. Although her convict conduct record states that there were four children on board with

Queen's Orphan Asylum, *c.* 1863. (Reproduced with permission of the Tasmanian Archive and Heritage Office)

her, her indent says that she had four children but only three were on board.[21] The surgeon's report mentions only three children. The records of the Orphan Schools show three children: Eliza, aged 11; Mary Ann, aged 6; and Edward, aged 3. Eliza, Mary and Edward were all admitted on 9 December 1845, the same date their mother was admitted to the Colonial Hospital.[22]

Mary Wall's daughter Mary Ann was admitted to the Female Orphan School on arrival but there is no record of an admission for her younger brother Patrick. He may have stayed with his mother or been placed in one of the convict nurseries. Patrick died of dysentery in April 1846.[23] Catherine Kelly, aged 20 months, daughter of Margaret, also died of dysentery, in March 1846.[24] Kippen concluded that 41 per cent of deaths of children under the age of three in convict nurseries from 1838 to 1858 resulted from diarrhoea, compared to 12 per cent of those of the same age outside convict nurseries.[25]

Some of those admitted to the Orphan Schools on arrival were still toddlers. Jane Bradshaw's 2-year-old daughter Mary Jane Connor was one of those taken from her mother and placed in the Female Orphan School on 9 December. She remained there until February 1847, when she was released to her mother.

Sarah Brennan's son Joseph Carroll or Rutherford, aged 2½, was also separated from his mother shortly after arrival and placed in the Female Orphan School.[26] When he was three, he transferred to the Male Orphan School. He remained there for more than ten years, until March 1856, when he was apprenticed out.[27]

The youngest children remained with their mothers in a convict nursery. If they survived, they were admitted to the Orphan Schools after they were weaned (see Table 7). The weaning period was short – the recommended age was nine months – and, combined with early separation of mother and child, may have contributed to the infant mortality rate.[28] Mary Ann Butler, daughter of Margaret Butler 2nd, stayed with her mother until May 1846 and was admitted to the institution at the age of 2.

Three of the youngest children, Anne Byrne, Robert Burgess and John Docherty, died in the Orphan Schools. Anne, who was admitted to the Female Orphan School on arrival when she was 2 years and 3 months old, died of inflammation of the brain in May 1849.[29] Robert, aged 2½, died from inflammation of the lungs; John, aged 3 years 9 months, died of croup.[30]

In all, four children from the *Tasmania* (2) died in the Orphan Schools. The fourth was Sarah Ann Kelly, who died in May 1847, aged 11.[31]

| CHILD | AGE | MOTHER | ADMITTED | DISCHARGED OS |
|---|---|---|---|---|
| Robert Burgess | 2y | Esther Burgess | 13 May 1846 | died 15 Nov 1846 |
| Mary Ann Butler | 2y | Margaret Butler | 14 May 1846 | 10 June 1851 to mother TL # |
| James Keegan | 2y | Honora Cullen | 2 Oct 1846 | 8 Jun 1848 to mother |
| John Docherty | 1y9m | Anne Dogherty | 2 Oct 1846 | died 31 Dec 1849 |
| James Hearns | 2y | Elizabeth Hearns | 14 May 1846 | 10 April 1850 to mother TL |

# readmitted     TL = ticket of leave

Table 7: *Tasmania* (2) children on board admitted to the Queen's Orphan Schools once weaned [n=5], TAHO, SWD28/1/1

## WHAT BECAME OF THE *TASMANIA* (2) CHILDREN?

Margaret Butler's son, William Butler, was one of three children who came free with their convict mothers only to be apprenticed out to masters in Port Phillip (now Victoria), then a separate colony across Bass Strait.[32] He left the Male Orphan School on 17 January 1847, apprenticed to Revd Richard Walsh. The other two who were sent to Port Phillip were Eliza Griffin and Rose Murphy.

It is likely that William's younger sister Mary Ann initially stayed with her mother, probably in the bleak and cramped Dynnyrne House, not

Dynnyrne House. (TAHO, PH30/1/8546, reproduced with permission of the Tasmanian Archive and Heritage Office)

William Butler and his wife Margaret (*née* McIntyre), date unknown. (Authors' Collection)

far from the Cascades Female Factory. When she was 2, she was considered old enough to be admitted to the Female Orphan School, another cold and miserable institution. Brothers and sisters were separated in the Orphan Schools, on the same site but in different buildings, and we can only guess at the contact William and Mary Ann had. Similarly problematic is the amount of contact the children had with their mother. In any event, William left the colony when Mary Ann was only about 4. Mary Ann remained in the Female Orphan School for five years until she was released to her mother, who had remarried and who was then a ticket of leave holder. Four years after Mary Ann was reunited with her mother, Margaret was beaten to death by her colonial husband. Mary Ann, then 11, was again admitted to the Female Orphan School and stayed there for four years until she was apprenticed to Mrs Mary O'Boyle in Hobart.[33] By this time, William was settled in the Monaro region of New South Wales, where he married in 1858. Against all odds, at some stage William and Mary Ann reunited. She settled on the south coast of NSW, marrying George Ward in 1865 when she was 18 and having a large family. William died in 1909 in Cooma and his obituary mentions that he was survived by a sister, Mrs George Ward of Bemboka. William and Mary Ann's story is a remarkable one of courage, resilience and survival and the strength of family ties under difficult and complex circumstances.[34]

## THE OTHER TULLOW CHILDREN

In all, the Tullow women brought ten children with them. Of the four surviving Burgess children, Elizabeth was apprenticed from the Female Orphan School in February 1846.[35] Alicia was discharged to Elizabeth in January 1849.[36] Jane was discharged in September 1849 to her mother, but was readmitted in June 1850, when she was 12½; it is not clear why, although her mother's conduct records stated that she was at Oatlands about this time. Jane was apprenticed out in March 1853 to F. Martin at New Norfolk.[37] William Burgess spent eight years in the Male Orphan School. In March 1853, when he was about 13, he was released to his mother, 'now free'.[38] No record of him has been located after this date.

The first of the Burgess children to marry was Alicia or Alice Burgess, who married Thomas Rice in Hobart in December 1854. There were nine Rice children. Both Alice and Thomas died in Maryborough, Victoria.[39] A detailed obituary for Alice, subtly glossing over the fine points of her family background, was published in the *Geraldton Guardian*:

THE VICTORIAN GOLDFIELDS.
OLD PIONEER PASSES.

Mrs. Alice Rice, who died recently at Maryborough, Victoria, was born in Co. Carlow, Ireland, in 1834, and came to Australia with her parents in 1842, which made her a colonist of 79 years. She married the late Mr. Thomas Rice, who operated the Maryborough diggings by discovering gold on the 4th or 5th of June, 1854, at a place near the bridge on the Avoca Road. Mrs. Rice came to Maryborough in 1857, and as a recollection of the early days of Maryborough she records an episode worth chronicling. Living in a tent at Blackman Lead in the early part of 1858 she was washing and preparing dinner, and whilst inside the tent her brother-in-law dropped a 537 oz. nugget in the tub amongst the clothes she had washed. She had repeated many times the surprise she got when she discovered the nugget in the tub. She was also present at the opening of the goldfields at Inglewood and other places. Going to Inglewood proved rather an unlucky venture, as through being there they missed seeing the Government Gazette giving a grant for the discovery of new goldfields, and though in after years application was made for the reward, it proved futile owing to the lapse of time between the discovery and its application, and no Government award was ever paid for the discovery of the Maryborough field. Although only eight years old when she left the Old Country, she always cherished a love for Ireland, and followed the happenings of that unhappy country with the keenest interest. The deceased lady, who was an invalid for a number of years, leaves a large grown-up family.[40]

Elizabeth, who was also known as Eliza, married Joshua Page in Sandhurst Victoria in February 1855. At the time of her marriage, Eliza was a laundress aged 25; Joshua was a miner. A son Joshua, aged 17 months, drowned four months before his parents married. In all, they had 10 children. Elizabeth died on 20 August 1896 at Kangaroo Flat, Victoria.[41]

Jane married Irish ex-convict Augustus Brady in October 1862 in Hobart.[42] Augustus, an 'imperfect painter', was transported on the *London* in 1851 after being tried in Dublin for stealing a book.[43] His indent noted that his proper name was Owen Brady.[44]

By the time Jane and Augustus married, they already had two sons. The first, Augustus Brady, was born in December 1859; he died two days later on Christmas Eve. The second was born a year later, in December 1860.[45] They had three more children between 1865 and 1873: William Francis, Jane, and Edwin George.[46] Jane may have had a child, James Francis Brady, in 1892.[47]

Augustus Brady died of 'delirium tremens' in Hobart in February 1874 when he was 45, leaving Jane economically vulnerable with several young children.[48] Perhaps it was not surprising then that Jane was a frequent inmate of the Campbell Street Gaol in Hobart. Surviving under these circumstances was difficult. In July 1888, with another woman, Jane was charged with living in an unoccupied house in Campbell Street. They were both sent to gaol for one month.[49] Jane had several convictions for being idle and disorderly as well as for using 'filthy and abusive language'. She was sent to gaol again in April 1893, this time for three months for 'her own protection'; at the time she was living in an old shed in Murray Street.[50] Jane died in gaol in Hobart in June 1893:

> An inquest was held in gaol this morning on the body of Jane Brady, aged 53 years, a widow, who was undergoing a sentence of three months. The jury returned a verdict of death from chronic disease of the lungs.[51]

Campbell Street Gaol, Hobart. (AB713/1/7988, reproduced with permission of the Tasmanian Archive and Heritage Office)

Contagious Diseases Hospital, Yard 4, Cascades, South Hobart (foreground). (TAHO, NS1013/1/48, reproduced with permission of the Tasmanian Archive and Heritage Office)

In 1893, Esther Burgess' granddaughter, Jane Brady, escaped from the Lock Hospital: 'The police have been notified of the fact, and are on the look-out to bring her back'.[52] The outcome of her escape is not known. The Lock Hospital (or Contagious Diseases Hospital) was established by the government on the site of the former Cascades Female Factory for women and girls suffering from sexually transmitted diseases. In 1895, it was taken over by the Home of Mercy, a rescue home.[53]

Of Mary Griffen's three children, Eliza remained at the Female Orphan School until August 1847 when she was apprenticed 'by Agreement' to R. Shadforth at Port Phillip. Her sister, Mary Ann, was apprenticed to John French Esq. of Longford Hall, after six years in the Female Orphan School. Mary Griffen's youngest child Edward, admitted at the age of 3, was discharged to his mother, 'now free', in December 1853 when he was about 11.[54]

## MARGARET CONNELL, 'THE IRISH NURSEMAID'

When Cork widow Mary Connell was transported, she brought three children with her.[55] Margaret aged 11, Patrick aged 7 and James aged 3, were all admitted to the Orphan Schools in December 1845.[56]

In March 1849, Margaret was discharged from the Female Orphan School to H. Huish, Hobart. Her mother married in July that year but Mary's sons were not released to her until April 1851.[57] Shortly afterwards, in July 1851, Mary's colonially born son William Connell, aged 4, was admitted to the Male Orphan School.[58] He was discharged in April 1858, to his mother, 'now free'.[59] Tracing Patrick, James and William has proved difficult from the time they were discharged from the Male Orphan School; in contrast, their sister's life is well documented.

Margaret Connell, a minor at 17, married farmer George Cotton, 'of full age', in July 1851 at the Hobart residence of Independent minister Revd Frederick Miller.[60]

George Cotton was part of a well-known and respectable Quaker family. He arrived in the colony in 1828 with his parents, Francis and Anna Maria Cotton (née Tilney). The family settled at Kelvedon on the east coast.[61]

Gwen Webb, in her history *Pyengana: The New Country*, erroneously stated that Margaret Connell, an Irish nursemaid, arrived with the Cotton family in 1828.[62] Another version of Margaret Connell's story appeared in 1986 in Frances Cotton's history of the Cotton family, *Kettle on the hob: a family in Van Diemen's Land*.[63] Frances Cotton wrote:

When George was 22 years of age, he travelled to Hobart Town to stay with his sister Maria in Liverpool Street. Maria's children had a nursemaid named Margaret Connell, the daughter of a woman convict. Here was a situation ready to take fire and soon George was in what his father termed "a pitiable state". George insisted on getting married at once and the ceremony took place at the Registry Office in Hobarton on July 7th, 1851.[64]

As already noted, Margaret and George married at the residence of Independent minister Revd Miller; no record of a registry office marriage has been located. Webb suggests that George Cotton married 'the Irish nursemaid' in the Quaker meeting house in Hobart.[65]
Cotton continues:

Margaret claimed to be the daughter of a French Lady, but Father's enquiries at the Orphan School proved this to be incorrect. She had arrived with her mother on a convict ship. "We are filled with distress and apprehension", writes George's mother, but she is kind enough to ask her daughter Maria to see that Margaret has a suitable dress to be married in.[66]

According to Cotton, George and Margaret were allocated 'some acres' of land and a cottage 3 miles from Kelvedon: 'After the birth of the first infant, Margaret decided to go to Hobarton with her husband, leaving the child in the care of the policeman's wife at Rocky Hill'. It seemed that in the eyes of her in-laws Margaret could do nothing right![67]

George's father Francis considered his son profligate: 'Any money George earns is soon spent'. George's mother bemoaned the marriage. George left the colony for the gold rushes in February 1852 with his brothers Henry, Thomas and Tilney, but had little to show for it on his return.[68] In 1864, George was appointed superintendent of police for the Glamorgan municipality.[69] He was drawn into ongoing bickering between the Cottons and their neighbours and, in court, allegations were made about George's behaviour.[70] In June 1870, the warden of Glamorgan, John Meredith, advertised for a new superintendent of police to fill a vacancy created by George Cotton's resignation.[71] In September 1870, 'in a case of great public interest', George appeared in the police court at Swansea, charged by John Meredith, of *Cambria*, with trespass.[72] The case was dismissed but Meredith warned George against doing it again.

St Columba Falls, W. Pyengana, Portland, photograph J.W. Beattie W.K. (Crowther
Collection, reproduced with permission of the Tasmanian Archive and Heritage Office)

The following month, politician Charles Meredith presented a petition in the House of Assembly from George Cotton, 'late Superintendent of Police in the Municipality of Glamorgan'. George wanted 'a searching inquiry' into the circumstances of his dismissal as superintendent of police, which he attributed to the action of the warden.[73]

For a time, Margaret and George lived at Mathinna, where their youngest son Clement O'Connell was born in 1873.[74] Later they moved further north, settling on the South George River on a rich and fertile piece of land which Margaret named St Columba.[75] Margaret's two sons, Gus and Charles, discovered the St Columba Falls, which, according to Webb, were named by Margaret.[76]

Margaret and George Cotton had a large family, born between 1854 and 1873. The youngest, Clement O'Connell Cotton, was named for his mother's family.

Margaret's children were educated at Catholic colleges in Hobart and Melbourne. A daughter, Pearlie, conducted the first private school in Pyengana. Charlie and Gus were noted runners.[77] One daughter eloped with a man who worked for the Cottons, giving rise to some colourful folklore about Margaret. The couple arranged for the priest at St Helen's to marry them and some family members and locals combined to distract Margaret and George. Webb's romanticised account reads:

> A capable horse-woman, Mrs Cotton was soon in hot pursuit, along narrow tracks, over logs and through the bogs she rode, as fast as she dared, only to arrive at the church at midnight as the couple emerged, man and wife; she never forgave them.[78]

Margaret was probably never reconciled with George's family. Frances Cotton concluded her account with the comment: 'Old people about the district say they still remember seeing a wild-looking old lady driving a horse and cart at breakneck speed'.[79] Gwen Webb's account was more generous:

> Mrs. Cotton was a hardworking woman, but she had a most generous heart. Many a mouth would have been empty but for her in those early days of struggle and hardship. She had wonderful ideas for making money – and spending it. The fine river flats were cleared and cultivated with a single furrow plough which the boys carried over the hills from Mathinna on their backs. These paddocks were set out

with fruit trees, mainly apples and to this woman must go the honour of being the first woman to export apples from Tasmania. The reason was circumstantial as the only outlet for her crop was by ship from St. Helens. The boat brought supplies direct from Melbourne and the apples, together with tin from surrounding districts, made up the return freight.[80]

Margaret's husband George died in 1916:

> Mr. George Cotton, an old resident of the North-East Coast, died at the residence of his daughter (Mrs. M. Grace) at Derby on Monday. Deceased was born at Swansea 87 years ago, and has been a resident of that part ever since. He was at one time superintendent of police, and harbourmaster for a number of years. His wife died a few months ago. There are four daughters and four sons left to mourn their loss. One son, Mr. George Cotton, and a daughter, Mrs. M. Grace, are resident at Derby, and Mr. Gus Cotton at Ringarooma.[81]

No record of Margaret's death has been located. Margaret and George's last surviving child, Margaret Mary Singline, died in 1953 at Ringarooma.[82]

## THE OTHER *TASMANIA* (2) CHILDREN

Tracing many of the *Tasmania* (2) children is difficult. Ann Ferguson's story is typical: 9-year-old Ann, daughter of Mary McGowan or Magowan, arrived with her mother and was admitted to the Female Orphan School with several other children from the ship on 9 December 1845. The last record of her was in September 1847 when she was released to her mother, who had married Edward Littlejohn.[83]

Mary Reardon, whose mother Ellen Sullivan died during the voyage, has not been traced. She was still a baby when she arrived.

In 1855, Jane Bradshaw advertised for the whereabouts of her young daughter:

> MARY JANE CONNOR.—Should this meet the eye of anyone acquainted with MARY JANE CONNOR, aged 12 years, formerly in the service of Mrs. Hooper, Barrack-street, Hobarton; was known to be in the service of Mrs. Hooper twelve months ago. Any one knowing

the whereabouts of the above girl, and making the same known at the office of this paper will be rewarded, and receive the heartfelt thanks of her broken-hearted mother.

JANE BRADSHAW
Launceston, June 26.[84]

After two years in the Female Orphan School, in February 1847, Mary Jane had been 'delivered to her mother', who had a ticket of leave.[85] Mary Jane was then about 4. Her mother married in February 1848.[86] Some time after this, Mary Jane went into service. No further record of Mary Jane has been located.

While they were serving their sentence, the women were powerless to keep their Irish-born children with them. For many of these children, their formative years were spent in a range of austere institutions. Little work has been done on the impact of this on them. Families were fragmented as a result of death, desertion and rigid rules and regulations. Mothers and children lost contact with each other; many were not reunited. Like Ann Ferguson, many of the children who arrived on the *Tasmania* (2) disappeared from the records once they were released from the Orphan Schools.

# New Families in a New Land

Of the *Tasmania* (2) women, 43 per cent are known to have given birth to children in Van Diemen's Land. Some of the children were stillborn and others did not survive infancy. Some were illegitimate, some were born in institutions and spent their early years there. Some got into trouble with the law but many lived settled lives, producing numerous grandchildren for their convict mothers.

Eliza Davis was one of only fourteen women who had children in Ireland and in Van Diemen's Land. She was also the first to give birth in the colony: her twin daughters were born in St John's Hospital, Launceston, on 20 May 1847.[1] Ironically, Eliza had been transported for infanticide.

Three days later, at the other end of the colony, Catherine Grace gave birth to a son, John Grace, in the Cascades Female Factory.[2] Although Catherine's husband was also transported, no father's name was included on the birth certificate.[3]

In all, nine children were born in 1847, within two years of the ship's arrival. Ann Flood's child was stillborn.[4] Three of the 1847 births were legitimate: Catherine Grace's son, John Grace; Harriet Madine's son, William 'Vernham';[5] and Martha Martin's unnamed daughter, who lived only six days before dying of convulsions.[6]

## CHILDREN BORN IN INSTITUTIONS

Nurseries were established within female factories and in separate institutions for pregnant convict women and their infant children. These institutions were often overcrowded. Infant mortality rates were high, partly because of unhygienic and cold living conditions, but also because of the premature separation of mothers from their infants.[7] Poor maternal diet was another factor. Many of the institutionally born infants died from preventable diseases such as malnutrition, diarrhoea and similar illnesses. There were intermittent attempts to improve the conditions at the nurseries but they were seldom effective.

As Table 8 shows, the location of convict nurseries in the 1840s and 1850s frequently changed. The Dynnyrne Nursery, located between the Cascades Female Factory and Hobart Town, was the main nursery from 1842 to 1851.

| Nursery | Location | Operating Years |
|---|---|---|
| Brickfields Depot | Hobart | 1849–1851 |
| Dynnyrne House | Hobart | 1842–1851 |
| Launceston Female Factory | Launceston | 1834–1848 |
| Liverpool Street Nursery | Hobart | 1838–1842 |
| Ross Female Factory | Ross | 1848–1851 |

Table 8: Nurseries operating in Van Diemen's Land between 1841 and 1851.

Dynnyrne Nursery. (PH30/1/5134, reproduced with permission of the Tasmanian Archive and Heritage Office)

A pregnant convict woman in a female factory was usually transferred to a convict nursery to await the birth of her child. As a rule, she remained there until her infant was weaned, sometime between six and nine months. After this, the usual practice was for the convict mother to be sent to the factory crime-class yard to serve six months' hard labour as punishment for giving birth to an illegitimate child. Infants remained in the nurseries until they were old enough to be transferred to the Orphan Schools at New Town, usually at the age of about 2 or 3. However, if in the interim the convict mother had been granted a ticket of leave or had become free and could prove that she could support her child, the child could be released to her.

In some instances, a convict woman's colonial marriage resulted in her illegitimate children being rejected by her new husband; her children remained in the Orphan Schools. Others, however, became part of their convict mother's colonial family.

## 'I HAVE NOTHING TO SAY'

In January 1849, Mary Byrne was charged with leaving her master in Liverpool Street without permission. Absent for one day, she was found 'residing in a house in Bathurst Street, Hobart Town, having been delivered of an illegitimate child'. Mary pleaded guilty to the charge, adding 'I have nothing to say'.[8] She was sent to the Cascades Female Factory for six months as punishment for being absent without leave and for having given birth to an illegitimate child, James 'Burns'.[9] While she was serving this sentence, her Irish-born daughter Ann died at the Female Orphan School, where she had been since arriving in the colony.[10] After her marriage in September 1851 to Thomas Cann, Mary gave birth to a son, Henry, in February 1852.[11] Mary had another daughter named Ann, in 1854, who died at the age of three in 1858[12] and then Charlotte in 1856. It seems likely that James remained with his mother while she was alive. However, after Mary's death in 1858, Thomas no longer took responsibility for James. In July 1859, James Kerr of Liverpool Street, Hobart, applied to have James 'Burns', a Roman Catholic boy aged 8, admitted to the Male Orphan School:

> The Father is unknown, and the mother died in November last. It is impossible to give any further particulars than those … and but for the kindness of Mr Kerr [the] Boy would be turned out into the streets.

James was considered 'a genuine case' for the Orphan Schools. A further application was made by James Kerr in August 1859. The earlier application had been mislaid at the Comptroller's Office. In the August application, James was recorded as 10 years 8 months old. James Kerr wrote to the Colonial Secretary:

> I most respectfully beg leave to bring under your consideration the case of an Orphan Boy, who has been left completely destitute in consequence of the death of his mother, Mary McCann, who resided in Harrington Street near the 'Queen's Arms'—After the mother's death I took the boy into my house, clothed and sent him to school but owing to the vicious habits contracted by him, he is quite incorrigible, and all amendment, under me, at least, is hopeless. Being therefore under no parental control I would respectfully suggest that the State takes him under its protection by placing him in the 'Orphan School' before he becomes absolutely irreclaimable.[13]

James was admitted to the Male Orphan School as James McCann in September 1859. He remained there until February 1863, when he was apprenticed to George Pickford in Launceston.[14]

Of the colonially born children, at least twenty-seven were born in one of the female factories – fourteen at Cascades Female Factory, ten at Launceston Female Factory and three at Ross Female Factory. Of these children, seven died in the factories.

As Casella highlights, 'Within the female factories of Australia, up to one third of the human occupants had never committed any crime.'[15] The children of convict women born in female factories were incarcerated in the same institutions designed for the punishment of their mothers.

In 1841, Matron Slea of the Liverpool Street Nursery observed that 'there are few [convict women] who do not conduct themselves as good mothers'.[16] According to Damousi, it was a commonly held nineteenth-century belief that 'no woman could love the living proof of her sin'[17] and that an 'unwed mother was not fit to be called a mother at all'.[18] Prominent Hobart Police Magistrate John Price stated at an enquiry into female convict prison discipline that it would be 'beneficial to the children to cut off the connexion with the mother'.[19] Revd Thomas Ewing, master of the Queen's Orphan Schools, firmly believed convict mothers should not be able to associate with their children because they would be contaminated by their vice.[20]

## CHILDREN BORN IN THE CASCADES FEMALE FACTORY

Bridget Stankard, from Leitrim, transported at the age of 24 for perjury, gave birth to two children in the Cascades Female Factory: William in 1848 and Jane in 1851.[21] William died in the factory in August 1850; his mother had been released and was leading 'an idle and disorderly life'.[22] On the day William died, Bridget was sentenced to three months' imprisonment with hard labour in the Cascades Factory.[23]

Mary Wall (or Watt), a farm servant from Cork, had four children in Ireland, two of whom came with her. Her infant son, Patrick Wall, died from 'dysentery' when he was 2 but it is not clear where he was when he died.[24] Mary's daughter, Mary Ann, aged 3½, was admitted to the Female Orphan School on arrival in the colony. Eight years later, in August 1853, she was discharged to her mother. In December 1847, a son, James, was born in the Cascades Female Factory. In September 1849, Mary was charged with being absent without leave. When she was apprehended, she was found in bed with a man. She was sentenced to six months' hard labour, again in the Cascades Female Factory. At the time, she was pregnant – while she was in the factory, in January 1850, she gave birth to a daughter, Margaret.[25] In January 1852, when she was 2, Margaret was admitted to the Female

Cascades Female Factory. (TAHO, NS1013/1/45, reproduced with permission of the Tasmanian Archive and Heritage Office)

Orphan School. She died there two years later aged 4, from 'dysentery after measles'.[26] Her brother, James, aged 4, was admitted to the institution at the same time and remained there until 1862.[27]

Sarah Ryan's son, John Ryan, was born at the Cascades Female Factory in May 1848, while his mother was serving a sentence of six months' hard labour for being absent without leave. Sarah was readmitted to the factory five months after John's birth, charged with neglect of duty. She was barely out when she was sent back for another one-month stint for drunkenness. There was no mention of John. Sarah married in 1850 and had another son in 1851.[28]

Jane Bradshaw, a thief from Queen's County, was in the Cascades Female Factory from September 1846 to January 1849 for several offences. While she was there, Jane gave birth to a daughter, Ann Bradshaw, in September 1848. In June 1849, Ann, aged 8 months, died at the Dynnyrne Nursery of 'acute catarrh'.[29] Jane's older daughter, Mary Jane Connor, arrived with her mother from Ireland when she was 2. Admitted to the Female Orphan School on arrival, she was there until February 1847 when she was discharged to her mother. Jane married in February 1848 but not long afterwards she was readmitted to the Cascades Female Factory for six months for disobedience of orders and disorderly conduct. It is not known what became of Mary Jane Connor, although she was apparently sent into service at a young age.[30]

Bell (or Isabella) Amos, from Fermanagh, was only 19 when she arrived in the colony. In February 1849, she gave birth to a son, Joseph Amos, at the Cascades Female Factory. He died there of 'convulsions' the following month.[31] An inquest into his death, held in March at the 'House of Correction for Females at the Cascades Hobart Town' concluded 'the said Joseph Amos being the infant child of Isabella Amos a Prisoner in the House of Correction … By the visitation of God in a natural way To wit of Convulsions did die'.[32] Joseph appears to have been Bell's only child.

## CHILDREN BORN IN THE LAUNCESTON FEMALE FACTORY

At least twenty-seven of the *Tasmania* (2) women were imprisoned in the Launceston Female Factory and ten children were born there, including a set of twins.

Sarah McArdle, transported for vagrancy, was in the Launceston Female Factory several times, having started her factory 'career' at Cascades not long after she left the *Anson*.[33] During the voyage to Van Diemen's Land, Sarah gave birth to a son, James, who did not survive: he died of 'gastro-enteritis' in January 1846.[34] Another son, Charles Lee McArdle, was born in July 1848 while Sarah was in private service in Launceston; he was 'received' at the Launceston House of Correction in September 1849.[35] Sarah's twins, James and Mary Ann, were born in the Launceston Female House of Correction in June 1851. Sarah married the month after her twins were born.[36] Her daughter lived only a few months, dying in the factory in October 1851. Sarah was not with her. The following day, she was charged with being drunk and sent to the factory for two months. Charles was admitted to the Male Orphan School when he was 4; his mother was undergoing a sentence in the house of correction. He was released to his mother from the school in March 1853. It is not clear what happened to James. Records relating to the birth of Sarah's children are confused and there are gaps in information: her son, Charles was recorded as James on Sarah's conduct record. There is no record of where he was for the first year of his life and why he was received into the house of correction when he was 14 months old.

Margaret Henry, Margaret Connor and Deborah Connor all gave birth to children in the Launceston Factory. Margaret Henry, who had also been in the Cascades Factory, gave birth to a son, James Henry, in February 1848.[37] Margaret Connor's daughter, Ellen, was born in March 1850; the child did not survive, dying in the factory shortly after birth.[38] Deborah Connor gave birth to a son, Francis, in August 1850.[39]

## CHILDREN BORN AT THE ROSS FEMALE FACTORY

In 1847, John Hampton, Comptroller General of Convicts, proposed establishing Ross Female Factory as a depot for pregnant women.[40] There had been increasing concern at high infant mortality rates at the Launceston and Cascades factories:

> There is no separate Nursery Establishment in Launceston, and the Female House of Correction there is so crowded by lying-in women and young children as to interfere very seriously with both the discipline and the health of the inmates, I ... intend to remove a number of these woman and children to Ross and ... to make Ross a depot for pregnant women.[41]

Better facilities, including three large nurseries and healthier nutrition, as well as the education of convict mothers in the care of their children, contributed to a lower infant mortality rate.[42] Two months after the Ross Female Factory opened, Hampton wrote:

> The healthy situation and pure atmosphere at Ross also render this newly-formed establishment peculiarly eligible for lying-in women, a considerable number of whom have already been moved there. Arrangements have been made, by the purchase of cows, and by the cultivation of the large vegetable garden attached to the station, to reduce the cost of the establishment and at the same time provide for the better maintenance of the inmates.[43]

Convict women were punished for not looking after children in their care. Others were placed in charge of the 'weaned' nursery.

Catherine Burnet, transported at the age of 18 from Tyrone, entered the Ross Female Factory not long after it opened in March 1848, and was in its hiring depot at least from June 1848, when she was sentenced to three days in the cells for misconduct. There is nothing on Catherine's conduct record to indicate when or why she was sent to the factory, although presumably she was waiting to be rehired. She was, however, in the early stages of pregnancy and her son George Burnet was born in the factory hospital in February 1849. Little George spent his entire life within the high walls of the factory compound, his only home the convict nursery, where he died on 31 December 1852 when he was almost 3. Perhaps he had not been transferred to the Orphan Schools, as he might have been when he turned 2, because he had never flourished. The wasting disease from which he died, marasmus, is caused by malnutrition or the inability to digest protein and since he should not have been malnourished on the diet in the nursery, his severe loss of body weight may have originated in problems which the factory's doctor could not identify or treat. Catherine was not in the factory when George died.[44]

In all, four women from the *Tasmania* (2) either gave birth in the Ross Female Factory or were accompanied by a child on admission.

Sarah Brennan, a housemaid, cook and laundress from Meath, was transported at the age of 29. In March 1849, while assigned to Kermode – presumably William Kermode of *Mona Vale* – Sarah was sentenced to seven days in the cells for not returning home at a reasonable time. She was sent to the Ross Female Factory, where her daughter, Sarah

Jane Brennan, was born on 16 December 1849. Sarah was most likely just pregnant when she was admitted to the factory, perhaps the result of not returning to the factory at a reasonable time! Sarah Jane was Sarah's third child: she brought a son, Joseph Rutherford, with her on board the *Tasmania* (2). Aged 2½, Joseph was separated from his mother on arrival and admitted to the Queen's Orphan Schools at New Town. He remained there for nearly eleven years until March 1856. Sarah's second child had been born in the Launceston Female Factory in 1847. Registered as William Brennan, he may be the child admitted to the Male Orphan School as Henry Brennan in June 1854, aged 7. He was there seven years. No record has been located for Sarah Jane Brennan after her birth at the Ross Female Factory.[45]

Margaret Meara – or O'Meara, ancestor of the late novelist Christopher Koch – was another who was admitted pregnant to the Ross Factory. Married in 1848, Margaret absconded three years later and was living in 'open adultery' with ex-convict John Nadin, a labourer from the north of England. In June 1851, Margaret was sentenced to eight months' imprisonment with hard labour in the Ross Factory for the two offences; John does not appear to have been punished. Margaret gave birth to a son, James Meara, in the Ross Factory in January 1852. She had already given birth to a son, John, in the Launceston Female Factory in February 1848, four months before she married; the only record of this child is on his mother's conduct

*Mona Vale* at the time Sarah Brennan was assigned to Kermode. (AUTAS0011126183300, reproduced with permission of the Tasmanian Archive and Heritage Office)

record. Less than two months after giving birth to James, Margaret was charged with neglecting a child committed to her care, but there is nothing to indicate who the child was. For this, she was sentenced to six months' imprisonment with hard labour. Three days later, she received thirty days in the cells for insubordination. Four days after this sentence, Margaret's infant son James, aged 2 months, died of 'convulsions'.[46]

In January 1848, Mary Russell gave birth to a son, Henry, in Hobart. By October 1848, Mary was in the Ross Factory; she was admonished for cruelly beating her child. The child was not named but given that Henry was just over 9 months old, and Mary does not appear to have had more children, it is probable that he accompanied her to the Ross Female Factory. After she left the factory, Mary Russell had no more colonial offences. She applied three times to marry different men but appears to have married none: she died as Mary Russell in November 1868. Henry has not been traced.

During an outbreak of disease at Ross in 1851–1852, 102 babies died. An enquiry found this loss was due to mismanagement and neglect.[47]

## ILLEGITIMATE CHILDREN

In the absence of detailed studies, it is difficult to establish whether colonial patterns of illegitimacy varied from those in the United Kingdom or Ireland.[48] It is impossible to say what determined the rate of illegitimate births in Van Diemen's Land: while social dislocation and sexual exploitation were undoubtedly factors, they were not solely responsible. Furthermore, an area yet to be explored by historians is the knowledge and practice of birth control by convict women.

In penal Van Diemen's Land, however, sexual behaviour was subject to a certain amount of official scrutiny. When the women were under sentence, pregnancy was difficult to conceal. In addition, it had an impact on women's ability to work and so the women were punished for becoming pregnant. Convict women were also valued as 'economic reproducers'.[49] Illegitimacy, to a certain extent, appears to have been accepted as part and parcel of the convict system.

It was the sexual behaviour and the alleged immorality of the convict women that was in question, not the fact that they had given birth to an illegitimate child.[50] The records of the convict women in Van Diemen's Land were marked 'delivered of an illegitimate child', but this seems to have been more a matter of administrative necessity than social comment.

The recording of the births of legitimate children of convict women under sentence was sometimes similarly annotated. In some instances, when the mother had married and the child was legitimate, her record stated 'delivered of a legitimate child', perhaps indicating that the status of the child was of concern to the government authorities, most likely for financial reasons. While illegitimacy was not condoned, it did not result in the same social stigma or loss of character leading to inability to obtain secure employment as it did in contemporary Britain.[51] It is not surprising, then, that some convict women had more than one illegitimate child.

## CHILDREN IN THE ORPHAN SCHOOLS

Not only illegitimate children of convict women were admitted to the Orphan Schools. Other children were also admitted, usually because they were destitute, due to the death, illness, imprisonment or desertion of one or both of their parents. Some of the children spent considerable time in the Orphan Schools before being reunited with their mothers. Others, like William Butler, were never reunited.

Queen's Orphan School, New Town, c. 1859. (AUTAS001126252212, reproduced with permission of the Tasmanian Archive and Heritage Office)

St Joseph's Orphanage Hobart. (Reference: H22406, reproduced with permission of the State Library of Victoria)

The Orphan Schools (by then known as the Queen's Asylum for Destitute Children) closed in May 1879. Ellen Johnson, daughter of Mary Salmon or Lyons, was one of the last remaining residents. Admitted in May 1879, Ellen transferred the same day to St Joseph's Orphanage, run by the Sisters of Charity, in Hobart. In May 1881, she was sent to Mrs Dalton in Lansdowne Crescent, West Hobart.

Tracing the children admitted to the Queen's Orphan Schools is complicated by variations in names and discrepancies in ages.

## LARGE FAMILIES

Some of the *Tasmania* women produced large colonial families. Eliza Davis had nine children from two marriages.

One of the biggest families was that of Bridget Gallagher.[52] Transported when she was 19, Bridget was sentenced to transportation for seven years for stealing potatoes. She was from Cavan; she could not read or write and was Roman Catholic. She was tried with her mother Rose Fitzpatrick, who was 45. Bridget's aunt Ann Fitzpatrick and her older brother James Donovan were also transported.[53] Bridget married William Peter Briggs in 1848.[54] Bridget and William had twelve children between 1849 and 1870. All but two survived: Henry died of 'convulsions' in 1854 when he was a month old and Edward died of pneumonia only a few days after his first birthday in 1860.[55]

In what was perhaps a patriotic twist, Bridget's last two children were called Albert and Victoria. Bridget died in 1876 and William, who was one of ten children, had five more children with his second wife, Matilda or Tilly (*née* Knapper). Bridget's daughter, Elizabeth Mary 'Lily' Wignall, also had twelve children.

Ann Delany, a nursemaid from County Kildare, was transported at the age of 17 for stealing potatoes. She married George Hooper,

Sarah Hughes *née* Eastwood, daughter of Eliza Davis. (Courtesy of Bryan Lucas)

a cabinet turner aged 26, in Hobart in February 1848. Their eldest child, George, was born five months later. Ann and George had eleven children between 1848 and 1868.[56]

Alice Jones *née* Eastwood, daughter of Eliza Davis. (Courtesy of Bryan Lucas)

Mary Burgess, one of the Tullow women, married Thomas Jones, a convict who arrived on the *London* in 1844. Mary was 19 when she married; her husband, a cabinetmaker, was 32.[57] Mary and Thomas had eleven children. Their first child, Amy, was born in Hobart in 1850.[58] Thomas established a successful cabinetmaking business in Launceston and the family moved there shortly after Amy's birth (and after Mary had been granted a certificate of freedom). Their remaining children were born in Launceston from 1852 to 1876.[59] Amy Jones married Richard Harvey Ferrall in 1872; they had ten children.[60]

Mary McBride was another who had a large family. Mary's story highlights the fragility and vulnerability of colonial childhood. Mary, a pass-holder aged 22, married Robert McLeod, aged 30, in Christ Church, Longford.[61] Mary and Robert had a family of twelve, including three sets of twins, on their small parcel of land at Carrick. Two children did not survive infancy: Robert died in Longford of 'inflammation of the chest' before his second birthday.[62] Mary's first set of twins, John and Thomas, were born in the district of Longford in 1851.[63] Of the twins, only Thomas survived; he

Harriet Whitton *née* Eastwood, daughter of Eliza Davis. (Courtesy of Bryan Lucas)

later worked and lived on the Woolmers Estate at Longford – he was living there at the time of the marriage of his brother Daniel in 1884.[64] John, nearly 3, accidentally drowned.[65] Another son named Robert was born after John died.[66] At this time, the family were living at Emu Bay where the father was a farmer. Not long after the birth of twins in 1855, the family moved back to Norfolk Plains (Longford).[67] A son, Henry, was born there in 1858.[68] Another son ,William, was born about 1859 followed by another set of twins, Florence Lydia and Roland, about 1865.[69].

Hannah Chatwin *née* Eastwood, daughter of Eliza Davis, with infant Athol Kemp. (Courtesy of Bryan Lucas)

Daughter Ellen was born in 1868 and the youngest child, Annie Eva, was born about 1878.[70] Mary's three surviving children, Thomas, Mary (Rose) and Daniel, produced thirty grandchildren for her. The next generation also produced large families: Thomas and his wife Mary Ann (*née* Bresnehan) had ten children; all but two survived infancy. Mary (Rose) and her husband James Maher also had ten children, including twins. Daniel and his wife Lydia (Davis) had eleven children; one daughter, Dorothy Ilene, died as an infant.[71]

Amos Eastwood, son of Eliza Davis. (Courtesy of Bryan Lucas)

Alice Carroll *née* Jones and family in New Zealand. (Courtesy of Kevin Reed)

Catherine Grace brought three young daughters with her from Ireland – a son, James, died as a baby. Catherine was one of the first of the *Tasmania* (2) women to start a family in Van Diemen's Land. Her husband Pierce was also transported and the couple were reunited in the colony, although their Irish children were sent to the Female Orphan School on arrival. Their son John was born in the female factory in 1847 but was baptised Phillip in St Joseph's Church, Hobart, when he was 3 days old. He was known as Pierce or Pierre. In December 1848, a son, John Whelan Grace, was baptised in St John's Church, Richmond.[72] (Catherine's family name was Whelan.) A daughter, Eliza, was born in 1851 at New Town. She was followed by Michael in 1853 and William Patrick in 1855.[73] The family eventually settled at Port Cygnet and had land at Glaziers Bay. After some skirmishes with the law, they became quietly respectable.[74] Catherine Grace died of cancer at Port Cygnet on 16 August 1887, aged 71.[75] In March 1890, her husband Pierce died in the New Town Charitable Institution, where he had been since 1888.[76]

Colonial family life was fragile. Catherine Grace's grandchildren died in tragic circumstances in 1879:

> The Graces, an industrious young couple, live at Glazier's Bay, and, on Saturday last, Grace being absent at his work in the bush, Mrs. Grace left the hut about 4 o'clock in the afternoon to pick raspberries, leaving the three children shut up in the hut. The youngest, a female 6 months old, in bed; the others, a male and a female, aged 1 year and 9 months, and 3 years, playing about the floor. Mrs. Grace was about 300 yards away at work, and had not been absent over twenty minutes, when she was alarmed by hearing some neighbours shouting. Upon going up to her hut she found it enveloped in flames and partly on the ground. After the fire had abated sufficiently to allow a search, what remained of the three children was found, the two eldest near where the door was, the infant in the smouldering remains of the bed-clothes. Mrs. Grace states there was no fire when she left the hut, but it is probable there might have been some live embers under the ashes. The fire was first observed near the chimney. The building was a two-roomed hut. A verdict of accidentally burned was recorded.[77]

Family information was often recorded on the convict indent; this provides a record of relatives left behind. Families were an important part of the convict experience yet there has been very little research done on convict families, the families left behind and colonial families. Convict families

Woolmers Estate, 2011. (Authors' collection)

were created in three ways: firstly, children left behind and later sent for; second children accompanying convict parents; and, third, children born in Van Diemen's Land or other colonies. There were also various arrangements of family structure, with some families resembling modern, 'blended' families.

When she arrived in the colony, Mary Meaghar, aged 46, stated that she was a widow with ten children. She was tried in Tipperary for stealing sheep with her son and father-in-law. She was well conducted in the colony and in August 1847 she married convict John Steambridge, a shoe- and boot-maker who arrived on the *Lord Lyndoch* in 1841.[78] Just over two years later, Mary successfully applied for a free passage for her family, which consisted of Ellen, 18; William, 14, Bridget, 12, and Michael (age not recorded). They were living in Castle Town, Tipperary. It is possible that only Ellen and Michael came to the colony but the evidence is not certain.[79] John Steambridge left the colony in July 1853 and Mary has not been traced beyond 1849.[80]

As the Molesworth Committee recognised, exile caused the greatest pain for convicts.[81] The impact of psychological factors – 'feelings, emotions, dignity, social and cultural ties, love of place …'[82] – cannot be overestimated. The psychological dislocation that formed a fundamental part of the migrant experience applied also to convicts: 'Uprooting from one's homeland is often a traumatic experience … leaving the stability of one's own parish or town, cutting one's ties with a supportive network of family and friends ...'[83] Families were recreated in Van Diemen's Land, despite the difficulties and heartache caused by the removal and institutionalisation of children. The women had no say in the removal of the children they had brought with them; many were not reunited. Some women had family members living in the colony and there is some evidence that they maintained family links. Others formed strong bonds with their shipmates. Many new families were created in Van Diemen's Land. Above all, a study of the families of the *Tasmania* (2) demonstrates the importance of not categorising the women as 'good' or 'bad' mothers: their family experiences were diverse and complex, as were those of their children.

# 12

# Journey's End

For a large part of their lives in Van Diemen's Land, Eliza Davis and Margaret Butler were all but invisible in the records. As with many working-class women, they left no written records. Unlike many of their shipmates, they had no contact with the law or institutions, both rich sources of information about individual lives. Only from the records of birth, death and marriage can a little of Eliza and Margaret's colonial lives be gleaned.

The deaths of Eliza Davis and Margaret Butler could not have been more different. Eliza died at home with her family; Margaret Butler was beaten to death by her colonial husband.

Eliza died of 'cerebral apoplexy' (a stroke) at Emu Bay on 19 October 1898.[1] She married Amos Eastwood the week before her death, almost forty years after the birth of their first child.[2] Eliza was remembered as an esteemed member of her community:

> A very old resident of Burnie in the person of Mrs. Amos Eastwood passed away at her late residence on Wednesday morning. Deceased, who had reached the advanced age of 78 years, had been failing in health for some time, and a short while back was attacked with paralysis, from which she never recovered. Her demise is regretted by a large circle of friends, as she was universally liked and respected.[3]

In contrast, Margaret died at the hands of her husband, John Shakleton. She died in hospital and her only memorial were the gruesome details of her post mortem and inquest in several local newspapers.[4]

John Shakleton arrived on the *Marquis of Hastings* (2) in 1842. He was a 42-year-old drover and waggoner, from Yorkshire. Margaret Butler married John in 1850 in St Joseph's Church, Hobart. Two years later

John was awarded his free certificate. After little more than five years of marriage, on Sunday 4 November 1855, Margaret Butler died in the Colonial Hospital of fractures and contusions to most of her body. It was just over ten years since Margaret had left Ireland. Her son, William, had left the colony eight years before and her daughter, Mary Ann, aged 11, was once again admitted to the Female Orphan School.

John was a large man – his convict conduct record described him as 'stout made' – and he was over 5ft 9in tall. Margaret, on the other hand, was barely 5ft and no match for his strength. John had cruelly beaten Margaret on Monday 29 October 1855 at their Hobart home. She was admitted to hospital on Friday 2 November and she died a slow and painful death there on the evening of Sunday 4 November.[5]

Margaret Butler's inquest was held on 7 November 1855:

> Yesterday, an inquest was held at Mr. Parson's, the Waterman's Arms, Liverpool-street, before A.B. Jones, Esq, coroner, to enquire into the death of Margaret Snackleton [sic], who died on Sunday evening last, in Her Majesty's General Hospital, from injuries supposed to have been inflicted by her husband …
>
> Before the jury proceeded to view the body the coroner said that it might be expedient to adjourn the inquiry to another day; it was not necessary to mention the cause, except that it was to further the ends of justice. The jury then proceeded to the Colonial Hospital to view the body of the deceased. It exhibited the appearance of having been severely beaten—on the face, neck, and upper part of the body being one mass of bruises, and the upper part of the left humerus being fractured.

Margaret's young daughter, Mary Ann Butler, 'a girl of 10 years of age', appeared at the inquest, stating that:

> she was at her mother's house on Sunday week, when she told her that Shackleton had beat her; they appeared on good terms that day; there were other persons in the house, who were drunk, as was deceased; witness saw the deceased on Friday, who told her that Shackleton had beaten her.

Witness Mary Ann Ward testified that she had known Margaret for two years, and that she lived next door to her in Lansdowne Crescent. On 29 October, a neighbour called and asked her:

for God's sake … go to Shackleton's, as John was beating his wife. Witness went there and found the deceased standing naked outside the door. She said, "see how John has been beating me." Witness asked him, why had he done so, when he replied, that he had given the deceased a pound on Saturday to procure some things, and she had not even provided a dinner for Sunday. Witness saw a woman named Steward [sic] put some clothes on the deceased, and did not see her again until Friday, when she said to witness—"Jack has beaten and killed me" … She told witness that Jack would give her nothing to eat or drink … witness took her some tea, and bread and butter, and went for Dr Stokell. Witness afterwards saw Shackleton feeding the deceased with gruel and marmalade. Dr Stokell told her she would soon be well. Shackleton told witness that if his wife got over this, he would never beat her again, but would go out of the country; he would pay a woman £1 a week to wait upon her, rather than she should go to the hospital. The deceased and Shackleton both drank, and regularly on Saturday, Sunday and Monday. When they were drinking they were always quarrelling.

A member of the jury asked Mary Ann Ward whether Margaret was drunk when she was standing naked in the road; Mary Ann Ward replied that she could not say because 'she was covered in blood'.

At the inquest, several other neighbours testified to the couple's violent relationship. Angelina Stewart heard cries of murder in Shackleton's house and when she went there, she saw Margaret on the floor and Shackleton standing over her, striking her with his fists: 'he said he would kill her, if he got seven years for it'. On another occasion, she had seen Shackleton strike Margaret 'two or three times, across the mouth' and heard him threaten to kill her.

Angelina's husband, Joseph Stewart, was returning from the bush with a load of wood when his wife called out to him to go to Shackleton's because he was beating his wife. He saw Margaret lying on the floor in her chemise: 'Shackleton tore it off, and kicked her'. Stewart and his wife took Margaret from the house, covering her with a blanket, and Stewart 'fastened' Shackleton in the house.

Another witness, gardener Lawrence Benson, was at work on Monday at half past twelve when he heard Shackleton making 'a great noise' and 'cries of murder'. He saw Margaret outside, naked. She asked Benson if she could hide in his water closet to get away from her husband. He later saw her crawl into a gutter. He saw Margaret again on Friday, 'crippled up in bed', and he asked Shackleton how it had happened: 'he replied that he had been working all day on Monday at Kangaroo Point, and when he returned he found his wife under the fence'.

Dr Downing conducted a post mortem on Margaret's body. At the inquest, he stated:

> that he was house surgeon to Her Majesty's General Hospital; the deceased was admitted into that institution on the evening of 2nd November, labouring from the effects of injuries received five days before; witness found extensive bruises on various parts of her body, especially on the head, face and eyes; the scalp, also, was much bruised, and exhibited some bloody tumours; the left humerus (the upper part of the arm) was fractured; the pulse was low and feeble, and the surface of the body was cold; the patient was sensible at times, but required rousing; she slept during the night, but was occasionally delirious; witness was called to her next morning, when he found her worse, and sinking rapidly; she did not rally, and died at seven o'clock on Sunday evening. A *post mortem* examination was made sixty-five hours after death; the surface of the body was bruised, and there were scratches on both hands …

Dr Downing noted that Margaret's liver had the nutmeg appearance of that of an alcoholic: she was of 'a debilitated constitution from dissipated habits of hard drinking, and the injuries had taken greater effect than if she had been in a healthy state'. He thought that her head injuries were sufficient to cause death 'by concussion of the brain'.

Dr Downing was the first of several medical witnesses. Dr F.G. Brock, the surgeon in charge of Her Majesty's Hospital, mostly concurred with Dr Downing but attributed Margaret's death to the shock given to her nervous system and not concussion of the brain.

Dr W.L. Crowther and Dr Stokell had both visited Margaret before she died. Dr Crowther testified he had been called by a man in Bathurst Street [*sic*] to see his wife, who had been drinking and fighting with the neighbours. Crowther found Margaret in bed, suffering from great pain from injuries on several parts of her body, which he believed had been caused by a severe beating. He asked Margaret, in front of Shackleton and another witness, Mrs Ward, how the injuries had been caused; Margaret hesitated but Mrs Ward replied that Margaret's husband had beaten her and turned her out of the house naked on Monday night; 'the man did not deny it'.

He believed the injuries were inflicted by a severe beating with a fist while Margaret was lying on the ground. He considered her to be in great danger of dying. He informed the police and had Margaret taken to hospital. Dr Crowther described Shackleton as 'a tall, sharp-featured man, red-faced with light hair'.

Dr Stokell visited Margaret at her residence in Lansdowne Crescent. She told him that her husband had beaten her but she refused to go to hospital. Dr Stokell testified that 'the fracture of the arm could not have been caused by a blow from a fist but it could have been caused by a kick with a boot'.[6]

John Shackleton, described as an 'atrocious brute', was found guilty of manslaughter and the coroner issued a warrant for his arrest on that charge. A month later, it was reported that he had been apprehended by Constable Gordon and lodged in Her Majesty's Gaol:

> John Shackleton, the fellow taken into custody on the Coroner's warrant, on a charge of manslaughter by kicking and beating his wife to death, was also arraigned on the more serious charge of murder. The prisoner was found guilty of manslaughter, and was sentenced to be transported for life.[7]

This was John Shackleton's third sentence of transportation. He had previously been transported for seven years for stealing potatoes and, in 1842, for ten years for stealing cotton cloth. As already mentioned, it was possible to have more than one sentence of transportation. No details of Shackleton's first transportation sentence have been uncovered, except that, according to his conduct record in 1842, he served three years of this sentence at the penitentiary in England.[8]

In the Supreme Court on 4 December 1855, 'John Shakleton, charged with the wilful murder of Margaret Shakleton, his wife, on the 3rd November pleaded not guilty'.[9] Shakleton was sent to Port Arthur for manslaughter.[10]

A man named John 'Shackelton', a labourer aged 83, died of 'senilis' (old age) at the Brickfields Pauper Establishment in Hobart on 7 April 1870.[11] He was probably Margaret Butler's widower.

A study of the deaths of the women and children who arrived on the *Tasmania* (2) – looking at their age at death, where and how they died, where they were buried and how they were remembered – reveals aspects of their colonial experience, their living conditions and their relationships. The inquest for Judith Dooling or Dowling, for example, shows that she was living in a timber hut when she was accidentally killed.[12] The inquest of Margaret Butler 2nd reveals that she was living in a violent relationship but that she had retrieved her daughter from the Female Orphan School. Mary Russell's inquest revealed that she was in a long-term *de facto* relationship.[13] Snippets like this shed light on the lives of individual convict women.

Of the 138 convict women who sailed on the *Tasmania* (2), deaths have been found for approximately fifty-four women (39 per cent). Lack of evidence or discrepancies in the records make certainty difficult in some instances: Sarah Ryan, for example, married John Turnbull and may have died as Sarah Turnbull in April 1856 but there are some discrepancies which make it difficult to be sure that she is the *Tasmania* (2) convict.[14]

Age at death (or the age given at any other time) cannot always be relied on. Incorrect ages on death certificates can also make it difficult to find deaths for the women. Ages were often provided by someone who did not know the person well: for example, a hospital registrar, coroner or undertaker.

Surprisingly, given the harsh conditions that characterised the lives of many of the women, several lived a long time: Mary McBride, a thief from County Down, was 85 when she died from 'senility' (old age) and 'exhaustion' in the Launceston Invalid Depot in 1907.[15] Harriet Madine, another thief from County Down, was 84 when she died in 1898 in the Benevolent Asylum in Launceston.[16]

If transportation provided a chance at a better life, as some have suggested, some of the women had no opportunity to test this theory. Several died before they had any hope of starting a new life. Ellen Sullivan, as already noted, died during the voyage, but there were others who died shortly after arriving in the colony.[17]

## DIED UNDER SENTENCE

Of the *Tasmania* (2) women, at least seven died, usually in one of the colonial institutions, before regaining their freedom. Convicts became free by serving their sentence (free by servitude) or by receiving a conditional or absolute pardon. For some of these women, only the basic details of the circumstances of their deaths were recorded. Mary McVeagh, for example, simply had 'dead' starkly stated on her convict conduct record.[18] Similarly, Anne Mullan's conduct record bluntly stated, 'Died Cascades Factory 11 February 1847', with no other details.[19] The conduct record of

Mary McVeagh's conduct record. (TAHO, CON41/1/8, reproduced with permission of the Tasmanian Archive and Heritage Office)

Catherine Foy, transported at the age of 22, stated 'Died 23 March 1851 at the General Hospital Hobart'.[20]

Two women died on board the *Anson*, moored in the River Derwent: Mary Murphy died on 9 January 1846 and Fanny Doherty died on 26 March 1846. Their inquests were held on board the *Anson*. In Mary Murphy's case, the inquest determined that she died 'by the visitation of God in a natural way to wit, from inflammation of the lungs'.[21]

Three witnesses testified at the inquest. The first was Dr Edmund Bowden Esq.,[22] superintendent on the *Anson*, who stated:

I am a legally qualified medical practitioner. I knew the deceased Mary Murphy, a Prisoner of the Crown serving Probation on board this vessel of which I have the charge. She has been on board about a month, she was ailing when received. She was taken into Hospital a few days after suffering from cough and inflammation of the lungs. She was treated by me for that disease. She continued in Hospital up to the ninth instant when she died of natural causes, inflammation of the lungs. The Government allows every sort of medical comfort on board. I am not under any restriction as to what I give.[23]

The next to testify was Mrs Margaret Power who stated:

I am a Warder on board the Anson and have charge of the sick. I knew the deceased Mary Murphy, she has been in Hospital since the second day she came on board this vessel. She was treated by Dr Bowden up to the time of her death, he saw her everyday and frequently twice. She received everything she required and expressed her [thanks] of the kindness shewn her by everyone and more especially by Dr and Mrs. Bowden. I never heard her make any complaint.[24]

The last testimony was that of Margaret Newman, 'a Prisoner of the Crown and nurse' in the hospital on the *Anson*, who cared for Mary. Her evidence was similar to that of the other two.[25]

Fanny Doherty, transported from Londonderry at the age of 27, died in March 1846 on board the *Anson*. She was taken from there to the General Hospital and then buried in the ground of the prisoners' barracks in Hobart on 31 March.[26] An inquest into her death was held on 28 March.[27] Dr Bowden and Margaret Power both gave evidence to the inquest, which determined that Fanny died 'by the Visitation of God in a natural way'.

Dr Bowden testified:

I am a legally qualified Medical Practitioner and have charge of the Prisoners in her Majesty's ship Anson. The deceased Fanny Dogherty was one of these prisoners. She came in the Tasmania the second. She had been here about four months, her age was about twenty seven, she died on the twenty sixth instant of dysentery. She was admitted at first into the Hospital on the eleventh of January the first time and was under my charge. She was discharged convalescent on the sixth of February. She was readmitted on the tenth of the same

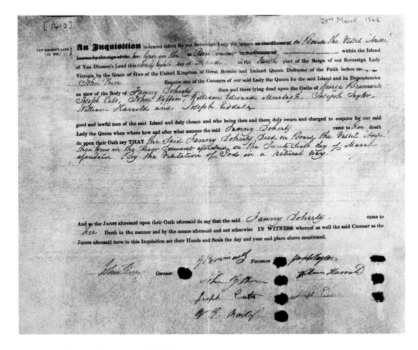

Inquest of Mary Murphy. (TAHO, SC195/1/17 Inquest 1384, p.1, reproduced with permission of the Tasmanian Archive and Heritage Office)

Inquest of Fanny Doherty. (TAHO, SC195/1/17 Inquest 1410, p. 1, reproduced with permission of the Tasmanian Archive and Heritage Office)

month suffering under the same symptoms ... She was of consump-
tive habit and was occasionally better but ultimately weak under
the dysentery. I saw her daily whilst in Hospital, she had everything
necessary and proper for her. I am in no way restricted as to the
medical comforts required.[28]

The hospital warder on the *Anson*, Margaret Power, testified:

I knew the deceased Fanny Dogherty, she has been under my charge
with the intermission of three or four days since the eleventh of January
last during that period she was attended by Dr Bowden, he saw her
once every day and latterly twice. I never heard her make any complaint
during her illness, she had everything she could wish for. We are not
restricted in any way in the Hospital here under the direction of the
Doctor, the patients obtain all they wish.[29]

Mary McManus was another who died under sentence. She died on
New Year's Eve 1850, six weeks after she married.[30]

Mary Hetherington died in hospital on 1 April 1847 and was buried in
the grounds of the prisoners' barracks in Hobart.[31]

## CAUSE OF DEATH

Cause of death can shed light on a convict's way of life and standard of living.
It can be difficult, however, to determine and classify cause of death.[32] It was
not always recorded. Until 1895 in Tasmania, certification of cause of death
by a registered medical practitioner was not legally required.[33] Even when a
cause of death was recorded, detail was often sparse.

In her study of death in colonial Tasmania, Rebecca Kippen suggested
the following as significant causes of mortality: disease of the respiratory
system and tuberculosis; diseases of the circulatory system; old age and
decay; and accidents.[34]

In some instances, multiple causes of death were recorded: for example,
Ann Mallon, a farmer's widow aged 76, died on 2 November 1891 from
'senility and bronchitis' at Deloraine.[35]

From time to time, an inquest was held to determine cause of death.
There was an inquest, for example, into the death of Mary Russell, who
passed away at her home on the Swamp in Launceston at the age of 47

in November 1868.[36] The inquest on 7 November determined that she died of natural causes.[37] The *Cornwall Chronicle* reported the details of the inquest, starting with Mary's *de facto* husband Samuel Leonard:

> Samuel Leonard deposed—I am a carpenter, and reside on the Swamp. The body of the woman shown to the jury in my presence is that of Mary Russell, who lived with me as my wife for the last 15 or 16 years. She was a single woman and I am a single man. She was 47 years of age. I last saw her alive a little after 1 o'clock yesterday, at her own residence. She had been ill for a length of time; she had not been confined to bed but used to lie down occasionally for an hour or two. Yesterday she complained of a tightness in the chest. About 16 months ago she was an out-patient of the Hospital. She has never since had any medical adviser. About breakfast time she complained of being ill, and I sent for Dr Ranson, who wrote a prescription, which I took to Messrs. Hatton and Laws. I got it made up, and brought it home about 2 o'clock, and when I returned she was lying in the gateway apparently lifeless. I called my neighbours, and Messrs. Clayfield and Chandler come, and we took deceased into the house. I sent for Dr Ranson and he sent a message to say it was useless for him to come. Deceased was in the habit of drinking beer to excess. She told me she had applied to Mr. Marrison on Saturday night, and she brought home some medicine, which she took. On Tuesday she brought some more pills and liquid in a phial; I have some of the liquid left.

Evidence was also given by the chemist, who outlined the treatment he had provided, adding 'Deceased appeared to be suffering from heart disease, but he did not like to tell her lest it should alarm her'! The doctor who visited Mary thought perhaps the medication she received might have contributed to her symptoms – that is, rapid pulse, 'great disturbance of the heart action' and difficulty breathing – but so would heart disease. He had declined to visit Mary again: 'the man who brought the message to him told him that the woman was quite dead'. The jury's verdict was that Mary died of natural causes.[38]

Often the doctor with his limited knowledge could only describe the cause of death as a fever, apoplexy or convulsions or what was visible, such as a head wound, or evidence of a lifestyle, such as over-indulgence of drink. Where death was inexplicable, the cause of death was often described as 'a Visitation of God'. It later came to mean that the person died of natural causes.[39]

## ILLNESS AND DISEASE

The most common cause of death among the *Tasmania* (2) women was some form of respiratory illness, including tuberculosis and phthisis (pulmonary tuberculosis). At least nine women died from respiratory illness. Four died from 'phthisis' or 'phthisis pulmonalis'.[40] Mary Cann (*née* Byrne), an engineer's wife aged 38, died of consumption in 1858.[41]

Mary Burgess, transported at the age of 18, died on 31 March 1898 as Mary Jones. She was a widow aged 68 and died of pneumonia.[42] Her mother, Esther Burgess, died in 1855 from 'a rupture of a blood vessel in the left lung'.[43]

Several women died because they were simply worn out. Officially, they died from debility, old age and decay. Debility was generally defined as a weakness or lack of strength, uniform exhaustion of all the organs of the body without specific disease.[44] Eliza Hunter, a house servant aged 50, died of 'debilitas' in 1854 in the Colonial Hospital Hobart.[45] Her new life had taken its toll after less than ten years in the colony.

Often, old age and debility went hand in hand: a possible death for Ann Fitzpatrick is that of a widow of that name who died of 'old age and debility' in 1865, aged 74.[46]

At least three of the *Tasmania* (2) women died from a form of cancer. Sarah McGinley died as Sarah Pritchard, a labourer's wife aged 63, in Oatlands in 1881. She had 'cancer of the breast'.[47] Mary McCarthy died as Mary Kent, a labourer's wife aged 55, in Hobart in 1884. She had 'cancer of [the] tongue and mouth'.[48] In 1889, Ann Flood died of 'epithalamia and stricture of [the] oesophagus'.[49]

Only one childbirth-related death has been located for the *Tasmania* (2) women. Catherine McNally or Shaw, a shoemaker's wife aged 28, died in childbirth on 23 March 1853 in Launceston.[50] Her son lived only an hour, dying from 'convulsions'.[51]

## ALCOHOL-RELATED DEATHS

Interestingly, given the place of alcohol in colonial society and the number of drink-related offences committed by the *Tasmania* (2) women, only a handful appear to have died from alcohol-related conditions. However, as Kippen noted, alcohol, like suicide, syphilis and tuberculosis, falls into the category of stigmatised causes of death. In 1858, Hobart medical practitioner Edward Swarbreck Hall noted that death from alcoholism was under-reported:

> Except from the Public Hospitals, this cause of death is scarcely ever registered. Private persons will not record a cause of death so disgraceful to their friends or relatives. Intemperance forms, directly or indirectly, a very large portion of adult deaths.[52]

As already noted, alcohol played a large part in the violent death of Margaret Butler at the hands of her husband. Alcohol was also mentioned as a factor in the death of Mary Russell: her *de facto* husband testified at her inquest that Mary was 'in the habit of drinking beer to excess'.[53]

## ACCIDENTAL DEATH AND SUICIDE

At least two of the *Tasmania* (2) women died accidentally. Mary Hurley, who was granted a ticket of leave, was found drowned in October 1850 in the River Derwent near the bathing house on the Government Domain.[54] The *Courier* reported the inquest into her death:

> INQUEST.—On the 3rd instant, inquest was held at the Gordon Castle, Liverpool-street, on the body of Mary Hurley, ticket-of-leave, who was found drowned in the Government Domain, near the bathing-house, the previous morning. Verdict—Found drowned, and no evidence to show in what way she came into the water.[55]

Judith Dooling or Dowling was living at Jerusalem (now Colebrook) near Richmond when she was accidentally killed in June 1856.[56] An inquest into her death determined that she died when timber in a shed on James Corrigan's property at Altamont fell on her.[57] Judith had been tried with her son, John, who was crippled. He was murdered on the Richmond Road three years after his mother died.[58]

## PLACE OF DEATH

There is no evidence that any of the *Tasmania* (2) women returned to Ireland. In theory, those who were free by servitude (or had been granted an absolute pardon) could return, but practically it was difficult. Perhaps some of those who cannot be traced successfully returned home.

Like many convict women, some women of the *Tasmania* (2) died in penal and colonial institutions. These institutions included the colonial hospitals, the Cascades Female Factory, the Launceston Female Factory, the New Norfolk Asylum, the New Town Charitable Institution and various invalid depots.[59]

At least five *Tasmania* (2) women died in hospital in Hobart; some were still under sentence. Mary Hetherington, from Galway, died in April 1847. She was 25.[60] Mary Gillespie, a thief from Londonderry, died in September 1850 in the Colonial Hospital, Hobart. She was 42.[61] Maria Johnson, transported from Dublin when she was 24, died in the General Hospital in February 1870. Free by servitude, she was admitted with 'phthisis pulmonalis' from Franklin as Maria Johnson 'ux' Derbyshire.[62]

Others died in penal or charitable institutions. Anne Mullan, originally from Woolwich but tried in Antrim, was less than a week into a two-month sentence with hard labour for misconduct at the Cascades Female Factory when she died there, aged about 28.[63]

Charitable institutions were a response to an increasing number of paupers. In southern Tasmania, pauper invalids, the aged, infirm and 'incurables' were separated from the existing general hospital population and accommodated

Colonial (General) Hospital Hobart, J.W. Beattie, 'Colonial Hospital, Liverpool Street, main entrance', 1880. (W.L. Crowther Library, reproduced with permission of the Tasmanian Archive and Heritage Office)

in separate institutions.[64] Increasingly, there was pressure on existing facilities because of the number of aged ex-convicts who had no family support. Conditions were generally unsuitable for aged care or care of the chronically ill, as Brown, writing about the invalid depot on the site of the former Cascades Female Factory, highlighted:

New Town Charitable Institution (Women's Division). (TAHO, PH30/1/7641, reproduced with permission of the Tasmanian Archive and Heritage Office)

> This old female prison, damp and depressing, was a most unsuitable building for old people suffering from rheumatism and respiratory diseases, the most common conditions on admission.[65]

The New Town Charitable Institution, also known as the New Town Pauper Establishment, was founded in 1874 to care for the aged poor, many

Holyrood, home of Mary Jones, Launceston. (Courtesy of Kevin Reed)

of whom were former convicts. It separated male and female residents.[66] Before that, invalids and paupers were housed in unsuitable buildings at Port Arthur, the Cascades, the Brickfields and the Launceston depots.

In the north, from 1895, the Launceston Benevolent Society operated the Launceston Benevolent Asylum.[67] At least three of the *Tasmania* (2) women died there in the 1890s. Mary Salmon, a domestic aged 66, died as Mary Salmon or Kewley in 1896.[68] Ellen Maguire, a domestic aged 77, died as Ellen Gregory in 1897.[69] Harriet Madine, a domestic aged 84, died as Harriet Vernon in 1898.[70] Ellen and Harriet both died of 'senility'; Mary died of 'apoplexy'.

By the 1890s, the *Launceston Examiner* was publishing monthly reports of those in the Benevolent Asylum, including those who died there. In November 1897, Ellen Gregory, 'native of Ireland', aged 72, appeared in the lists.[71] According to her death certificate, she was a domestic aged 77 and she died of 'senility'.[72]

As noted elsewhere, at least five of the *Tasmania* (2) women died in the 'Hospital for the Insane' at New Norfolk.[73]

Margaret Kelly, described as 'a poor imbecilic helpless creature … dirty in her habits and tottering on her feet … and doubtless, the victim of intemperance', was admitted to the asylum with 'amentia' in 1856. She died there in the same year, aged 55.[74]

Not all of the women died in institutions. As with Eliza Davis, some of the women died at home, surrounded by family. Mary Cann (*née* Byrne) died at home in Harrington Street, Hobart.[75] Bridget Briggs (*née* Gallagher) died at home in Francis Street, Battery Point in 1876.[76] Mary Jones (*née* Burgess), a widow aged 68, died at home at Invermay in 1898.[77]

## WILLS, PROBATE AND LETTERS OF ADMINISTRATION

In the same way as headstones and published funeral notices, wills served as an indication of wealth and status. Most people who owned land or other substantial assets had a will. However, if they died intestate with property, probate or letters of administration could be sought through the courts.

The only will located for a *Tasmania* (2) woman was for Mary Jones (*née* Burgess), transported at the age of 18. Mary was a beneficiary of her husband's will and in turn made a will of her own. In her will, she left a parcel of land in York Street, Launceston (now prime real estate), to her son, Alfred. She left property to her daughters Clara Thureau and Amy

Bridget Gallagher's headstone. (Authors'
collection)

Reinterment of Judith Dowling, 2015.
(Courtesy of Brian Andrews)

Headstone of Judith Dowling, Colebrook (formerly Jerusalem), 2013. (Authors'
collection)

Ferrall. Her plate, linen, china, glass, books, pictures, and other household effects were bequeathed to her daughter Alice Carroll. Her remaining four children each received £500 with the residue to be divided equally amongst all her children. Mary was a wealthy women when she died but she still signed her mark [x].[78]

## REMEMBERING THE DEAD

Few burial places for the *Tasmania* (2) women have been located and even fewer headstones have been found. Headstones were often expensive and a sign of status and depended upon a surviving family member or friend being able to mark the grave. Many of the women were buried in unmarked or pauper graves. Not all unmarked graves, however, were

Headstone of Judith Dowling, relocated 2015. (Courtesy of Brian Andrews)

paupers' plots. Fanny Doherty and Mary Hetherington were buried in unmarked graves in the Prisoners Burial Ground at Trinity Cemetery (now a school playground!)

When Bridget Briggs (*née* Gallagher) died in 1876, she was buried in the Roman Catholic section of the Cornelian Bay Cemetery in Hobart. In all, there are eleven family members in this grave, including Bridget's husband, William Peter Briggs, who died in 1906, and his second wife, Matilda Catherine (*née* Knapper), who died in 1913.[79]

Judith Dowling or Dooling was buried at Jerusalem. Her headstone may have been erected by her son, John, who was tried with her and transported in 1849.[80] It read:

GLORIA IN EXCELSIS DEO

+

IHS

SACRED TO THE MEMORY

OF JUDITH DOWLING WHO

DIDE IN JUNE 23 1856 IN THE

68 YEAR OF HER AGE MAY

THE LORD HAVE MERCY ON

HER SOUL

AMEN

In 2015, Judith's headstone, which was adjacent to a railway line, was removed when Judith was reinterred in the main cemetery.

## OBITUARIES, DEATH AND FUNERAL NOTICES

The dead were also remembered by obituaries published in local newspapers, but, like headstones, these are rare. Only a handful of death notices have been uncovered for the women and their husbands.

Mary (Burgess) Jones' husband, Thomas Winton Jones, died in 1886:

Deaths
JONES.—On Saturday morning, the 3rd July, at the age of 75 years and nine months, Mr. Thomas Winton Jones, after a long and painful illness, at his residence, New Parade, St. John-street, Launceston. (Victorian and New South Wales papers please copy).

Funeral Notice

The friends of Thomas, Henry, Edward, and Alfred Jones are respectfully invited to follow the remains of their late beloved father, Mr. Thomas JONES, which are to leave his late residence, New Parade, St. John-street, for interment in the General Cemetery, at 3.30p.m. on Tuesday, July 6.

The friends of Richard Ferrall, John P. Roles, and John Carroll are respectfully invited to attend the funeral of their late respected father-in-law, Mr. Thomas Jones, which will leave his late residence at 3.30 p.m. on Tuesday, July 6.[81]

Interestingly, the notices do not mention his daughters, only their husbands and brothers. Mary (Burgess) Jones died on 31 March 1898 in Launceston:

The funeral of the late Mrs. Mary Jones will leave her late residence, Holyrood, Invermay, this day (Saturday), at a quarter to three, arriving at the bridge at three o'clock. Friends respectfully invited to attend.—H. POLLINGTON, Undertaker, 82 St. John-street.[82]

Ann Flood also had a death notice, as did her husband Samuel Ford:

FORD.—On August 5, 1889, in the 67th year of her age, Ann, the dearly beloved wife of Samuel R. Ford, of New Town.[83]
FORD.—On October 12 [1889], at Fallside, New Town, Samuel Richard Ford, in the 71st year of his age. The funeral will move from his late residence on TUESDAY, October 15, at 9 o'clock.[84]

Mary McBride, aged 85, died as Mary Jane McLeod in the Launceston Invalid Depot on 2 April 1907. A widow for twenty-one years, she died of senility and exhaustion. She was buried in St Andrew's Church at Carrick. A funeral notice was published in the *Examiner*:

Funeral Notice
The funeral of the late Mrs. M'Leod will leave Launceston This Day (Thursday), the 5th [*sic*] inst., reaching Carrick at a quarter-past 1. Friends are invited to attend.[85]

Mary had lived in Van Diemen's Land for sixty-two years and her story is a remarkable one of longevity and resilience. Descendant Cheryl Griffin has meticulously researched her ancestor and writes:

> Mary stayed on in Carrick, but eventually moved into Launceston, living in a small cottage near St George's Square. Her son Dan provided a poignant picture of his mother in old age, sitting with great dignity at her kitchen table, drinking what appeared to be a cup of tea, but which he knew was boiling water because she was too poor to afford to buy tea. He would bring in firewood for her, but she refused to take it because she could not pay. Despite her extreme poverty, she was a fussy housekeeper and kept her little cottage meticulously clean.[86]

The deaths of the *Tasmania* (2) women reveal much about their lives. As Cowley and Snowden write:

> Not only is death symbolically the end of their journey but many aspects of dying help [our] understanding [of] the criminal, convict and colonial experiences of the women. Their treatment in death reflected their treatment in life – largely ignored unless the colonial administration was somehow involved. Some of the women died before they had a chance to make a new start in Van Diemen's Land. Others could not shake off the legacy of their homeland, dying impoverished and alone in institutions. These, however, were a minority. Supported economically by the convict system while under sentence, many struggled to survive once emancipated. A few, though, established large and stable families, dying at home in relative comfort; their deaths were marked with newspaper funeral notices and they were remembered with headstones. The unmarked pauper graves … remain a potent symbol of the poverty which haunted the … women.[87]

Conclusion

# The Legacy of Eliza Davis and Margaret Butler

Some historians have suggested that transportation was a lottery and the life stories of Eliza Davis, transported for infanticide, and Margaret Butler 2nd, transported with a group of women for stealing potatoes, demonstrate this.

Eliza Davis, as a foundling, had no known family. Margaret Butler, on the other hand, was a widow with six children, two of whom accompanied her to Van Diemen's Land. Margaret's children, William aged 10 and Mary Ann aged 2, were both admitted to the colonial Orphan School. William was separated from his mother on arrival and left the colony in 1847 after two years, apprenticed from the Male Orphan School to Catholic priest Revd Richard Walsh in Port Phillip (now Melbourne). William settled in the Cooma district of New South Wales, where his descendants still live. Mary Ann spent her first few months in Van Diemen's Land with her mother before being admitted to the Female Orphan School in May 1846. She was there until 1851, when she was released to her recently married mother. After her mother's death in 1855, Mary Ann was readmitted to the school and remained there until 1859. At some stage, she moved to Bemboka on the south coast of New South Wales, marrying there in 1865 when she was 18. Margaret's other children, who remained in Ireland, have not been located.[1]

Both Eliza Davis and Margaret Butler married twice and both married men from Yorkshire. Eliza married in Van Diemen's Land in 1847 and then again in 1896, a week before she died.[2] Margaret married in Ireland (although no record of this has been found) and then again in Hobart in 1850. Eliza and Margaret's colonial marriages were to fellow convicts.

Eliza created a large colonial family and died at home in 1896. Her first marriage was fraught; her husband Joseph Roebuck was admitted to the New Norfolk Asylum. Margaret's colonial marriage to John Shakelton had tragic consequences. In 1855, she was cruelly beaten to death by her husband ten years after arriving in the colony and was buried in an unmarked grave in an unknown cemetery. Her daughter, Mary Ann, then 11, was readmitted to the Female Orphan School.

Eliza Davis and Joseph Roebuck had three children. Eliza had six children to her second husband Amos Eastwood before they married. During the years of this second union, the family travelled from the south of Tasmania up the country, eventually settling in Burnie on the north-west coast, where Amos worked as a wheelwright.[3] Eliza, mother of ten, became a respected midwife. Eliza's children were highly regarded members of their local community. Her son Amos Eastwood worked for a mining company and later became a train driver. He bought a 34-acre dairy farm and worked there until his death in 1931. Her grandson, Cliff, bought a 270-acre property which he worked until his retirement in 1969. He donated 8 acres to the Burnie Council in 1964 – now a tennis court and park known as the Eastwood Reserve. Cliff left a considerable estate.[4]

Eastwood Reserve Burnie, Tasmania, 2012. (Authors' collection)

Margaret Butler's children and grandchildren formed a much-needed rural labouring class. Her son William, a stockman when he married, was later a police constable, mail contractor and municipal employee, rising to the position of sheriff's bailiff and later Inspector of Nuisances in Cooma. Many of his sons were rural labourers; his daughters married labourers. Margaret's daughter Mary Ann Butler married George Ward, a stockman, who as a young man had survived the wreck of the *Admella*.[5] He was later a dairy farmer on the south coast of New South Wales. One of Mary Ann's sons, William George Ward, was

Agnes Margaret *née* Butler, granddaughter of Margaret Butler, and her children. (Authors' collection)

Margaret Lundie *née* Butler, granddaughter of Margaret Butler, and her husband Daniel. (Courtesy of Janet Hammon)

a newsagent; his brother George was a hotel manager. Another son, Erasmus Ward, was a school teacher. Daughters, including Admella Ward and Muriel Pansy Ernestine Centennial Ward, married public school teachers. Another married a postmaster. The family was not prominent but did manage to lead quietly respectable lives and stay out of trouble – with one notable exception, that of Margaret's great-granddaughter, Maggie Lundie, who shot her violent father when she was 13 to protect her mother.[6] In court, Maggie stated: 'I really thought father would kill mother by the look in his eyes. Father was a violent man. I did it to save mother.'[7] Maggie was convicted of manslaughter and sent to the Tempe Convent as there was no appropriate reformatory. Margaret later married three times, in 1918, 1933 and 1944.

Between them, Eliza Davis and Margaret Butler had at least sixty grandchildren. This figure is all the more remarkable because Margaret's twenty-seven grandchildren were produced by only two of her children: William had a family of thirteen, Mary Ann fourteen. Margaret may have had more grandchildren from the four children – her 'wretched orphans' – she left behind in Ireland. Her grandchildren were the first Australian-born members of her family.

Alfred William, Bertram 'Terry' and Mick Hughes, c. 1916. (Courtesy of Beverley Gellatly)

Eliza Davis' grandchildren were born in the Emu Bay (Burnie) district of north-west Tasmania and, because she didn't die until 1898, she probably knew most of them.

Lizzie, Elaine, Ella and Milton Hughes, 1960s. (Courtesy of Beverley Gellatly)

Sadly, Margaret Butler died in 1855, when her children were still young, so she did not know her grandchildren. They were born in New South Wales in the Cooma district between 1860 and 1889 and on the south coast between 1864 and *c.* 1889. Her son, William, named his second daughter Margaret.[8]

Crispena Maud Butler, granddaughter of Margaret Butler. (Authors' collection)

Margaret Butler's oldest known surviving child died in 1920. Her oldest surviving Butler grandchild, Crispena Maud (Butler) Snowden, died in 1948; her oldest surviving Ward grandchild, Harry Erasmus Ward, lived until 1960.[9]

Eliza's oldest surviving child, William James Eastwood, died in 1939 and her oldest surviving grandchild, Ellen May 'Nell' Lucas (*née* Whitton), died in 1998.

Descendants of the *Tasmania* (2) women are spread throughout Australia and other parts of the world. There are descendants of Eliza Davis, Esther and Mary Burgess, Rose Fitzpatrick and Bridget Gallagher in New Zealand and there are descendants of Mary Burgess in the United States.

Crispena Maud Butler, mother Margaret *née* McIntyre and niece May Butler. (Authors' collection)

The convict story is an integral part of Australian history. Initially regarded by historians as 'damned whores', convict women are now acknowledged as 'founding mothers'. In 2015, the year of the ANZAC centenary, convict women are also recognised as having an important

Crispena Maud Snowden *née* Butler and husband, John. (Authors' collection)

Ellen May 'Nell' Lucas *née* Whitton, 1925 and *c.* 1984. (Courtesy of Bryan Lucas)

Eliza Davis' descendants George Hughes (d. 2015), Beverley Gellatly and Linda Hughes Dunedin, 2014. (Authors' collection)

Shirley Joyce (NZ), on the chair carved by her ancestor W.P. Briggs, husband of Bridget Gallagher, Legislative Council chamber, Hobart. (Courtesy of Harriet Taylor)

connection to the ANZAC story as grandmothers and great-grand-mothers of the ANZACs.

Like many Tasmanian convict women, Eliza Davis and Margaret Butler produced descendants who enlisted in the Boer War, the First or Second World War.

Margaret Butler's third grandson, William, a labourer, served in the South African War (Boer War) with the 6th Imperial Bushmen for just over two years, and wrote letters home to the local newspaper.[10] In February 1915, he enlisted in Keswick South Australia but was discharged because he was considered 'unlikely to become an efficient soldier'.[11] He again enlisted

Caroline and Emily Williams (USA), descendants of Esther and Mary Burgess, Orphan Memorial Garden, Hobart 2014. (Authors' collection)

in June 1917 in Petersburg, South Australia, as a sapper, a year after his wife, Mary, died of 'enteric fever' at Broken Hill.[12] William, aged 43, died of asthma in England in August 1918, having been admitted to hospital in Weymouth with influenza. He was buried in Melcombe Regis Cemetery, Weymouth.

Headstone of William Butler, Melcombe Regis Cemetery, Weymouth, England. (Reproduced with permission of The War Graves Photographic Project)

William's younger brother, Paul Butler, enlisted on 16 March 1916. He served as a private with the 18th Battalion, 14th Reinforcement. He was awarded a Military Medal and returned to Australia on 8 January 1919.[13] Paul, described as a returned soldier and labourer aged 52, died of 'pneumonia following meningitis', in hospital in Leeton, NSW.[14]

Margaret Butler's great-grandson, Arthur Paul Lundie, who was born in Captain's Flat in 1894, enlisted on 9 November 1914 in Sydney when he was 20. Lance Corporal Lundie served with the 13th Battalion, G Company and was killed in action on 8 August 1918 at Villers-Bretonneux, France.[15] His exact place of burial has not been located but he is remembered in the Australian National War Memorial at Villers-Bretonneux, with 11,000 members of the Australian Imperial Force who died in France and have no known grave.

Eliza Davis had several descendants who served in the Australian and New Zealand defence forces. Her grandson, William Raymond Chatwin, enlisted at the age of 18 in August 1915, the third of the Chatwin brothers to enlist. He served as a private in the 15th Battalion, 11th Reinforcement. He was killed in action on 31 December 1916 in France and was buried at Montauban, France.[16] His brothers, Alton Chatwin and Roy Alfred Chatwin, also served in the First World War.[17]

Paul Butler, grandson of Margaret Butler. (Courtesy of Les Butler)

Montauban, France, burial place of William Raymond Chatwin. (Reproduced with permission of The War Graves Photographic Project)

At least two of Eliza's four Hughes grandsons living in New Zealand fought in the First World War. Private Joseph Henry Hughes, son of Alfred Hughes of Laproireya, Wynyard, Tasmania, served with the Otago Regiment, New Zealand Expeditionary Force (NZEF). Aged 30, he died in the military hospital (England) in April 1916 of gunshot wounds to the chest. He was buried in the Plymouth Western Mill Cemetery, England.[18] His brother Bertram (known as Terry) also served in the war; he was badly wounded at Passchendaele. A bushman from Tuatapere, he was killed in a tree-felling accident in 1936.[19]

Joseph Hughes with Duncan McKenzie.
(Courtesy of Beverley Gellatly)

As well as Eliza Davis and Margaret Butler 2nd, several other *Tasmania* (2) women had descendants who served in the defence forces; some died in active service. Bridget Gallagher lost two grandsons: David Joseph Charles Ringrose, from New Zealand, who died in Ypres, France, in 1917 and Henry Charles Briggs, who died in France in 1918.

Tasmanian-born Private David Ringrose was the son of Sarah Ringrose of North Dunedin. He served with the Otago Regiment and is remembered in the Messines Ridge (NZ) Memorial.

Plymouth Western Mill Cemetery, England, burial place of Private Joseph Henry Hughes. (Reproduced with permission of The War Graves Photographic Project)

**RINGROSE**.—Killed in action, somewhere in France, on July 31st, 1917, David J. C., eldest son of Sarah and the late David Ringrose, of Hobart. Beloved brother of Mrs C. Baird, Ann street, Williamstown.[20]

Private Charles Briggs, grandson of Bridget Briggs (*née* Gallagher) and great-grandson of Rose Fitzpatrick, was killed in action in August 1918, not long after he rejoined his battalion following a prolonged bout of

Messines Ridge (N.Z.) Memorial, David Joseph Charles Ringrose. (Reproduced with permission of The War Graves Photographic Project)

Borre British Cemetery, Charles Briggs. (Reproduced with permission of The War Graves Photographic Project)

influenza. He was buried at Borre British Cemetery. His personal effects were returned to his father and included '2 wallets, 1 testament, 1 birthday book, 1 metal cigarette case, 1 comb, 1 fountain pen, 1 curio, photos, 1 mirror (damaged) and 4 coins'.[21] Charles was awarded a War Service Medal (Western Front) as well as the British War Medal and Victory Medal.[22]

Descendants of Esther and Mary Burgess also enlisted in the First World War.[23] Brothers Sergius Christopher Martin (1895–1939) and Cyril Livingstone Martin (1897–1933) were great-grandsons of Esther and grandsons of Mary. Sergius enlisted in August 1915 and served in the 17th Battery, Army Field Artillery (AFA) in Egypt, France and Belgium. He was wounded in November 1917 and sent to England to recuperate. In July 1918 he rejoined his unit in France. He was gassed in October and was again sent to hospital in England. He was awarded the 1914–15 Star, British War Medal and the Victory Medal.[24] Cyril enlisted in April 1917 and served in the 2nd Australian Light Railway Operating Company in France and Belgium. Sergius was awarded the 1914–15 Star, British War Medal and the Victory Medal.[25] Mary Burgess had at least three other grandsons who served in the First World War: Harold George Winton Jones, AIF; Joseph Winton Carroll, NZIF; and John Bernard Carroll, NZIF.[26]

As well as those who served in the defence forces, other descendants of the women of the *Tasmania* (2) left an enduring legacy in other ways. The family of Mary Jones (*née* Burgess) were quietly successful and prominent in Tasmanian and interstate circles: the Roles family, for example, were well known in the hotel trade in Launceston and later in Sydney.[27] Annie Roles (*née* Jones) ran hotels after her husband's death and owned property in Sydney.

Perhaps the most prominent of Esther and Mary Burgess'

Alice Carroll *née* Jones and son Joseph Winton Carroll before his departure from New Zealand. (Courtesy of Kevin Reed)

descendants was Sir Raymond Ferrall, one of ten children born to Richard Harvey and Amy (*née* Jones) Ferrall. Kevin Reed writes: 'A sportsman of note, Ray played fullback for the Tasmanian Football XVIII in 1932 and captained the Tasmanian Cricket XI in 1934'.[28] He worked as a journalist for the *Examiner* and in the family wholesale grocery business, beginning Four Roses Pty Ltd. Sir Raymond Ferrall was awarded his CBE in 1969 for services to the community. He wrote several books, the last, *90 Years On: A Tasmanian Story*, when he was 90. The Sir Raymond Ferrall Centre at the University of Tasmania was named for him.

Annie Roles *née* Jones, daughter of Mary Burgess and granddaughter of Esther Burgess. (Courtesy of Kevin Reed)

Margaret Meara, a 20-year-old country servant and housemaid from County Limerick, was tried in Tipperary and transported for seven years for stealing clothes.[29] Margaret was the great-great-grandmother of internationally renowned novelist Christopher Koch, AO (1932–2013).[30] His convict connection was successfully hidden: 'Like many other Tasmanians, I was innocent of any serious knowledge of the history of my island'. He spoke of the discovery of his convict ancestor:

> The past – still so close to us – was full of curious gaps. It was a past which many Tasmanians still did not want to know about, in 1960, for fear of disturbing an ancestor in chains … The Hidden Convict has been until recently the ghost at the feast for many Tasmanians. He (or she) was hidden by our parents and grandparents with great cunning.

Alison Alexander recorded Christopher Koch's eloquent picture of his great-great-grandmother on the *Anson*:

> clad in a brown serge skirt, a jacket of brown and yellow gingham, a dark blue cotton kerchief, a white calico cap, knitted blue stockings, and a masculine pair of half boots … I see her in this outfit, standing on deck in some moment of respite, perhaps in the late afternoon: a small,

brown-haired figure in her white cap and clumsy boots, staring at the far silver reaches of the river … this bereft Irish peasant girl from Tipperary.

Koch's search for Margaret took him to the site of the Ross Female Factory in the Tasmanian Midlands:

> Wandering there recently, among those quiet mounds, I thought of my reckless and foolish great-great-grandmother … a loneliness and sorrow that were not entirely my own enclosed me like a wave. The dead are not really close, as we sometimes like to imagine; it is their pain and annihilation that hang so near in the air.

In all Margaret Meara had five children; her youngest, Julia, was Christopher Koch's great-grandmother. Margaret died from inflammation of the lungs when she was 34. Julia was only three.[31] Christopher Koch, dual Miles Franklin Award winner, died on 23 September 2013.

Surgeon Superintendent of the *Tasmania* (2) Jason Lardner described the women in his charge as 'these unfortunate females'.[32] Margaret Butler 2nd was described by the matron of the county gaol as 'a desperate character'.[33] Unfortunate and desperate they may have been, but being sentenced to transportation was a mixed blessing. For some, it was a continuation of their previous lives, living on the edge, skirting the law and repeating past behaviour. It also meant leaving behind parents, siblings, husbands, friends and, for those such as Margaret Butler, children – a heartrending experience. But for others, like Eliza Davis, the sentence of transportation was an opportunity to start anew, an opportunity perhaps to make amends for the past. In some ways, too, the women and children were fortunate. For the 138 women who

Sir Raymond Ferrall, grandson of Mary Burgess and great-grandson of Esther Burgess. (Courtesy of Kevin Reed)

Christopher Koch AO, great-great-grandson of Margaret Meara. (Courtesy of
Random House Australia)

sailed on the *Tasmania* (2) in September 1845 and the thirty-five children
who accompanied them, the sentence of transportation beyond the seas
on the eve of the Great Famine was in hindsight a fortuitous escape:
escape from poverty, disease and starvation. For many, then, transportation marked the start of a new and potentially better life. Alicia Burgess,
daughter of Esther and sister of Mary, was only a young child when she
arrived in Van Diemen's Land but she remained a proud Irishwoman up
until her death.

Henry Carter's poem provides a sardonic perspective on the concept
of British transportation: 'We left our country for our country's good.'[34]
While for many convicts, transportation was a positive experience that
provided an opportunity for a new life, Britain also benefitted through the
removal of unwanted outcasts who provided labour in its new colonies.

The stories of Margaret Butler 2nd and Eliza Davis, and their acknowl-
edgment by their descendants, form part of a significant historical

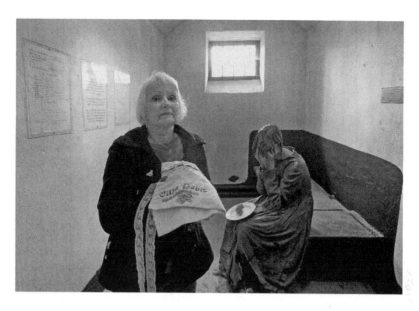

Gail Mulhern, descendant of Eliza Davis, Wicklow Gaol interpretation 'Eliza Davis', 2012. (Reproduced with permission of ©PA)

Beverley Gellatly, descendant of Eliza Davis, Wicklow Gaol interpretation 'Eliza Davis', 2014. (Authors' collection)

revision: no longer is a convict past seen as shameful; rather, it is celebrated. Recently, historians such as Alexander, Smith and Boyce have explored the cultural amnesia of convictism and the impact it has had on more recent generations.[35] Margaret and Eliza's descendants exemplify this. Perhaps more importantly, their narratives highlight that there is much more to a convict life than a crime, trial and sentence. Daniels, noting the complexity of individual convict lives, warned against stereotyping; and this is borne out by the stories of Margaret, Eliza and their *Tasmania* (2) shipmates.[36] Their individual lives were diverse and complex; they were not one-dimensional characters. In particular, Eliza's many descendants have embraced the difficult details of her early years, as a foundling, as a woman who committed infanticide, and as an Irish convict sentenced to transportation for life. She is accepted with compassion and understanding. Margaret's descendants are still discovering the details of their ancestor's life, searching for an understanding of their past and their convict ancestor. For all of the women and children of the *Tasmania* (2), the search for lost voices goes on, in a continuing process of sifting through the fragments of the past.

# Appendix I

# Trial Statistics

## TRIAL PLACE OF *TASMANIA* (2) WOMEN [N =138]

| Trial Place | Number | Percentage |
|---|---|---|
| Dublin City and County | 17 | 12.3 |
| Antrim | 11 | 8 |
| Tipperary | 9 | 7 |
| Carlow | 8 | 6 |
| Cork Co. | 8 | 6 |
| Fermanagh | 8 | 6 |
| Down | 7 | 5 |
| Cavan | 6 | 4 |
| Limerick City | 3 | 2 |
| Limerick Co. | 3 | 2 |
| | Total: 6 | |
| Kerry | 5 | 4 |
| Queen's Co. | 5 | 4 |
| Waterford City | 4 | 3 |
| Waterford County | 1 | 1 |
| | Total: 5 | |
| Kilkenny City | 1 | 1 |
| Kilkenny | 3 | 1 |
| | Total: 4 | |
| Longford | 4 | 3 |
| Tyrone | 4 | 3 |
| Kildare | 3 | 2 |
| Londonderry | 3 | 2 |

| Roscommon | 3 | 2 |
|---|---|---|
| Westmeath | 3 | 2 |
| Wicklow | 3 | 2 |
| Armagh | 2 | 1.5 |
| Clare | 2 | 1.5 |
| King's Co. | 2 | 1.5 |
| Meath | 2 | 1.5 |
| Monaghan | 2 | 1.5 |
| Wexford | 2 | 1.5 |
| Donegal | 1 | 1 |
| Leitrim | 1 | 1 |
| Louth | 1 | 1 |
| Mayo | 1 | 1 |

Source: TAHO, CON41/1/8

## COMPARISON OF TRIAL PLACES
## BY PROVINCE AND COUNTY

| County/City | All Irish Female Convicts to VDL (%) | *Tasmania* (2) Convicts (%) | *Australasia* Convicts (%) |
|---|---|---|---|
| **Leinster** | | | |
| Carlow | 2 | 6 | 0.0 |
| Dublin City | 11 | 12 | 0.5 |
| Dublin County | 3 | 0 | 3.5 |
| Kildare | 3 | 2 | 5.0 |
| Kilkenny City | 1 | 1 | 0.0 |
| Kilkenny County | 2 | 2 | 1.0 |
| King's County[1] | 2 | 1.5 | 2.0 |
| Longford | 1 | 3 | 2.0 |
| Louth | 1 | 1 | 1.5 |
| Meath | 2 | 1.5 | 3.5 |
| Queen's County[2] | 2 | 4 | 1.5 |
| Westmeath | 2 | 2 | 0.5 |
| Wexford | 2 | 1.5 | 2.5 |
| Wicklow | 2 | 2 | 0.0 |
| | **36** | **39.5** | **23.5** |
| **Munster** | | | |
| Clare | 4 | 1.5 | 13.5 |
| Cork City | 3 | 0 | 1.0 |
| Cork County | 9 | 6 | 12.0 |

| | | | |
|---|---|---|---|
| Kerry | 3 | 4 | 5.5 |
| Limerick City | 2 | 2 | 2.0 |
| Limerick County | 4 | 2 | 3.0 |
| Tipperary | 4 | 7 | 3.0 |
| Waterford City | 0 | 3 | 0.5 |
| Waterford County | 3 | 1 | 4.0 |
| | **32** | **26.5** | **44.5** |
| **Ulster** | | | |
| Antrim | 4 | 8 | 2.5 |
| Armagh | 2 | 1.5 | 2.0 |
| Cavan | 2 | 4 | 1.5 |
| Donegal | 1 | 1 | 0.0 |
| Down | 2 | 5 | 0.0 |
| Fermanagh | 3 | 6 | 1.5 |
| Londonderry | 2 | 2 | 0.0 |
| Monaghan | 1 | 1.5 | 3.5 |
| Tyrone | 4 | 3 | 4.5 |
| | **21** | **32** | **15.5** |
| **Connaught** | | | |
| Galway Town | 0 | 0 | 1.5 |
| Galway County | 5 | 0 | 11.0 |
| Leitrim | 1 | 1 | 2.0 |
| Mayo | 2 | 1 | 2.0 |
| Roscommon | 1 | 2 | 0.0 |
| Sligo | 1 | 0 | 0.0 |
| | **10** | **4** | **16.5** |

All Irish female convicts to Van Diemen's Land (n=3,687), *Tasmania* (2) convicts 1845 (n=138) and *Australasia* convicts 1849 (n=200)

## NATIVE PLACE OF *TASMANIA* (2) WOMEN [N=138]

| Native Place | Number | Percentage |
|---|---|---|
| Dublin | 15 | 10.9 |
| Tipperary | 10 | 7.2 |
| Cavan | 9 | 7 |
| Fermanagh | 9 | 7 |
| Cork | 8 | 6 |
| Carlow | 7 | 5 |
| Down | 6 | 4 |
| Antrim | 5 | 4 |
| Kerry | 5 | 4 |
| Limerick | 5 | 4 |
| Queen's County | 5 | 4 |
| Tyrone | 5 | 4 |
| Kildare | 4 | 3 |
| Kilkenny | 4 | 3 |
| Roscommon | 4 | 3 |
| Waterford | 4 | 3 |
| Meath | 3 | 2 |
| Londonderry (Derry) | 3 | 2 |
| Wexford | 3 | 2 |
| Wicklow | 3 | 2 |
| Clare | 2 | 1.5 |
| Galway | 2 | 1.5 |
| Longford | 2 | 1.5 |
| Louth | 2 | 1.5 |
| Westmeath | 2 | 1.5 |
| Armagh | 1 | 1 |
| Donegal | 1 | 1 |
| King's Co. | 1 | 1 |
| Leitrim | 1 | 1 |
| Mayo | 1 | 1 |
| Monaghan | 1 | 1 |
|  |  |  |
| Not Ireland | 4 | 3 |
| Not recorded | 1 | 1 died on board[3] |

Percentage points rounded up to nearest ½ percent
Source: TAHO, CON41/1/8 & CON15/1/3

## *TASMANIA* (2) WOMEN
## TRIED AWAY FROM NATIVE PLACE [N=36]

| Name | Trial Place | Native Place |
|------|-------------|--------------|
| Anne Agnew | Dublin City | Dundoch, Louth |
| Sarah Brennan | Dublin City | Meath |
| Maria Brien | Wicklow | Dublin |
| Ellen Callaghan | Dublin City | London (brought up in Ireland) |
| Bridget Clifford | Waterford | Wexford |
| Bridget Cunningham | Longford | Tipperary |
| Bridget Dignan | Longford | Drogheda |
| Margaret Gibson | Antrim | Woolwich |
| Catherine Grace | Carlow | Tipperary |
| Margaret Grady | King's Co. | Tipperary |
| Mary Griffen | Carlow | Wicklow |
| Elizabeth Hearns | Kilkenny | Carlow |
| Catherine Heenan | Tipperary | Galway |
| Catherine Hughes | King's Co. | Athlone, Westmeath |
| Ellen Jackson | Westmeath | Roscommon |
| Margaret Kelly | Antrim | Monaghan |
| Ellen King | Antrim | Down |
| Margaret Lee | Down | Cavan |
| Maria Lynch | Roscommon | Galway |
| Annie McNeill | Westmeath | Roscommon |
| Mary McVeagh | Armagh | Antrim |
| Anne Mallon | Antrim | Armagh |
| Margaret Meara | Tipperary | Limerick |
| Anne Mullon | Antrim | Woolwich |
| Ellen Maguire | Cavan | Fermanagh |
| Mary Murphy | Monaghan | Cavan |
| Eliza Perry | Dublin City | Wicklow |
| Catherine Preston | Louth | Cavan |
| Mary Ryan | Wicklow | Kildare |
| Catherine Stewart | Armagh | Paisley, Scotland |
| Mary Sullivan 1st | Limerick | Killarney, Kerry |
| Elizabeth Waring | Down | Dublin |
| Isabella Warnock | Antrim | Dublin |
| Ann Williams | Dublin | King's Co. |
| Margaret Wilson | Monaghan | Cavan |
| Elizabeth Wright | Londonderry | Tyrone |

Source: TAHO, CON41/1/8 & CON15/1/3

# Appendix II

# The Women of the *Tasmania* (2)

| Surname | Given Name | Height | Age | When Committed | Trial Date | Trial Place | Native Place | Crime | Sentence | Convicted Before | When received into Grangegorman | Days Awaiting Trans | Trade Grange Gorman | Trade Indent | Rel | R/W | Marital Status | CRF |
|---|---|---|---|---|---|---|---|---|---|---|---|---|---|---|---|---|---|---|
| Agnew | Anne | 5ft ¼in | 27 | 02/07/1845 | 17/07/1845 | Dublin City | Louth, Dundoch(k) | Felony – stealing a gold watch | 7 | Y | 18/07/1845 | 62 | Bonnet maker | Dressmaker and milliner | CE | Yes | S | N/A |
| Amos | Bell | 5ft 1¼in | 19 | Not known | 17/07/1845 | Fermanagh | Fermanagh | Larceny – stealing a gown | 7 | N | 13/08/1845 | 47 | Spinster | Farm servant | CE | R | S | N/A |
| Barry | Mary | 5ft ¼in | 25 | 20/05/1845 | 18/07/1845 | Limerick City | Limerick | Larceny – stealing a sheet | 7 | Y | 15/08/1845 | 105 | Servant | Housemaid | RC | N | S | N/A |
| Beresford | Henrietta | 5ft | 24 | Not Known | 18/10/1844 | Limerick Co. | Waterford | Larceny – stealing muslin | 7 | N | 06/06/1845 | 319 | None | Housemaid/laundress | RC | R | S | N/A |
| Bradshaw | Jane | 4ft 11½in | 26 | 06/01/1845 | 07/01/1845 | Queens | Queens | Larceny – stealing a frying pan | 7 | Y | 06/06/1845 | 239 | Spinster | Farm servant | RC | Yes | S | CRF 1845 B28 |
| Brennan | Sarah | 5ft 1½in | 29 | 05/03/1845 | 29/03/1845 | Dublin City | Meath | Felony – stealing a cloak | 7 | Y | 31/03/1845 | 181 | Servant | Housemaid/laundress/cook | RC | R | S | N/A |
| Brien | Maria | 5ft 4½in | 21 | Not Known | 19/06/1845 | Wicklow | Dublin | Larceny – stealing a watch | 10 | Y | 12/08/1845 | 75 | None | Housemaid | RC | R | S | N/A |
| Brown | Mary | 5ft 1½in | 23 | Not Known | 16/07/1845 | Waterford City | Kilkenny | Vagrancy | 7 | Y | 15/08/1845 | 48 | None | Housemaid | RC | N | S | N/A |
| Burgess | Esther | 5ft 4in | 40 | Not Known | 02/04/1845 | Carlow | Carlow | Larceny – stealing 6 stone potatoes | 7 | Y | 06/06/1845 | 153 | None | Washer-woman | RC | N | W | CRF 1845 B15 |
| Burgess | Mary | 5ft 3¾in | 18 | Not Known | 02/04/1845 | Carlow | Carlow | Larceny | 7 | N | 06/06/1845 | 153 | None | Country servant | RC | N | S | N/A |
| Burnet | Catherine | 5ft 3in | 18 | Not Known | 08/03/1845 | Tyrone | Tyrone | Larceny – receiving a shawl | 7 | Y | 05/06/1845 | 178 | None | Housemaid | CE | R | S | N/A |
| Burns | Anne | 5ft 4in | 24 | 03/08/1844 | 07/11/1844 | Tipperary | Tipperary | Sheep stealing – five sheep | 7 | N | 06/06/1845 | 395 | None | Professed cook | RC | Yes | M | N/A |

| Butler | Margaret 1st | 5ft 1in | 22 | Not known | 17/10/1844 | Carlow | Carlow | Larceny – stealing 5yds of cashmere | 7 | Y | 06/06/1845 | 320 | None | Country servant | RC | N | S | N/A |
|---|---|---|---|---|---|---|---|---|---|---|---|---|---|---|---|---|---|---|
| Butler | Margaret 2nd | 5ft 3¼in | 40 | Not known | 02/04/1845 | Carlow | Carlow | Larceny – stealing potatoes | 7 | Y | 06/06/1845 | 153 | None | Farm servant | RC | R | W | CRF 1845 B14 |
| Byrne | Mary | 5ft 1¾in | 30 | Not known | 02/04/1845 | Carlow | Carlow | Larceny – stealing 2 stone potatoes | 7 | Y | 06/06/1845 | 153 | None | Country servant | RC | N | S | N/A |
| Cahil | Ellen | 4ft 10½in | 24 | Not known | 04/01/1845 | Kerry | Kerry | Larceny – stealing money (£10 10s) | 7 | Y | 04/06/1845 | 241 | None | Housemaid wash | RC | N | S | N/A |
| Callaghan | Ellen | 5ft 4in | 20 | Not known | 05/02/1845 | Dublin City | London brought up in Ireland | Felony – stealing money from a man | 7 | Y | 06/02/1845 | 209 | None | Plain laundress | CE | N | S | N/A |
| Carroll | Mary | 5ft 2in | 20 | 21/04/1845 | 26/04/1845 | Dublin City | Dublin | Felony – stealing a bonnet | 7 | Y | 26/04/1845 | 134 | None | Housemaid | RC | N | S | N/A |
| Clifford | Bridget | 5ft 1¾in | 30 | Not known | 16/07/1845 | Waterford City | Wexford | Vagrancy | 7 | Y | 15/08/1845 | 48 | None | Housemaid | RC | N | S | N/A |
| Coleman | Catherine | 4ft 9¾in | 20 | Not known | 31/12/1844 | Cavan | Cavan | Larceny – stealing a pair of boots | 7 | Y | 04/06/1845 | 245 | None | Kitchen maid | CE | N | S | N/A |
| Collins | Ann | 4ft 9in | 21 | Not known | 11/10/1844 | Cork Co. | Cork | Receiving stolen goods – stealing money. Tried with Margaret Daly | 7 | Y | 04/06/1845 | 326 | None | Country servant | RC | N | S | N/A |
| Connell | Mary | 5ft 1¾in | 30 | Not known | 11/10/1844 | Cork Co. | Cork | Receiving stolen goods – a cloak | 7 | Y | 04/06/1845 | 326 | None | Dairy woman | RC | N | W | N/A |
| Connor | Deborah | 5ft 3½in | 18 | Not known | 15/04/1845 | Kerry | Kerry | Larceny – stealing clothes | 7 | Y | 04/06/1845 | 140 | None | Housemaid | RC | N | S | N/A |
| Connor | Margaret | 4ft 6¾in | 25 | Not known | 11/06/1845 | Dublin City | Dublin | Felony – stealing a watch | 7 | Y | 14/06/1845 | 83 | None | House servant and plain laundress | CE | R | M | N/A |

| Surname | First name | Height | Age | | | County | Place | Offence | Sentence | Y/N | Date | No. | Status | Occupation | Religion | | | Ref |
|---|---|---|---|---|---|---|---|---|---|---|---|---|---|---|---|---|---|---|
| Conolly | Ellen | 5ft 5in | 22 | 04/09/1844 | 21/10/1844 | Cork Co. | Cork | Larceny – receiving a stolen frock | 7 | Y | 04/06/1845 | 363 | None | Housemaid | RC | N | S | N/A |
| Cullen | Honora | 5ft | 23 | Not known | 02/05/1844 | Tipperary | Tipperary | Larceny | 7 | N | 06/06/1845 | 488 | None | Plain laundress | RC | N | S | CRF 1844 C63 |
| Cummane | Ellen | 5ft ¼in | 23 | Not known | 16/10/1844 | Kerry | Kerry | Larceny – stealing money | 7 | Y | 04/06/1845 | 321 | None | Dairy woman | RC | N | S | N/A |
| Cunningham | Bridget | 5ft 1½in | 20 | Not known | 05/07/1844 | Longford | Tipperary | Vagrancy – obtaining money by means of begging letters | 7 | N | 03/06/1845 | 424 | None | Laundress | RC | N | S | N/A |
| Daly | Margaret | 4ft 11½in | 20 | Not known | 11/10/1844 | Cork Co. | Cork | Receiving stolen goods – money from a soldier. Tried with Ann Collins | 7 | Y | 04/06/1845 | 326 | None | Country servant | RC | N | S | N/A |
| Daly | Eleanor | 4ft 9in | 25 | Not known | 18/04/1845 | Queens | Queens | Larceny – stealing a mantle | 7 | Y | 06/06/1845 | 137 | Spinster | Country servant | RC | N | S | N/A |
| Daly | Ann | 5ft 3½in | 30 | 11/05/1845 | 03/07/1845 | Tipperary Clonmel | Tipperary | Larceny – stealing a cloak from a hawker | 7 | Y | 13/08/1845 | 114 | Spinster | Country servant | RC | N | W | N/A |
| Davis | Bridget | 4ft 11in | 28 | Not known | 14/04/1845 | Clare | Clare | Larceny – stealing two shirts | 7 | Y | 06/06/1845 | 141 | None | Country servant | RC | N | S | N/A |
| Davis | Eliza | 5ft 1in | 22 | Not known | 08/07/1845 | Wicklow | Dublin | Infanticide | Life | N | 12/08/1845 | 56 | Servant | Housemaid | CE | R | S | CRF 1844 D18 |
| Delany | Anne | 5ft 1in | 17 | Not known | 03/01/1845 | Kildare (Athy) | Kildare | Felony – stealing 8lbs of potatoes. Tried with Mary Russell | 7 | Y | 06/06/1845 | 242 | None | Nursemaid | RC | R | S | N/A |
| Dignan | Bridget | 5ft 3¾in | 22 | Not known | 02/01/1845 | Longford | Louth, Drogheda | Larceny – stealing a shawl | 7 | Y | 03/06/1845 | 243 | None | Housemaid | RC | N | W | N/A |
| Dogherty | Anne | 5ft 2¼in | 21 | Not known | 02/01/1845 | Longford | Longford | Larceny – stealing clothes | 7 | Y | 03/06/1845 | 243 | None | Laundress and housemaid | RC | R | S | N/A |

| Surname | First name | Height | Age | | | | | Offence | | | | | | Occupation | | | | |
|---|---|---|---|---|---|---|---|---|---|---|---|---|---|---|---|---|---|---|
| Doherty | Fanny | 5ft 6in | 27 | Not known | 29/07/1845 | Londonderry | Londonderry | Larceny – stealing a ring from a man | 7 | Y | 15/08/1845 | 35 | None | Laundress | CE | N | S | N/A |
| Dooling | Judith | 4ft 9in | 60 | Not known | 31/10/1844 | Kilkenny Co. | Kilkenny | Receiving stolen goods – a horse cover | 7 | Y | 06/06/1845 | 306 | None | Housemaid | RC | N | W | CRF 1845 D7 |
| Dwyer | Elizabeth | 5ft 1½in | 21 | Not known | 11/07/1845 | Wexford | Wexford | Larceny – stealing linen | 7 | N | 14/08/1845 | 53 | Servant | Housemaid | CE | N | M | N/A |
| Egan | Bridget | 5ft 1½in | 20 | 11/07/1844 | 25/07/1844 | Tipperary | Tipperary | Vagrancy | 7 | Y | 06/06/1845 | 418 | None | Housemaid | RC | N | S | CRF 1845 E1 |
| Fanning | Bridget | 4ft 11½in | 16 | Not known | 28/03/1845 | Westmeath | Westmeath | Larceny – stealing a table cloth | 7 | Y | 05/06/1845 | 158 | None | Nursemaid | RC | N | S | N/A |
| Farrell | Catherine | 5ft 1in | 21 | Not known | 30/12/1844 | Meath | Meath | Larceny – stealing from a man | 7 | N | 04/06/1845 | 246 | None | Country servant | RC | N | S | N/A |
| Farrell/ Dwyer | Judith | 5ft 2in | 62 | 21/06/1845 | 03/07/1845 | Tipperary, Clonmel | Tipperary | Larceny – stealing two shirts | 7 | Y | 15/08/1845 | 73 | Servant | Housemaid | RC | N | W | N/A |
| Fitzpatrick | Anne | 5ft 1½in | 54 | Not known | 05/04/1845 | Cavan | Cavan | Having stolen goods in her possession – stealing caps | 7 | Y | 04/06/1845 | 150 | None | House servant | RC | N | S | N/A |
| Fitzpatrick | Rose | 4ft 11½in | 45 | Not known | 03/03/1845 | Cavan | Cavan | Larceny – stealing 10 stone of potatoes. Tried with daughter Bridget Gallagher, on board, and son James Donovan | 7 | Y | 04/06/1845 | 183 | None | Laundress | RC | N | W | N/A |
| Flannery | Anne | 5ft 2in | 24 | Not known | 27/02/1845 | Ros-common | Roscommon | Arson – burning a house | 15 | Y | 05/06/1845 | 187 | None | Housemaid | RC | N | S | CRF 1845 F6 |
| Flood | Anne | 4ft 11¼in | 24 | Not known | 19/10/1844 | Dublin City | Dublin | Felony – stealing shirts | 7 | Y | 21/10/1844 | 318 | Servant | Laundress and house servant | RC | R | S | N/A |

| Surname | First name | Height | Age | | Date | County | Place tried | Crime | Sentence | | Date | No. | Former occupation | Occupation | | | | |
|---|---|---|---|---|---|---|---|---|---|---|---|---|---|---|---|---|---|---|
| Foy | Catherine | 4ft 10¾in | 22 | Not known | 17/07/1845 | Fermanagh | Fermanagh, Enniskillen | Larceny – stealing stockings | 7 | Y | 13/08/1845 | 47 | Spinster | Laundress | RC | | S | N/A |
| Francis | Mary | 4ft 11in | 20 | 25/07/1845 | 26/07/1845 | Dublin City | Dublin | Felony – shoplifting and stealing ribbon | 7 | Y | 28/07/1845 | 39 | None | Farm servant and dairy woman | RC | Yes | M | N/A |
| Gallagher | Jane | 5ft ½in | 24 | Not known | 28/10/1844 | Antrim | Antrim | Larceny – stealing 3s 6d. Tried with Sarah Morrow | 10 | Y | 03/06/1845 | 309 | Mill-worker | Housemaid and plain cook | RC | N | S | N/A |
| Gallagher or Toland | Margaret | 5ft 1½in | 53 | Not known | 02/01/1845 | Donegal | Donegal | Larceny – stealing soap | 7 | Y | 05/06/1845 | 243 | Servant | House servant, laundress and plain cook | RC | N | W | N/A |
| Gallagher | Bridget | 4ft 11¾in | 19 | Not known | 03/03/1845 | Cavan | Cavan | Larceny – stealing potatoes. Tried with mother Rose Fitzpatrick and brother James Donovan. Aunt Ann Fitzpatrick on board | 7 | Y | 04/06/1845 | 183 | None | House servant | RC | N | S | N/A |
| Gardiner or Harrison | Anne | 5ft 1¼in | 64 | Not known | 16/10/1844 | Fermanagh | Fermanagh | Larceny – stealing a stocking & 2d | 7 | Y | 04/06/1845 | 321 | None | Housemaid, laundress and dairy maid | CS | N | W | N/A |
| Gibson | Margaret | 4ft 11¾in | 24 | Not kown | 08/03/1845 | Antrim | Woolwich | Larceny – stealing 2s from the person | 10 | Y | 14/08/1845 | 178 | None | Housemaid and plain laundress | CE | R | M | N/A |
| Gillespie | Mary | 5ft 1½in | 35 | Not known | 27/06/1845 | Londonderry | Londonderry | Larceny – stealing a gig cover and chain | 7 | Y | 15/08/1845 | 67 | None | Laundress | CE | R | S | N/A |
| Grace | Catherine | 4ft 9½in | 30 | Not known | 17/10/1844 | Carlow | Tipperary | Larceny – stealing a tea 'catty' | 7 | Y | 06/06/1845 | 320 | Bonnet maker | Housemaid and kitchen maid | RC | R | M | N/A |
| Grady | Margaret | 4ft 11½in | 25 | Not known | 03/01/1845 | Kings | Tipperary | Larceny – stealing a calico sheet | 7 | Y | 06/06/1845 | 242 | None | Laundress and knitter | RC | N | S | N/A |

| | | | | | | | | | | | | | | | | | | |
|---|---|---|---|---|---|---|---|---|---|---|---|---|---|---|---|---|---|---|
| Griffen | Mary | 4ft 9in | 30 | Not known | 02/04/1845 | Carlow | Wicklow | Larceny – stealing potatoes | 7 | Y | 06/06/1845 | 153 | None | House maid | CE | R | M | N/A |
| Hearns | Elizabeth | 5ft 3in | 25 | Not known | 26/07/1845 | Kilkenny City | Carlow | Stealing 6yds of cashmere | 7 | N | 15/08/1845 | 38 | Servant | Housemaid and dairy woman | RC | N | W | N/A |
| Heenan | Catherine | 5ft 1in | 24 | Not known | 02/08/1845 | Tipperary Nenagh | Galway | Larceny – stealing clothes | 7 | N | 15/08/1845 | 31 | None | Plain cook | RC | Yes | S | N/A |
| Henry | Margaret | 5ft 1in | 30 | Not known | 18/08/1845 | Dublin City | Dublin | Felony – stealing a cloak | 7 | Y | 19/08/1845 | 15 | Servant | Housemaid, nurse and needle woman | CE | Yes | S | N/A |
| Hethering-ton | Mary | 5ft 3½in | 24 | Not known | 22/10/1844 | Queens Co. | Queens | Larceny – stealing a petticoat | 7 | Y | 06/06/1845 | 315 | Spinster | Housemaid | CE | R | S | N/A |
| Hughes | Catherine | 5ft 3¾in | 20 | Not known | 28/10/1844 | Kings Co. | Westmeath, Athlone | Larceny – stealing from the person | 7 | N | 06/06/1845 | 309 | None | Housemaid | RC | R | M | CRF 1844 H34 |
| Hunter | Eliza | 5ft ½in | 41 | Not known | 09/11/1844 | Dublin City | Dublin | Felony – stealing boots | 7 | Y | 09/11/1844 | 297 | None | Plain cook | RC | R | W | N/A |
| Hurley | Bridget | 5ft 4½in | 23 | Not known | 08/04/1845 | Waterford Co. | Waterford | Larceny – stealing clothes and shoes | 7 | Y | 02/06/1845 | 147 | None | House servant and country servant | RC | N | S | N/A |
| Hurley | Mary | 5ft ¾in | 29 | Not known | 16/10/1844 | Kerry | Kerry | Larceny – stealing a gown and petticoat | 7 | Y | 04/06/1845 | 321 | None | Housemaid | RC | R | S | N/A |
| Jackson | Ellen | 4ft 11in | 23 | Not known | 16/10/1844 | Westmeath | Roscommon | Larceny – stealing woollen ware | 7 | N | 05/06/1845 | 321 | None | Housemaid and country servant | RC | N | M | N/A |
| Johnson | Maria | 5ft 4in | 24 | Not known | 15/01/1845 | Dublin City | Dublin | Felony – stealing brass cock and steal pipes | 7 | Y | 16/01/1845 | 230 | None | Farm servant and country servant | RC | R | S | N/A |
| Keeffe | Catherine | 4ft 9¾in | 30 | 26/12/1844 | 01/01/1845 | Cork Co. | Cork | Receiving stolen goods – blankets. Tried with Johanna Murray | 7 | Y | 04/06/1845 | 250 | None | Housemaid and wash | RC | N | W | N/A |

| | | | | | | | | | | | | | | | | | | |
|---|---|---|---|---|---|---|---|---|---|---|---|---|---|---|---|---|---|---|
| Kelly | Margaret | 5ft 1in | 40 | Not known | 28/10/1844 | Antrim | Monaghan | Larceny – stealing a cloak. Tried with Ann Mallon | 7 | Y | 03/06/1845 | 309 | None | Housemaid | RC | R | M | N/A |
| Kelly | Bridget | 5ft | 25 | Not known | 09/01/1845 | Dublin Co. | Dublin | Stealing a gold watch | 7 | Y | 22/01/1845 | 236 | None | Nurse maid | RC | R | S | N/A |
| King | Ellen | 4ft 11½in | 25 | Not known | 09/01/1845 | Antrim | Down | Larceny – stealing money from the person | 10 | Y | 03/06/1845 | 236 | Servant | Housemaid | CE | N | S | N/A |
| Langan | Elizabeth | 5ft 1in | 23 | Not known | 21/06/1845 | Limerick Co. | Limerick | Larceny – stealing £30 | 7 | N | 15/08/1845 | 75 | Servant | Housemaid | RC | N | S | N/A |
| Lee | Margaret | 4ft 11in | 23 | Not known | 21/10/1844 | Down | Cavan | Larceny – stealing a shawl | 7 | Y | 03/06/1845 | 316 | None | Housemaid and plain laundress | RC | N | S | CRF 1844 L27 |
| Leonard | Mary | 5ft 1in | 31 | Not known | 17/10/1844 | Fermanagh | Fermanagh | Larceny – stealing a cow | 7 | Y | 04/06/1845 | 320 | None | Housemaid and dairy woman | RC | N | S | N/A |
| Liston | Mary | 5ft 3½in | 27 | 11/07/1844 | 25/07/1844 | Tipperary | Tipperary | Vagrancy | 7 | Y | 06/06/1845 | 418 | None | Housemaid and plain laundress | RC | R | S | N/A |
| Lynam or Egan | Mary | 4ft 10¾in | 40 | Not known | 05/04/1845 | Longford | Longford | Larceny – stealing a pitch | 7 | Y | 03/06/1845 | 150 | None | Housemaid, wash and iron | RC | N | M | N/A |
| Lynch | Maria | 5ft 3½in | 20 | Not known | 10/07/1845 | Roscommon | Galway | Arson – setting fire to a cart house | 15 | N | 14/08/1845 | 54 | None | Farm servant and housemaid | RC | N | S | N/A |
| Madine | Harriet | 5ft 1¼in | 28 | Not known | 18/06/1845 | Down | Down | Larceny – stealing £5 | 10 | Y | 14/08/1845 | 76 | P worker | Shirt maker and staymaker | P | Yes | S | N/A |
| Magowan | Mary | 4ft 10¾in | 30 | Not known | 17/10/1844 | Fermanagh | Fermanagh | Larceny – stealing a watch | 7 | Y | 04/06/1845 | 320 | None | Farm servant and dairy woman | RC | N | M | N/A |
| Magrath | Mary | 5ft | 24 | 07/04/1845 | 26/04/1845 | Dublin City | Dublin | Vagrancy | 7 | Y | 02/05/1845 | 148 | None | housemaid | RC | R | S | N/A |

| Surname | First name | Height | Age | | Date of trial | Place of trial | Native place | Offence | Sentence | | Date arrived | Ship no | Former occupation | Occupation | Religion | Read | Status | |
|---|---|---|---|---|---|---|---|---|---|---|---|---|---|---|---|---|---|---|
| Maguire | Margaret | 5ft 2in | 30 | Not known | 27/12/1844 | Fermanagh | Fermanagh | Larceny – stealing potatoes. Mother Mary Scallon on board for same | 7 | Y | 04/06/1845 | 249 | None | Country servant | RC | R | S | N/A |
| Maguire | Ellen | 5ft 3in | 23 | Not known | 11/04/1845 | Cavan | Fermanagh | Larceny – stealing a watch | 10 | Y | 13/08/1845 | 144 | Spinster | Farm servant and country servant | RC | R | S | N/A |
| Mallon | Anne | 5ft 3in | 23 | Not known | 28/10/1844 | Antrim | Armagh | Larceny – stealing a cloak | 7 | Y | 03/06/1845 | 309 | P worker | Needle woman, nursemaid and laundress | RC | Yes | S | N/A |
| Martin | Martha | 5ft | 20 | Not known | 21/10/1844 | Cavan | Cavan | Larceny £11 from the person | 10 | Y | 04/06/1845 | 316 | None | Needle woman, laundress and housemaid | P | N | S | N/A |
| Marrow | Sarah Jane | 5ft 3in | 20 | Not known | 28/10/1844 | Antrim | Antrim | Larceny – stealing money | 10 | Y | 03/06/1845 | 309 | Mill-worker | Nurse girl and housemaid | RC | R | S | N/A |
| McArdle | Sarah | 5ft 1in | 28 | Not known | 16/07/1845 | Waterford City | Waterford | Vagrancy | 7 | Y | 15/08/1845 | 48 | None | Housemaid | RC | R | S | N/A |
| McAvine | Anne | 5ft 1½in | 22 | Not known | 17/07/1845 | Fermanagh | Fermanagh | Larceny – stealing a gown | 7 | Y | 13/08/1845 | 47 | Spinster | Country servant | RC | N | S | N/A |
| McBride | Mary | 5ft ½in | 22 | Not known | 05/04/1845 | Down | Down | Larceny – stealing a handkerchief. Tried with Eleanor McKiverigan | 10 | N | 03/06/1845 | 150 | None | Housemaid | P | N | S | N/A |
| McCarmack | Annie | 5ft 6½in | 30 | Not known | 15/01/1845 | Wexford | Wexford | Receiving stolen goods – printed cotton | 7 | Y | 04/06/1845 | 230 | None | Plain cook and dairymaid | | | M | N/A |
| McCarthy | Mary | 4ft 11in | 20 | Not known | 17/03/1845 | Cork Co. | Cork | Larceny – housebreaking and stealing clothes | 7 | Y | 04/06/1845 | 169 | None | Country servant | RC | N | S | N/A |
| McGinley | Sarah | 5ft 1in | 21 | Not known | 08/04/1845 | Antrim | Antrim, Belfast | Larceny – stealing £6 | 10 | Y | 03/06/1845 | 147 | Mill-worker | Housemaid | RC | R | S | N/A |

| | | | | | | | | | | | | | | | | | | |
|---|---|---|---|---|---|---|---|---|---|---|---|---|---|---|---|---|---|---|
| McKiverigan | Eleanor | 4ft 9in | 20 | Not known | 05/04/1845 | Down | Down, Newry | Larceny – stealing a handkerchief. Tried with Mary McBride | 10 | N | 03/06/1845 | 150 | | Laundress and Needle woman | RC | R | S | N/A |
| McMackin or O'Neill | Margaret | 4ft 11½in | 45 | Not known | 08/03/1845 | Tyrone | Tyrone | Larceny – stealing two frocks | 7 | Y | 05/06/1845 | 178 | Servant | Servant, Washer-woman, Housemaid and Dairywoman | RC | Yes | W | N/A |
| McManus | Mary | 5ft 1in | 27 | Not known | 28/10/1844 | Antrim | Antrim, Belfast | Larceny – stealing a watch | 10 | Y | 03/06/1845 | 309 | Mill-worker | Housemaid can wash | RC | R | S | N/A |
| McNally or Shaw | Catherine | 5ft | 25 | 27/05/1845 | 23/06/1845 | Meath | Meath | Larceny – stealing a petticoat | 7 | Y | 13/08/1845 | 98 | None | House servant and Nurse maid | RC | N | M | N/A |
| McNeil | Annie | 5ft 2½in | 30 | Not known | 01/01/1845 | Westmeath | Roscommon | Larceny – stealing a shirt | 7 | Y | 05/06/1845 | 244 | None | Country servant | RC | N | S | N/A |
| McVeagh | Mary | 5ft 3½in | 53 | Not known | 02/11/1844 | Armagh | Antrim | Larceny – stealing a shirt | 7 | Y | 05/06/1845 | 304 | None | Country servant | RC | R | W | CRF 1844McS1 |
| Meagher | Mary | 5ft 2in | 46 | 03/02/1845 | 20/03/1845 | Tipperary | Tipperary | Sheep stealing | 10 | N | 06/06/1845 | 211 | 30 | Country servant, Housemaid and Laundress | RC | N | W | N/A |
| Meany | Catherine | 5ft 4½in | 24 | Not known | 14/03/1845 | Kilkenny Co. | Kilkenny | Manslaughter – poisoning her husband | Life | N | 06/06/1845 | 172 | None | Country servant & Laundress | RC | N | W | N/A |
| Meara | Margaret | 5ft 4½in | 20 | Not known | 11/04/1845 | Tipperary | Limerick | Larceny – stealing clothes | 7 | Y | 06/06/1845 | 144 | Servant | Country servant and Housemaid | RC | N | S | N/A |
| Meehan | Mary | 5ft 1¼in | 30 | Not known | 21/02/1845 | Clare | Clare | Larceny – stealing 9yds of cotton | 7 | Y | 06/08/1845 | 193 | None | Housemaid | RC | N | S | N/A |
| Merryfield | Martha | 5ft 2½in | 21 | Not known | 25/06/1845 | Antrim | Antrim, Belfast | Larceny | 7 | Y | 14/08/1845 | 69 | Servant | Housemaid can wash | P | Yes | S | N/A |

| Mugan | Honor | 4ft 8in | 30 | Not known | 27/06/1845 | Mayo | Mayo | Larceny – stealing £2 17s 6d | 7 | N | 14/08/1845 | 67 | None | House servant | RC | N | S | N/A |
|---|---|---|---|---|---|---|---|---|---|---|---|---|---|---|---|---|---|---|
| Mullan | Anne | 5ft 2½in | 26 | Not known | 09/01/1845 | Antrim | Woolwich | Larceny – stealing a clock | 7 | Y | 03/06/1845 | 236 | Servant | Housemaid can wash | RC | N | S | N/A |
| Murphy | Mary | 4ft 10½in | 52 | Not known | 01/01/1845 | Monaghan | Cavan | Larceny – receiving a piece of cloth stolen by her daughter, Margaret Wilson | 7 | N | 05/06/1845 | 244 | None | Housemaid | RC | Yes | W | N/A |
| Murray | Johannah | 5ft 1in | 24 | Not known | 01/01/1845 | Cork Co. | Cork | Receiving stolen goods. Tried with Catherine Keefe | 7 | Y | 04/06/1845 | 244 | None | Housemaid can wash | RC | N | S | N/A |
| Neill | Ellen | 4ft 10¾in | 20 | Not known | 09/07/1844 | Carlow | Carlow | Larceny – stealing a watch from the person | 7 | Y | 07/09/1844 | 420 | None | Housemaid | RC | N | S | N/A |
| O'Brien | Mary 1st | 5ft 1½in | 29 | Not known | 25/02/1845 | Dublin City | Dublin | Felony – stealing a shawl | 7 | Y | 25/02/1845 | 189 | None | Housemaid | RC | R | S | N/A |
| O'Brien | Mary 2nd | 4ft 11½in | 35 | Not known | 18/07/1845 | Limerick City | Limerick | Larceny – stealing a sheet | 7 | Y | 15/08/1845 | 46 | None | Housemaid | RC | N | W | N/A |
| O'Neill | Sarah Ann | 4ft 11½in | 21 | Not known | 20/06/1844 | Tyrone | Tyrone | Larceny – stealing a dress | 7 | N | 05/06/1845 | 439 | P worker | Laundress | RC | R | S | CRF 1844 O11 |
| Perry | Eliza | 5ft | 27 | Not known | 08/01/1845 | Dublin City | Wicklow | Felony – stealing a watch, coat and money | 7 | Y | 16/01/1845 | 237 | None | Housemaid | RC | Yes | S | N/A |
| Preston | Catherine | 4ft 11in | 22 | Not known | 08/04/1844 | Louth | Cavan | Larceny – stealing £43 | 7 | Y | 06/09/1844 | 512 | None | Nursemaid | P | R | S | N/A |
| Randall or Reilly or Mary Reynolds | Margaret | 5ft 5in | 31 | 13/06/1845 | 14/06/1845 | Dublin City | Dublin | Stealing money and wearing apparel | 10 | Y | 20/06/1845 | 81 | Servant | Midwife | RC | Yes | M | N/A |
| Riley | Catherine | 5ft 1in | 30 | Not known | 18/10/1844 | Roscommon | Roscommon | Larceny – stealing a suit of clothes | 7 | Y | 05/06/1845 | 319 | None | Housemaid, country servant | RC | N | S | CRF 1845 R6 |

| | | | | | | | | | | | | | P worker | | P | R | S | |
|---|---|---|---|---|---|---|---|---|---|---|---|---|---|---|---|---|---|---|
| Rooney | Bell | 5ft 8¾in | 28 | Not known | Down | Down | 18/06/1845 | Larceny – stealing 10s 4d from the person | 10 | Y | 14/08/1845 | 76 | | Needle-woman, housemaid, can wash | | | S | CRF 1845 R-27 |
| Russell | Mary | 5ft ½in | 23 | Not known | Kildare (Athy) | Kildare | 03/01/1845 | Felony – stealing eight barrels of potatoes. Tried with Anne Delany | 7 | Y | 06/06/1845 | 242 | None | Nursemaid | RC | R | S | N/A |
| Ryan | Mary | 5ft ½in | 21 | Not known | Wicklow | Kildare | 24/10/1844 | Larceny – stealing clothes | 7 | Y | 05/06/1845 | 313 | None | Housemaid | RC | R | S | N/A |
| Ryan | Sarah | 5ft 2in | 26 | 13/12/1844 | Limerick City | Limerick | 08/03/1845 | Stealing from the person – a watch | 10 | Y | 15/08/1845 | 263 | Servant | Housemaid, laundress, milk | RC | N | S | N/A |
| Salmon or Lyons | Mary | 5ft 3¾in | 21 | Not known | Kildare (Naas) | Kildare | 25/06/1845 | Larceny – stealing clothes | 7 | Y | 15/08/1845 | 69 | None | Housemaid | RC | Yes | S | N/A |
| Sawyer or Gardiner | Margaret | 5ft 4½in | 26 | Not known | Queens | Queens | 07/01/1845 | Larceny – stealing plaid clothes | 7 | Y | 06/06/1845 | 238 | Milliner | Dressmaker, country servant | P | R | W | N/A |
| Scallon | Mary | 5ft 3in | 60 | Not known | Fermanagh | Fermanagh | 27/12/1844 | Larceny – stealing potatoes. Tried with her daughter Margaret Maguire | 7 | Y | 04/06/1845 | 249 | None | Plain cook and house servant | RC | N | S | N/A |
| Shaughnessy | Eleanor | 5ft 1in | 19 | Not known | Kilkenny Co. | Kilkenny | 17/10/1844 | Larceny and burglary – stealing a veil | 10 | N | 06/06/1845 | 320 | None | Nursemaid | RC | R | S | N/A |
| Sloane | Margaret | 5ft 3¾in | 40 | Not known | Tyrone | Tyrone | 11/01/1845 | Larceny – stealing a gown and a quilt | 7 | Y | 05/06/1845 | 234 | None | Farm servant and plain llundress | P | N | W | CRF 1845 S8 |
| Smyth or Swan | Mary Anne | 5ft 1in | 27 | Not known | Dublin City | Dublin | 28/12/1844 | Felony – stealing blankets | 7 | Y | 30/12/1844 | 248 | Servant | Plain cook and laundress | P | R | S | N/A |
| Stankard | Bridget | 5ft 4in | 24 | Not known | Leitrim | Leitrim | 31/12/1844 | Perjury | 7 | N | 03/06/1845 | 245 | None | House and farm servant | RC | N | S | N/A |
| Stewart | Catherine | 4ft 9½in | 28 | Not known | Armagh | Paisley | 25/06/1845 | Larceny – stealing 12s 8d | 7 | Y | 14/08/1845 | 69 | None | Housemaid can wash | P | R | S | N/A |

| Surname | First name | Height | Age | | Date | | | Crime | | | Date | | | Occupation | | | | | |
|---|---|---|---|---|---|---|---|---|---|---|---|---|---|---|---|---|---|---|---|
| Sullivan | Mary 1st | 5ft 3in | 62 | Not known | 03/01/1845 | Limerick | Kerry, Killarney | Larceny – stealing 16s. Claimed tried with Henrietta Beresford | 7 | N | 06/06/1845 | 242 | None | Laundress Plain cook | RC | N | W | N/A |
| Sullivan | Mary 2nd | 5ft 1in | 45 | Not known | 16/07/1845 | Waterford | Waterford | Vagrancy | 7 | Y | 15/08/1845 | 48 | None | Nurse servant | RC | N | S | N/A |
| Sullivan D. 28/11/1845 on voyage | Ellen | 4ft 11in | 20 | Not known | 15/03/1844 | Kerry | Kerry | Burglary | 10 | N | 04/06/1845 | 536 | None | Not known | C | R | S | CRF 1844 S24 |
| Thompson | Mary | 5ft | 27 | Not known | 14/01/1845 | Down | Down | Larceny – stealing yarn and butter | 7 | Y | 03/06/1845 | 231 | None | Housemaid can wash | RC | R | S | N/A |
| Wade | Anne | 4ft 10in | 23 | Not known | 22/10/1844 | Queens | Queens | Larceny – stealing calico | 7 | Y | 06/06/185 | 315 | Spinster | Farm servant | P | N | S | N/A |
| Wall | Mary | 5ft 1½in | 29 | Not known | 11/10/1844 | Cork Co. | Cork | Receiving stolen goods – a coat and cloak | 7 | Y | 04/06/1845 | 326 | None | Farm servant | RC | N | M | N/A |
| Waring | Elizabeth | 5ft 1in | 40 | Not known | 14/03/1845 | Down | Dublin | Perjury | 7 | N | 03/06/1845 | 172 | Servant | House servant | Jew-ess | R | W | N/A |
| Warnock | Isabella | 5ft 3½in | 24 | Not known | 08/04/1845 | Antrim | Dublin | Larceny – stealing a watch from the person | 10 | Y | 03/06/1845 | 147 | Dress-maker | Dressmaker | P | Yes | S | N/A |
| Williams | Ann | 5ft 6in | 24 | Not known | 11/10/1844 | Dublin City | King's | Felony – stealing ribbon | 7 | Y | 12/10/1844 | 326 | None | House and nursemaid | P | R | S | N/A |
| Wilson | Margaret | 5ft | 17 | Not known | 01/01/1845 | Monaghan | Cavan | Larceny – stealing a shoe | 7 | Y | 05/06/1845 | 244 | Servant | Nursemaid | RC | R | S | N/A |
| Wright | Elizabeth | 4ft 9in | 40 | Not known | 17/03/1845 | Londonderry | Tyrone | Having instruments for coining in her possession | 10 | N | 05/06/1845 | 169 | None | Laundress | P | R | M | CRF 1845 W2 |

# Appendix III

# The Children of the *Tasmania* (2)

## *TASMANIA* (2) CHILDREN IN GRANGEGORMAN FEMALE CONVICT DEPOT 1845 (N = 35)[4]

| Name | Child | Age | Admission |
|---|---|---|---|
| Sarah Brennan | Joseph Carroll | 1y9m | 31 Mar 1845 |
| Anne Doherty | John Reynolds[5] | 1y | 3 Jun 1845 |
| Margaret Kelly | Sarah Anne Kelly | 7y6m | 3 Jun 1845 |
| | Catherine Kelly | 1y2m | 3 Jun 1845 |
| Mary Lynam or Egan | Jane Lynam | b.5 Jul | 3 Jun 1845 |
| Mary Connell | Margaret Connell | 8y | 4 Jun 1845 |
| | Patrick Connell | 4y9m | 4 Jun 1845 |
| | James Connell | 2y | 4 Jun 1845 |
| Mary Leonard | Mary Leonard or McCaffrey | 10m | 4 Jun 1845 |
| Mary Magowan | Anne Ferguson | 8y | 4 Jun 1845 |
| | Patrick Ferguson or Bradley | 4m | 4 Jun 1845 |
| Ellen Sullivan | Mary Reardon | 6m | 4 Jun 1845 |
| Mary Wall | Mary Anne Wall | 3y6m | 4 Jun 1845 |
| | Patrick Wall | 1y1m | 4 Jun 1845 |
| Anne McNeil[6] | William Moran | 1y6m | 5 Jun 1845 |
| Mary Murphy | Rose Murphy[7] | 9y | 5 Jun 1845 |
| Jane Bradshaw | Mary Jane Connor | 1y9m | 6 Jun 1845 |
| Esther Burgess | Elizabeth Burgess | 11y | 6 Jun 1845 |
| | Alice Burgess | 9y | 6 Jun 1845 |
| | James (Jane) Burgess[8] | 7y | 6 Jun 1845 |

| | William Burgess | 4y6m | 6 Jun 1845 |
|---|---|---|---|
| | Robert Burgess | 1y | 6 Jun 1845 |
| Margaret Butler 2nd | William Butler | 6y | 6 Jun 1845 |
| | Mary Ann Butler | 1y | 6 Jun 1845 |
| Mary Byrne | Anne Byrne | 1y | 6 Jun 1845 |
| Honora Cullen[9] | James Keegan | 9m | 6 Jun 1845 |
| Catherine Grace | Mary Grace | 7y | 6 Jun 1845 |
| | Bridget Grace | 4y | 6 Jun 1845 |
| | Catherine Grace | 2y | 6 Jun 1845 |
| Margaret Grady | James Austin | 3y6m | 6 Jun 1845 |
| Mary Griffen | Eliza Griffen | 9y | 6 Jun 1845 |
| | Mary Anne Griffen | 6y | 6 Jun 1845 |
| | Edward Griffen | 2y | 6 Jun 1845 |
| Elizabeth Hearns | Jane (James) Hearns[10] | 1y2m | 15 Aug 1845 |
| Mary O'Brien 2nd | Margaret O'Brien | 6y6m | 15 Aug 1845 |

Source: NAI, PRIS 1/09/07 Grangegorman Prison Registry of Female Convicts, Grangegorman Female Convict Depot, 11 July 1840 – 22 December 1853.

## NUMBER OF CHILDREN BORN TO *TASMANIA* (2) CONVICTS BEFORE AND AFTER TRANSPORTATION (N=14)

| Convict Name | Total Children | Children Before Transportation | Children After Transportation |
|---|---|---|---|
| Jane Bradshaw | 2 | 1 | 1 |
| Sarah Brennan | 3 | 1 | 2 |
| Mary Byrne | 4 | 1 | 3 |
| Mary Connell | 5 | 3 | 2 |
| Eliza Davis | 10 | 1 | 9 |
| Anne Dogherty | 2? | 1 | 1 |
| Catherine Grace | 5 | 3 | 2 |
| Margaret Grady | 4 | 1 | 3 |
| Elizabeth Hearns | 2 | 1 | 1 |
| Sarah McArdle | 5 | 1 | 4 |
| Margaret McMackin | 4? | 3? | 1 |
| Annie McNeill | 2 | 1 | 1 |
| Harriet Madine | 4 | 1 | 3 |
| Mary Wall or Watt | 6 | 4 | 2 |

# Appendix IV

# The Sick List of the *Tasmania* (2)

Copy of the Daily Sick Book in the FC ship *Tasmania* between 28 August and 9 December 1845. An additional column has been included showing the present-day term for the disease described by Mr Lardner. (Starts overleaf)

| When put on Sick List | Name | Age | No. on S.B. | Disease | (Present-day term) | When put off the List | Disposal |
|---|---|---|---|---|---|---|---|
| 30 Aug | Mary McGowan's child | 6 mths | | Phthisis | Tuberculosis | 20 Sep | Died |
| 8 Sep | Honor Cullen | 22 | 26 | Ophthalmia | Inflammation of the eye (infection) | 15 Sep | N/A |
| 9 Sep | Jane Gallagher | 24 | 55 | Constipation | | 14 Sep | N/A |
| 9 Sep | Mary McManus | 25 | 28 | Phlogosis | Skin inflammation | 25 Sep | N/A |
| 9 Sep | Mary Scallon | 66 | 27 | Rheumatism | | 18 Sep | N/A |
| 10 Sep | Mary Griffon | 30 | 84 | Dyspepsia | Stomach complaint, pain indigestion | 3 Oct | N/A |
| 10 Sep | Mary Murphy | 50 | 80 | Dyspepsia | Stomach complaint, pain indigestion | 3 Oct | N/A |
| 12 Sep | Ellen Neill | 20 | 126 | Rheumatism | | 26 Oct | N/A |
| 13 Sep | Ann Fitzpatrick | 54 | 90 | Dyspepsia | Stomach complaint, pain indigestion | 26 Oct | N/A |
| 14 Sep | Jane Bradshaw | 21 | 54 | Dyspepsia | Stomach complaint, pain indigestion | 29 Sep | N/A |
| 14 Sep | Eliz Hearns | 25 | 93 | Dyspepsia | Stomach complaint, pain indigestion | 30 Sep | N/A |
| 15 Sep | Ellen Cahil | 20 | 96 | Cynanche | Throat/Tonsillitis infection | 20 Sep | N/A |
| 16 Sep | Ellen Cummane | 23 | 95 | Dyspepsia | Stomach complaint, pain indigestion | 5 Oct | N/A |
| 16 Sep | Henri [sic] Beresford | 24 | 69 | Dyspepsia | Stomach complaint, pain indigestion | 20 Sep | N/A |
| 16 Sep | Cath Farrell | 21 | 116 | Rheumatism | | 28 Sep | N/A |
| 16 Sep | Rose Fitzpatrick | 52 | 88 | Dyspepsia | Stomach complaint, pain indigestion | 22 Sep | N/A |
| 20 Sep | Cathe Meaney | 19 | 76 | Diarrhœ | | 23 Sep | N/A |
| 20 Sep | Mary Ryan | 23 | 61 | Dyspepsia | Stomach complaint, pain indigestion | 29 Sep | N/A |
| 21 Sep | Anne McAvine | 22 | 114 | Ulcus | An ulcer | 3 Sep | N/A |
| 21 Sep | Ann Wade | 26 | 13 | Dyspepsia | Stomach complaint, pain indigestion | 28 Sep | N/A |

| | | | | | | | |
|---|---|---|---|---|---|---|---|
| 21 Sep | Mary Russell | 22 | 57 | Dyspepsia | Stomach complaint, pain indigestion | 26 Sep | N/A |
| 21 Sep | Mary Gillespie | 38 | 92 | Dyspepsia | Stomach complaint, pain indigestion | 28 Sep | N/A |
| 22 Sep | Sarah Ryan | 25 | 45 | Dyspepsia | Stomach complaint, pain indigestion | 30 Sep | N/A |
| 22 Sep | Margt Butler | 40 | 85 | Diarrhœ | | 26 Sep | N/A |
| 22 Sep | Margt [Mary] Barry | 25 | 46 | Dyspepsia | Stomach complaint, pain indigestion | 28 Sep | N/A |
| 23 Sep | Cath Foy | 22 | 115 | Synanche [sic] | Throat/Tonsillitis infection | 12 Oct | N/A |
| 23 Sep | Ann Flannery | 25 | 110 | Hæmetemosis | Vomiting blood | 30 Sep | N/A |
| 23 Sep | Mary Connell | 30 | 138 | Synanche | Throat/Tonsillitis infection | 5 Nov | N/A |
| 29 Sep | Sarah Kelly's child | 8 | | Ophthalmia | Inflammation of the eye (infection) | 4 Oct | N/A |
| 2 Oct | Margt Wilson | 16 | 81 | Scropula | Tuberculosis of the lymph nodes | 2 Nov | N/A |
| 2 Oct | Bridt Kelly | 25 | 103 | Phlogosis | Skin inflammation | 7 Oct | N/A |
| 8 Oct | Mary McManus | 25 | 27 | Ulcus | | 9 Dec | *Anson* |
| 9 Oct | Ann Gardiner | 52 | 71 | Contusio | Bruising | 15 Oct | N/A |
| 9 Oct | Bell Amos | 18 | 56 | Ophthalmia | Inflammation of the eye (infection) | 15 Oct | N/A |
| 12 Oct | Cath Shaw | 25 | 134 | Ulcus | | 30 Nov | N/A |
| 15 Oct | Mary McCarthy | 19 | 133 | Verruca | Skin disease, warts | 31 Oct | N/A |
| 16 Oct | Mary Griffon's child | 10 | | Cynanche | Throat/Tonsillitis infection | 23 Oct | N/A |
| 23 Oct | Mary Leonard | 28 | 112 | Phlogosis | Skin inflammation | 31 Oct | N/A |
| 25 Oct | Ann McAvine | 22 | 114 | Diarrhœ | | 1 Nov | N/A |
| 25 Oct | Bridt Kelly | 25 | 103 | Diarrhœ | | 5 Nov | N/A |
| 25 Oct | Cath Foy | 22 | 115 | Rheumatism | | 9 Dec | Colonial Hosp. |
| 25 Oct | Mary Scallon | 56 | 1 | Herpes | | 10 Nov | N/A |

| 25 Oct | Mary Frances | 24 | 108 | Contusio | Bruising | 30 Oct | N/A |
|---|---|---|---|---|---|---|---|
| 25 Oct | Mary McGowan | 29 | 113 | Haemonhois | Vomiting blood | 14 Nov | N/A |
| 29 Oct | Ellen Cahil | 23 | 96 | Contusio | Bruising | 3 Nov | N/A |
| 1 Nov | Brid Clifford | 30 | 135 | Rheumatism | | 30 Nov | N/A |
| 1 Nov | Mary McCarthy | 19 | 133 | Vulnus | Multiple wounds | 14 Nov | N/A |
| 5 Nov | Fanny Doherty | 26 | 98 | Pleuritis | Pleurisy | 24 Nov | N/A |
| 6 Nov | Elen Shaughnessy | 19 | 127 | Hysteria | Emotionally unwell | 14 Nov | N/A |
| 7 Nov | Mary [Sarah] McArdle | 28 | 136 | Parturition | Child birth | 20 Nov | N/A |
| 11 Nov | Mary Meagher | 50 | 48 | Diarrhea | | 28 Nov | N/A |
| 13 Nov | Mary McGrath | 31 | 120 | Diarrhæ | | 19 Nov | N/A |
| 13 Nov | Cath Reilly | 25 | 122 | Diarrhæ | | 24 Nov | N/A |
| 14 Nov | Ellen Sullivan | 20 | 94 | Dysentery | Intestinal inflammation. Diarrhoea with blood and mucus | 28 Nov | Died |
| 14 Nov | Honor Cullen | 23 | 55 | Diarrhæ | | 20 Nov | N/A |
| 15 Nov | Ann Fitzpatrick | 54 | 90 | Diarrhæ | | 24 Nov | N/A |
| 18 Nov | Elizabeth Hearns | 24 | 93 | Diarrhæ | | 1 Dec | N/A |
| 18 Nov | Mary Scallon | 66 | 1 | Diarrhæ | | 24 Nov | N/A |
| 18 Nov | Bell Amos | 18 | 56 | Catarrhus | Flu-like illness. Runny nose mucus | 24 Nov | N/A |
| 18 Nov | Cath Meany | 22 | 76 | Diarrhæ | | 24 Nov | N/A |
| 18 Nov | Mary Hetherington | 23 | 66 | Catarrhus | Flu-like illness. Runny nose mucus | 24 Nov | N/A |
| 19 Nov | Ann Delany | 17 | 58 | Diarrhæ | | 28 Nov | N/A |
| 19 Nov | Mary Leonard | 28 | 112 | Diarrhæ | | 24 Nov | N/A |
| 19 Nov | Ann Burns | 28 | 47 | Vulnus | Wound | 28 Nov | N/A |

| | | | | | | | |
|---|---|---|---|---|---|---|---|
| 21 Nov | Mary Gillespie | 38 | 92 | Diarrhœa | | 30 Nov | N/A |
| 22 Nov | S Brennan's Child | 1½ | | Vulnus | Wound | 4 Dec | N/A |
| 22 Nov | Ellen Neill | 20 | 126 | Rheumatism | | 9 Dec | Colonial Hosp. |
| 27 Nov | Eliz Dwyer | 22 | 79 | Synache | Throat/Tonsillitis infection | 3 Dec | N/A |
| 27 Nov | Ann Williams | 26 | 39 | Diarrhœa | | 1 Dec | N/A |
| 27 Nov | Mary Griffon | 30 | 84 | Dyspepsia | Stomach complaint, pain indigestion | 9 Dec | Colonial Hosp. |
| 27 Nov | Elizh Waring | 40 | 52 | Diarrhœa | | 1 Dec | N/A |
| 27 Nov | Johanh Murray | 35 | 99 | Synache | Throat/Tonsillitis infection | 4 Dec | N/A |
| 27 Nov | Margt Grady | 29 | 121 | Catarrhus | Flu-like illness. Runny nose mucus | 5 Dec | N/A |
| 28 Nov | Mary Byrne | 30 | 117 | Diarrhœa | | 5 Dec | N/A |
| 28 Nov | Mary McBride | 22 | 74 | Diarrhœa | | 4 Dec | N/A |
| 28 Nov | Brid Dignan | 22 | 91 | Synache | Throat/Tonsillitis infection | 5 Dec | N/A |
| 28 Nov | Mary Murphy | 50 | 80 | Catarrhus | Flu-like illness. Runny nose mucus | 5 Dec | N/A |
| 28 Nov | Ellen McGuire | 23 | 111 | Dyspepsia | Stomach complaint, pain indigestion | 4 Dec | N/A |
| 28 Nov | Mary Frances | 24 | 108 | Catarrhus | Flu-like illness. Runny nose mucus | 3 Dec | N/A |
| 28 Nov | Ann Wade | 26 | 13 | Synache | Throat/Tonsillitis infection | 2 Dec | N/A |
| 28 Nov | Mary Thompson | 27 | 51 | Synache | Throat/Tonsillitis infection | 3 Dec | N/A |
| 28 Nov | Mary Hetherington | 23 | 66 | Catarrhus | Flu-like illness. Runny nose mucus | 5 Dec | N/A |
| 29 Nov | Cath Burnett | 20 | 59 | Dyspepsia | Stomach complaint, pain indigestion | 7 Dec | N/A |
| 2 Dec | Esther Burgess | 36 | 100 | Diarrhœa | | 6 Dec | N/A |
| 4 Dec | Mary McCarthy | 20 | 133 | Verruca | Skin disease, warts | 9 Dec | Colonial Hosp. |

## CAUSES OF DEATH OF THE WOMEN OF THE TASMANIA (2) (N=41)

| Convict | Cause of Death | Place | Date | Death Age |
|---|---|---|---|---|
| Burgess, Esther | Rupture of blood vessel, left lung | Hobart | 1855 | 46 |
| Burgess, Mary | Pneumonia | Launceston | 1898 | 68 |
| Butler, Margaret 2nd | Manslaughter | Hobart | 1855 | 31 [sic] |
| Byrne, Mary | Consumption | Hobart | 1858 | 38 |
| Connelly, Ellen | Dropsy | Launceston | 1872 | 42 |
| Davis, Eliza | Cerebral apoplexy | Emu Bay | 1898 | 69 |
| Dignan, Bridget | Dysentery | Longford | 1857 | 32 |
| Doherty, Fanny | Visitation of God | Hobart | 1846 | 26 |
| Dooling or Dowling, Judith | Killed by falling timber in a hut | | 1856 | 50 or 68 |
| Fitzpatrick, Ann | Old age and debility | Hobart | 1865 | 74 |
| Fitzpatrick, Rose | Icterus (jaundice) | Hobart | 1856 | 60 |
| Flood, Ann | Cancer: epithalamia and stricture of oesophagus | Hobart | 1889 | 66 |
| Gallagher, Bridget | Intestinal inflammation | Hobart | 1876 | 47 |
| Gallagher, Jane | Kidney disease | Hobart | 1876 | 45 |
| Gardiner or Harrison, Ann | Not known | Brighton | 1850 | |
| Gillespie, Mary | Not known | Hobart | 1850 | 42 |
| Hughes, Catherine | Phthisis pulmonalis | Hobart | 1881 | 50 |
| Hunter, Eliza | Debilitas | Hobart | 1854 | 50 |
| Hurley, Mary | Drowned, River Derwent | | 1850 | |
| Jackson, Ellen | Not known | New Norfolk | | |
| Johnson or Derbyshire, Maria | Phthisis pulmonalis | Hobart | 1870 | 43 |
| Kelly, Margaret | Not known | New Norfolk | 1856 | 55 |
| McArdle or Thompson, Mary | Senility | Launceston | 1888 | 72 |
| McBride, Mary | Not known | Launceston | 1907 | 85 |
| McCarthy, Mary | Cancer of the tongue and mouth | Hobart | 1884 | 55 |
| McMackin, Margaret | Phthisis | Hobart | 1853 | 44 |
| McNally or Shaw, Catherine | Childbirth | Launceston | 1853 | 28 |
| Madine, Harriet | Not known | Launceston | 1898 | 84 |
| Maguire, Ellen | Senility | Launceston | 1897 | 77 |
| Mallon, Ann | Senility and bronchitis | Deloraine | 1891 | 76 |
| Merryfield, Martha | Vascular disease of the heart | New Norfolk | 1891 | 68 |

| | | | | |
|---|---|---|---|---|
| Molloy, Catherine | Paralysis | New Norfolk | 1884 | 72 |
| Murray, Johannah | Disease of the brain | New Norfolk | 1876 | 54 |
| Murphy, Mary | Visitation of God (inflammation of lungs) | | | |
| O'Brien, Mary 2nd | Dementia | New Norfolk | 1900 | |
| Perry, Eliza | Debility | Launceston | 1871 | 52 |
| Pritchard, Sarah | Cancer of the breast | Oatlands | 1881 | 63 |
| Riley, Catherine | Phthisis pulmonalis | Hobart | 1854 | 40 |
| Russell, Mary | Natural causes | Launceston | 1868 | 47 |
| Salmon or Lyons, Mary | Not known | Launceston | 1896 | 66 |
| Suitor or Fanning, Bridget | Paraplegia | Launceston | 1856 | 45 |

# Select Bibliography

## BOOKS

Alford, Katrina. *Production or Reproduction? An economic history of women in Australia, 1788–1850*, Melbourne, Oxford University Press, 1984.

Alexander, Alison (ed.). *The Companion to Tasmanian History*, Hobart, Centre for Tasmanian Historical Studies, University of Tasmania, 2005.

Alexander, Alison. *Tasmania's Convicts: How Felons Built a Free Society*, Sydney, Allen & Unwin, 2010.

Bardon, Jonathan. *A History of Ireland in 250 Episodes*, Dublin, Gill and Macmillan, 2009.

Bateson, Charles. *The Convict Ships 1787–1868*, Sydney, Library of Australian History, 1983.

Beckett, J.C. *A Short History of Ireland. From Earliest Times to the Present Day*, first published London, 1952; this edition, Random House, 1979.

Boyce, James. *Van Diemen's Land*, Melbourne, Black Inc., 2008.

Brand, Ian. *The convict probation system, Van Diemen's Land 1839–1854: a study of the probation system of convict discipline, together with C.J. La Trobe's 1847 report on its operation and the 1845 report of James Boyd on the probation station at Darlington, Maria Island*, Hobart, Blubber Head Press, 1990.

Brown, Joan C. *'Poverty is not a crime': the development of social services in Tasmania, 1803–1900*, Hobart, Tasmanian Historical Research Association, 1972.

Coad, David. *Port Cygnet Irish Convicts*, Kingston, David Coad, 2012.

Coad, David. *Port Cygnet 1792–1860. A History of Tasmania,* Volume 1, Kingston, David Coad, 1st published 2009, revised edition 2010.

Coad, David. *Port Cygnet 1860–1900. A History of Tasmania*, Kingston, David Coad, 2010.

Coad, David. *Port Cygnet 1900. A History of Tasmania,* Volume 3, Kingston, David Coad, 2011.

Coad, David. *Port Cygnet 1914–1919. A History of Tasmania*, Volume 4, Kingston, David Coad, 2014.

Connolly, S.J. *Oxford Companion to Irish History*, Oxford, Oxford University Press, 1998.

Cotton, Frances. *Kettle on the hob: a family in Van Diemen's Land, 1828–1885*, Orford, Tasmania, Joan Roberts, 1986.

Cowley, Trudy and Snowden, Dianne. *Patchwork Prisoners: The Rajah Quilt and the women who made it*, Hobart, Research Tasmania, 2013.

Cuffley, Peter (ed.). *Send the Boy to Sea: The Memoirs of a Sailor on the Goldfields by James Montagu Smith*, Noble Park, Victoria, Five Mile Press, 2001.

Damousi, Joy. *Depraved and Disorderly*, Cambridge, Cambridge University Press, 1997.

Daniels, Kay. *Convict Women*, St Leonards, NSW, Allen & Unwin, 1998.

Dún Laoghaire Harbour Company. *The Construction of Dun Laoghaire Harbour*, Dun Laoghaire Harbour Company, 2003.

Emsley, Clive. *Crime and Society in England, 1750–1900*, London and New York, Longman, 1987.

Finane, Mark. *Insanity and the Insane in Post-Famine Ireland*, London, Croom Helm, 1981.

Fitzpatrick, Sir Jeremiah. *An essay on gaol-abuses, and on the means of redressing them; together with the general method of treating disorders to which prisoners are most incident*. Dublin, 1784.

Foster, R.F. *Modern Ireland 1600–1972*, London, Penguin Books, 1988.

Frost, Lucy. *Footsteps and Voices: An historical look into the Cascades Female Factory*, Hobart, Female Factory Historic Site Ltd., 2004.

Frost, Lucy (ed.). *Convict Lives at the Ross Female Factory*, Hobart, Convict Women's Press, 2011.

Fry, Katherine and Rachel Cresswell (eds). *Memoir of the life of Elizabeth Fry, with extracts from her journals and letters, edited by two of her daughters*, London, C. Gilpin, J. Hatchard, 1847–48.

Geoghegan, Patrick M. *Liberator: The Life and Death of Daniel O'Connell 1830–1847*, Dublin, Gill & Macmillan, 2012.

Gray, Peter. *The Irish Famine*, London, Thames and Hudson, 1995.

Gowlland, Ralph W. *Troubled asylum: the history of the Royal Derwent Hospital, R.W. Gowlland*, New Norfolk, 1981.

Griffin, Brian. *Sources for the Study of Crime in Ireland 1801–1921*, Dublin, Four Courts Press, 2005.

Grundy, Joan E. *A Dictionary of Medical & Related Terms for the Family Historian,* Rotherham, South Yorkshire, Swansong Publications, 2006.

Harrington, John P. (comp. & ed.). *The English Traveller in Ireland; Accounts of Ireland and the Irish Through Five Centuries*, Dublin, Wolfhound Press, 1997.

Howard, Patrick. *To Hell or to Hobart*, Sydney, Kangaroo Press, 1993.

Kennedy, Liam; Ell, Paul S.; Crawford, E.M.; & Clarkson, L.A. *Mapping the Great Irish Famine*, Dublin, Four Courts Press, 1999.

Killeen, Richard. *A Timeline of Irish History*, Dublin, Gill & Macmillan, 2003.

Lewis, Samuel. *A Topographical Dictionary of Ireland*, 2 volumes, first published London, 1837; reprinted Baltimore, 1984.

Neal, David. *The Rule of Law in a Penal Colony: Law and Power in Early New South Wales*, Melbourne, Cambridge University Press, 1992.

McClaughlin, Trevor, *Barefoot and Pregnant. Irish Famine Orphans in Australia*, Volume 1, Melbourne, Genealogical Society of Victoria, 1991.

McDowell, R.B. *The Irish Administration, 1801–1914*, London, Routledge & Kegan Paul, 1964.

MacLysaght, Edward. *The Surnames of Ireland*, Dublin, Irish Academic Press, 1991.

McMahon, Anne. *Convicts at Sea; the voyages of the Irish convict transports to Van Diemen's Land, 1840–1853*, Victoria, Anne McMahon, 2011.

Maxwell-Stewart, Hamish. *Closing Hell's Gates – the closing of a convict station*, Sydney, Allen & Unwin, 2008.

Meredith, Louisa Ann. *My home in Tasmania, during a residence of nine years by Mrs. Charles Meredith,* London, John Murray, 1852; facsimile edition, Glamorgan Spring Bay Historical Society (Tas.), 2003.

Mitchel, John. *Jail Journal*, Dublin, University Press of Ireland, 1982.

Mundy, Lieutenant Colonel G.C., *Our Antipodes, or, Residences and Rambles in the Australasian Colonies*, 4th edition, London, 1857.

Nicholson, Asenath. *Ireland's Welcome to the Stranger or An Excursion Though Ireland in 1844 & 1845*, New York, Baker and Scribner, 1847.

O'Connor, John. *The Workhouses of Ireland. The fate of Ireland's Poor*, Dublin, Anvil Books, 1995.

O'Donnell, Ruán. *A Short History of Ireland's Famine*, Dublin, O'Brien Press, 2008.

Ó Gráda, Cormac. *Ireland: A New Economic History*, Oxford, Oxford University Press, 1994.

Ó Tuathaigh, Gearóid. *Ireland before the Famine: 1798–1848*, Dublin, Gill & Macmillan, 2007.

Oxley, Deborah. *Convict Maids. The Forced Migration of Women to Australia*, Melbourne, Cambridge University Press, 1996.

Perrott, Monica. *A Tolerable Good Success. Economic Opportunities for Women in New South Wales 1788–1830*, Sydney, Hale & Iremonger, 1983.

Phillips, David. *Crime and Authority in Victorian England*, London, Croom Helm, 1977.

Rayner, Tony. *Female factory, female convicts: the story of the more than 13,000 female convicts sent to Van Diemen's Land*, Dover, Esperance Press, 2004.

Reed, Kevin. *The Widows of Tullow*, Hamilton, Victoria, K&R Reed, 1998.

Robins, Joseph. *The Lost Children: A Study of Charity Children 1700–1900*, Dublin, Institute of Public Administration, 1980.

Robinson, Portia. *The Hatch and Brood of Time: A study of the first generation of native-born White Australians 1788–1828*, Volume 1, Melbourne, Oxford University Press, 1985.

Robinson, Portia. *The Women of Botany Bay: A Reinterpretation of the Role of Women in the Origins of Convict Society*, revised edition, Ringwood, Victoria, Penguin, 1993.

Rudé, George. *Criminal and Victim: Crime and Society in Early Nineteenth-Century England*, Oxford, Clarendon Press, 1985.

Shaw, A.G.L. (ed.). John West, *The History of Tasmania*, Sydney, Angus and Robertson, 1971.

Smith, Babette. *Australia's Birthstain: The startling legacy of the convict era*, Sydney, Allen & Unwin, 2008.

Smith, Howard. *Ireland: Some Episodes from Her Past*, BBC, 1974.

Summers, Anne. *Damned Whores and God's Police: The Colonization of Women in Australia*, Ringwood, Victoria, Penguin, 1975.

Vaughan, W.E. and Fitzpatrick, A.J. (eds). *Irish Historical Statistics: Population, 1821–1971*, Dublin, Royal Irish Academy, 1978.

Vaughan, W.E. *Murder Trials in Ireland 1836–1914*, Dublin, Four Courts Press, 2009.

Wall, Maureen. *The Penal Laws, 1691–1760*, Dublin Historical Association, Dundalgan Press, 1967.

Webb, Gwen. *Pyengana: A new country*, Hobart, Mercury-Walch, 1975.

Whitaker, Anne-Maree. *Unfinished Revolution: United Irishmen in New South Wales 1800–1810*, Sydney, Crossing Press, 1994.

White, Charles, *Early Australian History: Convict Life in New South Wales and Van Diemen's Land*, Parts I & II, Bathurst, 1889, esp. Ch. VII, 'Life on Board Convict Ships', published at http://gutenberg.net.au/ebooks12/1204081h.html.

Wilkes, Charles. *Narrative of the United States Exploring Expedition*, London, Wiley & Putnam, 1845.

Williams, John. *Ordered to the Island – Irish Convicts and Van Diemen's Land*, Sydney, Crossing Press, 1994.

Woodham-Smith, Cecil. *The Great Hunger: Ireland 1845–9*, London, Hamish Hamilton, 1962.

## ARTICLES, CHAPTERS AND PAPERS

Alexander, Alison. 'A Novelist Pictures His Convict Ancestor: Margaret O'Meara and Christopher Koch ', in Lucy Frost (ed.) and Female Convicts Research Group Tas., *Convict Lives at the Ross Female Factory*, Hobart, Convict Women's Press, 2011, pp. 210–214.

Alexander, Alison. 'Benevolent Societies', in Alison Alexander (ed.), *The Companion to Tasmanian History*, Hobart, Centre for Tasmanian Historical Studies, 2005, pp. 43–44.

Aveling, Marian. 'She Only Married to Be Free; Or Cleopatra Vindicated', *Push from the Bush*, No. 2, November 1978, pp. 116–124.

Bartlett, Anne. 'The Launceston Female Factory', *Tasmanian Historical Research Association Papers and Proceedings*, Vol. 41, No. 2, pp. 115–124.

Breen, Shayne. 'Outdoor poor relief in Launceston, 1860–1880', *Tasmanian Historical Research Association Papers and Proceedings*, Vol. 38, No. 1, 1991, pp. 19–50.

Carr, John. 'The Stranger in Ireland Or, a Tour in the Southern and Western Parts of that Country in the Year 1805', in John P. Harrington, *The English Traveller in Ireland; Accounts of Ireland and the Irish Through Five Centuries*, in Harrington, John P. (comp. & ed.)., Dublin, Wolfhound Press, 1997.

Casella, Eleanor Conlin. 'Playthings: Archaeology and the Material Ambiguities of Childhood', in K. Lesnik-Oberstein, *Children in Culture, Revisited: Further Approaches to Childhood*, Basingstoke, Palgrave, 2011.

Casella, Eleanor Conlin. 'Where are the Children? Archaeology of the Nursery Ward', in Lucy Frost (ed.), *Convict Lives at the Ross Female Factory*, Hobart, Convict Women's Press, 2011, pp. 33–42.

Clarkson, L.A. and Crawford, E. Margaret. 'A Non-Famine History of Ireland', in *History Ireland*, Issue 2, Summer 2002, 'The Famine', Vol. 10, at www.historyireland.com/18th-19th-century-history/a-non-famine-history-of-ireland.

Crawford, E. Margaret. 'Food and Famine', in Cathal Póirtéir (ed.), *The Great Irish Famine*, Cork, Mercier Press, 1995, pp. 60–73.

Currey, C.H. 'The law of marriage and divorce in New South Wales (1788–1858)', *Royal Australian Historical Society Journal*, Vol. 41, No. 3, 1955, pp. 97–114.

Davis, Richard. 'Exile', in Alison Alexander (ed.), *The Companion to Tasmanian History*, Hobart, Centre for Tasmanian Historical Studies, University of Tasmania, 2005, pp. 432–437.

Geary, Laurence M. 'The whole country was in motion: mendicancy and vagrancy in pre-Famine Ireland', in *Luxury and austerity: Historical Studies*, xxi, Dublin, UCD Press, 1999.

Glassford, R.W. 'A fleet of hulks', *Royal Australian Historical Society Journal and Proceedings*, Vol. 39, No. 5, 1953, pp. 217–252.

Hall, E.S. 'On the medical topography and vital statistics of the city of Hobarton, Tasmania, and its southern subdistricts, for 1855', *Australian Medical Journal*, Vol. 3, pp. 85–105.

Howlin, Niamh. 'Review of W.E. Vaughan, Murder Trials in Ireland, 1836–1914', in *Irish Journal of Legal Studies*, Vol. 2, Issue 2, 2011, pp. 104–111.

Kavanagh, Joan. 'From Mullinacuffe to Emu Bay Eliza Davis Revisited', *Tasmanian Ancestry*, Genealogical Society of Tasmania, Vol. 17, No. 3, December 1996, pp. 169–175.

Kavanagh, Joan. 'From Mullinacuffe to Emu Bay: Eliza Davis Revisited', *Wicklow Historical Society*, Vol. 2, No. 2, July 1996, pp. 2–8.

Kavanagh, Joan. 'The Case of Eliza Davis', *Tasmanian Ancestry*, Genealogical Society of Tasmania, Vol. 17, No. 2, September 1996, pp. 101–106 and *Wicklow Historical Society*, Vol. 1, No. 7, July 1994, pp. 36–42.

Kavanagh, Joan and Snowden, Dianne. 'From Cronelea to Emu Bay, to Timaru and Back: Uncovering the Convict Story', in Angela McCarthy (ed.), *Ireland in the World: Comparative, Transnational, and Personal Perspectives* (Routledge Studies in Modern History, 2015).

Kavanagh, Joan and Snowden, Dianne. 'Mary Salmon, a "sad spectacle of humanity", and other women of the *Tasmania* in the Launceston Female Factory', in Lucy Frost and Alice Meredith Hodgson (eds), *Convict Lives at the Launceston Female Factory*, Hobart, Female Convicts Research Centre, 2013, pp. 55–62.

Kent, David. 'Decorative Bodies: The Significance of Convict Tattoos', *Journal of Australian Studies*, LV, 1997, pp. 78–88.

Kent, David, and Townsend, Norma. 'Some Aspects of Colonial Marriage', *Labour History*, Vol. 74, 1998, pp. 40–53.

Kippen, Rebecca and Gunn, Peter. 'Convict bastards, common-law unions and shotgun weddings: premarital conceptions and ex-nuptial births in nineteenth-century Tasmania', *Journal of Family History*, 36, No. 4 (2011) pp. 387–403.

Lennox, G.R. 'A private and confidential despatch of Eardley-Wilmot: implications, comparisons and associations concerning the probation system for convict women', *Tasmanian Historical Research Association Papers and Proceedings*, Vol. 29, No. 2, June 1982, pp. 80–92.

Lohan, Rena. 'Sources in the National Archives for research into the transportation of Irish convicts to Australia (1791–1853)', www.nationalarchives.ie/topics/transportation/Ireland_Australia_transportation.pdf.

McDowell, R.B. 'Parliamentary Independence, 1782–9', in T.W. Moody & W.E. Vaughan, *A New History of Ireland IV: Eighteenth Century Ireland 1691–1800*, Oxford, Clarendon Press, 1986.

Maxwell-Stewart, Hamish and Duffield, Ian. 'Skin Deep Devotions: Religious Tattoos and Convict Transportation to Australia', in Caplan,

Jane, *Written on the Body. The Tattoo in European and American History*, London, 2000, pp. 118–135.

Newham, Lois. 'Women and Children at Ross Female Factory', in Lucy Frost (ed.) & Female Convicts Research Centre, *Convict Lives at the Ross Female Factory*, Hobart, Convict Women's Press, 2011, pp. 43–49.

Nicholas, Stephen and Shergold, Peter. 'Convicts as Migrants', in Stephen Nicholas (ed.), *Convict Workers*, Cambridge, Cambridge University Press, 1988.

O'Brien, Gerard. 'Workhouse Management in Pre-Famine Ireland', *Proceedings of the Royal Irish Academy,* Vol. 86C (1986), pp. 113–134.

O'Connor, John. *The Workhouses of Ireland. The fate of Ireland's Poor*, Dublin, Anvil Books, 1995.

O'Donnell, Ruán. *A Short History of Ireland's Famine*, Dublin, The O'Brien Press, 2007.

Ó Gráda, Cormac. 'Poverty, population, and agriculture, 1801–45', in W.E.Vaughan (ed.), *A New History of Ireland, V: Ireland under the Union, I: 1801–70*, Oxford, Clarendon Press, 1989.

Parker, James. 'The Female Factory at Ross', in Lucy Frost (ed.) and Female Convicts Research Group, *Convict Lives at the Ross Female Factory*, Hobart,Convict Women's Press, 2011, pp. 111–112.

Piper, Andrew. 'Launceston Invalid Asylum', in Alison Alexander (ed.), *The Companion to Tasmanian History*, Hobart, Centre for Tasmanian Historical Studies, 2005, p. 210.

Price, Liam. *The Place Names of County Wicklow 6: The Barony of Shillelagh*, Dublin, The Dublin Institute of Advances Studies, 1958.

Rimon, Wendy. 'Royal Hobart Hospital', in Alison Alexander (ed.), *The Companion to Tasmanian History*, Hobart, Centre for Tasmanian Historical Studies, University of Tasmania, 2005, pp. 315–316.

Ryan, Lyndall. 'The Governed: Convict women in Tasmania, 1803–1853', *Bulletin of the Centre for Tasmanian Historical Studies*,Vol. 3, 1990–1991, pp. 37–51.

Ryan, Lyndall. 'From Stridency to Silence: The Policing of Convict Women 1803–1853', in Diane Kirkby (ed.), *Sex, Power and Justice: Historical Perspectives on Law in Australia*, Melbourne, Oxford University Press, 1995, pp. 70–85.

Snowden, Dianne. '"These Unfortunate Females"', in Anne M. Bartlett (comp.), *Our heritage in history: papers of the sixth Australasian congress on genealogy and heraldry*, Launceston,Tasmania, May 1991, pp. 332–52.

Snowden, Dianne. '"A Most Humane Regulation?" Free children transported with convict parents', *Tasmanian Historical Research Association Papers and Proceedings*,Vol. 58, No. 1, April 2011, pp. 33–36.

Snowden, Dianne. 'Convict Marriage: "the best instrument of reform"',

*Tasmanian Historical Studies*, Vol. 9, 2004, pp. 63–71.

Snowden, Dianne. 'Female Convicts', in Alison Alexander (ed.), *The Companion to Tasmanian History*, Hobart, Centre for Tasmanian Historical Studies, University of Tasmania, 2005, p. 131.

Snowden, Dianne. 'Margaret Butler "A Desperate Character?"', in *Pros and Cons of Transportation, A collection of convict stories*, Tasmanian Family History Society Inc., Hobart Branch, 2004, pp. 72–8.

Snowden, Dianne. 'The Matron's Quarters, 8 Degraves Street South Hobart, Yard 4 Female Factory Historic Site', unpublished manuscript, 2011.

Snowden, Dianne. 'Mental distress and forced migration: Irish convict women in the Asylum for the Insane at New Norfolk, Van Diemen's Land', unpublished paper presented to the 19th Australasian Irish Studies Conference, Otago, New Zealand, 9 November 2012.

Snowden, Dianne. 'Voices from the Orphan School: Margaret Connell & St Columba Falls', *Tasmanian Ancestry*, Vol. 35, No. 2, September 2014, pp. 77–80.

Snowden, Dianne and Kavanagh, Joan. 'Irish Shipmates from the *Tasmania*', in Lucy Frost (ed.) & Female Convicts Research Centre, *Convict Lives at the Ross Female Factory*, Hobart, Convict Women's Press, 2012, pp. 73–76.

Sprod, Michael. 'The Probation System', in Alison Alexander (ed.), *The Companion to Tasmanian History*, Hobart, Centre for Tasmanian Historical Studies, University of Tasmania, 2005, p. 290.

Sturma, Michael. 'The Eye of the Beholder: The Stereotype of Women Convicts 1788–1852', *Labour History*, No. 34, May 1978, pp. 3–10.

*The Englishwoman's Domestic Magazine. An Illustrated Journal combining Practical Information, Instruction, and Amusement*, 'Life on Board a Female Convict Ship', Vol. 1, London, S.O. Beeton, 1866, pp. 311–317.

Tooth, John. 'The Royal Derwent Hospital', in Alison Alexander (ed.), *The Companion to Tasmanian History*, Hobart, Centre for Tasmanian Historical Studies, University of Tasmania, 2005, p. 315.

Townsend, Norma. 'Penelope Bourke Revisited', *Labour History*, Vol. 77, 1999, pp. 207–218.

Tuffin, Richard. 'Assignment', in Alison Alexander (ed.) *The Companion to Tasmanian History*, Hobart, Centre for Tasmanian Historical Studies, University of Tasmania, 2005, pp. 30–31.

Whelan, Kevin. 'Pre and Post-Famine Landscape Change', in Cathal Póirtéir (ed.), *The Great Irish Famine*, Cork, Mercier Press, 1995, pp. 19–33.

Whitlock F.A. 'A Note on Moral Insanity and Psychopathic Disorders', *Psychiatric Bulletin*, Vol. 6, 1982, pp. 57–59, viewed at http://pb.rcpsych.

org/content/6/4/57.full.pdf.

Williams, Brad. 'The archaeological potential of colonial prison hulks: The Tasmanian case study', *Bulletin of the Australasian Institute for Maritime Archaeology*, Vol. 29, 2005, pp. 77–86.

## ONLINE ARTICLES

'Brickfields Hiring Depot', Female Convicts Research Centre, www.femaleconvicts.org.au/index.php/convict-institutions/ hiring-depots/brickfields (accessed on line 11 June 2013).

Brand, Ian and Staniforth, Mark. 'Care and control: female convict transportation voyages to Van Diemen's Land, 1818–1853.' *The Great Circle*, 1994, Vol. 16. No. 1. pp. 23–42, Academia.edu, www.academia. edu/1465912/Care_and_control_female_convict_transportation_ voyages_to_Van_Diemens_Land_1818–1853 (accessed on line 19 April 2015).

Cowley, Trudy. 'A Statistical Overview of the Voyages', Female Convicts Research Centre, www.femaleconvicts.org.au/docs/seminars/ Voyages_TrudyCowley.pdf (accessed 14 November 2014).

Kippen, Rebecca. '"And the Mortality Frightful": Infant and Child Mortality in the Convict Nurseries of Van Diemen's Land', Female Convicts Research Centre, www.femaleconvicts.org.au/docs/seminars/ RebeccaKippen_InfantMortality.pdf (accessed 11 June 2013).

'Prison Registers', The National Archives of Ireland, www.nationalarchives.ie/topics/transportation/transp7.html.

Snowden, Dianne. 'These Unfortunate Females', *Carlow Past and Present*, Vol. 1, No. 5, 1996, www.rootsweb.ancestry.com/~irlcar2/convicts_burgess_2.htm (accessed 12 May 2010)

Warke, Oonagh, 'The Law Must Take its Course', *Carlow Past and Present*, Vol. 1, No. 4, 1993, www.rootsweb.ancestry.com/~irlcar2/convicts_burgess.htm.

## BIOGRAPHICAL DICTIONARIES

Bateson, Charles. 'Bowden, Edmund (1801–1847)', *Australian Dictionary of Biography*, National Centre of Biography, Australian National University, http://adb.anu.edu.au/biography/bowden-edmund-1807/text2057. Published in hard copy in 1966 by Melbourne University Press. Accessed online 11 November 2014.

Boyce, Peter. 'Hampton, John Stephen (1810–1869)', *Australian Dictionary of Biography*, National Centre of Biography, Australian National

University, http://adb.anu.edu.au/biography/hampton-john-stephen-2151/text2745. Published in hard copy in 1966 by Melbourne University Press. Accessed online 25 September 2014.

Rudé, G. 'Mitchel, John (1815–1875)', *Australian Dictionary of Biography*, National Centre of Biography, Australian National University, http://adb.anu.edu.au/biography/mitchel-john-2461/text3293. Published in hard copy in 1967 by Melbourne University Press (accessed online 25 September 2014).

O'Neill, Sally. 'Meredith, Charles (1811–1880)', *Australian Dictionary of Biography*, National Centre of Biography, Australian National University, http://adb.anu.edu.au/biography/meredith-charles-4187/text6731. Published in hard copy in 1974 by Melbourne University Press accessed online 25 September 2014).

Royal Irish Academy, *Dictionary of Irish Biography*, Cambridge, Cambridge University Press, 2009.

## THESES

Bailey, Inez. 'Women and Crime in Nineteenth Century Ireland', MA thesis, National University of Ireland, Maynooth, 1992.

Casella, Eleanor Conlin. 'Dangerous Girls and Gentle Ladies: Archaeology and Nineteenth Century Australian Female Convicts', PhD thesis, University of California, Berkeley, 1999.

Heath, Laurel May. 'The Female Convict Factories of New South Wales and Van Diemen's Land: An examination of their role in the control, punishment and reformation of female prisoners between 1804 and 1854', MA thesis, Australian National University, 1978, pp. 234–239.

Kippen, Rebecca. 'Death in Tasmania: Using civil death registers to measure nineteenth-century cause-specific mortality', PhD thesis, Australian National University, 2002.

Lawlor, Rebecca Sharon. 'Crime in nineteenth-century Ireland: Grangegorman female penitentiary and Richmond male penitentiary, with reference to juveniles and women, 1836–60', MLitt thesis, National University of Ireland Maynooth, 2012.

Leppard-Quinn, Christine. 'The Unfortunates': Prostitutes transported to Van Diemen's Land, 1822–1843', PhD thesis, University of Tasmania.

Lohan, Rena. 'The Management of female convicts sentenced to transportation and penal servitude 1790–1898', MLitt. Thesis, Trinity College, University of Dublin, 1989.

Nolan, Bláthnaid. 'Power, Punishment and Penance: An Archival Analysis of the Transportation of Irish Women from Grangegorman in Dublin to Hobart Town in Van Diemen's Land (Tasmania)', PhD thesis, Dublin, University College Dublin, 2013.

Piper, Andrew. 'Beyond the Convict System: the Aged Poor and Institutionalisation in Colonial Tasmania', PhD thesis, Tasmania, University of Tasmania, 2003.

Reid, Kirsty M. 'Work, Sexuality and Resistance: The Convict Women of Van Diemen's Land, 1820–1839', PhD thesis, Edinburgh, University of Edinburgh, 1995.

Rushen, Elizabeth Anne. 'Free, single and female: The women of the first scheme for female emigration to Australia, 1833–1837', PhD thesis, Melbourne, Victoria, Monash University, 1999.

Snowden, Dianne. '"A White Rag Burning": Irish women who committed arson in order to be transported to Van Diemen's Land', PhD thesis, Tasmania, University of Tasmania, 2005.

## NEWSPAPERS: IRELAND

*Carlow Sentinel*

*Drogheda Conservative Journal*

*Dublin Evening Packet and Correspondent*

*Freeman's Journal* (Dublin)

*Kerry Evening Post*

*Kilkenny Journal*

*Longford Journal*

*Nenagh Guardian*

*Roscommon and Leitrim Gazette*

*Statesman and Dublin Christian Record*

*Tipperary Vindicator*

*Tralee Chronicle*

*Wexford Conservative*

## NEWSPAPERS: AUSTRALIA

*Advocate* (Melbourne)

*Argus* (Melbourne)

*Braidwood Dispatch*

*Colonial Times* (Hobart)

*Cornwall Chronicle* (Launceston)

*Courier* (Hobart)

*Examiner* (Launceston)

*Freeman's Journal* (Sydney)

*Geelong Advertiser*

*Geraldton Guardian*

*Goulburn Evening Penny Post*
*Hobart Town Courier and Government Gazette*
*Launceston Advertiser*
*Launceston Examiner*
*Manaro Mercury* (Cooma, NSW)
*Mercury* (Hobart)
*North-Eastern Advertiser*
*Observer* (Hobart)
*Sydney Morning Herald*
*The Hobarton Mercury*
*The Hobart Town Daily Mercury*
*Williamstown Advertiser*
*Zeehan and Dundas Herald*

## ARCHIVAL RECORDS: TNA (UK)

TNA, Adm. 101/5/11 Surgeon's Report *Asia V* 1847.
TNA, Adm. 101/71/2 Surgeon's Report *Tasmania* (2) 1845.
TNA, Adm. 101/75/3 Surgeon's Report *Woodbridge* 1843.
TNA, Adm. British Parliamentary Papers, Transportation, Vol. 9.

*British Parliamentary Papers and Reports*
Sixteenth Report of Inspectors-General on the General State of Prisons
    in Ireland, 1837: with Appendices HC 1837–8 (186), xxix, 475.
Nineteenth Report of the Inspectors-General on the State of the Prisons
    of Ireland, 1840: with Appendices [299], HC 1841, XI, 759.
Twenty-Third Report of the Inspectors-General on the General State of
    the Prisons of Ireland, 1844: with Appendices [620], HC1845, XXV, 231.
Twenty-Fifth Report of the Inspectors-General on the State of the
    Prisons of Ireland, 1846 with Appendices [805], HC 1847, XXIX, 151.

## ARCHIVAL RECORDS: NAI AND COUNTY ARCHIVES

Louth County Archives, Louth Gaol GJ/004.
NAI, BR/WAT/28/7 Waterford Harbour Records.
NAI, Chief Secretary's Office Registered Papers (CSORP).
NAI, Convict Letter Books (LB).
NAI, Convict Reference Files (CRF) 1845 M29 List of all the female
    convicts aboard the *Tasmania* (2).
NAI, Crown Books at Assizes Kilkenny City and County 1833–1846.
NAI, General Prisons Registers.
NAI, GPO/CN 13, 1842–48, Prisoners' Commutation Book.

NAI, Outrage Papers 1844 Kilkenny 14/13113.

NAI, Outrage Papers 1844 Tipperary 27/8029 & 27/8551 14/13113.

NAI, PRIS 1/09/07 Grangegorman Prison, Registry of Female Convicts, Grangegorman Female Convict Depot, 11 July 1840–22 December 1853.

NAI, Prisoners' Petitions and Cases (PPC).

Wicklow Archives Office, Wicklow Grand Jury Presentment Book, 1836–1847.


## ARCHIVAL RECORDS: TAHO

TAHO, CON15/1/3 Convict indent *Tasmania* (2).

TAHO, CON19/1/5 Convict Description List *Tasmania* (2).

TAHO, CON30/1/1-2 Register of Employment of Probation-Passholders.

TAHO, CON33 Convict conduct record (male).

TAHO, CON37 Reconvictions.

TAHO, CON41/1/8 Convict conduct record *Tasmania* (2).

TAHO, CON52 Convict applications for permission to marry.

TAHO, GO33 Governor's Duplicate Despatches received by the Colonial Office.

TAHO, HSD145 Royal Hobart Hospital Return of deaths.

TAHO, HSD285 Royal Derwent Hospital Patient records.

TAHO, LC251 Lower court records Hobart (female).

TAHO, NS1190/1/3 Parish of Campbell Town.

TAHO, POL220 Returns of crews and passengers on ships departing from Launceston.

TAHO, POL709 Reports of Crime.

TAHO, RGD32, 33, 34, 35, 36, 37 birth, marriage and death certificates.

TAHO, SC195 Inquests.

TAHO, *Statistics of Tasmania* 1847.

TAHO, SWD28/1/1 Register of children admitted and discharged from the Male and Female Orphan School.

TAHO, SWD6/1/1 Register of children admitted and discharged from the Infant School.


## ARCHIVAL RECORDS: OTHER

New South Wales birth, marriage and death certificates.

Mitchell Library, CY 1077 'Log Book of HBM Hired Convict Ship *Tasmania* commencing 1st August 1844, Ending 30th December 1844'.

Mitchell Library, ML 84/304, *Instructions for Surgeon Superintendents on Board Convict Ships proceeding to New South Wales or Van Diemen's Land and for the Masters of those Ships*, London, W. Clowes & Sons, 1846.

Victoria birth, marriage and death certificates.

## INDEXES

Davidson, Rosemary (compiler) for the Friends of the Orphan Schools St John's Park Precinct Research Group New Town, Hobart, Tasmania. *Deaths and Burials in the Parish of St John's New Town*, [Friends of the Orphan Schools and St. John's Park Precinct], 2010.

Mesecke, Coralie (compiler). *Convict applications to bring out families to Van Diemen's Land* (also NSW, Vic. and WA), Tasmanian Family History Society Inc., reprint, 2005.

Purtscher, Joyce (compiler). *Deaths at General Hospital Hobart, January 1864–June 1884*, Mt Stuart, Joyce Purtscher, 1999.

Purtscher, Joyce (compiler) for the Friends of the Orphan Schools St John's Park Precinct [New Town]. *Deaths at the New Town Charitable Institution July 1895–December 1912*, Joyce Purtscher and the Friends of the Orphan Schools, 2012.

# Notes

## PRELIMS

1   Shakespeare, *King Lear*, act 3, scene 2, 57060.

2   Hamish Maxwell-Stewart and Rebecca Kippen, 'Sickness and Death on Male and Female Convict Voyages to Australia', www.femaleconvicts.org.au/docs/seminars/Voyages_HamishMaxwellStewart.pdf (accessed 14 November 2014).

3   Dianne Snowden, 'Female Convicts', in Alison Alexander (ed.), *The Companion to Tasmanian History*, Hobart, Centre for Tasmanian Historical Studies, 2005, p. 131; Trudy Cowley, 'A Statistical Overview of the Voyages', www.femaleconvicts.org.au/docs/seminars/Voyages_TrudyCowley.pdf (accessed 14 November 2014).

4   Recent studies include Dianne Snowden, '"A White Rag Burning": Women who Committed Arson in Order to be Transported to Van Diemen's Land', PhD thesis, University of Tasmania, 2005; Trudy Cowley, *A Drift of Derwent Ducks*, Hobart, Research Tasmania, 2004; Lucy Frost, *Abandoned Women: Scottish Convicts Exiled Beyond the Seas*, Sydney, Allen & Unwin, 2012; Trudy Cowley and Dianne Snowden, *Patchwork Prisoners: The Rajah Quilt and the women who made it*, Hobart, Research Tasmania, 2013.

5   Because it was the second voyage of the *Tasmania* as a convict ship, it was styled the *Tasmania* (2).

6   NAI, TR5 p. 256; NAI, Convict Reference File (CRF) 1845 S24 Ellen Sullivan; TAHO, CON41/1/8 No. 684 Ellen Sullivan.

7   For the Surgeon's Report, see TNA, Adm. 101/71/2. For the women, see NAI, CRF 1845 M29 List of all the female convicts aboard the *Tasmania* (2).

8 There were two women named Margaret Butler on the *Tasmania* (2). The colonial authorities labelled them Margaret Butler 1st and Margaret Butler 2nd to distinguish them. Margaret Butler 1st was a 22–year-old country servant, single with no children.

9 Joan Kavanagh and Dianne Snowden, 'From Cronelea to Emu Bay, to Timaru and Back: Uncovering the Convict Story', in Angela McCarthy (ed.), *Ireland in the World. Comparative, Transnational, and Personal Perspectives* (Routledge Studies in Modern History, 2015). See also Joan Kavanagh, 'The Case of Eliza Davis', *Wicklow Historical Society*, Vol. 1, No. 7, July 1994, pp. 36–42; Joan Kavanagh, 'From Mullinacuffe to Emu Bay: Eliza Davis Revisited', *Wicklow Historical Society*, Vol. 2, No. 2, July 1996, pp. 2–8; Joan Kavanagh, 'The Case of Eliza Davis', *Tasmanian Ancestry*, Genealogical Society of Tasmania, Vol. 17, No. 2, September 1996, pp. 101–6; Joan Kavanagh, 'From Mullinacuffe to Emu Bay Eliza Davis Revisited', *Tasmanian Ancestry*, Genealogical Society of Tasmania, Vol. 17, No. 3, December 1996, pp. 169–175.

10 Joseph Robins, *The Lost Children: A Study of Charity Children 1700–1900*, Dublin, Institute of Public Administration, 1980, p. 11.

11 Robins, *The Lost Children*, p. 45.

12 Robins, *The Lost Children*, pp. 39–40.

13 Robins, *The Lost Children*, pp. 39–40.

14 Robins, *The Lost Children*, p. 53.

15 NAI, CRF 1845 D18 Elizabeth Davis.

16 For administrative purposes, Ireland was divided into provinces, counties, baronies, parishes and townlands and in 1838 into Poor Law Unions for the administration of workhouses. Townlands are the smallest division of land and their origins date back to the Gaelic clan system with adjustments made during the mapping of Ireland by the Ordnance Survey from the 1820s. They were used as a basis for levying tithes in the 1820s and 1830s and for land valuation from the 1840s. For Cronelea, see Liam Price, *The Place Names of County Wicklow 6: The Barony of Shillelagh*, Dublin, The Dublin Institute of Advanced Studies, 1958, p. 356.

17 The Fitzwilliam or Coollattin estate was approximately 80,000 acres in size. It stretched from Collattin House in Shillelagh in the south up to Wicklow town.

18 NAI, CRF 1845 D18 Elizabeth Davis.

19 *Nenagh Guardian*, 16 July 1845, p. 4.

20　NAI, CRF 1845 D18 Elizabeth Davis.

21　*Nenagh Guardian*, 16 July 1845, p. 4.

22　*Statesman and Dublin Christian Record*, 25 July 1845, p. 4.

23　TAHO, CON41/1/8 No. 515 Elizabeth Davis; TAHO, CON15/1/3
　　pp. 228–229 No. 515 Elizabeth Davis.

24　See Dianne Snowden, '"These Unfortunate Females"', in Anne
　　M. Bartlett (comp.), *Our heritage in history: papers of the sixth Australasian
　　congress on genealogy and heraldry*, Launceston, Tasmania, May 1991, pp.
　　332–352; Dianne Snowden, 'Margaret Butler "A Desperate Character?"'
　　in *Pros and Cons of Transportation: A collection of convict stories*, Tasmanian
　　Family History Society Inc., Hobart Branch, 2004, pp. 72–8.

25　NAI, CRF 1845 B14 Margaret Butler.

26　The potato crop was planted in spring (March) and harvested in
　　autumn (September/October). It was stored in a pit for safekeeping.

27　NAI, CRF 1845 B14 Margaret Butler.

28　NAI, CRF 1845 B14 Margaret Butler.

29　William's age was recorded as 6 when he entered
　　Grangegorman: NAI, PRIS 1/09/07 Grangegorman Prison,
　　11 July 1840–22 December 1853, Registry of Female Convicts,
　　Grangegorman Female Convict Depot. His age when he was
　　admitted to the Male Orphan School in Van Diemen's Land in
　　December 1845 was 10: TAHO, SWD28/1/1 p. 20. Mary Ann was 2.

30　*Hobart Town Courier and Government Gazette*, 13 December 1845 p. 4.

31　NAI, TR6 p. 361; NAI, CRF 1845 D18 Elizabeth Davis.

32　NAI, TR5 p. 263.

33　Lyndall Ryan, 'The Governed: convict women in Tasmania,
　　1803–1853', *Bulletin of the Centre for Tasmanian Historical Studies*,
　　Vol. 3, 1990–1991, pp. 37–51. See also Lyndall Ryan, 'From Stridency
　　to Silence: The Policing of Convict Women 1803–1853', in Diane
　　Kirkby (ed.), *Sex, Power and Justice: Historical Perspectives on Law in
　　Australia*, Oxford University Press, Melbourne, 1995, pp. 70–85.

34　Michael Sturma, 'Eye of the Beholder: the stereotype of female
　　convicts 1788–1852', *Labour History*, Vol. 34, May 1978, pp. 3–10.

35　Kay Daniels, *Convict Women*, St Leonards, NSW, Allen & Unwin, 1998,
　　p. 2; Deborah Oxley, *Convict Maids. The Forced Migration of Women to
　　Australia*, Melbourne, Cambridge University Press, 1996; Kirsty M. Reid,
　　'Work, Sexuality and Resistance: The Convict Women of Van Diemen's
　　Land, 1820–1839', PhD thesis, University of Edinburgh, 1995.

36  Reid, 'Work, Sexuality and Resistance', p. 275.

37  Age calculated from conduct record: TAHO, CON41/1/1 No. 770
     Margaret Butler 2nd 1845

# CHAPTER 1

1   NAI, CRF 1845 B14 Margaret Butler.

2   J.C. Beckett, *A Short History of Ireland. From Earliest Times to the
     Present Day*, first published London, 1952; this edition, 1979, pp.
     125–126; R.F. Foster, *Modern Ireland 1600–1972*, London, Penguin
     Books, 1988, p. 318.

3   W.E. Vaughan and A.J. Fitzpatrick (eds), *Irish Historical Statistics:
     Population, 1821–1971*, Dublin, Royal Irish Academy, 1978, pp. 2–3.

4   Exact population numbers are difficult to establish. The first
     Irish Census took place in 1821 and was thereafter conducted at
     ten-yearly intervals. The first reliable figures, however, are considered
     to be the Census of 1841. Compulsory civil registration of births
     did not commence until 1864. For a discussion of the reasons for
     population growth, see Cecil Woodham-Smith, *The Great Hunger:
     Ireland 1845–9*, London, Hamish Hamilton, 1962, pp. 29–31. See also
     Cormac Ó Gráda, 'Poverty, population, and agriculture, 1801–45', in
     W.E. Vaughan (ed.), *A new history of Ireland, V: Ireland under the union, I:
     1801–70*, Oxford, Clarendon Press, 1989, pp. 108–36.

5   Ruán O'Donnell, *A Short History of Ireland's Famine*, Dublin,
     The O'Brien Press, 2008, p. 7.

6   Beckett, *A Short History of Ireland*, p. 126.

7   Peter Gray, *The Irish Famine*, London, Thames and Hudson, 1995, p. 26.

8   Cormac Ó Gráda, *Ireland: A New Economic History*, Oxford, Oxford
     University Press, 1994, p. 5. According to Ó Gráda, the agricultural
     population per tilled acre was probably the highest in Europe.
     See also Kevin Whelan, 'Pre and Post Famine Landscape Change',
     in Cathal Póirtéir (ed.), *The Great Irish Famine*, Cork, Mercier Press,
     1995, pp. 19–33; Woodham-Smith, *The Great Hunger*, pp. 31–35.

9   Woodham-Smith, *The Great Hunger*, p. 32.

10  Ó Gráda, *Ireland*, p. 20.

11  Beckett, *A Short History of Ireland*, p. 126.

12  Howard Smith, *Ireland. Some Episodes from her Past*, BBC, 1974, pp. 22–23.

13  Samuel Lewis, *A Topographical Dictionary of Ireland,* 2 volumes,
     first published London, 1837; reprinted Baltimore, 1984, Vol. 2, p. 265.

14  Quoted in Smith, *Ireland*, p. 22.

15  Edward MacLysaght, *The Surnames of Ireland*, Dublin, Irish
    Academic Press, 1991.

16  Examples include: Fitzpatrick, the only Fitz name of Gaelic Irish
    origin and was originally Mac Giolla Phádraig, meaning a devotee
    of St Patrick. While Salmon is an English name, it can also be a
    translation of Ó Bradáin, the Gaelic word for a salmon. Similarly,
    Smyth can be an English name but in County Cavan it is usually
    a synonym of MacGowan or Mac an Ghabhann, son of the
    blacksmith. Warnock might seem the name of a settler family but
    it can be traced back to an old County Down name, Mac Giolla
    Mhearnóg, a devotee of St Mearnog. Rose and Anne Fitzpatrick,
    Mary Salmon, Mary Anne Smyth and Isabella Warnock sailed on
    the *Tasmania* (2), CRF 1845 M29.

17  Richard Killeen, *A Timeline of Irish History*, Dublin, Gill &
    Macmillan, 2003. For an overview of the Penal Laws, see Maureen
    Wall, *The Penal Laws, 1691–1760*, Dublin, Dundalgan Press, Dublin
    Historical Association, 1967.

18  Bardon, *A History of Ireland*, pp. 2, 36–242.

19  Foster, *Modern Ireland*, p. 215.

20  John Wesley quoted in Foster, *Modern Ireland*, p. 212.

21  Ó Gráda, 'Poverty, population, and agriculture, 1801–45', p. 141.

22  John Dunton, 'Conversation in Ireland' (1705), in John P.
    Harrington (comp. & ed.), *The English Traveller in Ireland; Accounts of
    Ireland and the Irish Through Five Centuries*, Dublin, Wolfhound Press,
    1997, p. 149.

23  Joseph Robins, *The Lost Children: A Study of Charity Children
    1700–1900*, Dublin, Institute of Public Administration, 1980, p. 11.

24  R.B. McDowell, 'Parliamentary Independence, 1782–9', in
    T.W. Moody and W.E. Vaughan, *A New History of Ireland IV Eighteenth
    Century Ireland 1691–1800*, Oxford, Clarendon Press, 2005, pp. 265–287.

25  For example, radical Presbyterian Society of United Irishmen,
    formed in Belfast in 1791. See Foster, *Modern Ireland*, p. 215.

26  Richard Killeen, *A Timeline of Irish History*, p. 70.

27  Anne-Maree Whitaker, *Unfinished Revolution United Irishmen in New
    South Wales 1800–1810*, Sydney, Crossing Press, 1994, p.v.

28  *Union with Ireland Act* 1800 (39 & 40 Geo. 3 c. 67), an Act of the
    Parliament of Great Britain, and *The Act of Union (Ireland)* 1800

(40 Geo. 3 c. 38), an Act of the Parliament of Ireland.

29  The Union Flag signified the unification of the three kingdoms, with each kingdom's patron saint represented by a cross: that of St George, the patron saint of England; that of St Andrew, the patron saint of Scotland and that of St Patrick, the patron saint of Ireland.

30  *Roman Catholic Relief Act of 1829* (10 Geo. IV, c. 7).

31  R.B. McDowell, *The Irish Administration, 1801–1914,* London, Routledge & Kegan Paul, 1964, pp. 52–77.

32  *Roman Catholic Relief Act of 1829* (10 Geo. IV, c. 7). The dismantling of the penal laws had commenced with the passing of the Catholic Relief Act of 1778 which allowed Catholics who had taken an oath of allegiance to bequeath land to a single heir and to take leases of 999 years. Further relief acts in 1782 allowed Catholics to buy land and removed restrictions in relation to education and the Catholic clergy. Catholics could practise law under legislation passed in 1792. Voting rights were given under an act passed in 1793 under which Catholics could now also hold most civil and military posts. However, the ban on sitting in parliament remained. See *The Oxford Companion to Irish History*, Oxford, Oxford University Press, 1998, p. 77–78.

33  Patrick M. Geoghegan, *Liberator: The Life and Death of Daniel O'Connell 1830–1847*, Dublin, Gill & Macmillan, 2012, p. 19.

34  Liam Kennedy, Paul S. Ell, E.M. Crawford, and L.A. Clarkson, *Mapping the Great Irish Famine*, Dublin, Four Courts Press, 1999, p. 69.

35  L.A. Clarkson and E. Margaret Crawford, 'A Non-Famine History of Ireland', *History Ireland,* Issue 2, Summer 2002, The Famine, Vol. 10 at www.historyireland.com/18th-19th-century-history/a-non-famine-history-of-ireland (accessed 19 February 2015). The potato diet was healthy; mashed potatoes and milk made a convenient weaning food, enabling babies to be weaned earlier. This also had an impact on fertility; mothers lost the contraceptive benefits of extended lactation.

36  Extract from John Carr, *The Stranger in Ireland Or, a Tour in the Southern and Western parts of that Country in the Year 1805* in Harrington, *The English Traveller in Ireland*, p. 202.

37  Foster, *Modern Ireland 1600–1972*, p. 318.

38  Ruán O'Donnell, *A Short History of Ireland's Famine*, O'Brien Press, Dublin, 2008, p. 14.

39  Ó Gráda, *Ireland*, p. 93.

40  O'Connor, *The Workhouses of Ireland*, p. 48.

41  Great Britain, *Parliamentary Papers,* 1826, Report from the Select Committee on the State of Ireland 1825 quoted in O'Connor, *The Workhouses of Ireland*, p. 49.

42  Quoted in O'Connor, *The Workhouses of Ireland*, p. 49.

43  Quoted in O'Connor, *The Workhouses of Ireland*, p. 51.

44  Bardon, *A History of Ireland*, p. 372.

45  See S.J. Connolly, *The Oxford Companion to Irish History*, Oxford, Oxford University Press, 1998, p. 5.

46  Gearóid Ó Tuathaigh, *Ireland before the Famine; 1798–1848*, Dublin, Gill & Macmillan, 2007, pp. 83–4.

47  *Drogheda Conservative Journal*, 16 November 1844, p. 1.

48  *Dublin Evening Packet and Correspondent*, 24 June 1845, p. 2.

49  See, for example, Clive Emsley, *Crime and Society in England 1750–1900,* London and New York, Longman, 1987; David Phillips, *Crime and Authority in Victorian England*, London, Croom Helm, 1977; and George Rudé, *Criminal and Victim in Early Nineteenth Century England*, Oxford, Clarendon Press, 1985.

50  See, for example, *Freeman's Journal*, 14 February 1842, p. 3 col. 3; *Freeman's Journal*, 23 February 1842, p. 3 col. 4.

51  Rudé, *Criminal and Victim*, p. 84.

52  Rudé, *Criminal and Victim*, pp. 81–85. See also Emsley, *Crime and Society* and Phillips, *Crime and Authority*.

53  Woodham-Smith, *The Great Hunger*, pp. 94–102.

54  S.J. Connolly, *Oxford Companion to Irish History*, pp. 248–51; Whelan, 'Pre- and Post-Famine Landscape Change', pp. 19–33; E. Margaret Crawford, 'Food and Famine', in Póirtéir (ed.), *The Great Irish Famine*, pp. 60–73.

55  O'Donnell, *A Short History of Ireland's Famine*, p. 7.

## CHAPTER 2

1  NAI, CRF 1845 B14 Margaret Butler. This was the response of the Lord Lieutenant of Ireland to Margaret Butler's memorial or petition seeking commutation of her sentence, as it was to the majority of those who petitioned him.

2  These memorials or petitions are held in the National Archives of Ireland. Correspondence appealing to the Lord Lieutenant for

clemency, referred to as Prisoners' Petitions and Cases (PPC), date from 1788 to 1835. From 1836 to 1853 such correspondence became known as Convict Reference Files (CRFs).

3   Brian Griffin, *Sources for the Study of Crime in Ireland 1801–1921*, Dublin, Four Courts Press, 2005, p. 30. Collections such as the State of the Country Papers, the Outrage Papers and the Chief Secretary's Office Registered Papers held in the National Archives of Ireland give accounts of events, opinions and observations of the police, magistrates and gentry throughout the country during the period 1796 to 1924.

4   7 Geo. IV. C. 74. All previous Prison Acts were consolidated or repealed under this act by the Chief Secretary, Henry Goulburn.

5   For an insight into the running of a county gaol and the workings of a Board of Superintendence, see Minute Book of the Board of Superintendence of Louth County Gaol, March 1837–August 1852, GJ/004, Louth County Archives Service.

6   See, for example, Twenty-Third Report of the Inspectors-General on the General State of the Prisons of Ireland, 1844: with Appendices [620], HC1845, XXV, 231.

7   S.J. Connolly, *The Oxford Companion to Irish History*, Oxford, Oxford University Press, 1998, p. 448. See also R.B. McDowell, *The Irish Administration, 1801–1914*, London, Routledge & Kegan Paul, 1964, pp. 135–45. The Chief Secretary's Office Registered Papers (CSORP) collection held in the National Archives of Ireland (NAI) contain reports from the police on crime and reports on activities happening in their area.

8   The title 'Royal' was added in 1867 in recognition of the role played by the force in quashing the Fenian Rising of that year.

9   NAI, CRF 1844 H34 Catherine Hughes.

10  NAI, CRF 1844 H34 Catherine Hughes.

11  *Kerry Evening Post* (Tralee Quarter Sessions), 11 January 1845, p. 3.

12  NAI, CRF 1845 B14 Margaret Butler.

13  Sir Jeremiah Fitzpatrick, *An essay on gaol-abuses, and on the means of redressing them; together with the general method of treating disorders to which prisoners are most incident*, Dublin, 1784; John Howard, *An account of the present Lazarettos in Europe*, London, 1791; *Report addressed to the Marquess Wellesley, Lord Lieutenant of Ireland by Elizabeth Fry and Joseph John Gurney, respecting their late visit to the country*, London, 1827.

14  Twenty-Third Report of the Inspectors-General, p.vii. Twenty-eight *Tasmania* (2) women were in gaol in 1844. See TAHO, CON41/1/8 *Tasmania* (2) 1845.

15  Twenty-Third Report of the Inspectors-General. Only Belfast, Clonmel and Waterford gaols were profitable and articles produced there were readily marketable.

16  Twenty-Third Report of the Inspectors-General, 1844, pp. 64–65.

17  Twenty-Third Report of the Inspectors-General, 1844, pp. 41–43.

18  Twenty-Third Report of the Inspectors-General, 1844, p. 42. For *Tasmania* (2) women in Carlow County Gaol, see NAI, CRF 1845 M29.

19  See Wicklow County Archives, County Wicklow Grand Jury: Abstracts of Presentments (1819–1899). Eliza Davis was tried in July 1845 but had been committed to Wicklow Gaol in February of that year: NAI, CRF 1845 D18 Elizabeth Davis.

20  Twenty-Third Report of the Inspectors-General, 1844: with Appendices, Dublin, 1846, pp. 84–85.

21  TNA, Adm. 101/71.

22  By 1796 six circuits had been established; Home, North East, North West, Connaught, Munster, and Dublin and Leinster Circuits.

23  W.E. Vaughan, *Murder Trials in Ireland*, Dublin, Four Courts Press, 2009, p. 90.

24  Vaughan, *Murder Trials*, p. 90.

25  This figure has been calculated using the Convict Reference Files, newspaper accounts and prison registers.

26  NAI, CRF 1845 B14 Margaret Butler.

27  NAI, CRF 1845 D18. Elizabeth Davis. Chief Justice Doherty, (1783–1850), MP and member of the Irish bar, was Solicitor General and one of the judges at the William Smith O'Brien trial in 1848: *Dictionary of Irish Biography*, Royal Irish Academy, Cambridge, Cambridge University Press, 2009, pp. 356–357.

28  For the role of the grand jury, see www.carlowlibraries.ie/ documents/archives/grandjury.pdf, accessed 5 December 2014.

29  True Bills were recorded in the Crown and Peace Papers for Elizabeth Hearne: NAI, Crown Books at Assizes Kilkenny City 1833–46, 1D-57–18; and Judith Dooling: NAI, Crown Books at Assizes Kilkenny County 1833–46, 1D-57–24.

30  NAI, CRF 1845 D18 Elizabeth Davis.

31   NAI, CRF 1845 D18 Elizabeth Davis; NAI, CSO LB 394. While
     the newspaper account in the *Wexford Conservative* of Eliza Davis'
     trial refers to a Mr Rolleston addressing the jury on behalf of the
     defendant, an entry in the Crown Solicitors Book of 1845 refers
     to a payment of £4 19s 7d to Henry Harris Esq., solicitor, 'To
     pay his taxed Bill of costs in defending Elizabeth Davis', dated
     20 July 1845. In September the sum of £5 18s 4d was recorded
     as the 'Bill of costs in the case of the Queen against Elizabeth
     Davis' to be paid to W.F. Rogers, Esq., Crown Solicitor of No. 29
     Peters Street, Dublin.

32   Niamh Howlin, 'Review of W.E. Vaughan, Murder Trials in Ireland,
     1836–1914', *Irish Journal of Legal Studies*, Vol. 2, Issue 2, 2011, p. 105.

33   Catherine Meany was convicted of poisoning her husband: NAI,
     Outrage Papers 1844 Kilkenny 14/13113; See also *Freeman's Journal*,
     29 July 1844, p. 3; *Tipperary Vindicator*, 19 March 1845, p. 2; *Statesman
     and Dublin Christian Record*, 18 March 1845, p .2.

34   NAI, CRF 1845 D18 Elizabeth Davis.

35   NAI, Outrage Papers 1844 Kilkenny 14/13113.

36   NAI, Crown Books at Assizes Kilkenny County 1833–46, 1D-57–24.

37   NAI, CRF 1845 B14 Margaret Butler.

38   NAI, Crown Books at Assizes Kilkenny County 1833–46, 1D-57–24.

39   Vaughan, *Murder Trials*, p. 89.

40   Vaughan, *Murder Trials*, p. 304.

41   Rena Lohan, 'The treatment of women sentenced to transportation
     and penal servitude 1790–1898', MLitt thesis, Trinity College,
     University of Dublin, 1989, p. 67. See also Lohan, 'Sources in
     the National Archives for research into the transportation of
     Irish convicts to Australia (1791–1853)', www.nationalarchives.
     ie/topics/transportation/Ireland_Australia_transportation.pdf
     (accessed 14 June 2010). However, see Inez Bailey, 'Women and
     Crime in Nineteenth Century Ireland', MA thesis, National
     University of Ireland, Maynooth, 1992, p. 81. Bailey suggests that
     there were more petitions submitted to the Lord Lieutenant than
     originally estimated. She calculated that between 1800 and 1855,
     just over 23,000 petitions were received and of that number 1,891
     (8.2 per cent) were from women.

42   NAI, CRF 1844 G19 Margaret Gardiner or Sawyer. Maryborough
     is now Portlaoise.

43   NAI, CRF 1845 K33 Anne Kelly.

44  NAI, CRF 1845 F6 Ann Flannery; NAI CRF 1844 L27 Margaret Lee. Catherine claimed she had only one sister, namely Margaret. On the ship's Indent Margaret stated she had three sisters, Ann, Kitty and Rose. See TAHO, CON15/1/3 No. 352 pp. 238–9 Margaret Lee.

45  Hamish Maxwell-Stewart, *Closing Hell's Gates – the closing of a convict station*, Sydney, Allen & Unwin, 2008, p. 222.

46  Wicklow Gaol documents sighted by Joan Kavanagh in the NAI.

47  Bláthnaid Nolan, 'Power, Punishment and Penance: An Archival Analysis of the Transportation of Irish Women from Grangegorman in Dublin to Hobart Town in Van Diemen's Land (Tasmania) from 1844–1853', PhD thesis, University College Dublin, 2013, pp. 224–225.

48  Lohan, 'Treatment of women sentenced to transportation', p. 67.

49  See, for example, Ellen Sullivan, Bridget Egan and Ann Flannery, who claimed that others had led them astray; Honora Cullen who claimed to have been 'seduced by a promise of marriage'; and Esther Burgess, Margaret Butler and Margaret Sloan who claimed poverty and distress: see NAI, CRF 1844 C63 Honora Cullen; NAI, CRF 1844 S24 Ellen Sullivan; NAI, CRF 1845 B15 Esther Burgess; NAI, CRF 1845 B14 Margaret Butler; NAI, CRF 1845 S8 Margaret Sloan.

50  NAI, CRF 1844 S24 Ellen Sullivan.

51  NAI, CRF 1844 H34 Catherine Hughes.

52  NAI, CRF 1844 O11 Sarah Ann O'Neill.

53  NAI, CRF 1845 W2 Elizabeth Wright.

54  The names of Elizabeth (Eliza) Davis and Anne Kelly are recorded in the Prisoners' Commutation Book: NAI, GPO/CN 13, 1842–48; NAI, CRF 1845 B14 Margaret Butler.

55  NAI CRF 1845 B28 Jane Bradshaw.

56  NAI, CRF 1845 C63 Honora Cullen.

57  TAHO, CON41/1/8 No. 777 Honora Cullen.

58  NAI, Outrage Papers 1844 Tipperary 27/8029 and 27/8551.

59  NAI, CRF 1845 D7 Judith Dooling or Dowling.

60  NAI, CRF 1845 F6 Ann Flannery. See also Dianne Snowden '"A White Rag Burning": Irish Women who committed arson in order to be transported to Van Diemen's Land', University of Tasmania, PhD Thesis, 2005.

61  NAI, CRF 1845 K33 Anne Kelly.

62  NAI PRIS 1/09/07 Grangegorman Prison,

11 July 1840–22 Decemver 1853, Registry of Female Convicts, Grangegorman Female Convict Depot.

63 *Carlow Sentinel*, 13 September 1845, p. 3.

64 NAI, CRF 1845 B15 Esther Burgess.

65 Her daughter Mary Burgess was tried with her and another daughter Ann (or Mary Ann) Burgess came out as a free migrant in 1849 on the *Lismoyne*: see Trevor McClaughlin *Barefoot and Pregnant: Irish Famine Orphans in Australia*, Vol. 1, Genealogical Society of Victoria, Melbourne, 1991, p. 75: 'Ann Burgess'. We are indebted to Barbara Simpson and Perry McIntyre for information about Ann Burgess per *Lismoyne*. See also www.irishfaminememorial.org. The Burgess children were Elizabeth, Alicia, Jane, William, and Robert.

66 Oscar Wilde, *The Ballad of Reading Gaol*, lines 535–540 at www.ucc.ie/celt/online/E850003–023/text002.html (accessed on 11 December 2014).

## CHAPTER 3

1 TNA Adm. 101/71/2.

2 John Williams, *Ordered to the Island: Irish Convicts and Van Diemen's Land*, Sydney, Crossing Press, 1994, p. 101.

3 Dianne Snowden, 'Female Convicts', in Alison Alexander (ed.) *The Companion to Tasmanian History*, Hobart, Centre for Tasmanian Historical Studies, University of Tasmania, 2005, p. 131.

4 For details, see Appendix I: The Women of the *Tasmania* (2) 1845.

5 Williams, *Ordered to the Island*, p. 20.

6 NAI, CRF 1845 M29.

7 NAI, CRF 1844 C63 Honora Cullen.

8 For details, see Appendix I: The Women of the *Tasmania* (2) 1845.

9 For details, see Appendix I: The Women of the *Tasmania* (2) 1845.

10 TAHO, CON41/1/8 No. 196 Anne Agnew; TAHO, CON41/1/8 No. 290 Maria Johnson; TAHO, CON41/1/8 No. 383 Mary Russell.

11 TAHO, CON41/1/8 No. 684 Ellen Sullivan.

12 TAHO, CON41/1/8 No. 686 Eleanor Shaughnessy.

13 For details, see Appendix I: The Women of the *Tasmania* (2) 1845.

14 TAHO, CON41/1/8 No. 627 Mary Hurley.

15 *Tralee Chronicle*, 19 October 1844, p. 2 (Mary 'Hurly').

16  TAHO, CON41/1/8 No. 775 Deborah Connor.

17  TAHO, CON41/1/8 No. 385 Catherine Riley; TAHO, CON15/1/3 pp. 248–249 Catherine Riley 1845. An ostler takes care of horses in a stable, usually at an inn.

18  *Roscommon and Leitrim Gazette*, 19 October 1844, p. 2 (Catherine McCormack alias Reilly).

19  Those transported for stealing were Bridget Kelly (watch); Sarah Ryan (stealing a watch from the person); Margaret Randall or Reilly or Mary Reynolds (money and wearing apparel); and Elizabeth Hearns (6 yards of cashmere).

20  TAHO, CON41/1/8 No. 353 Mary Leonard.

21  *Nenagh Guardian*, 29 March 1845, p. 2 (Mary 'Meagher').

22  TAHO, CON41/1/8 No. 397 Bridget Gallagher; TAHO, CON41/1/8 No. 323 Rose Fitzpatrick 1845; TAHO, TAHO, CON14/1/20 No. 16168 James Gallagher 1st *Ratcliffe* (1) 1845.

23  TAHO, CON41/1/8 No. 630 Margaret Maguire; TAHO, CON41/1/8 No. 683 Mary Scallon.

24  TAHO, CON41/1/8 No. 507 Ann Delany; TAHO, CON41/1/8 No. 383 Mary Russell.

25  For details, see Appendix I.

26  TAHO, CON33/1/37 No. 9071 John Wright *North Briton* 1843.

27  TAHO, CON41/1/8 No. 657 Elizabeth Waring.

28  TAHO, CON41/1/8 No. 687 Bridget Stankard.

29  *Tipperary Vindicator*, 27 July 1844, p. 2 (Bridget Egan, Mary Liston and Mary Mansfield).

30  Williams, *Ordered to the Island*, p. 20: 13 per cent of those who admitted to being 'on the town' were transported for vagrancy.

31  Mary Brown, Bridget Clifford, Bridget Cunningham, Bridget Egan, Mary Liston, Sarah McArdle, Mary Magrath and Mary Sullivan 2nd: TAHO, CON41/1/8 No. 778 Mary Brown; TAHO, CON41/1/8 No. 778 Bridget Clifford; TAHO, CON41/1/8 No. 776 Bridget Cunningham; TAHO, CON41/1/8 No. 144 Bridget Egan; TAHO, CON41/1/8 No. 357 Mary Liston; TAHO, CON41/1/8 No. 639 Sarah McArdle; TAHO, CON41/1/8 No. 628 Mary Magrath; TAHO, CON41/1/8 No. 688 Mary Sullivan.

32  TAHO, CON41/1/8 No. 776 Bridget Cunningham; TAHO, CON15/1/3 No. 776, pp. 226–227 Bridget Cunningham.

33 *Longford Journal*, 6 July 1844, p. 4 (Bridget Cunningham).

34 Mary Mansfield's sentence was commuted; she was bailed and discharged on 17 July 1845. No reason was stated in the Tipperary Register.

35 *Nenagh Guardian*, 27 July 1844, p. 2. See also *Freeman's Journal*, 27 July 1844, p. 1.

36 For more about Irish women committing arson, see Dianne Snowden, '"A White Rag Burning": Irish women who committed arson in order to be transported to Van Diemen's Land', PhD thesis, University of Tasmania, 2005.

37 Williams, *Ordered to the Island*, pp. 76–77. See also Laurence M. Geary, 'The whole country was in motion: mendicancy and vagrancy in pre-Famine Ireland' in *Luxury and austerity: Historical Studies*, xxi, Dublin, UCD Press, 1999, pp. 121–136.

38 TAHO, CON41/1/8 No. 329 Ann Flannery.

39 TAHO, CON41/1/8 No. 356 Maria Lynch.

40 TAHO, CON41/1/8 No. 631 Catherine Meany. Elsewhere the man was named as Lennon: see NAI, Outrage Papers 27/14453.

41 Williams, *Ordered to the Island*, p. 66.

42 TAHO, CON41/1/8 No. 778 Bridget Clifford.

43 TAHO, CON41/1/8 *Tasmania* (2) 1845.

44 *Longford Journal*, 4 January 1845, p. 4.

45 *Longford Journal*, 4 January 1845, p. 4.

46 TAHO, CON41/1/8 No. 511 Anne Dogherty.

47 TAHO, CON41/1/8 No. 775 Deborah Connor.

48 *Kerry Evening Post*, 16 April 1845, p. 2.

49 TAHO, CON41/1/8 No. 619 Mary McVeagh.

50 NAI, CRF 1844 Mc51 Mary McVeagh.

51 NAI, CRF 1844 Mc51 Mary McVeagh.

52 NAI, CRF 1844 Mc51 Mary McVeigh; TAHO, CON41/1/8 No. 619 Mary McVeagh: this states that Mary had ten children.

53 TAHO, CON41/1/8 No. 619 Mary McVeagh.

54 NAI, CRF 1844 Mc51 Mary McVeagh.

55 NAI, Clonmel Gaol Register 1840–1924.

56 NAI, Outrage Papers (OP) 27/14453.

57 TAHO, CON41/1/8 Eliza Perry.

58  NAI, Grangegorman Female Prison Register. In twenty-three instances the native place is listed as Baltinglass and once each as Blessington and Hacketstown, a village on the border between Counties Wicklow and Carlow.

59  NAI, Grangegorman Female Prison Register 1/9/1.

60  NAI, General Prison Registers.

61  Several entries were found in gaol registers for Anne Collins and Margaret Daly, both from Cork, Margaret Henry, Eliza Hunter, Mary Liston, Sarah McArdle, Sarah Ryan and Ann Williams. While these names appear multiple times in the gaol registers, it is often difficult to prove a link to the *Tasmania* (2) because the surnames are common. These records can be viewed at findmypast.ie: http://search.findmypast.ie/search-world-records-in-institutions-and-organisations?_ga=1.97990426.445005954.1403025992 (accessed 19 April 2015).

62  TAHO, CON41/1/8 No. 196 Anne Agnew.

63  NAI, Grangegorman Female Prison General Register 1831–1838 Book No 1/9/1.

64  TAHO, CON41/1/8 No. 774 Mary Barry.

65  NAI, Limerick General Register 1838–1847 Book No 1/24/4.

66  TAHO, CON41/18 No. 58 Mary O'Brien 2nd; *Limerick Chronicle*, 19 July 1845, p. 2.

67  TAHO, CON41/18 No. 773 Ellen Cummane; *Kerry Evening Post*, 23 October 1844 (Tralee Quarter Sessions), p. 2. Ellen's surname is spelt Kimmane in the newspaper report.

68  NAI, CRF 1845 B14 Margaret Butler.

69  NAI, CRF 1845 S8 Margaret Sloan.

70  Few studies have examined deliberate offenders in detail and so it is difficult to gauge the extent of the phenomenon of committing crime in order to be transported. See Snowden, "'A White Rag Burning'", esp. Ch 3.

71  TAHO, CON41/1/8 No. 352 Margaret Lee.

72  TAHO, CON40/1/6 No. 288 Anne Lee *East London* 1843.

73  TAHO, CON41/1/8 No. 357 Mary Liston.

74  *Nenagh Guardian*, 27 July 1844, p. 2.

75  *Roscommon and Leitrim Gazette*, 12 July 1845, p. 2, col. 1. See also Snowden "'A White Rag Burning'".

76 For details, see Appendix III: The Sick List of the *Tasmania* (2) 1845. For a discussion of prostitution, see Christine Leppard-Quinn, '"The Unfortunates": Prostitutes transported to Van Diemen's Land, 1822–1843', PhD thesis, University of Tasmania, 2013.

77 TAHO, CON41/1/8 No. 329 Ann Flannery.

78 Bridget Clifford, aged 31 and tried in Waterford, stated she had been 'on the town' six or seven years; Mary Brown, tried in Waterford city and four times convicted as a vagrant, was 23, and admitted to four and a half years 'on the town'; Mary Liston, aged 27 and tried in Tipperary, had been 'on the town' two years; and Bridget Egan, aged 20 and tried in Tipperary, was twelve months 'on the town': TAHO, CON41/1/8 No. 778 Bridget Clifford; TAHO, CON41/1/8 No. 778 Mary Brown; TAHO, CON41/1/8 No. 357 Mary Liston; and TAHO, CON41/1/8 No. 516 Bridget Egan.

79 TAHO, CON41/1/8 No. 770 Ellen Callaghan; TAHO, CON15/1/31 No. 770 pp. 224–225 Ellen Callaghan.

80 TAHO, CON41/1/8 No. 197 Bell Amos.

81 TAHO, CON15/1/3 No. 510 pp. 228–229 Bridget Dignan.

82 TAHO, CON41/1/8 No. 769 Ann Collins; TAHO, CON41/1/8 No. 769; TAHO, CON41/1/8 No. 506 Margaret Daley.

83 TAHO, CON41/1/8 No. 615 Sarah Jane Marrow; TAHO, CON41/1/8 No. 393 Jane Gallagher.

84 TAHO, CON41/1/8 No. 283 Catherine Keeffe; TAHO, CON41/1/8 No. 623 Johannah Murray.

85 TAHO, CON41/1/8 No. 625 Mary McBride; TAHO, CON15/1/3 No. 625 pp. 242–243 Mary McBride; TAHO, CON41/1/8 No. 626 Elleanor McKiverigan.

86 TAHO, CON41/1/8 No. 625 Mary McBride.

87 TAHO, CON41/1/8 No. 691 Mary Sullivan 1st.

88 TAHO, CON41/1/8 No. 773 Henrietta Beresford.

89 TAHO, CON41/1/8 No. 769 Esther 'Burges'; TAHO, CON41/1/8 No. 7671 Esther 'Burges'.

90 TAHO, CON41/1/8 No. 323 Rose Fitzpatrick; TAHO, CON41/1/8 No. 397 Bridget Gallagher; TAHO, CON14/1/20 No. 16168 James Gallagher 1st *Ratcliffe* (1) 1845; TAHO, CON33/1/69 No. 16168 James Gallagher 1st *Ratcliffe* (1) 1845.

91 TAHO, CON41/1/8 No. 324 Ann Fitzpatrick.

92 TAHO, CON41/1/8 No. 636 Mary Meaghar; TAHO, CON15/1/3

No. 636 pp. 244–245 Mary Meaghar.

93    TAHO, CON33/1/69 No. 16240 Stephen Meagher *Ratcliffe* (1) 1845; TAHO, CON33/1/69 No. 16238 John Meagher 1st *Ratcliffe* (1) 1845; TAHO, CON33/1/69 No. 16241 John Meagher 2nd *Ratcliffe* (1) 1845.

94    TAHO, CON33/1/69 No. 16240 Stephen Meagher *Ratcliffe* (1) 1845; TAHO, CON14/1/20 No. 16240 pp. 306–307 Stephen Meagher *Ratcliffe* (1) 1845.

95    TAHO, CON14/1/20 No. 16238 pp. 304–305 John Meagher 1st *Ratcliffe* (1) 1845.

96    TAHO, CON33/1/69 No. 16241 John Meagher 2nd *Ratcliffe* (1) 1845.

97    TAHO, CON41/1/8 No. 508 Judith Dooling or Dowling; TAHO, CON15/1/3 No. 508 pp. 226–227 Judith Dooling or Dowling: her indent stated that she had a brother, Pat, four children, 'John Dooling transported 12 months ago'; Pat, Jeremiah and William at her native place; TAHO, CON33/1/69 No. 16137 John Dooling *Ratcliffe* (1) 1845.

98    TAHO, CON14/1/20 No. 16137 pp. 266–267 John Dooling *Ratcliffe* (1) 1845.

99    TAHO, RGD35/1/25 Richmond 1856/207 Judith Dowling; TAHO, SC195/1/38 Inquest No. 3791 Judith Dowling; TAHO, RGD35/1/28 Richmond 1859/744 John 'Dowling'.

100   TAHO, CON15/1/3 No. 627 pp. 242–243 Harriet Madine; TAHO, CON15/1/3 No. 381 pp. 246–247 Bell Rooney.

101   TAHO, CON15/1/3 Convict Indent *Tasmania* (2) 1845.

102   TAHO, CON15/1/3 No. 685 Mary Salmon or Lyons. A James Salmon, an English convict, arrived in 1844, but he is not a good match: see TAHO, CON14/1/30 No. 14611 pp. 196–197 James Salmon *Lord Auckland* (1) 1844.

103   TAHO, CON15/1/3 No. 615 pp. 240–241 Sarah Jane Marrow. The length of time is overwritten: it could be three or eight years, providing a date of *c.* 1841 or *c.* 1837. A James Morrow, tried in Antrim, arrived from Dublin in 1843 but the family members do not match: TAHO, CON14/1/27 No. 11162 pp. 160–161 Patrick Morrow *Orator* 1843. His family members were father James, mother Mary, brothers James and Joseph. Sarah Jane's family members were father Jeremiah, mother Amelia, brothers James and Patrick, sisters Mary and Ann.

104   TAHO, CON15/1/3 No. 622 pp. 240–241 Mary Meehan. A Patrick Meahan (or Mealan) was transported in 1828: TAHO, CON31/1/29

No. 328 Patrick 'Mealan' *William Miles* 1828, tried Lancaster 1827. There is no surviving indent for this ship.

105  TAHO, CON15/1/3 No. 284 pp. 236–237 Bridget Kelly.

106  TAHO, CON15/1/2 pp. 196–197 Anne Lee *East London* 1843.

107  TAHO, CON15/1/3 No. 657 pp. 252–253 Elizabeth Waring.

108  TAHO, CON41/1/8 No. 399 Anne Gardiner or Harrison.

109  TAHO, CON41/1/8 No. 331 Bridget Fanning.

110  TAHO, CON41/1/8 No. 515 Elizabeth Davis.

111  TAHO, CON41/1/8 No. 770 Margaret Butler 2nd.

112  TAHO, CON41/1/8 No. 772 Margaret Connor. For details, see Appendix I: The Women of the *Tasmania* (2) 1845.

113  TAHO, CON41/1/8 No. 381 Bell Rooney; TAHO, CON41/1/8 No. 641 Annie McCarmack; TAHO, CON41/1/8 No. 509 Fanny Doherty; TAHO, CON41/1/8 No. 658 Ann Williams.

114  TAHO, CON41/1/8 No. 778 Bridget Clifford; TAHO, CON19/1/5 No. 778 Bridget Clifford; TAHO, CON15/1/3 No. 778 Bridget Clifford.

115  NAI, PRIS 1/09/07 Grangegorman Prison Registry of Female Convicts, Grangegorman Female Convict Depot, 11 July 1840 – 22 December 1853.

116  TAHO, CON19/1/5 No. 621 Ellen Maguire; TAHO, CON41/1/8 No. 690 Margaret Sloane.

117  TAHO, CON19/1/5 No. 621 Ellen Maguire; TAHO, CON41/1/8 No. 690 Margaret Sloane.

118  TAHO, CON41/1/8 No. 508 Judith Dooling or Dowling.

119  TAHO, CON41/1/8 No. 625 Eliza Hunter.

120  TAHO, CON41/1/8 No. 681 Catherine Stewart.

121  TAHO, CON41/1/8 No. 516 Bridget Egan.

122  TAHO, CON41/1/8 No. 511 Anne Dogherty.

123  TAHO, CON41/1/8 No. 778 Bridget Clifford.

124  TAHO, CON41/1/8 No. 513 Anne Daley; TAHO, CON41/1/8 No. 632 Anne McAvine.

125  TAHO, CON41/1/8 No. 148 Ellen Neill.

126  TAHO, CON41/1/8 No. 509 Fanny Doherty.

127  TAHO, CON41/1/8 No. 324 Ann Fitzpatrick; TAHO, CON41/1/8 No. 355 Mary Lynam or Egan.

128  TAHO, CON41/1/8 No. 661 Ann Wade.

129  TAHO, CON41/1/8 No. 687 Bridget Stankard.

130  TAHO, CON41/1/8 No. 686 Eleanor Shaughnessy.

131  TAHO, CON41/1/8 No. 691 Mary Sullivan 1st.

132  TAHO, CON41/1/8 No. 636 Mary Meaghar.

133  TAHO, CON41/1/8 No. 624 Mary McCarthy.

134  TAHO, CON41/1/8 No. 638 Margaret McMackin.

135  *Colonial Times* (Hobart), 15 February 1850, p. 2.

136  David Kent, 'Decorative Bodies: The Significance of Convict Tattoos', *Journal of Australian Studies*, LV, 1997, pp. 78–88. See also Hamish Maxwell-Stewart and Ian Duffield, 'Skin Deep Devotions: Religious Tattoos and Convict Transportation to Australia', in Jane Caplan, *Written on the Body: The Tattoo in European and American History*, London, Princeton University Press, 2000, pp. 118–135.

137  Maxwell-Stewart and Duffield, 'Skin Deep Devotions', p. 128.

138  TAHO, CON41/1/8 No. 394 Margaret Gibson.

139  TAHO, CON41/1/8 No. 323 Rose Fitzpatrick.

140  TAHO, CON41/1/8 No. 393 Jane Gallagher.

141  TAHO, CON41/1/8 No. 690 Margaret Sloane.

142  TAHO, CON41/1/8 No. 771 Mary Carroll.

143  TAHO, CON19/1/5 No. 618 Martha Merryfield.

144  TAHO, CON41/1/8 No. 326 Mary Francis.

145  TAHO, CON41/1/8 No. 614 Mary McManus.

146  TAHO, CON41/1/8 No. 616 Anne Mullan.

147  TAHO, CON41/1/8 No. 329 Ann Flannery.

148  TAHO, CON41/1/8 No. 627 Mary Hurley.

149  TAHO, CON41/1/8 No. 776 Bridget Cunningham; TAHO, CON41/1/8 No. 392 Bridget Fanning.

## CHAPTER 4

1   5 George IV c.84: An Act for the Transportation of Offenders from Great Britain (1824).

2   For a detailed account of the administration and provision of shipping to convey the convicts to the penal colonies in Australia,

see Charles Bateson, *The Convict Ships 1787–1868*, Sydney, Library of
Australian History, 2004, pp. 10–57.

3   Sixteenth Report of Inspectors-General on the General State of Prisons
     in Ireland, 1837: with Appendices HC 1837–8 (186), xxix, 475, p. 8.

4   NAI, PRIS 1/09/07, Grangegorman Prison, Registry of Female
     Convicts, Grangegorman Female Convict Depot, 11 July 1840 –
     22 December 1853. See also Rebecca Sharon Lawlor, 'Crime in
     nineteenth-century Ireland: Grangegorman female penitentiary and
     Richmond male penitentiary, with reference to juveniles and women,
     1836–60', MLitt thesis, National University of Ireland Maynooth, 2012.

5   Lawlor, 'Grangegorman', p. 67.

6   *Freeman's Journal*, 16 November 1842, p. 3.

7   Nineteenth Report of the Inspectors-General on the State of the
     Prisons of Ireland, 1840: with Appendices [299], HC 1841, XI, 759, p. 21.

8   Lawlor, 'Grangegorman', p. 39.

9   NAI, CRF 1845 M29.

10  NAI, CON LB 1 Letter from E. Lucas Dublin Castle to the
     Superintendent of Constabulary, 30 July 1845.

11  NAI, CON LB 1 Letter from E. Lucas.

12  Charles Bateson, *The Convict Ships 1787–1868*, Sydney, Library of
     Australian History, 1983, pp. 368–369. A barque is a sailing ship with
     three masts, square-rigged on the fore and main and with only fore
     and aft sails on her mizzen mast. We are grateful to John Woods,
     Local Studies Department, Sunderland Library, Sunderland City
     Council, for his assistance in providing information about the
     building of the *Tasmania*.

13  For detail, see Bateson, *The Convict Ships*, pp. 38–57. See also Ian
     Brand and Mark Staniforth, 'Care and Control: Female Convict
     Transportation Voyages to Van Diemen's Land, 1818–1853',
     www.academia.edu/1465912/Care_and_control_female_convict_
     transportation_voyages_to_Van_Diemens_Land_1818–1853
     (accessed 14 November 2014).

14  Bateson, *The Convict Ships*, pp. 38–57.

15  TNA Adm. 101/71/2 'Journal of His Majesty's Convict Ship *Tasmania*,
     Mr. Jason Lardner Surgeon Between the 28th of August 1845 and
     the 9th of December 1845'; Australian Medical Pioneer Index www.
     medicalpioneer.com (accessed 22 September 2011). For qualifications of
     Surgeons Superintendent, see Ian Brand and Mark Staniforth, *The Great
     Circle*, Vol. 16, No. 1 (1994), *Australian Association for Maritime History*,

pp. 23–42. A period of at least three years serving as an Assistant Surgeon was required before promotion to the post of Surgeon. Lardner was appointed Assistant Surgeon in 1827 and served on the *Spartiate* from 1832 in that role. By 1838, he had been promoted to Surgeon and served on the *Jaseur* in the Mediterranean fleet: John Murray, *The Navy List,* London, 1834, pp. 50, 80; Simpkin, *The Navy List*, London, Marshall & Co., 1840, p. 209; John Murray, *The Navy List*, London, 1848, p. 127.

16  For detail, see Bateson, *The Convict Ships*, pp. 38–57.

17  *Instructions for Surgeon Superintendents on Board Convict Ships proceeding to New South Wales or Van Diemen's Land and for the Masters of those Ships*, London 1846, p. 42.

18  For the *Lady Juliana*, see Bateson, *The Convict Ships*, pp. 120–123.

19  *Instructions for Surgeon Superintendents on Board Convict Ships proceeding to New South Wales or Van Diemen's Land and for the Masters of those Ships*, p. 38.

20  Reprinted in the *Hobart Town Courier and Government Gazette*, 13 December 1845, p. 4.

21  NAI, CON LB 1 Letter from E. Lucas Dublin Castle to the Superintendent of Convicts, Major Cottingham, 14 August 1845.

22  NAI, CON LB 1 Major Cottingham to [RN] Sir J. Fremantle, 21 August 1845.

23  NAI, CON LB 1 Letter from E. Lucas Dublin Castle to the Superintendent of Constabulary, 28 May 1845. Twenty-six of the thirty-two counties were referred to in the correspondence. Counties Cork, Clare, Dublin, Louth, Mayo and Sligo were not included.

24  NAI, CRF 1845 Misc 15.

25  NAI, PRIS 1/09/07, Grangegorman Prison, Registry of Female Convicts, Grangegorman Female Convict Depot, 11 July 1840–22 December 1853.

26  *Carlow Sentinel*, 16 August 1845, p. 3.

27  From Tipperary, Judith Farrell or Dwyer (Clonmel); Anne Daley (Clonmel); Catherine Heenan (Nenagh); and from Waterford, Bridget Clifford; Mary Browne; Mary Sullivan; and Sarah McArdle.

28  NAI, CSORP 1845 G6572.

29  NAI, CSORP 1845 G6572. Eight of the ten Cork women were for the *Tasmania* (2): Mary Connell, Mary Wall, Ann Collins and Margaret Daly had been convicted at the Mallow Sessions on 11 October 1844. Ellen Connolly had been convicted at Fermoy

Sessions on 21 October. Johannah Murray and Catherine Keeffe were also convicted at the next Fermoy Sessions on 1 January 1845. Mary McCarthy was tried at the Spring Assizes on 17 March. The other two women were Ellen Moylan, 'in Hospital, incurable', who was tried at the Spring Assizes on 19 March 1844 and Eliza Hayes, tried on 21 October in Fermoy. Mary Connell had three children with her and Mary Wall had two. The children, it was noted, were 'to be sent by permission of the Government'.

30  NAI, CRF 1845 Misc 17.

31  NAI CRF 1845 M29.

32  TAHO, CON41/1/8 No. 396 Mary Griffen.

33  *Instructions for Surgeon Superintendents*, p. 11.

34  TNA, Adm. 101/71/2.

35  Anne McMahon, *Convicts at Sea: the voyages of the Irish convict transports to Van Diemen's Land, 1840–1853,* Anne McMahon, Victoria, 2011, p. 42.

36  NAI, CRF 1845 R31/15.

37  NAI, CRF 1845 R31/15. Scrofula is a form of tuberculosis.

38  The harbour was originally known as Dunleary and later Dún Laoghaire. In honour of the departure of King George IV from the new harbour in Dún Laoghaire in 1821, the town was renamed Kingstown and remained so until 1920. See also *The Construction of Dún Laoghaire Harbour*, Dún Laoghaire Harbour Company, pp. 3–5, 14.

39  Bateson, *The Convict Ships*, pp. 346–375. While the place of departure was given as Dublin for the convict ships, it was in fact Kingstown that had become the port for Dublin. The *Phoebe Dunbar* bound for Western Australia in 1853 with 295 male convicts, is the only vessel Bateson recorded with a departure location of Kingstown. It was the last convict ship to sail from Ireland.

40  NAI, Convict Letter Book, CON LB 22, 27 August 1845.

41  NAI, Convict Letter Book, CON LB 22, 15 April 1845.

42  NAI, Convict Letter Book, CON LB 22, 28 May 1845.

43  NAI, CON LB 22 1843–1846. See also www.nationalarchives.ie/topics/transportation/transp5.html (accessed 14 June 2014).

44  NAI, CON LB 22 1843–1846.

45  NAI, CON LB 1 Letter from Lucas to Cottingham, 22 August 1845.

46  Bateson, *The Convict Ships*, p. 17.

47  NAI, Convict Letter Book, CON LB 22, 28 August 1845.

48  *Hobart Town Courier*, 13 December 1845, p. 4.

49  *Hobart Town Courier*, 13 December 1845, p. 4.

50  *Hobart Town Courier*, 13 December 1845, p. 4.

51  *Hobart Town Courier*, 13 December 1845, p. 4.

52  *Hobart Town Courier*, 13 December 1845, p. 4.

53  *Hobart Town Courier*, 13 December 1845, p. 4.

54  *Hobart Town Courier*, 13 December 1845, p. 4.

55  NAI, CON LB 1 Letter from R. Pennefather, Dublin Castle to the Superintendent of Convicts, Major Cottingham, 1 September 1845.

56  NAI, CON LB 22, 29 August 1845; NAI; CRF 1845 M29.

57  NAI, PRIS 1/09/07.

58  NAI, CON LB 22 Correspondences from Convict Office 23, 24 and 26 January and 3 February 1846.

59  NAI, CON LB 22.

60  NAI, CON LB 1 Letter from R. Pennefather, Dublin Castle to R. Peel, MD Deputy Inspector General of Hospitals, 31 January 1846.

61  NAI, PRIS 1/09/07.

## CHAPTER 5

1  'Scene on Board the Tasmania Convict Ship', *Hobart Town Courier*, 13 December 1845, p. 4.

2  NAI, CRF 1845 M29.

3  Meteorological observations made in the year 1845 at the Ordnance Survey Office, Phoenix Park, Dublin pp. 301–302. The Pilot Station at Passage, Waterford, recorded 'cloudy weather but dry and fine with moderate breezes' and north-east to east-north-east winds that Tuesday. The following day the winds had shifted east-south-east to south-south-east with gloomy weather and light winds initially, then clear and fine with moderate breezes. See NAI, BR/WAT/28/7, Waterford Harbour Records.

4  For John Mitchel, see G. Rudé, 'Mitchel, John (1815–1875)', *Australian Dictionary of Biography*, National Centre of Biography, Australian National University, http://adb.anu.edu.au/biography/mitchel-john-2461/text3293,

published first in hard copy in 1967 (accessed online 17 March 2014).

5 John Mitchel, *Jail Journal*, Dublin, The University Press of Ireland, 1982, p 4.

6 TAHO, CON15/1/3 *Tasmania* (2) 1845.

7 NAI, CRF 1845 W2 Elizabeth Wright.

8 NAI, CRF 1844 Mc51 Mary McVeagh.

9 Mitchel, *Jail Journal*, p. 4. Mitchel wrote this as he was being transferred from Newgate Prison in Dublin to Spike Island, where he remained until he was sent to the convict hulks in Bermuda. In 1850 he was removed to Van Diemen's Land.

10 Though tried in Carlow and Dublin, Mary Griffen and Eliza Perry stated their native place was Wicklow; Bridget Clifford was tried in Waterford City but, like Elizabeth Dwyer and Annie McCarmack, she was a Wexford woman; while she was tried in Limerick, Henrietta Beresford's native place was Waterford, as it was for Bridget Hurley, Sarah McArdle and Mary Sullivan 2nd; and Ann Collins, Mary Connell, Ellen Connelly, Margaret Daly, Catherine Keeffe, Mary McCarthy, Johanna Murray and Mary Wall were all from Cork.

11 *Geraldton Guardian*, 8 March 1921, p. 1.

12 Mitchell Library, CY 1077 'Log Book of HBM Hired Convict Ship *Tasmania* Commencing 1st August 1844, Ending 30th December 1844'. We are indebted to Captain John Barlow, harbour master, Wicklow Town, for reading a copy of the original log and for his knowledge, expertise and patience in explaining the nautical terminology.

13 Originally those who take their meals together, a mess being the dining compartment on a naval ship.

14 Anne McMahon, *Convicts at Sea: the voyages of the Irish convict transports to Van Diemen's Land, 1840–1853,* Victoria, Anne McMahon, 2011, p. 38.

15 Twenty-fifth Report of the Inspectors General on the State of the Prisons of Ireland, 1846 with Appendices, [805], HC 1847, XXIX, 151, p. 28.

16 *Hobart Town Courier*, 13 December 1845, p. 4.

17 *Hobart Town Courier*, 13 December 1845, p. 4.

18 Mitchell Library, CY 1077 'Log Book *Tasmania*, 1844'.

19 *Hobart Town Courier*, 13 December 1845, p. 4.

20 Charles Bateson, *The Convict Ships 1787–1868*, Library of Australian History, Sydney, 1983, esp. Chapter 5. See also McMahon, *Convicts*

at Sea, pp. 39–40. For the *Lady Juliana*, see Bateson, pp. 120–3. See also Charles White, *Early Australian History. Parts I & II … New South Wales and Van Diemen's Land*, Bathurst, 1889, esp. Ch. VII, 'Life on Board Convict Ships', published as http://gutenberg.net.au/ebooks12/1204081h.html (accessed 17 March 2014). The procedures pioneered in the convict voyages laid the foundations for later free immigration voyages to Australia.

21  'Life on Board a Female Convict Ship', *The Englishwoman's Domestic Magazine. An Illustrated Journal*, London, S.O. Beeton, 1866, p. 314.

22  TNA, Adm 101/75/3, *Woodbridge* 1843. For information about shipboard activity on another English ship, see Trudy Cowley and Dianne Snowden, *Patchwork Prisoners: The Rajah Quilt and the women who made it*, Hobart, Research Tasmania, 2013, esp. Chs 2 and 4.

23  'Scene on Board the Tasmania Convict Ship', *Hobart Town Courier*, 13 December 1845, p. 4.

24  See, for example, Mitchell Library, CY 1077 'Log Book *Tasmania*, 1844'. Mr Black regularly 'performed divine service' on Sunday mornings at 10.30 a.m., depending on the weather, as he noted on Sunday 6 October 1844 'baffling winds and sultry weather prevented the performance of divine Service'.

25  TNA, Adm. 101/71/2, *Tasmania* 1845. See also McMahon, *Convicts at Sea*, p. 25.

26  TNA, Adm. 101/71/1, *Tasmania* 1844.

27  TNA, Adm. 101/75/3, *Woodbridge* 1843.

28  For other examples, see Dianne Snowden, '"A Most Humane Regulation?": Free children transported with convict parents', *Tasmanian Historical Research Association Papers and Proceedings*, Vol. 58, No. 1, April 2011, p. 36.

29  TNA, Adm. 101/71/2, *Tasmania* 1845.

30  Mitchell Library, CY 1077 'Log Book *Tasmania*, 1844'.

31  TNA, Adm. 101/71/2, *Tasmania* 1845.

32  For examples of the use of the solitary box on the *Tasmania* (1), see Mitchell Library, CY 1077 'Log Book *Tasmania*, 1844'.

33  'Life on Board a Female Convict Ship', *The Englishwoman's Domestic Magazine*, p. 313.

34  Charles Wilkes, *Narrative of the United States Exploring Expedition*, London 1845, p. 127.

35  McMahon, *Convicts at Sea*, pp. 39–40. On the 1844 voyage of the

*Tasmania*, one woman was kept in the box for three and a half days: see Mitchell Library, Sydney, CY 1077 Log Book of HBM Hired Convict ship *Tasmania, 1844.*

36  TNA, Adm. 101/71/2, *Tasmania* 1845.

37  TNA, Adm. 101/71/2, *Tasmania* 1845.

38  TNA, Adm. 101/71/2, *Tasmania* 1845. We are grateful to Dr John McManus GP and Dr Conor Fitzgerald GP for reading Jason Lardner's journal and commenting on the medical conditions of the women and the present-day treatment for such complaints.

39  TNA, Adm. 101/71/2, *Tasmania* 1845. A summary of the sick list appears as Appendix III. The women who suffered from diarrhoea ranged in age from 17 to 60. Catherine Meany was afflicted twice, in October and again in November, spending nine days in all on the Sick List. Esther Burgess was put on the sick list on 2 December close to land and remained on it for four days.

40  TNA, Adm. 101/71/2, *Tasmania* 1845.

41  TNA, Adm. 101/71/2, *Tasmania* 1845.

42  NAI, TR5, p. 302; NAI, CRF 1845 F6; TNA, Adm. 101/71/2, *Tasmania* 1845.

43  TAHO, CON41/1/8 No. 329 Ann Flannery.

44  NAI, PRIS 1/09/07 Grangegorman Prison, Registry of Female Convicts, Grangegorman Female Convict Depot, 11 July 1840–22 December 1853 Mary 'McMannus'; TNA, Adm. 101/71/2, *Tasmania* 1845.

45  TAHO, CON41/1/8 No. 614 Mary McManus.

46  TNA, Adm. 101/71/2 *Tasmania* 1845.

47  TAHO, CON41/1/8 No. 509 Fanny Doherty; TAHO, RGD34/1/2 Hobart 1846/1500 Fanny Doherty.

48  NAI, PRIS 1/09/07, Ellen O'Neill.

49  TNA, Adm. 101/71/2 *Tasmania* 1845.

50  TAHO, POL220/1/2 p. 18.

51  TNA, Adm. 101/71/2 *Tasmania* 1845.

52  TAHO, CON63/1/2 No. 327 Catherine Foy. She died in Launceston Hospital.

53  TAHO, CON15/1/3 No. 327 Catherine Foy.

54  TAHO, CON41/1/8/92 No. 624 Mary McCarthy; TNA, Adm. 101/71/2 *Tasmania* 1845.

55  TNA, Adm. 101/71/2 *Tasmania* 1845.

56  For the link between mental illness and fever, see Dianne Snowden,
    'Mental distress and forced migration: Irish convict women in the Asylum
    for the Insane at New Norfolk, Van Diemen's Land', unpublished paper
    presented to the 19th Australasian Irish Studies Conference, Otago,
    New Zealand, 9 November 2012. See also Mark Finane, *Insanity and the
    Insane in Post-Famine Ireland*, London & New Jersey, 1981, p. 142.

57  TNA, Adm. 101/71/2 *Tasmania* 1845. An analysis of Mr Lardner's
    notes on Mary Griffen by Dr Conor Fitzgerald GP suggests Mary
    was delirious or had an underlying illness, appearing at this point to
    be paranoid.

58  Dr Conor Fitzgerald GP suggests the pain may have been a
    symptom of a possible mental illness.

59  For a list of the children, see Appendix III: The Children of the
    *Tasmania* (2).

60  Ages are those recorded on the Grangegorman Admission register.
    There is a significant discrepancy in some of the ages: Elizabeth Burgess,
    for example, is recorded as 11 at Grangegorman but 14 when she was
    admitted to the Female Orphan School in Van Diemen's Land.

61  Sarah Kelly's child was Margaret; Mary Griffen's child was Eliza and
    Sarah Brennan's child was Joseph.

62  TAHO, RGD33/1/2 Hobart 1835/1379 male McArdle.

63  TAHO, RGD35/1/2 Hobart 1846/948 James McArdle. His place of
    death and burial have not been located.

64  TNA, Adm. 101/75/3, *Woodbridge* 1843; TNA, Adm. 101/5/11
    *Asia V*. No convicts died on the *Woodbridge* or the *Asia V*, although
    four children died on both voyages.

65  TNA, Adm. 101/71/2, *Tasmania* 1845.

66  TNA, Adm. 101/71/2, *Tasmania* 1845. Patrick was buried at
    11 degrees 55 minutes north latitude and 19 degrees 54 minutes
    west longitude.

67  NAI, TR5, p. 256; NAI, CRF 1845 S24.

68  TNA, Adm. 101/71/2, *Tasmania* 1845.

69  NAI, CRF 1844 S24 Ellen Sullivan.

70  'Life on Board a Female Convict Ship', *The Englishwoman's Domestic
    Magazine*, p. 315.

71  For burial at sea, see McMahon, *Convicts at Sea*, p. 29.

72  *Hobart Town Courier*, 13 December 1845, p. 4.

73  TNA, Adm. 101/71/2 *Tasmania* (2) 1845.

74  TNA, Adm. 101/71/2 *Tasmania* (2) 1845.

75  This was Maria Lynch: TAHO, CON41/1/8 No. 256 Maria Lynch.

76  This was Mary Griffen: TAHO, CON41/1/8 No. 396 Mary Griffen.

77  McMahon, *Convicts at Sea*, p. 31.

78  *Colonial Times* (Hobart), 9 December 1845, p. 3.

## CHAPTER 6

1  *Colonial Times* (Holbart), 9 December 1845, p. 3.

2  TAHO, CON41/1/8 No. 515 Elizabeth Davis.

3  TAHO, CON41/1/8 No. 770 Margaret Butler.

4  See Glossary.

5  Dianne Snowden, 'Female Convicts', in Alison Alexander (ed.),
*The Companion to Tasmanian History*, Hobart, Centre for Tasmanian
Historical Studies, University of Tasmania, 2005, p. 131.

6  For the assignment period, see Richard Tuffin, 'Assignment',
in Alexander (ed.), *Companion*, pp. 30–31. For the probation system, see
Michael Sprod 'The Probation System' in Alexander (ed.), *Companion*,
p. 290. See also G.R. Lennox, 'A private and confidential despatch of
Eardley-Wilmot: implications, comparisons and associations concerning
the probation system for convict women', *Tasmanian Historical Research
Association Papers and Proceedings*, Vol. 29, No. 2, June 1982, pp. 80–92;
Laurel May Heath, 'The Female Convict Factories of New South Wales
and Van Diemen's Land: an examination of their role in the control,
punishment and reformation of female prisoners between 1804 and
1854', MA thesis, Australian National University, 1978, pp. 234–239; and
Ian Brand, *The convict probation system, Van Diemen's Land 1839–1854: a
study of the probation system of convict discipline, together with C.J. La Trobe's
1847 report on its operation and the 1845 report of James Boyd on the probation
station at Darlington, Maria Island*, Hobart, Blubber Head Press, 1990.

7  Snowden, 'Female Convicts', p. 131.

8  Sprod, 'The Probation System', p. 290.

9  Sprod, 'The Probation System', p. 290.

10  Richard Davis, 'Exile', in Alexander (ed.), *Companion*, p. 433; Sprod,
'The Probation System', p. 290.

11  Regulations within these stages changed during the period in

which the probation system operated: Brand, *The Convict Probation System*; Lyndall Ryan, 'The Governed: Convict women in Tasmania, 1803–1853', *Bulletin of the Centre for Tasmanian Historical Studies*, Vol. 3, 1990–1991, pp. 46–50. See also *BPP, Transportation,* Vol. 7, p. 38: Franklin to Russell 9 July 1841.

12 For Elizabeth Fry and her impact on the convict system, see Trudy Cowley and Dianne Snowden, *Patchwork Prisoners: The Rajah Quilt and the women who made it*, Hobart, Research Tasmania, 2013, pp. 5–11.

13 Brand, *The Convict Probation System*, pp. 103–105. The *Anson* establishment was moved from Risdon to Hobart in July 1849; it operated on a smaller scale until the following year: Lennox, 'A Private and Confidential Despatch', pp. 88–89.

14 Brand, *The Convict Probation* System, pp. 103–105; TAHO, GO1/48 p. 165 Secretary of State Stanley to Lt Governor Franklin, 25 November 1842 No. 175.

15 Brad Williams, 'The archaeological potential of colonial prison hulks: The Tasmanian case study', *Bulletin of the Australasian Institute for Maritime Archaeology* (2005), Vol. 29, pp. 77–86; A.G.L Shaw (ed.), John West *The history of Tasmania*, Sydney, Angus and Robertson, 1971, pp. 510–511; Patrick Howard, *To hell or to Hobart*, Kangaroo Press, 1993, esp. Ch 12.

16 *Geelong Advertiser*, 16 August 1843, p. 2.

17 Williams, 'The archaeological potential of colonial prison hulks', p. 80.

18 *Courier* (Hobart), 21 July 1843, p. 2; *Geelong Advertiser*, 16 August 1843, p. 2. See also Williams, 'The archaeological potential of colonial prison hulks', p. 80.

19 *Launceston Examiner*, 7 February 1844, p. 5.

20 *Colonial Times* (Hobart), 6 February 1844, p. 2. See also *Launceston Advertiser*, 6 January 1844, p. 3: the military guard included three sergeants, five corporals, and forty-four privates, of the 58th Regiment. Other military on board, to join their regiments already in the colony, were the 51st, the 96th, and the 80th.

21 *Hobart Town Courier*, 23 February 1844, p. 2. Oyster Cove is in the D'Entrecasteaux Channel, south of Hobart.

22 Williams, 'The archaeological potential of colonial prison hulks', p. 80.

23 Katherine Fry and Rachel Cresswell (eds), *Memoir of the life of Elizabeth Fry, with extracts from her journals and letters, edited by two of her daughters*, C. Gilpin, J. Hatchard, London, 1847–48, Vol. 1, p. 202, Vol. 2, p. 473.

24  *Launceston Examiner*, 26 April 1845, pp. 2–3.

25  *Courier* (Hobart), 29 October 1844, p. 2. See also *Cornwall Chronicle* (Launceston), 6 November 1844, p. 2.

26  *Courier* (Hobart), 29 October 1844, p. 2.

27  *Launceston Examiner*, 26 April 1845, p. 2.

28  *Launceston Examiner*, 26 April 1845, p. 2.

29  *Launceston Examiner*, 26 April 1845, p. 2.

30  See, for example, *Launceston Examiner*, 26 April 1845, pp. 2–3.

31  West, p. 510.

32  West, p. 510.

33  West, pp. 510–511.

34  Brand, *The Convict Probation Station*, p. 104; *Launceston Examiner*, 16 November 1850, p. 3.

35  TAHO, CON30/1/1-2 Probation-Passholders.

36  *Launceston Examiner*, 14 November 1846, p. 3.

37  For Meredith, see Sally O'Neill, 'Meredith, Louisa Ann (1812–1895)', *Australian Dictionary of Biography*, National Centre of Biography, Australian National University, http://adb.anu.edu.au/biography/meredith-louisa-ann-4435/text6731, published in hardcopy 1974 (accessed online 24 July 2014). This article was first published in hardcopy in Australian Dictionary of Biography, Vol. 5, MUP, 1974.

38  Louisa Ann Meredith, *My home in Tasmania, during a residence of nine years by Mrs. Charles Meredith*, London, John Murray, 1852, facsimile edition, Glamorgan Spring Bay Historical Society (Tas.), 2003, pp. 207–209.

39  *Launceston Examiner*, 14 November 1846, p. 3.

40  *Launceston Examiner*, 14 November 1846, p. 3.

41  TAHO, CON41/1/8 No. 58 Mary O'Brien 2nd.

42  TAHO, SC195/1/17 Inquest No. 1384 (10 January 1846) Mary Murphy.

43  TAHO, SC195/1/17 Inquest No. 1410 (26 March 1846) Fanny Doherty.

44  TAHO, CON41/1/8 No. 770 Margaret Butler 2nd; TAHO, CON15/1/3 pp. 220–221 Margaret Butler 2nd; TAHO, CON19/1/5 Margaret Butler 2nd.

45  TAHO, CON41/1/8 No. 515 Elizabeth Davis; TAHO, CON15/1/3 pp. 228–229 Elizabeth Davis; TAHO, CON19/1/5 Elizabeth Davis.

46  TAHO, CON41/1/8 No. 382 Margaret Randall or Reilly or Reynolds.

47  TAHO, CON41/1/8 No. 4 Bell Amos; TAHO, CON41/1/8 No. 779 Maria Brien.

48  All tried in Antrim.

49  Tried Down, Antrim and Tyrone.

50  As Ellen Sullivan died en route, the details of only 137 women were recorded on landing.

51  TAHO, CON30/1/1-2 Probation-Passholders.

52  Brand, *The Convict Probation System*, p. 210; Ryan, 'The Governed', p. 82. For a first-hand account, see Lieutenant Colonel G.C. Mundy, *Our Antipodes, or, Residences and Rambles in the Australasian Colonies*, fourth edition, London, 1857, p. 222.

53  TAHO, CON41/1/8 No. 355 Mary Lynam or Egan. The death was not registered.

## CHAPTER 7

1  Trudy Cowley and Dianne Snowden, *Patchwork Prisoners: The Rajah Quilt and the women who made it,* Research Tasmania, Hobart, 2013, pp. 143–144.

2  Cowley and Snowden, *Patchwork Prisoners*, pp. 143–144.

3  Kay Daniels, *Convict Women*, St Leonards, NSW, Allen & Unwin, 1998, p. 133.

4  Cowley and Snowden, *Patchwork Prisoners*, p. 146. See also www.victorianlondon.org/prisons/millbank.htm (accessed 14 June 2012): 'On entering his cell, each prisoner's hair is cut, and the rules of the prison are read over to him, the latter process being repeated every week, and the hair cut as often as required.' An investigation of the Female Convicts in Van Diemen's Land database shows that by 1850, cutting the hair and head-shaving were rarely used as punishments.

5  Peter Cuffley (ed.), *Send the Boy to Sea: the Memoirs of a Sailor on the Goldfields by James Montagu Smith,* Noble Park, Victoria, Five Mile Press, 2001, p. 29.

6  TAHO, CON41/1/8 No. 618 Martha Merryfield; TAHO, RGD37/1/9 Fingal 1850/85 Martha Merryfield and Elias Morton. See also Dianne Snowden and Joan Kavanagh, 'Irish Shipmates from the *Tasmania*', in Lucy Frost (ed.), *Convict Lives at the Ross Female Factory*, Hobart, Convict Women's Press, 2012, pp. 73–74.

7  TAHO, CON41/1/8 No. 655 Isabella Warnock.

8   TAHO, CON41/1/8 No. 506 Margaret Daley; TAHO, CON41/1/8
     No. 514 Elizabeth Dwyer; TAHO, CON41/1/8 No. 331 Bridget
     Fanning; and TAHO, CON41/1/8 No. 326 Mary Francis.

9   Tony Rayner, *Female factory, female convicts: the story of the more than
     13,000 female convicts sent to Van Diemen's Land*, Dover, Tasmania,
     Esperance Press, *c.* 2004, pp. 171–172; Daniels, *Convict Women*, esp. Ch 5;
     Lucy Frost, *Footsteps and Voices: An historical look into the Cascades Female
     Factory*, Hobart, Female Factory Historic Site Ltd, 2004.

10  TAHO, RGD33/1/3 Hobart 1849/1281 Ann Bradshaw; TAHO,
     RGD35/1/2 Hobart 1849/2499 Ann Bradshaw. Catarrh is the
     build-up of mucous membrane in the nose or throat.

11  TAHO, CON41/1/8 No. 768 Mary 'Bryne'.

12  TAHO, CON41/1/8 No. 773 Henrietta Beresford.

13  For *Tasmania* (2) women in the Launceston Female Factory, see
     Joan Kavanagh and Dianne Snowden, 'Mary Salmon, a "sad
     spectacle of humanity", and other women of the *Tasmania* in the
     Launceston Female Factory', in Lucy Frost and Alice Meredith
     Hodgson (eds), *Convict Lives at the Launceston Female Factory*, Hobart,
     Female Convicts Research Centre, 2013, pp. 55–62.

14  Anne Bartlett, 'The Launceston Female Factory', *Tasmanian Historical
     Research Association Papers and Proceedings*, Vol. 41, No. 2, p. 117.

15  TAHO, CON41/1/8 No. 623 Johannah Murray.

16  TAHO, CON41/1/8 No. 355 Mary Lynam or Egan; TAHO,
     CON41/1/8 No. 621 Ellen Maguire.

17  TAHO, CON41/1/8 No. 613 Anne Mallon.

18  TAHO, CON41/1/8 No. 148 Ellen Neil.

19  TAHO, CON41/1/8 No. 68 Bridget Hurley; TAHO, RGD33/1/23
     Launceston 1849/2400 Dennis Hurley.

20  Eleanor Conlin Casella, *Archaeology of the Ross Female Factory: female
     incarceration in Van Diemen's Land, Australia*, Launceston, Queen
     Victoria Museum and Art Gallery, 2002. See also Eleanor Conlin
     Casella, 'Dangerous Girls and Gentle Ladies: Archaeology and
     Nineteenth Century Australian Female Convicts', PhD thesis,
     University of California, Berkeley, 1999.

21  Lucy Frost (ed.), *Convict Lives at the Ross Female Factory*, p. 10.

22  *Hobart Town Gazette*, 4 April 1848, p. 348.

23  James Parker, 'The Female Factory at Ross', in Lucy Frost (ed.),
     *Convict Lives at the Ross Female Factory*, Hobart, Convict Women's

Press, 2011, p. 16.

24   Parker, 'The Female Factory at Ross', p. 18.

25   Parker, 'The Female Factory at Ross', p. 18.

26   Snowden and Kavanagh, 'Irish Shipmates from the *Tasmania*', in Frost (ed.), *Convict Lives at the Ross Female Factory*, pp. 70–76.

27   Sarah Brennan, Catherine Burnet and Margaret Meara all gave birth in the Ross factory; Mary Russell brought her son with her.

28   TAHO, CON41/1/8 No. 622 Mary Meehan.

29   TAHO, CON41/1/8 No. 382 Margaret Randall.

30   TAHO, CON41/1/8 No. 637 Margaret Meara.

31   TAHO, CON41/1/8 No. 772 Sarah Brennan.

32   TAHO, CON41/1/8 No. 772 Sarah Brennan.

33   TAHO, CON41/1/8 No. 772 Sarah Brennan; TAHO, CON41/1/8 No. 383 Mary Russell.

34   TAHO, CON41/1/8 No. 382 Margaret Randall.

35   TAHO, CON41/1/8 No. 637 Margaret Meara.

36   *Hobart Town Gazette*, 9 May 1848, p. 465.

37   For general background, see www.femaleconvicts.org.au/index.php/convict-institutions/hiring-depots/brickfields (accessed 14 June 2014).

38   TAHO, CON41/1/8 No. 197 Bell Amos; TAHO, RGD33/1/3 Hobart 1849/1326 Joseph Amos; TAHO, RGD35/1/2 Hobart 1849/2364 Joesph Amos.

39   TAHO, CON41/1/8 No. 775 Jane Bradshaw.

40   TAHO, CON41/1/8 No. 355 Mary Lynam or Egan; TAHO, CON41/1/8 No. 386 Mary Ryan.

41   *Observer* (Hobart), 13 March 1846, p. 2.

42   TAHO, CON41/1/8 No. 633 Honor Mugan.

43   TAHO, CON41/1/8 No. 687 Bridget Stankard.

44   TAHO, CON41/1/8 No. 779 Maria Brien; TAHO, CON41/1/8 No. 622 Mary Meehan; TAHO, CON41/1/8 No. 627 Mary Hurley; TAHO, CON41/1/8 No. 355 Mary Lynam or Egan.

45   TAHO, CON41/1/8 No. 775 Deborah Connor.

46   TAHO, CON41/1/8 No. 641 Annie McCarmack.

47   TAHO, CON41/1/8 No. 284 Bridget Kelly.

48  Generally, leisure.

49  *Observer* (Hobart), 13 March 1846, p. 2.

50  *Colonial Times* (Hobart), 26 October 1852, p. 2.

51  *Colonial Times* (Hobart), 26 November 1852, p. 3.

52  Dianne Snowden, 'The Matron's Quarters, 8 Degraves Street South Hobart, Yard 4 Female Factory Historic Site', unpublished manuscript, 2011.

53  Joan C. Brown, *'Poverty is not a Crime': Social Service in Tasmania 1803–1900*, Hobart, THRA, 1972, p. 65.

54  Tasmanian Reports of Crime Vol. III No. 153, 4 March 1864, p. 39.

55  TAHO, CON41/1/8 No. 624 Mary McCarthy.

56  Tasmanian Reports of Crime Vol. XIV No. 852, 19 November 1875, p. 184.

57  Kavanagh and Snowden, 'Mary Salmon', in Frost and Hodgson (eds), *Convict Lives at the Launceston Female Factory,* pp. 55–62.

58  Tasmanian Reports of Crime Vol. XXIV No. 1343, 17 April 1885, p. 64; Vol. XXIV No. 1349 p. 87 (Mary Ann Salmon).

59  *Launceston Examiner*, 6 June 1893, p. 5.

60  TAHO, CON41/1/8 No. 326: Catherine Foy.

61  TAHO, CON15/1/3 No. 690 pp. 250–251 Margaret Sloane.

62  The principal name changes, dated as accurately as possible, are as follows: Lunatic Asylum, New Norfolk 1829–1859, Hospital for the Insane, New Norfolk 1859–1915, Mental Diseases Hospital, New Norfolk 1915–1937, Lachlan Park Hospital 1937–1968, Royal Derwent Hospital 1968–2001. See R. Gowlland, Troubled Asylum, R.W. Gowlland, New Norfolk, 1981; John Tooth, 'Royal Derwent Hospital', in Alexander (ed.), *Companion*, p. 315.

63  NAI, TR 5, p. 216. See also Oonagh Warke, '"The Law Must Take its Course"', *Carlow Past and Present*, p. 120, Vol. 1, No. 4, 1993, www.rootsweb.ancestry.com/~irlcar2/convicts_burgess.htm (accessed 12 May 2007); TAHO, CON15/1/31 No. 397 pp. 232–233 Mary Griffen *Tasmania* (2) 1845. For the connection between fever and mental illness, see Dianne Snowden, 'Mental distress and forced migration: Irish convict women in the Asylum for the Insane at New Norfolk, Van Diemen's Land', unpublished paper presented to the 19th Australasian Irish Studies Conference, Otago, New Zealand, 9 November 2012.

64  TNA, Adm. 101/71/2 *Tasmania* (2) 1845. See Chapter 5.

65  TAHO, HSD246/1/5 Folio 13 (2 September 1847).

66  TAHO, HSD246/1/8 Folio 3, 34, 91, 154; TAHO, HSD246/1/9 Folio 3.

67  TAHO, SWD28/1/1 p. 20.

68  See Chapter 12.

69  TAHO, CON41/1/8 No. 8 Mary O'Brien; TAHO, HSD254/1/1 No. 235; TAHO, AB365/1/3 (1880) No. 235; TAHO, AB365/1/5 No. 235 (1884) Folio 177.

70  TAHO, Tasmanian Death Certificate 1900 No. 975 Mary White.

71  TAHO, CON41/1/8 No. 281 Margaret Kelly; TAHO, HSD285/1/1517 Margaret Kelly; TAHO, HSD52/1/2 Folio 121 Margaret Kelly; TAHO, RGD35/1/26 1857 New Norfolk 1856/568 Margaret Kelly (16 October 1856, registered 25 March 1857).

72  TAHO, HSD285/1/2094 Johannah Murray; TAHO, RGD35/1/45 New Norfolk 1876/463 Johannah Murray or Gillespie.

73  TAHO, HSD285/1/2000 Catherine Molloy.

74  TAHO, HSD285/1/2000 Catherine Molloy.

75  TAHO, RGD35/1/53 New Norfolk 1884/469 Catherine Molloy.

76  TAHO, HSD285/1/1992 No. 786; TAHO, HSD285/1/1993 No. 880.

77  TAHO, RGD35/1/60 New Norfolk 1891/578 Martha Mitchell.

78  TAHO, RGD35/1/42 New Norfolk 1872/374 Joseph Roebuck.

79  TAHO, CON41/1/8 No. 356 Maria Lynch.

80  TAHO, CON41/1/8 No. 628 Mary Magrath; TAHO, LC251/1/1 20 July 1851 Mary McGrath.

81  Brown, 'Poverty is not a crime', p. 122. Women had been accommodated at New Norfolk in the 1830s and 1840s, as well as in Hobart Hospital and Launceston's Cornwall Hospital. For Launceston, see www.launcestonhistory.org.au/2007/depot1.htm.

82  Brown, 'Poverty is not a crime', p. 122.

83  Brown, 'Poverty is not a crime', p. 122.

84  TAHO, RGD35/1/65 Launceston 1896/389 Mary Salmon or Kewley; TAHO, RGD35/1/66 Launceston 1897/264 Ellen Gregory; Australian Death Index 1907/0098 Mary Jane McLeod.

## CHAPTER 8

1  TAHO, CON41/1/8 No. 770 Margaret Butler 2nd.

2  TAHO, CON41/1/8 No. 515 Elizabeth (Eliza) Davis.

3 TAHO, CON41/1/8 No. 635 Mary Murphy; TAHO, CON41/1/8 No. 509 Fanny Doherty.

4 TAHO, CON41/1/8 No. 771 Mary Carroll. The last record located for Mary Carroll was when she was admitted to third class probation on 6 June 1846.

5 TAHO, CON41/1/8 No. 769 Esther Burgess; TAHO, LC251/1/1 (Esther Burgess).

6 TAHO, CON41/1/8 No. 657 Elizabeth Waring; TAHO, CON41/1/8 No. 512 Eleanor Daley.

7 TAHO, CON41/1/8 No. 616 Anne Mullan.

8 TAHO, CON41/1/8 No. 510 Bridget Dignan.

9 TAHO, CON41/1/8 No. 512 Eleanor Daley.

10 *Launceston Examiner*, 14 November 1846, p. 3.

11 *Cornwall Chronicle* (Launceston), 18 July 1868, p. 5.

12 TAHO, CON41/1/8 No. 331 Bridget Fanning.

13 TAHO, CON41/1/8 No. 331 Bridget Fanning; *Cornwall Chronicle* (Launceston) 19 November 1853 p. 8.

14 TAHO, CON41/1/8 No. 197 Bell Amos; TAHO, RGD33/1/3 Hobart 1849/1326 Joseph Amos; TAHO, RGD35/1/2 Hobart 1849/2364 Joseph Amos.

15 TAHO, CON41/1/6 No. 779 Maria Brien; TAHO, CON41/1/8 No. 769 Ann Collins; and TAHO, CON41/1/9 No. 613 Anne Mallon.

16 TAHO, CON41/1/8 No. 510 Bridget Dignan.

17 TAHO, CON41/1/8 No. 775 Jane Bradshaw.

18 TAHO, CON41/1/8 No. 357 Mary Liston; TAHO, CON41/1/8 No. 682 Mary Ann Smyth or Swan.

19 TAHO, CON41/1/8 No. 398 Margaret Gallagher or Toland; TAHO, CON41/1/8 Bridget Hurley 1845; *Launceston Examiner*, 29 November 1879, p. 2.

20 TAHO, CON41/1/8 No. 655 Isabella Warnock.

21 TAHO, CON41/1/8 No. 621 Ellen Maguire.

22 TAHO, CON41/1/8 No. 639 Sarah McArdle.

23 TAHO, CON41/1/8 No. 513 Anne Daley; TAHO, LC251/1 Monday 12 October 1846 Ann Daley now Fryer.

24 TAHO, LC251/1 23 November 1846 Ann Daley now Fryer.

25 TAHO, CON41/1/8 No. 513 Anne Daley.

26  TAHO, CON41/1/8 No. 290 Maria Johnson.

27  TAHO, LC251/1/1 16 November 1849 Catherine McNally now Stokes or Shaw; TAHO, CON41/1/8 No. 634 Catherine McNally or Shaw.

28  TAHO, LC251/1 16 November 1849 Catherine McNally now Stokes or Shaw.

29  TAHO, CON41/1/8 No. 687 Bridget Stankard; TAHO, RGD33/1/4 Hobart 1851/790 Jane Stankard.

30  TAHO, CON41/1/8 No. 401 Margaret Grady; TAHO, CON41/1/8 No. 641 Annie McCarmack; and TAHO, CON41/1/8 No. 623 Johannah Murray.

31  TAHO, CON41/1/8 No. 513 Anne Daley.

32  TAHO, CON41/1/8 No. 325 Ann Flood.

33  TAHO, CON41/1/8 No. 624 Mary McCarthy.

34  TAHO, CON41/1/8 No. 773 Henrietta Beresford.

35  TAHO, CON41/1/8 No. 506 Margaret Daley.

36  TAHO, CON41/1/8 No. 618 Martha Merryfield.

37  TAHO, CON41/1/8 No. 634 Catherine McNally or Shaw.

38  TAHO, CON41/1/8 No. 689 Margaret Sawyer.

39  TAHO, CON41/1/8 No. 658 Ann Williams.

40  TAHO, CON41/1/8 No. 628 Mary Magrath; TAHO, LC 251/1 Thursday 20 July 1851 (Mary Magrath).

41  TAHO, CON41/1/8 No. 639 Sarah McArdle; TAHO, CON41/1/8 No. 398 Margaret Gallagher or Toland.

42  TAHO, CON41/1/8 No. 771 Mary Burgess.

43  TAHO, LC251/1/1 13 October 1846 Ellen Cahill.

44  TAHO, LC251/1/1 14 October 1846 Catherine Heenan.

45  TAHO, LC251/1/1 22 August 1849 Eliza Hunter; TAHO, CON41/1/8 No. 625 Eliza Hunter.

46  TAHO, CON41/1/8 No. 383 Mary Russell.

47  TAHO, CON41/1/8 No. 516 Bridget Egan.

48  TAHO, CON41/1/8 No. 655 Isabella Warnock; TAHO, LC251/1/1 3 November 1846 Isabella Warnock.

49  TAHO, CON41/1/8 No. 778 Mary Brown.

50  TAHO, CON41/1/8 No. 511 Anne Dogherty.

51  TAHO, CON41/1/8 No. 385 Catherine Riley.

52 TAHO, CON41/1/8 No. 385 Catherine Riley.

53 TAHO, CON41/1/8 No. 768 Mary 'Bryne'.

54 TAHO, SWD28/1/1 p. 26.

55 TAHO, CON41/1/8 No. 325 Ann Flood.

56 TAHO, CON41/1/8 No. 353 Mary Leonard.

57 TAHO, LC25/1/1 16 October 1846 Ann McCormack and Mary Ann Smith.

58 TAHO, CON41/1/8 No. 634 Catherine McNally or Shaw; TAHO, LC25/1/1 4 January 1847 Catherine McNally alias Shaw.

59 TAHO, CON41/1/8 No. 196 Anne Agnew. Mary Swain was possibly the woman who arrived on the *America* in 1831. Tried in Middlesex in 1830, she was transported for seven years for stealing four pillows. At the time of her trial, she was married with one child. She had no colonial offences recorded against her and by the time of Anne's offence she would have been free by servitude. There is little information on her conduct record but she was in Campbell Town in 1844. Another possibility is the woman named Maria Swaine, who arrived on the *Angelina* in August 1844, but her first recorded offence was not until February 1847. A third possibility is Mary Ann Swaine, a former prostitute, transported on the *Emma Eugenia* (2), arriving in April 1844, but she had no colonial offences recorded until February 1853. Anne Agnew married Henry Bell in July 1847. She had lived with a man for five years before she was transported.

60 TAHO, RGD35/1/5 Hobart 1855/255 Esther Burgess.

61 *Mercury* (Hobart), 7 August 1873, p. 2.

62 TAHO, CON37/1/ p3096 Pierre Grace; TAHO, CON37/1/p3095 Michael Hassett; *Courier* (Hobart), 30 July 1858, p. 3.

63 TAHO, CON42/1/1 p. 6 Mary Bateman.

64 TAHO, CON52/1/2 p. 326 Mary Barry and William Bateman.

65 *Courier* (Hobart), 5 December 1854, p. 2. See also *Courier* (Hobart), 5 December 1854, p. 2; *Hobarton Mercury*, 6 December 1854, p. 2.

66 *Hobarton Mercury*, 6 December 1854, p. 2.

67 *Cornwall Chronicle* (Launceston), 10 January 1852, p. 24.

68 *Hobart Town Daily Mercury*, 11 October 1859, p. 2.

69 TAHO, CON41/1/8 No. 687 Bridget Stankard.

70 *Launceston Examiner*, 16 September 1875, p. 4. See also *Cornwall Chronicle* (Launceston), 15 September 1875, p. 2.

71  Tasmanian Reports of Crime Vol. XV No. 867, 3 March 1876, p. 36. This report says she was 42.

72  *Cornwall Chronicle* (Launceston), 11 September 1876, p .2; *Launceston Examiner*, 12 September 1876, p. 1.

73  *Cornwall Chronicle* (Launceston), 7 August 1876, p. 2.

74  *Cornwall Chronicle* (Launceston), 11 September 1876, p. 2.

75  TAHO, RGD35/1/60 Deloraine 1891/145 Ann Leach.

76  TAHO, CON31/1/34 No. 390 James Rourke *Chapman* 1824.

77  TAHO, SWD26/1/3 pp. 588, 704.

78  TAHO, CON41/1/8 No. 382 Margaret Randall or Reilly or Reynolds; TAHO, CON41/1/8 No. 766 Catherine Coleman.

79  TAHO, CON41/1/8 No. 618 Martha Merryfield.

80  Joan Kavanagh and Dianne Snowden, 'Mary Salmon, a "sad spectacle of humanity", and other women of the *Tasmania* in the Launceston Female Factory', in Lucy Frost and Alice Meredith Hodgson (eds), *Convict Lives at the Launceston Female Factory*, Hobart, Convict Women's Press, 2013, pp. 55–62.

81  TAHO, CON31/1/25 No. 620 John Kewley *Moffatt* (2) 1838.

82  *Cornwall Chronicle* (Launceston), 22 September 1849, p .881.

83  *Courier* (Hobart), 24 March 1854, p. 2.

84  TAHO, CON33/1/77 No. 17918 James Johnson *Joseph Somes* (1) 1846. He was transported for highway robbery. TAHO, SWD26/1/6 (25 May 1863) James Johnston and Thomas Johnston.

85  Then known as the Queen's Asylum for Destitute Children.

86  TAHO, SWD26/1/6 (25 May 1863) James Johnston and Thomas Johnston.

87  TAHO, SWD26/1/6 (25 May 1863) James Johnston and Thomas Johnston.

88  *Cornwall Chronicle* (Launceston), 6 June 1870, p. 2; *The Mercury* (Hobart), 7 November 1883, p. 3, 21 November 1884, p. 3.

89  *The Mercury* (Hobart), 1 September 1873, p. 2.

90  *Cornwall Chronicle* (Launceston), 16 May 1877, p. 3.

91  TAHO, RGD35/1/65 Launceston 1896/389 Mary Salmon or Kewley.

## CHAPTER 9

1  Louisa Ann Meredith, *My Home in Tasmania, during a residence of*

*nine years*, London, John Murray, 1852; reprint, Swansea, Glamorgan Spring Bay Historical Society, 2003, p. 209.

2  *Launceston Examiner*, 14 November 1846, p. 3. cf. *Launceston Advertiser*, 1 January 1846, p. 3.

3  The question of wives 'policing' convict morals has been addressed by Anne Summers, *Damned Whores and God's Police: The Colonization of Women in Australia*, Ringwood, Penguin, 1975. See also Dianne Snowden, 'Convict Marriage: "the best instrument of reform"', *Tasmanian Historical Studies*, Vol. 9, 2004, pp. 63–71.

4  For NSW, see Marion Aveling, 'She Only Married to Be Free; Or Cleopatra Vindicated', *Push from the Bush*, No. 2, November 1978, pp. 116–24; David Kent and Norma Townsend, 'Some Aspects of Colonial Marriage', *Labour History*, Vol. 74, 1998, pp. 40–53; Norma Townsend, 'Penelope Bourke Revisited', *Labour History*, Vol. 77, 1999, pp. 207–218. At least as late as 1837 in NSW, it was believed that a convict woman became free if she married: Aveling, 'She Only Married to Be Free', p. 122.

5  Snowden, 'Convict Marriage'.

6  TAHO, *Statistics of Tasmania* 1847.

7  Joan Kavanagh, 'The Case of Eliza Davis', in *Tasmanian Ancestry*, Genealogical Society of Tasmania, Vol. 17, September 1996, pp. 101–106; Joan Kavanagh, 'From Mullinacuffe to Emu Bay, Eliza Davis Revisited', *Tasmanian Ancestry*, Genealogical Society of Tasmania, Vol. 17, December 1996, pp. 169–176.

8  TAHO, CON33/1/13 No. 3081 Joseph Roebuck *David Clarke* 1841; TAHO, CON27/1/9 Appropriation List;

9  Skeleton keys are keys designed to fit many locks.

10 TAHO, CON33/1/13 No. 3081 Joseph Roebuck *David Clarke* 1841; University of Tasmania Library Special and Rare Collections 'The Leake Papers' L1/C80 Farm Management (servants, farm sales and supplies, correspondence and accounts).

11 TAHO, CON52/1/2 p. 178 Eliza Davis *Tasmania* and Joseph Roebuck *David Clarke*.

12 TAHO, NS1190/1/3 Parish of Campbell Town Register of Banns.

13 TAHO, RGD37/1/6 1847/624 Campbell Town Eliza Davis and Joseph Roebuck.

14 TAHO, RGD33/1/23 Launceston 1847/1722 female Roebuck and 1847/1723 female Roebuck.

15 TAHO, RGD32/1/3 No. 3204 Amelia Eleanor Davis and No. 3205

Elizabeth Davis.

16  *Hobarton Mercury*, 9 November 1855, p. 3.

17  *Colonial Times* (Hobart), 25 September 1856, p. 2.

18  *Hobarton Mercury*, 12 November 1855, p. 3.

19  *Colonial Times* (Hobart), 25 September 1856, p. 2. See also *Colonial Times* (Hobart), 25 September 1856, p. 27.

20  *Hobarton Mercury*, 26 September 1856, p. 2.

21  *Colonial Times* (Hobart), 25 September 1856, p. 27.

22  TAHO, HSD285/1/2581 Joseph Roebuck (Dr Bedford).

23  TAHO, HSD285/1/2581 Joseph Roebuck (Elizabeth Roebuck).

24  TAHO, HSD285/1/2581 Joseph Roebuck; TAHO, RGD35/1/42 New Norfolk 1873/374 Joseph Roebuck.

25  TAHO, NS1190/1/ Baptisms Campbell Town (Church of England); TAHO, RGD33/1/3 Hobart 2531/1850 Joseph Henry Roebuck.

26  TAHO, RGD33/1/38 Morven 1860/1590 Alice Eastwood.

27  Date calculated from marriage record: TAHO, RGD37/1/36 District of Wellington & West Devon (Ulverstone) 1877/812 Sarah Eastwood and Alfred Hughes.

28  TAHO, CON37/1/7 p. 2170 Amos Eastwood.

29  TAHO, RGD37/1/59 Emu Bay 1898/109 Elizabeth Roebuck and Amos Eastwood.

30  TAHO, CON41/1/8 No. 515 Elizabeth Davis.

31  TAHO, RGD35/1/67 Emu Bay 1898/193 Elizabeth Eastwood.

32  TAHO, CON33/1/29 No. 7021 John Shackleton *Marquis of Hastings* (2) 1842.

33  TAHO, CON52/1/3 p. 411 Margaret Butler *Tasmania* and John Shackleton *Marquis of Hastings*.

34  TAHO, RGD37/1/9 Hobart 1850/499 Margaret Butler and John Shakleton. X indicates that they could not sign their names.

35  TAHO, RGD37/1/9 Hobart 1850/499 Margaret Butler and John Shakelton.

36  TAHO, RGD35/1/5 Hobart 1855/439 Margaret Butler or Shakleton.

37  TAHO, CON41/1/8 No. 658 Ann Williams.

38  TAHO, CON41/1/8 No. 397 Mary Griffen; TAHO, CON15/1/31 No. 397 pp. 232–233 Mary Griffen.

39  TAHO, CON15/1/3 No. 772 pp. 224–225 Margaret Connor.

40  NAI, CRF 1845 D7 Judith Dooling or Dowling.

41  TAHO, CON15/1/3 No. 510 pp. 228–229 Bridget Dignan.

42  Her conduct record has both single and married: TAHO,
    CON41/1/8 No. 394 Margaret Gibson. Her indent states 'married':
    TAHO, CON15/1/3 No. 394 pp. 232–233 Margaret Gibson.

43  TAHO, CON15/1/3 No. 629 pp. 234–235 Catherine Hughes.

44  TAHO, CON33/1/75 No. 17595 Stephen Shaw *Samuel Boddington*
    1846; TAHO, CON14/1/35 No. 17595 pp. 50–51 *Samuel Boddington*
    1846; TAHO, SC195/1/21 Inquest 1789 Stephen Shaw.

45  TAHO, RGD35/1/22 Launceston 1853/841 Catherine Stokes.

46  TAHO, CON14/1/2 No. 9071 pp. 66–67 John Wright *North Briton*
    1843; TAHO, CON41/1/8 No. 659 Elizabeth Wright.

47  TAHO, CON33/1/37 No. 9071 John Wright *North Briton* 1843.

48  NAI, CRF 1844 H34 Catherine Hughes; TAHO, CON15/1/3
    No. 629 pp. 234–235 Catherine Hughes; TAHO, CON33/1/58
    No. 13735 James McMahon *Cadet* (1) 1844; TAHO, CON14/1/23
    No. 13735 pp. 130–131 James McMahon *Cadet* (1) 1844.

49  TAHO, CON33/1/58 No. 13662 Pierce Cantrill *Cadet* (1) 1844;
    TAHO, CON14/1/23 No. 13662 pp. 104–105 Pierce Cantrill
    *Cadet* (1) 1844.

50  TAHO, CON41/1/8 No. 395 Catherine Grace; TAHO,
    RGD33/1/3 Hobart 1847/35 John Grace.

51  TAHO, RGD33/1/4 Hobart 1851/103 Eliza Cantrell.

52  TAHO, CON37/1/ p3096 Pierre Grace; *Courier* (Hobart),
    30 July 1858, p. 3.

53  Dianne Snowden, '"A White Rag Burning": Irish women who
    committed arson in order to be transported to Van Diemen's Land',
    PhD thesis, University of Tasmania, 2005; Michael Sturma, 'The Eye
    of the Beholder: The Stereotype of Women Convicts 1788–1852',
    *Labour History*, No. 34, 1978, pp. 3–10; C.H. Currey, 'The law of
    marriage and divorce in New South Wales (1788–1858)', *Royal
    Australian Historical Society Journal*, Vol. 41, No. 3, 1955, pp. 97–114.

54  Portia Robinson, *The Hatch and Brood of Time: a study of the first
    generation of native-born white Australians 1788–1828*, Melbourne,
    Oxford University Press, 1985, p. 77.

55  TAHO, CON15/1/3 No. 768 pp. 220–221 Mary Byrne. Her name was
    recorded as Byrne on this record but 'Bryne' on her conduct record.

56  TAHO, CON15/1/3 No. 196 pp. 220–221 Anne Agnew.

57  TAHO, CON15/1/3 No. 772 pp. 220–221 Sarah Brennan.

58  TAHO, CON15/1/3 No. 512 pp. 228–229 Eleanor Daley.

59  TAHO, CON15/1/3 No. 640 pp. 244–245 Annie McNeil.

60  TAHO, CON15/1/3 No. 776 pp. 222–223 Anne Burns.

61  TAHO, CON15/1/3 No. 775 pp. 222–223 Jane Bradshaw.

62  TAHO, CON15/1/3 No. 400 pp. 232–233 Margaret Grady.

63  Elizabeth Anne Rushen, 'Free, single and female: the women of the first scheme for female emigration to Australia, 1833–1837', PhD Thesis, Monash University, 1999, pp. 226–228.

64  TAHO, RGD37/1/6 Campbell Town 1847/621 Mary McCarthy and James Rourke; TAHO, SWD26/1/3 pp. 508, 704 Application for admission to the Orphan School by James Rourke and Mary McCarthy for Esther Rourke September 1860.

65  TAHO, RGD35/1/10 Hobart 1884/1741 Mary Kent.

66  Cornwall Chronicle (Launceston), 11 November 1868, p. 3; TAHO, CON41/1/8 No. 381 Mary Russell.

67  Snowden, 'Convict Marriage', pp. 63–71.

68  Meredith, My Home in Tasmania, p. 209.

69  Snowden, 'Convict Marriage', pp. 63–71.

70  TAHO, CON52/1/2 p. 63 Ann Daly Tasmania and William Friar, free.

71  TAHO, RGD37/1/5 Hobart 1846/227 Ann Daley and William Friar.

72  Bell Rooney from County Down was 28 and single when she was transported; Martha Martin from County Cavan was 20 and single and Harriet Madine from County Down was 28 and single, although she had been five years 'on the town' and had one child: TAHO, CON52/1/2 p. 287; TAHO, CON52/1/2 p. 64; TAHO, CON52/1/2 p. 212.

73  TAHO, CON52/1/2 p. 316: Maria Johnson Tasmania and James Derbyshire John Renwick; TAHO, CON41/1/8 No. 290 Maria Johnson.

74  TAHO, RGD37/1/7 Brighton 1848/1437 Maria Johnson and James Derbyshire.

75  TAHO, CON52/1/3 p. 15 Margaret Randall and John Baker Sir Charles Napier. Refused (no reason stated); TAHO, CON52/1/4 Margaret Randall and William Cooke; TAHO, CON52/1/4 Margaret Randall and William Cook; CON52/1/4 p. 56 Margaret Randall and William Cooke.

76  TAHO, CON52/1/2 p. 327 April 1847 Anne McAvine and Richard

Bamford, free; TAHO, CON52/2 p. 443 February 1848 Anne
McAvine and Edward Smith, *Governor Ready*; TAHO, CON52/3
p. 345 24 October 1848 Anne McAvine & Aaron Patient; TAHO,
CON52/3 p. 352 8 October 1850 Anne McAvine & Aaron Patient.

77  TAHO, RGD37/1/9 Bothwell 1850/64 Anne 'McAvenie' and Aaron
Patient.

78  TAHO, CON52/1/3 p. 449 8 May 1849 Elizabeth Hearns and
Charles Thompson; TAHO, CON52/1/3 p. 449 27 August 1849
Elizabeth Hearns and Charles Thompson; TAHO, CON52/1/3
p. 451 8 January 1850 Elizabeth Hearns and Charles Thompson;
TAHO, RGD37/1/9 Hobart 1850/164 Elizabeth Hearns and
Charles Thompson.

79  TAHO, CON52/1/2 p. 258 Mary Watt and James Lines *Coromandel*.
He married Mary's shipmate Honora Cullen, *Tasmania*: see TAHO,
CON52/1/2 April 1848; TAHO, RGD37/1/7 Hobart 1848/1891
Honora Cullen and James Lines.

80  TAHO, CON52/1/2 p. 260 Honora Cullen and James Lines; TAHO,
RGD37/1/7 Hobart 1848/1891 Honora Cullen and James Lines.

81  TAHO, RGD37/1/12 Morven 1853/1294 Henrietta Beresford and
John Lenny.

82  TAHO, RGD37/1/16 Swanport 1857/93 Henrietta 'Linie' and
Elijah Harvey.

83  *Cornwall Chronicle* (Launceston), 8 January 1859, p. 4.

84  TAHO, RGD37/1/9 Brighton 1850/9 'Ann Gardener' and Peter Kelly.

85  TAHO, CON41/1/8 No. 399 Anne Gardiner or Harrison.

86  TAHO, CON52/1/3 p. 331 Mary McMannus and Moses Norcot;
TAHO, CON52/1/4 Mary McMannus and Moses Norcot; TAHO,
RGD37/1/9 Brighton 1850/14 Mary McManus and Moses Norcutt.

87  TAHO, CON41/1/8 No. 614 Mary McManus.

88  TAHO, RGD37/1/8 Hobart 1849/404 Mary Burgess and
Thomas Jones.

89  TAHO, RGD35/1/55 Launceston 1886/238 Thomas Winton Jones;
TAHO, RGD35/1/67 Launceston 1898/158 Mary Jones. See also
Kevin Reed, *The Widows of Tullow*, K & R Reed, Hamilton, Vic., 1998.

90  TAHO, RGD37/1/8 Hobart 1849/371 Margaret Leonard and John
Press.

91  TAHO, CON41/1/8 No. 353 Mary Leonard.

92  TAHO, RGD37/1/6 Hobart 1847/1044 Ann McNeil and John Spong.

93   TAHO, RGD33/1/3 Hobart 1850/2186 John Spong.

94   TAHO, LC251/1/1 30 July 1849.

95   TAHO, LC251/1/1 20 May 1850.

96   TAHO, CON41/1/8 No. 329 Ann Flannery.

97   TAHO, CON41/1/8 No. 655 Isabella Warnock; *Colonial Times* (Hobart), 6 April 1849, p. 3. The 'Cascade Convent' was the Cascades Female Factory.

98   Trudy Cowley and Dianne Snowden, *Patchwork Prisoners: the Rajah Quilt and the women who made it*, Hobart, Research Tasmania, 2013, p. 188.

## CHAPTER 10

1   Eleanor Conlin Casella, 'Where are the Children? Archaeology of the Nursery Ward', in Lucy Frost (ed.), *Convict Lives at the Ross Female Factory*, Hobart, Convict Women's Press, 2011, p. 33.

2   Casella, 'Where are the Children?' p. 33.

3   Dianne Snowden, '" A Most Humane Regulation?" Free children transported with convict parents', *Tasmanian Historical Research Association Papers and Proceedings*, Vol. 58, No. 1, April 2011, pp. 33–36. For Grangegorman, see Bláthnaid Nolan, 'Power, Punishment and Penance: An Archival Analysis of the Transportation of Irish Women from Grangegorman in Dublin to Hobart Town in Van Diemen's Land (Tasmania)', PhD thesis, University College Dublin, 2013; Rebecca Sharon Lawlor, 'Crime in nineteenth-century Ireland: Grangegorman female penitentiary and Richmond male penitentiary, with reference to juveniles and women, 1836–60', MLitt thesis, National University of Ireland Maynooth, 2012.

4   www.nationalarchives.ie/topics/transportation/transp7.html (accessed 14 June 2013).

5   Ages based on Grangegorman Admission Register: NAI, PRIS 1/09/07 Grangegorman Prison Registry.

6   Child's name recorded as Jane Hearns in Grangegorman records and James Hearns in Orphan Schools records: NAI, PRIS 1/09/07 Grangegorman Prison, Registry of Female Convicts, Grangegorman Female Convict Depot, 11 July 1840 – 22 December 1853; TAHO, SWD28/1/1 p. 20.

7   Jane Lynam died on 25 December 1846 at Brickfields Hiring Depot: TAHO, CON41/1/8 No. 355 Mary Lynam or Egan.

8   TAHO, RGD33/1/2 Hobart 1845/1379 male McArdle.

9   TAHO, RGD35/1/2 Hobart 1845/948 James McArdle.

10  William Burgess was recorded as 6 in Grangegorman and 10 when he was admitted to the Male Orphan School only months later: NAI, PRIS 1/09/07; TAHO, SWD28/1/1 p. 20.

11  TAHO, CON41/1/8 No. 395 Catherine Grace; TAHO, CON41/18 No. 767 Mary Connell.

12  TAHO, CON41/1/8 No. 281 Margaret Kelly; TAHO, CON41/1/8 No. 656 Mary Wall.

13  Joan C. Brown, *'Poverty is not a crime': the development of social services in Tasmania, 1803–1900,* Hobart, Tasmanian Historical Research Association, 1972.

14  Rebecca Kippen, 'Death in Tasmania: using civil death registers to measure nineteenth-century cause-specific mortality', PhD thesis, Australian National University, 2002.

15  TAHO, SWD28/1/1 pp. 20, 26.

16  NAI, CRF 1845 B15 Esther Burgess and Mary Burgess.

17  Ages based on Orphan Schools Admission Registers: TAHO, SWD28/1/1 pp. 20, 26.

18  TAHO, SWD28/1/1 p. 26.

19  TAHO, SWD28/1/1 p. 27; TAHO, RGD35/1/2 Hobart 1846/1236 Robert Burgess.

20  Trevor McClaughlin, *Barefoot and Pregnant: Irish Famine Orphans in Australia,* Vol. 1, Melbourne, Genealogical Society of Victoria, 1991, p. 75: 'Ann Burgess'. We are indebted to Barbara Simpson and Perry McIntyre for additional information about Ann Burgess per *Lismoyne.*

21  TAHO, CON41/1/8 No. 396 Mary Griffen; TAHO, CON15/1/3 No. 396 pp. 232–233 Mary Griffen.

22  TAHO, CON41/1/8 No. 396 Mary Griffen; TAHO, SWD28/1/1 pp. 20, 26.

23  TAHO, RGD35/1/2 Hobart 1846/1065 Patrick Wall.

24  TAHO, RGD35/1/2 Hobart 1846/995 Catherine Kelly.

25  Rebecca Kippen, '"And the Mortality Frightful": Infant and Child Mortality in the Convict Nurseries of Van Diemen's Land', www.femaleconvicts.org.au/docs/seminars/RebeccaKippen_InfantMortality.pdf (accessed 11 June 2013).

26  TAHO, SWD28/1/1 p. 2, 6.

27  TAHO, SWD28/1/1 p. 20. He was apprenticed to Thomas Rumney at Cambridge. His colonially born brother Henry Brennan, aged 7, was admitted to the Male Orphan School in June 1854, and remained there for seven years until September 1861: TAHO, SWD28/1/1, p. 33.

28  See Dianne Snowden, 'The Matron's Quarters, 8 Degraves Street South Hobart, Yard 4 Female Factory Historic Site', unpublished manuscript, 2011; Tony Rayner, *Female factory, female convicts*, Esperance Press, 2004, pp. 148–149.

29  TAHO, SWD28/1/1 p. 26; TAHO, RGD35/1/2 Hobart 1849/2419 Anne Byrne (9 May 1849).

30  TAHO, RGD35/1/2 Hobart 1846/1236 Robert Burgess (15 November 1846); TAHO, RGD35/1/2 Hobart 1849/2239 John Docherty (31 December 1848).

31  TAHO, RGD35/1/2 Hobart 1847/1469 Sarah Ann Kelly. The cause of death was recorded as 'pulmonary'.

32  TAHO, SWD28/1/1 p. 20.

33  TAHO, SWD28/1/1 pp. 27, 44.

34  Dianne Snowden, '" A Most Humane Regulation?" Free children transported with convict parents', *Tasmanian Historical Research Association Papers and Proceedings*, Vol. 58, no. 1, April 2011, pp. 33–36.

35  TAHO, SWD28/1/1 p. 26.

36  TAHO, SWD28/1/1 p. 26.

37  TAHO, SWD28/1/1 p. 36.

38  TAHO, SWD28/1/1 p. 20.

39  TAHO, RGD37/1/13 Hobart 1854/855 Alice Burgess and Thomas Rice; Victoria Death Certificate Maryborough 1878/9217 Thomas Rice; Victoria Death Certificate Maryborough 1921/2421 Alice Rice.

40  *Geraldton Guardian*, 8 March 1921, p. 1. See also *Argus* (Melbourne), 25 February 1921, p. 8; *Zeehan and Dundas Herald*, 1 March 1921, p. 2; *Advocate* (Melbourne), 10 March 1921, p. 26.

41  Victoria Marriage Certificate District of Bendigo 1855/857 Eliza Burgess and Joshua Page; Victoria Death Certificate District of Bendigo 1854/6136 Joshua Page; Victoria Death Certificate 1896/8691 Eliza Page.

42  TAHO, RGD37/1/21 Hobart 1862/351 Jane Burgess and Augustus Brady. Before he married Jane, Augustus (or Owen) had two children to a woman named Eliza Norton, in December 1853 and

in November 1856: TAHO, RGD33/1/5 Hobart 1854/447 daughter Brady, father named as Owen; TAHO, RGD33/1/6 Hobart 1856/1968 daughter Brady, father named as Augustus. The oldest died in October 1857 as Ellen Brady, aged 4: TAHO, RGD35/1/5 Hobart 1857/489 Ellen Brady.

43 TAHO, CON33/1/101 No. 23769 Augustus Brady *London* (2) 1851. He was granted his ticket of leave in October 1852 and his free certificate in April 1855.

44 TAHO, CON14/1/42 pp. 102–103 Augustus Brady *London* (2) 1851.

45 TAHO, RGD33/1/6 Hobart 1859/3001 Augustus Brady; TAHO, RGD35/1 Hobart 1858/1828 Augustus Brady; TAHO, RGD33/1 Hobart 1861/3967 male Brady.

46 TAHO, RGD33/1/9 Hobart 1865/7943 William Francis Brady; TAHO, RGD33/1/10 Hobart 1869/755 Jane Brady; TAHO, RGD33/1/10 Hobart 1873/3086 Edwin George Brady.

47 TAHO, RGD33/1/18 Hobart 1892/1146 James Francis Brady. He was born at 94 Melville Street.

48 TAHO, RGD35/1/8 Hobart 1874/1922 Augustus Brady.

49 *Mercury* (Hobart), 25 July 1888, p. 2.

50 *Mercury* (Hobart), 19 May 1891, p. 2; *The Mercury* (Hobart), 4 April 1892, p. 2.

51 *Launceston Examiner*, 6 June 1893, p. 5.

52 *Mercury* (Hobart), 16 November 1893, p. 2.

53 Kay Daniels (ed.), *So much hard work: women and prostitution in Australian history*, Sydney, Fontana/Collins, 1984, Ch 1.

54 TAHO, SWD28/1/1 pp. 20, 26.

55 TAHO, CON41/1/8 No. 767 Mary Connell.

56 TAHO, SWD 28/1/1 pp. 20, 26. See Dianne Snowden, 'Voices from the Orphan School: Margaret Connell & St Columba Falls', *Tasmanian Ancestry*, Vol. 35, Number 2, September 2014, pp. 77–80.

57 TAHO, RGD37/1/8 Hobart 1849/390 Mary Connell and Michael Cooke; TAHO, SWD28/1/1 p. 20.

58 TAHO, SWD6/1/1 p. 4 William Connell.

59 TAHO, SWD28/1/1 p. 33 William Connell.

60 TAHO, RGD37/1/602 1851 Hobart Margaret Connell and George Cotton.

61 *Mercury* (Hobart), 23 April 1883, p. 3 (obituary, Francis Cotton). See

also Michael Bennett, *Quaker Life in Tasmania: The First Hundred Years*, Hobart, University of Tasmania Library, 2007, p. 30.

62  Gwen Webb, *Pyengana: A new country*, Hobart, Mercury-Walch, 1975, p. 4.

63  Frances Cotton, *Kettle on the hob: A family in Van Diemen's Land, 1828–1885*, Orford, Tasmania, Joan Roberts, 1986.

64  Cotton, *Kettle on the hob*, p. 75.

65  Webb, *Pyengana*, p. 4.

66  Cotton, *Kettle on the hob*, p. 75.

67  Cotton, *Kettle on the hob*, p. 75.

68  TAHO, POL220/1/1 p. 564 *Tamar*; *Mercury* (Hobart), 26 July 1864, p. 1 (advertisement for position); Cotton, *Kettle on the hob*, p. 75.

69  *Mercury* (Hobart), 26 July 1864, p. 1 (advertisement for position).

70  *Mercury* (Hobart), 19 November 1867, p. 2.

71  *Mercury* (Hobart), 15 June 1870, p. 1. The salary was £182 per annum and included a uniform.

72  *The Mercury* (Hobart), 14 September 1870, p. 3.

73  *The Mercury* (Hobart), 19 October 1870, p. 2. For Charles Meredith, see Sally O'Neill, 'Meredith, Charles (1811–1880)', *Australian Dictionary of Biography*, National Centre of Biography, Australian National University, http://adb.anu.edu.au/biography/meredith-charles-4187/text6731, published in hard copy in 1974 (accessed online 12 July 2014).

74  Webb, *Pyengana*, p. 5; TAHO, RGD33/1/51 Fingal 1873/408 Clement O'Connell Cotton.

75  Webb, *Pyengana*, p. 5. St Columba was an Irish saint, also known as Colm, Colum and Columcille.

76  Webb, *Pyengana*, p. 5. cf. Cotton, *Kettle on the hob* p. 75, who credits George Cotton with the discovery of the Falls.

77  Webb, *Pyengana*, p. 5.

78  Webb, *Pyengana*, p. 6.

79  Cotton, *Kettle on the hob*, p. 75.

80  Webb, *Pyengana*, p. 5.

81  *Examiner* (Launceston), 15 November 1916, p. 3.

82  *North-Eastern Advertiser*, 4 December 1953, p. 5.

83  TAHO, SWD28/1/1 p. 26; TAHO, RGD37/1/6 Hobart 1847/1048 Mary 'Macgown' and Edward Littlejohn.

84  *Colonial Times* (Hobart), 28 June 1855, p. 3; 30 June 1855, p. 1;

2 July 1855, p. 1.

85  TAHO, SWD28/1/1 p. 26.

86  TAHO, RGD37/1/7 Hobart 1848/1613 Jane Bradshaw and Thomas Wilson.

## CHAPTER 11

1  TAHO, RGD33/1/23 Launceston 1847/1722 female Roebuck and 1847/1723 female Roebuck; TAHO, RGD32/1/3 No. 3204 Amelia Eleanor Davis and No. 3205 Elizabeth Davis.

2  TAHO, CON41/1/8 No. 385 Catherine Grace; TAHO, RGD33/1/3 Hobart 1847/35 John Grace (23 May 1847).

3  TAHO, CON33/1/58 No. 13662 Pierce Cantwill *Cadet* (1) 1844; TAHO, CON14/1/23 No. 13662 pp .104–105 Pierce Cantwill *Cadet* (1) 1844.

4  TAHO, CON41/1/8 No. 325 Ann Flood.

5  TAHO, RGD33/1/23 Launceston 1847/1886 William 'Vernham'.

6  TAHO, RGD35/1/18 Clarence 1847/3 female Blackmore.

7  A compilation of 1,148 children known to have died in the nurseries at Cascades Female Factory, Dynnyrne and Brickfields between 1829 and 1856 has been published on the website of the Female Convict Research Centre (Tasmania). It has been extracted from Registrar General's Department death records and includes those who died on the voyage to Van Diemen's Land. See www.femaleconvicts.org.au (accessed 14 June 2014).

8  TAHO, LC251/1/1 Mary Byrne 5 January 1849.

9  TAHO, CON41/1/8 No. 768 Mary 'Bryne'. The child was James Burns. He was admitted to the Male Orphan School in 1859 as James McCann, when he was 10, following his mother's death.

10  TAHO, SWD28/1/1 p. 26.

11  TAHO, RGD37/1/10 Hobart 1851/292 'Byran'/Cann; TAHO, RGD33/1/4 Hobart 1852/1189 Henry Cann. Thomas Cann, a convict, arrived on the *Maria Somes* (2) 1850: TAHO, CON33/1/96.

12  TAHO, RGD33/1/5 Hobart 1855/165 Ann Cann; TAHO, RGD35/1/5 Hobart 1858/1033 Ann Cann.

13  TAHO, SWD26/1/1 9 July 1859; 30 August 1859.

14  TAHO, RGD35/1/5 Hobart 1858/1166 Mary Cann; TAHO, SWD28/1/1 p. 39.

15  Eleanor Conlin Casella, 'Where are the Children? Archaeology of

the Nursery Ward', in Lucy Frost (ed.) and the Female Convicts Research Group, *Convict Lives at the Ross Female Factory*, Hobart, Convict Women's Press, 2011, p. 33.

16  Joy Damousi, *Depraved and Disorderly*, Cambridge, Cambridge University Press, 1997, p. 120: Mrs Slea, Testimony, 8 December 1841, Report, Inquiry into Female Convict Prison Discipline.

17  Damousi, *Depraved and Disorderly*, p. 123: John Price, Testimony.

18  Damousi, *Depraved and Disorderly*, p. 124.

19  Damousi, *Depraved and Disorderly*, p. 121: John Price, Testimony.

20  Damousi, *Depraved and Disorderly*, p. 120: Reverend Thomas Ewing, Testimony.

21  TAHO, CON41/1/8 No. 687 Bridget Stankard; TAHO, RGD33/1/3 Hobart 1848/1198 William Stankard; TAHO, RGD33/1/4 Hobart 1851/790 Jane Stankard.

22  TAHO, CON41/1/8 No. 687 Bridget Stankard; TAHO, RGD35/1/3 Hobart 1850/293 William Stankard.

23  TAHO, CON41/1/8 No. 687 Bridget Stankard.

24  TAHO, RGD35/1/2 Hobart 1846/1065 Patrick Wall. The informant appears to be the Colonial Surgeon, although the signature is difficult to read. Mary may have been on the *Anson* at the time.

25  TAHO, CON41/1/8 No. 656 Mary Wall (indexed as Mary Watt); TAHO, RGD33/1/3 Hobart 1850/203 Margaret Wall.

26  TAHO, SWD6/1/1 p .5.

27  TAHO, SWD6/1/1 p. 5. He was removed to the Male Orphan School: TAHO, SWD28/1/1 p. 33.

28  TAHO, CON41/1/8 No. 384 Sarah Ryan; TAHO, RGD33/1/3 Hobart 1849/1585 John Ryan; TAHO, RGD37/1/9 Hobart 1850/157 Sarah Ryan and John Turnbull; TAHO, RGD33/1/29 Spring Bay 1851/557 male Turnbull. Sarah may have died in 1856: TAHO, RGD35/1/25 Sorell 1856/171 Sarah Turnbull.

29  TAHO, RGD33/1/3 Hobart 1849/1281 Ann Bradshaw; TAHO, RGD35/1/2 Hobart 1849/2499 Ann Bradshaw.

30  *Colonial Times* (Hobart), 28 June 1855, p. 3 (advertisement). See also *Colonial Times* (Hobart), 30 June 1855, p. 1; 2 July 1855, p. 1.

31  TAHO, RGD33/1/3 Hobart 1849/1326 Joseph Amos; TAHO, RGD35/1/2 Hobart 1849/2362 Joseph Amos; TAHO, SC195/1/24/2041 p. 1 Joseph Amos.

32  TAHO, RGD33/1/3 Hobart 1849/1326 Joseph Amos;

TAHO, RGD35/1/2 Hobart 1849/2362 Joseph Amos; TAHO, SC195/1/24/2041 p. 1 Joseph Amos.

33 For Sarah McArdle, see Joan Kavanagh and Dianne Snowden, 'Mary Salmon, a "sad spectacle of humanity" and other women of the *Tasmania* in the Launceston Female Factory', in Lucy Frost and Alice Meredith Hodgson (eds), *Convict Lives at the Launceston Female Factory*, Hobart, Convict Women's Press, 2013, pp. 55–56.

34 TAHO, RGD35/1/2 Hobart 1846/948 James McArdle.

35 TAHO, RGD33/1/23 Launceston 1848/2120 Charles Lee McArdle.

36 TAHO, RGD37/1/10 Launceston 1851/757 Sarah 'McArdell' and William Ellis.

37 TAHO, RGD33/1/23 Launceston 1848/1957 James Henry.

38 TAHO, CON41/1/8 No. 772 Margaret Connor; TAHO, RGD33/1/23 Launceston 1850/2681 Eliza Conry Connor. Informant, J. Fraser, Superintendent, Launceston Female House of Correction. No death record located.

39 TAHO, RGD33/1/23 Launceston 1850/2830 Francis Connor. Informant, James Fraser, Superintendent, Female House of Correction, Launceston.

40 James Parker, 'The Female Factory at Ross', in Lucy Frost (ed.), 2011, pp. 14–20; Tony Rayner, *Female factory, female convicts*, Tasmania, Esperance Press, 2004, pp. 111–112. For Hampton, see Peter Boyce, 'Hampton, John Stephen (1810–1869)', *Australian Dictionary of Biography*, National Centre of Biography, Australian National University, http://adb.anu.edu.au/biography/hampton-john-stephen-2151/text2745, published in hard copy in 1966, accessed online 25 September 2014.

41 Rayner, *Female factory, female convicts*, p. 111.

42 Lois Newham, 'Women and Children at Ross Female Factory', in Frost (ed.) *Convict Lives at the Ross Female Factory*, pp. 43–49.

43 Rayner, *Female factory, female convicts*, p. 112.

44 TAHO, CON41/1/8 No. 777 Catherine Burnet; TAHO, RGD35/1/22 Campbell Town 1853/187 George Burnett. See also Dianne Snowden and Joan Kavanagh, 'Irish Shipmates from the *Tasmania*', pp. 70–71.

45 TAHO, CON41/1/8 No. 772 Sarah Brennan; TAHO, RGD33/1/26 Campbell Town 1849/928 Sarah Jane 'Brennon'; TAHO, SWD28/1/1 p. 33. See also Snowden and Kavanagh, 'Irish Shipmates from the *Tasmania*', p. 71.

46  TAHO, CON41/1/8 No. 637 Margaret Meara; TAHO, RGD33/1/30 Campbell Town 1852/80 James Meara; TAHO, RGD35/1/21 Campbell Town 1852/165 James Meara.

47  Damousi, *Depraved and Disorderly*, p. 122; Brown, 'Poverty is not a Crime', p. 65.

48  Rebecca Kippen and Peter Gunn, 'Convict bastards, common-law unions and shotgun weddings: premarital conceptions and ex-nuptial births in nineteenth-century Tasmania', *Journal of Family History* 36, No. 4, (2011), pp. 387–403.

49  Katrina Alford, *Production or Reproduction? An Economic History of Women in Australia, 1788–1850*, Melbourne, Oxford University Press, 1984, p. 80.

50  Alford, *Production or Reproduction*, p. 80.

51  Portia Robinson, *The Hatch and Brood of Time: A study of the first generation of native-born white Australians 1788–1828*, Melbourne, Oxford University Press, 1985, p. 37.

52  TAHO, RGD37/1/7 Hobart 1848/1904 Bridget Gallagher and William Peter Briggs.

53  TAHO, CON41/1/8 No. 397 Bridget Gallagher; TAHO, CON41/1/8 No. 323 Rose Fitzpatrick; TAHO, CON41/1/8 No. 324 Ann Fitzpatrick; TAHO, CON14/1/20 No. 16168 James Gallagher 1st *Ratcliffe* (1) 1845.

54  TAHO, RGD37/1/7 Hobart 1848/1904 Bridget Gallagher and William Peter Briggs.

55  TAHO, RGD35/1/4 Hobart 1854/1039 Henry Briggs; TAHO, RGD35/1/6 Hobart 1860/1976 Edward Briggs.

56  TAHO, CON41/1/8 No. 507 Ann Delany; TAHO, RGD37/1/7 Hobart 1848/1630 Ann Delany and George Hooper.

57  TAHO, RGD37/1/8 Hobart 1849/404 Mary Burgess and Thomas Jones.

58  TAHO, RGD33/1/3 Hobart 1850/2735 Amy Jones.

59  TAHO, RGD37/1/8 Hobart 1849/404 Mary Burgess and Thomas Jones. See also Kevin Reed, *The Widows of Tullow*, Hamilton, Victoria, K&R Reed, 1998.

60  Reed, *Widows of Tullow*, p. 115.

61  TAHO, RGD37/1/6 Norfolk Plains 1847/1331 Mary McBride and Robert McLeod.

62  TAHO, RGD33/1/3 Longford 1849/3609 Robert McLeod; TAHO, RGD35/1/1 Longford 850/329 Robert McLeod.

63   TAHO, RGD33/1/29 Longford 1851/320 John McLeod;
     TAHO, RGD33/1/29 Longford Thomas McLeod. Mother,
     Ann 'Killbride'.

64   Information from Mary McBride's descendant Ann Kiely.

65   TAHO, RGD35/1/23 1854 Horton John McLeod.

66   TAHO, RGD33/1/32 Horton 1854/350 male McLeod. Informant
     father, farmer, Emu Bay.

67   TAHO, RGD33/1/34 Westbury 1855/1563 male McLeod; TAHO,
     RGD33/1/34 Westbury 1855/1564 female McLeod.

68   TAHO, RGD33/1/36 Longford 1858/1468 Henry McLeod.

69   Information from Cheryl Griffin, 2 February 2011. Information
     calculated from death certificate (1862).

70   TAHO, RGD33/1/46 Westbury 1868/1759 Ellen McLeod.
     Information from Cheryl Griffin, 2 February 2011.

71   Information from Cheryl Griffin, 2 February 2011.

72   David Coad, *Port Cygnet Irish Convicts*, Kingston, David Coad, 2012,
     p. 84. Coad, *Irish Convicts*, p. 84.

73   Coad, *Irish Convicts*, p. 88.

74   Coad, *Irish Convicts*, pp .80–88.

75   TAHO, RGD35/1/56 Port Cygnet 1887/1073 Catherine Grace.

76   Coad, *Irish Convicts*, p. 86.

77   *The Mercury* (Hobart), 1 January 1879, p. 3.

78   TAHO, CON33/1/5 No. 1142 John Steambridge *Lord Lyndoch* 1841.

79   TAHO, GO33/70 p. 587; TAHO, CO386 Reel 987 p. 8 6.

80   TAHO, POL220/1/3 p. 227.

81   David Neal, *The Rule of Law in a Penal Colony: Law and Power in Early
     New South Wales*, Melbourne, Cambridge University Press, 1992, pp.
     38–39.

82   Neal, *The Rule of Law*, pp. 38–39.

83   Stephen Nicholas and Peter Shergold, 'Convicts as Migrants', in
     Stephen Nicholas (ed.), *Convict Workers*, p. 53.

## CHAPTER 12

1   TAHO, RGD35/1/67 Emu Bay 1898/193.

2   TAHO, RGD37/1/59 Emu Bay 1898/109.

3   *Launceston Examiner*, 21 October 1898, p. 7.

4   See, for example, *Hobarton Mercury*, 9 November 1855, p. 2;
    5 December 1855, p. 3.

5   TAHO, RGD35/1/5 Hobart 1855/439 Margaret Butler or
    Shakleton. Her age was recorded as 31 on her death certificate but
    she was 40 when she arrived and 35 when she married.

6   *Colonial Times* (Hobart), 8 November 1855, p. 2. See also *Courier*
    (Hobart), 8 November 1855, p. 2 (gives address as the top of
    Goulburn Street); *Hobarton Mercury*, 9 November 1855, p. 2;
    *Launceston Examiner*, 10 November 1855, p. 2.

7   *Courier* (Hobart), 3 December 1855; 5 December 1855, p. 3.

8   TAHO, CON33/1/29 No. 7021 John Shackleton *Marquis of
    Hastings* (2) 1842.

9   *Colonial Times* (Hobart), 5 December 1855, p. 2.

10  TAHO, CON37/1/ p. 2799 John Shackleton.

11  TAHO, RGD35/1/9 Hobart 1879/1820 John 'Shackelton'.

12  TAHO, SC195/1/38 Inquest No. 3791 Judith Dowling.

13  TAHO, CON41/1/8 No. 381 Mary Russell.

14  TAHO, RGD35/1/25 Sorell 1856/171 Sarah Turnbull. This death
    certificate stated that she was a single woman but she married
    John Turnbull in 1850 and they later lived in Sorell District: TAHO,
    RGD37/1/9 Hobart 1850/157 Sarah Ryan and John Turnbull.

15  Tasmanian Death Certificate Launceston 1907/98 Mary Jane McLeod.

16  TAHO, RGD35/1/67 Launceston 1898/208 Harriet Vernon.

17  TAHO, CON41/1/8 No. 684 Ellen Sullivan; TNA, Adm. 101/71/2.

18  TAHO, CON41/1/8 No. 619 Mary McVeagh.

19  TAHO, CON41/1/8 No. 616 Anne Mullan.

20  TAHO, CON41/1/8 No. 327 Catherine Foy.

21  TAHO, SC195/1/17 Inquest No. 1384 10 January 1846 Mary Murphy.

22  For Edmund Bowden, see Charles Bateson, 'Bowden, Edmund
    (1801–1847)', *Australian Dictionary of Biography*, National Centre of
    Biography, Australian National University, http://adb.anu.edu.au/
    biography/bowden-edmund-1807/text2057, published in hard copy
    in 1966 (accessed online 11 November 2014).

23  TAHO, SC195/1/17 Inquest No. 1384 pp. 2–3 (10 January 1846)
    Mary Murphy: Evidence of Dr Edmund Bowden.

24  TAHO, SC195/1/17 Inquest No. 1384 p. 4 (10 January 1846) Mary Murphy: Evidence of Margaret Powers.

25  TAHO, SC195/1/17 Inquest No. 1384 p. 4 (10 January 1846) Mary Murphy: Evidence of Margaret Newman.

26  TAHO, RGD34/1/2 Hobart 1846/1500 Fanny Doherty. Prisoners Barracks on a burial record refers to the Prisoners' Burial Ground at Hobart's Trinity Cemetery.

27  TAHO, SC195/1/17 Inquest No. 1410 28 March 1846 Fanny Doherty.

28  TAHO, SC195/1/17 Inquest No. 1410 Fanny Doherty pp. 2–3.

29  TAHO, SC195/1/17 Inquest No. 1410 Fanny Doherty p. 4.

30  TAHO, CON41/1/8 No. 614 Mary McManus. For her marriage, see TAHO, RGD37/1/9 Brighton 1850/14 Mary McManus and Moses Norcutt.

31  TAHO, CON41/1/8 No. 630 Mary Hetherington; TAHO, RGD34/1/2 Hobart 1847/1576 Mary Hetherington. 'Prisoners Barracks' on a burial record refers to the Prisoners Burial Ground at Trinity Cemetery Hobart.

32  For classification of cause of death, see Rebecca Kippen, 'Death in Tasmania: using civil death registers to measure nineteenth-century cause-specific mortality', PhD thesis, Australian National University, 2002, p. 74. In 1869 the Royal College of Physicians published *Nomenclature of Diseases*, which was issued to every doctor in the United Kingdom. It was an attempt to create a common standard of classification to the various causes of death and doctors were urged to use the guide when completing a death certificate.

33  Kippen, 'Death in Tasmania', p .74.

34  Kippen, 'Death in Tasmania', pp. 74–75.

35  TAHO, RGD35/1/60 Deloraine 1891/145 Ann Leach.

36  TAHO, RGD35/1/37 Launceston 1868/801 Mary Russell; TAHO, SC195/1/52 Inquest No. 6480; TAHO, POL 709/1/5 p. 188 (1868); TAHO, CON41/1/8 No. 381 Mary Russell.

37  TAHO, SC195/1/52 Inquest No. 6480 7 November 1868 Mary Russell; TAHO, POL709/1/5 p. 188 (1868) Crime Report 27.

38  *Cornwall Chronicle* (Launceston), 11 November 1868, p. 3.

39  Kippen, 'Death in Tasmania', p. 74.

40  Margaret McMackin, a house servant aged 44, died of 'phthisis' in 1853: TAHO, RGD35/1/3 Hobart 1853/2129 Margaret 'McMichan'. Catherine Riley died of 'phthisis pulmonalis' in hospital in Hobart

on 11 December 1854 (as Catherine Beckett), a house servant aged 40: TAHO, RGD35/1/4 Hobart 1854/1684 Catherine Beckett. Maria Johnson or Derbyshire, aged 43, died of phthisis pulmonalis in hospital in Hobart in 1870: Joyce Purtscher, *Deaths at General Hospital Hobart, January 1864–June 1884* [TAHO, HSD145], Mt Stuart, Joyce Purtscher, 1999. Catherine Hughes, a widow aged 50, also died of phthisis pulmonalis: TAHO, RGD35/1/9 Hobart 1881/3104 Catherine Hughes.

41   TAHO, RGD35/1/5 Hobart 1858/1166 Mary Cann.

42   TAHO, RGD35/1/67 Launceston 1898/158 Mary Jones.

43   TAHO, RGD35/1/5 Hobart 1855/255 Esther Burgess.

44   Joan E. Grundy, *A Dictionary of Medical & Related Terms for the Family Historian*, Rotherham, South Yorkshire, Swansong Publications, 2006, p. 31.

45   TAHO, RGD35/1/4 Hobart 1854/1688 Eliza Hunter. Others who died of debility or old age included Eliza Perry, a pauper aged 52, who died of 'debility' in 1871 in Launceston: TAHO, RGD35/1/40 Launceston 1871/1418 Elizabeth Dockins. Ellen Maguire, a domestic aged 77, died of 'senility' (old age) in 1897 in Launceston. Ellen Maguire, a domestic aged 77, died of 'senility' (old age) in 1897 in Launceston: TAHO, RGD35/1/66 Launceston 1897/264 Ellen Gregory. Mary Thompson or McArdle, who married George Hooper, may have died of 'senility' in hospital as Mary Hooper, a charwoman aged 72, but this has not been confirmed.

46   TAHO, RGD35/1/7 Hobart 1865/5044 Ann Fitzpatrick. Ann was single when she was transported and there is no record of a colonial marriage for her.

47   TAHO, RGD35/1/50 Oatlands 1881/477 Sarah Pritchard.

48   TAHO, RGD35/1/10 Hobart 1884/1741 Mary Kent.

49   Epithalamia is a cancer originating in the outermost layer of the mucous membranes and the skin: Grundy p. 37.

50   TAHO, RGD35/1/22 Launceston 1853/841 Catherine Stokes.

51   TAHO, RGD35/1/22 Launceston 1853/842 male Stokes.

52   E.S. Hall, 'On the medical topography and vital statistics of the city of Hobarton, Tasmania, and its southern subdistricts, for 1855', *Australian Medical Journal*, Vol. 3, pp. 85–105, quoted in Kippen, 'Death in Tasmania', p. 80.

53   *Cornwall Chronicle* (Launceston), 11 November 1868, p. 3.

54   TAHO, CON41/1/8 No. 627 Mary Hurley; TAHO, SC195/1/28

Inquest 2406; TAHO, CON41/1/8 No. 627 Mary Hurley.

55 *Courier* (Hobart), 5 October 1850, p. 3. A similar report was published in the *Colonial Times* (Hobart), 4 October 1850, p. 3.

56 TAHO, RGD35/1/25 Richmond 1856/207 Judith Dowling.

57 TAHO, SC195/1/38 No. 3791 26 June 1956 Judith Dowling.

58 TAHO, RGD35/1/28 Richmond 1859/744 John Dowling; TAHO, SC195/1/43 Inquest 4666 2 December 1859 John Dowling; *Hobart Town Daily Mercury*, 6 December 1859, pp. 2–3.

59 In 1856, responsibility transferred from the Imperial Government to the Colonial Government for a range of institutions.

60 TAHO, CON41/1/8 No. 630 Mary Hetherington; TAHO, RGD34/1/2 Hobart 1847/1576 Mary Hetherington.

61 TAHO, CON41/1/8 No. 401 Mary Gillespie; TAHO, RGD34/1/2 Hobart 1850/1879 Mary Gillespie.

62 Purtscher, *Deaths at the General Hospital Hobart* [TAHO, HSD145].

63 TAHO, CON41/1/8 No. 616 Anne Mullan.

64 Andrew Piper, *Beyond the Convict System: The Aged Poor and Institutionalisation in Colonial Tasmania*, PhD thesis, University of Tasmania, 2003, esp. Ch 4.

65 Joan C. Brown, *"Poverty is Not a Crime": The development of social services in Tasmania, 1803–1990*, THRA, Hobart, 1972, p. 123.

66 Joyce Purtscher (compiler) for the Friends of the Orphan Schools St John's Park Precinct [New Town], *Deaths at the New Town Charitable Institution July 1895–December 1912*, Joyce Purtscher and the Friends of the Orphan Schools, 2012. It became the New Town Infirmary in 1913, the New Town Rest Home in 1934 and St John's Park in 1944.

67 Alison Alexander, 'Benevolent Societies', in Alexander (ed.), *Companion*, pp. 43–44; Andrew Piper, 'Launceston Invalid Asylum', in Alexander (ed.), *Companion*, p. 210.

68 TAHO, RGD35/1/65 Launceston 1896/389 Mary Salmon or Kewley.

69 TAHO, RGD35/1/66 Launceston 1897/264 Ellen Gregory; *Launceston Examiner*, 3 November 1897, p. 4.

70 TAHO, RGD35/1/67 Launceston 1898/208 Harriet Vernon; *Launceston Examiner*, 8 June 1898, p. 5: Benevolent Asylum monthly report.

71 *Launceston Examiner*, 3 November 1897, p. 4.

72 TAHO, RGD35/1/66 Launceston 1897/264 Ellen Gregory. She arrived as Ellen Maguire.

73 See Chapter 7.

74 TAHO, CON41/1/8 No. 281 Margaret Kelly; TAHO, HSD285/1/1517 Margaret Kelly; TAHO, RGD35/1/26 New Norfolk 1856/568 Margaret Kelly.

75 TAHO, RGD35/1/5 Hobart 1858/1166 Mary Cann.

76 TAHO, RGD35/1/8 Hobart 1876/3422 Bridget Agnes Briggs.

77 TAHO, RGD35/1/67 Launceston 1898/158 Mary Jones.

78 TAHO, AD960/1/17 Will No. 3199 p. 33 (1886) Thomas Jones; TAHO, AD960/1/22 Will No. 5268 p. 251 (1898) Mary Jones.

79 SRCT, Cornelian Bay, Record ID 1150, RC, Section D, No. 8 (Bridget Agnes Briggs).

80 TAHO, CON33/1/659 John Dooling *Ratcliffe* (1) 30 August 1845 No. 16137.

81 *Launceston Examiner*, 5 July 1886, p. 1. See also *Argus* (Melbourne), 10 July 1886, p. 1.

82 *Launceston Examiner*, 2 April 1898, p. 1.

83 *The Mercury* (Hobart), 6 August 1889, p. 1; 7 August 1889, p. 1.

84 *The Mercury* (Hobart), 14 October 1889, p. 1.

85 *Examiner* (Launceston), 4 April 1907, p. 1. The newspaper is dated Thursday 4 April but the funeral notice states 'this day 5th inst'.

86 Cheryl Griffin, http://foundersandsurvivors.org/sites/newsletters, 9 December 2011, 'Robert McLeod and Mary McBride take their place in history' (accessed 21 December 2011).

87 Trudy Cowley and Dianne Snowden, *Patchwork Prisoners: the Rajah Quilt and the women who made it*, Hobart, Research Tasmania, 2013, p. 267.

## CONCLUSION

1 Dianne Snowden, '"A Most Humane Regulation": Free children transported with convict parents', *Tasmanian Historical Research Associations Papers & Proceedings*, Vol. 58, No. 1, April 2011, pp. 38, 41.

2 Joan Kavanagh, 'The Case of Eliza Davis', *Tasmanian Ancestry*, Genealogical Society of Tasmania, Vol. 17, September 1996, pp. 101–106; Joan Kavanagh, 'From Mullinacuffe to Emu Bay, Eliza Davis Revisited', *Tasmanian Ancestry*, Genealogical Society of Tasmania, Vol. 17, December 1996, pp. 169–175.

3 Tasmania was officially adopted as a name in place of Van Diemen's Land on 1 January 1856.

4 TAHO, AD960/1/186 Will No. 72909 (1983) Clifford William Eastwood.

5 www.admella.org.au (accessed 14 June 2010).

6 Margaret Lundie's crime received national coverage. See for example, *Goulburn Evening Penny Post*, 28 September 1909, p. 4; *Braidwood Dispatch*, 29 September 1909, p. 2; *Sydney Morning Herald*, 30 September 1909, p. 7; *Manaro Mercury*, 1 October 1909, p. 2.

7 *Sydney Morning Herald*, 6 September 1909, p. 6.

8 Margaret Cecilia Butler b.1868. William's wife was also Margaret.

9 NSW Death Certificate Cooma 1948/8735 Crispena Maud Snowden; NSW Death Certificate Sydney 1960/1860 'Henry' Erasmus Ward.

10 NAA, B2455 SERN 9583 William Butler. For Trooper Butler's letters, see *Manaro Mercury*, 16 July 1900, p. 2; 31 August 1900, p. 3; 23 November 1900, p. 2; 11 January 1901, p. 2; 4 February 1901, p. 2; 26 April 1901, p. 2; 4 March 1901, p. 2; 24 June 1901, p. 2; 6 December 1901, p. 4; 18 May 1901, p. 6 ; 24 June 1901, p. 2; 25 April 1902, p. 3; 23 November 1900, p. 2; 25 April 1902, p. 3; 9 May 1902, p. 3.

11 NAA, B2455 SERN 9583: William Butler pp .1–15.

12 NAA, B2455 SERN 9583: William Butler pp. 1–106; NSW Death Certificate Broken Hill 1916/9222 Mary Butler.

13 www.aif.adfa.edu.au Paul Butler No. 4158 (accessed 12 November 2012).

14 NSW Death Certificate Leeton 1937/2203 Paul Butler.

15 www.aif.adfa.edu.au Arthur Paul Lundie No. 181377; www.awm.gov. au/people/P10242259/rolls-and-awards (accessed 12 November 2012).

16 www.aif.adfa.edu.au, William Raymond Chatwin No. 51267 (accessed 12 November 2012).

17 Alton Chatwin enlisted on 26 January 1915. He served with the 12th Battalion, 4th Reinforcement as a driver and returned to Australia in April 1919: www.aif.adfa.edu.au/showPerson?pid=51260 (Alton Chatwin). 'Roy' Alfred Chatwin enlisted in May 1915 and served as a private with the 26th Battalion, C Company. He returned to Australia in May 1919: NAA, B2455 SERN 6554 pp. 1–41 Roy Alfred Chatwin enlisted; www.aif.adfa.edu.au, Roy Alfred Chatwin (accessed 12 November 2012).

18 NZ Archives R18050705 WW1 Joseph Henry Hughes.

19 NZ Archives R18050626 WWI Bertram Hughes; *Evening Post* (NZ), 28 January 1936, p. 11; *Auckland Star*, 28 January 1936, p. 8; *New Zealand Herald*, 29 January 1936, p. 14.

20 *Williamstown Advertiser*, 1 September 1917, p. 2.

21  NAA, B2455 Service Number 7231 Charles Briggs.

22  www.aif.adfa.edu.au, Charles Briggs No. 7231
    (accessed 12 November 2012).

23  For details, see Kevin Reed, *The Widows of Tullow*, Hamilton,
    Victoria, K&R Reed, 1998, pp. 190–4, 196–7, 218–228.

24  www.aif.adfa.edu.au, Sergius Christopher Martin No. 8203
    (accessed 25 April 2014).

25  www.aif.adfa.edu.au, Cyril Livingstone Martin No. 2029
    (accessed 25 April 2014).

26  NAA, B2455 Service Number 1716 Harold George Jones; NZ Archives
    WWI R21892520 Record No. 0023118 Joseph Winton Carroll; NZ
    Archives WWI R21892513 Record No. 0023111 John Bernard Carroll
    Additional information from Kevin Reed, 4 April 2015.

27  Reed, *The Widows of Tullow*, pp. 148–163.

28  Reed, *The Widows of Tullow*, p. 123.

29  TAHO, CON41/1/8 No. 637 Margaret Meara; TAHO, CON15/1/3
    pp. 244–245 Margaret Meara; TAHO, CON19/1/5 Margaret Meara.

30  Alison Alexander, 'A Novelist Pictures his Convict Ancestor: Margaret
    O'Meara and Christopher Koch', in Lucy Frost (ed.) and Female
    Convicts Research Group, *Convict Lives at the Ross Female Factory*,
    Hobart, Convict Women's Press, 2011, pp. 210–214. His works include
    *The Year of Living Dangerously* (1978), *The Doubleman* (1985), *Out of
    Ireland* (1999) and *Lost Voices* (2012). See also Dianne Snowden and
    Joan Kavanagh, 'Irish Shipmates from the *Tasmania*', in Frost (ed.)
    *Convict Lives at the Ross Female Factory*, pp. 70–76.

31  Alexander, 'Koch', pp. 210–214.

32  TNA, Adm. 101/71/2 Reel 3211 Surgeon's Report *Tasmania*.

33  NAI, CRF 1845 B14 Margaret Butler.

34  Bateson, *The Convict Ships*, p. 3.

35  Alison Alexander, *Tasmania's Convicts: How Felons Built a Free Society*,
    Sydney, Allen & Unwin, 2010; Babette Smith, *Australia's Birthstain:
    The startling legacy of the convict era*, Sydney, Allen & Unwin, 2008;
    James Boyce, *Van Diemen's Land*, Melbourne, Black Inc., 2008.

36  Kay Daniels, *Convict Women*, St Leonards, Allen & Unwin, 1998.

## APPENDIX

1  Now County Offaly.

2  Now County Laois.

3  Ellen Sullivan's trial place was recorded at Grangegorman;
   she was from Kerry. NAI PRIS 1/09/07. Grangegorman Prison
   Registry of Female Convicts in Grangegorman Female Convict
   Depot 11 July 1840- 22 December 1853.

4  Ages are those recorded in the Grangegorman Admission Register.
   There is a significant discrepancy in some of the ages: Elizabeth
   Burgess, for example, is recorded as 11 at Grangegorman but
   14 when she was admitted to the Female Orphan School in
   Van Diemen's Land: Child's name recorded as Jane Hearns in
   Grangegorman records and James Hearns in Orphan Schools
   records: NAI, PRIS 1/09/07; TAHO, SWD28/1/1 p. 26.

5  Known as John Docherty in Van Diemen's Land.

6  McNeal in Grangegorman Register: NAI, PRIS 1/09/07
   Grangegorman Prison Registry.

7  Mary Murphy had an older daughter, Margaret Wilson, on board,
   also transported: TAHO, CON41/1/8 No.635 Mary Murphy; TAHO,
   CON41/1/8 No.660 Margaret Wilson.

8  Child's name recorded as James Burgess in Grangegorman records
   and Jane Burgess in Orphan Schools records: NAI, PRIS 1/09/07;
   TAHO, SWD28/1/1 p. 26.

9  Culla in Grangegorman records: NAI, PRIS 1/09/07.

10  Child's name recorded as Jane Hearns in Grangegorman records
    and James Hearns in Orphan Schools records: NAI, PRIS 1/09/07;
    TAHO, SWD28/1/1 p. 20.

# Index

Compiled by Clodagh Jones

Illustrations and tables in **bold**
Appendix entries shown by A
Notes shown by n
VDL = Van Diemen's Land